S0-ACB-976

THE OHIO COMPANY
ITS INNER HISTORY

THE OHIO COMPANY *ITS INNER HISTORY*

BY

ALFRED P. JAMES

Professor Emeritus of History
University of Pittsburgh

UNIVERSITY OF PITTSBURGH PRESS

Library of Congress Catalog Card Number: 58-7176

Printed in the United States of America
American Book–Stratford Press, Inc., New York

To my Mother
Annie Elwood Shield James
stouthearted nonagenarian

Foreword

IT HAS long been known that many documents related to the Ohio Company of Virginia perished in disastrous fires, notably those at Williamsburg, Virginia (1781), those at William and Mary College (1859), those at Richmond, Virginia (1865), and those left by George Mason of *Gunston Hall.*

What papers of the Ohio Company had survived was a matter of conjecture for generations. Fortunately some papers were a matter of public record and others were in institutional depositories or in private hands. Significant use of this surviving material was made by Berthold Fernow, in his *The Ohio Valley in Colonial Days* (Albany, New York, 1890), and more particularly by Kenneth P. Bailey, in his *The Ohio Company of Virginia* (Glendale, California, 1939).

The Re-discovery of Papers

Readers of William Darlington's *Christopher Gists Journals with Historical, Geographical and Ethnological Notes and Biographies of his Contemporaries* (Pittsburgh, J. R. Weldin & Co., 1893), might well have understood that Mr. Darlington owned important Ohio Company papers, both originals and copies.

The library of Darlington was given to the University of Pittsburgh in 1918 and the estate of the Darlington family was donated by his descendants to the University in 1925. The William Darlington Library containing his books and maps was organized in 1936 and is a notable feature of the University. The real estate and personal property were devoted to library facilities and equipment. But it was twenty-two years after the donation of the library that, in 1940, the manuscript material relating to the Ohio Company was brought back into the Darlington Memorial Library. On examination this material was found to contain about two hundred thousand words. As printed later, even with some elimination of duplication in items, it filled more than three hundred pages of text.

The First Plan of Publication

On the fortunate acquisition of this material and its survey by several people, it was decided to publish not only the Darlington items but whatever additional relevant material might be located by whatever research and publication might be necessary.

The editor of this volume and Mrs. Lois Mulkearn, as assistant editor, accepted the responsibility of collecting and editing for publication by the University of Pittsburgh Press both the Darlington items and the relevant additional material.

Suspension of Operations, 1942–1948

In 1941 considerable progress was made in transcribing the manuscripts and collating typescripts. It seemed that it might be possible to complete the project in a few years. But the attack on Pearl Harbor and the entry of the United States into war changed prospects. For some time general and institutional circumstances were highly critical. A somewhat natural result was that the project was tabled. From 1942 to 1945, the University was swamped with military personnel and the faculty not in military service was much reduced. From 1945 to 1948, the registration in the University of thousands of service men occupied much of the time of the faculty. The project of 1941 remained in abeyance.

Resumption and Change

Increased stabilization came with years of peace. In 1948 it was decided to resume the editing of the Ohio Company historical papers. By agreement, a joint editorship was established. Later it was decided that Mrs. Lois Mulkearn, librarian of the Darlington collection, should edit the items from the Darlington estate. Later still it was decided that the *Case of the Ohio Company* published in 1770, of which a sole imprint was found in the New York Historical Society, should be published as an appendix to the Darlington material.

The relevant additional documents related to the Ohio Company, in number and quantity not then fully estimated, were assigned to this editor, as was the matter of the inner history of the Ohio Company as a résumé of the whole project. Unexpectedly and unfortunately for this editor, while the *George Mercer Papers* (University of Pittsburgh Press) could be published in 1954, the amount of other relevant material that could be and was found, assumed unexpected and relatively enormous proportions which prevented the bringing out of another volume in 1954, as a companion of the *George Mercer Papers.*

Limited Narrative

In the narrative below, the inner history of the Ohio Company, the treatment is definitely narrow. Much concomitant milieu has been consciously omitted. Relations with the Indians have been left to Charles H. McIlwain's introduction to his edition of Peter Wraxall's *Abridgement of Indian Affairs*; to Julian P. Boyd's "Indian Affairs in Pennsylvania, 1736–1762" in his edition of *Indian Treaties Printed by Benjamin Franklin, 1736–1762;* to Lawrence H. Gipson's *The British Empire Before the American Revolution*, Volumes IV-V; and to annotations and commentary in Lois Mulkearn's *George Mercer Papers.* The diplomatic relations of Great Britain and France are largely disregarded as already found well handled in Clarence W. Alvord's *The Mississippi Valley in British Politics*; in Theodore Calvin Pease's *Anglo-French Boundary Disputes in the West, 1749–1763*; and in the volumes of Lawrence H. Gipson's *British Empire Before the Revolution.* The military history of the struggle between the British and the French and of Pontiac's Conspiracy has been left, in its larger outlines, to the incomparable writings of Francis Parkman and to supplementary material found in the volumes of Gipson.

While little or no effort is made in this inner history to discuss the history of the period or state the broad milieu of the Ohio Company, much attention has been paid to available documentary material, whether old and familiar or newly found, and whether in the George Mercer Papers, in great depositories, or in regional and local archives. It is believed and hoped that not only additional data and new light may be furnished, but that a different and fuller interpretation of the Ohio Company and its place in history may result.

Classification of Material

No completely logical and satisfactory classification of the 1,228 items listed can be expected. Classification in general terms such as political, institutional, economic, financial, etc., gives no impression of the real factors. And many relevant items fit into several categories. But, roughly, about 340 items might be classified as political and institutional, including 180 letters, 58 minutes of the Board of Trade or Privy Council, 30 minutes or resolutions of the Ohio Company, 29 newspaper items (mainly advertisements of meetings or projected sales of lots)—a total of 42 items only in 10 other subdivisions. There are about 256 mercantile items, most of them in litigation records as petitions, declarations, warrants, accounts, promissory notes, bonds, dockets, judgments, etc. The land item documents, primary and secondary (the latter litigation items), number about 525, including 30 survey warrants, records of warrants and renewal of warrants, 18 surveys, 6 resurveys, 17 land entries, 37 land resolutions or laws, 8 land patents, 30 land dispute depositions, 12 land deeds, and sundry other items.

Some idea of this volume of relevant data about the Ohio Company is essential. An understanding of it is necessary as an explanation of a change in the plan of publication. Of more than 1,200 relevant items, only about 150 are found in the 37 manuscripts in the George Mercer Papers.

Limited Selection of Documents

Of the thousand or more remaining items many have long been known and some of them printed, notably by Fernow and Bailey. And although of more than two score different types, many of each type are highly similar and, in some cases highly repetitive. It has therefore been decided to include, in Appendix A, of this volume, only about ninety items, or in number, about one in thirteen of the documents found.

On the selection of the items for the Appendix certain principles seemed advisable and with some consistency have been followed. In the first place, it was made a rule to omit generally those items already in print in works found in the larger libraries. The second principle was that the item must be revealing and generally significant. The third principle was that unusual items hitherto unknown should be included. And, along with the above criteria, the idea has been pursued of including at least one item of each of the more important types found.

One who examines the Appendix will find included about 30 different types or species of documents. Twenty-five additional item types are found in the larger list of assembled items, but some of them are of minor significance and the illustrative items are often of less importance.

The Locations of Documents

The largest proportion of the extant and relevant papers of the Ohio Company of Virginia are found in six places, Pittsburgh,

Philadelphia, London, Washington, D. C., Annapolis, Maryland, Winchester, Virginia, and Frederick, Maryland.

In regard to Pittsburgh and the George Mercer Papers of the Darlington Memorial Library of the University of Pittsburgh, comment is unnecessary, for each item, well edited, is now available in print in the *George Mercer Papers*.

In Philadelphia, numerous items are found in the Manuscripts Division of the Historical Society of Pennsylvania, where material relevant to the Ohio Company of Virginia is found in ten or more collections, among which may be named the Cadwallader Collection, Dreer Collection, Etting Collection, Gratz Collection, Miscellaneous Collection, Penn Papers, Penn-Hamilton Correspondence, Penn Official Correspondence, Peters Papers, and Weiser Correspondence. A few items only are found in each of two other Philadelphia depositories.

As anyone familiar with the writings of Parkman, Fernow, Alvord, Gipson, Bailey, and others, would anticipate, many of the papers of the Ohio Company are drawn from the British Public Record Office, mainly from Colonial Office papers, Classification 5. About 67 such items are found in our complete list. References in the context of these and of other items involve, of course, many additional P.R.O. documents. The British Museum Library manuscripts, notably the Bouquet Papers and the Newcastle Papers, furnish a considerable number of items in our files and more yet for footnote reference. Fortunately much of this London material has been transcribed, photostated, or microfilmed and can be consulted in Washington, D. C.; Ottawa, Canada; and elsewhere.

In the Division of Manuscripts of the Library of Congress are found not only the transcripts, photostats, and microfilms of the British Public Record Office and British Museum items, but additional items in the Washington Papers, George Mason Papers, and Campbell-Preston Papers.

In the mere number of items relevant to the Ohio Company, Annapolis, Maryland, comes first as a location of material. In fact it is a place of triple significance. In the Hall of Records building are both the Maryland Land Office and the legal records. Among the latter are not only central archives of the Western Shore General Court and of the Court of Appeals, but also the early original records of Frederick County, whether docket books or judgment records or, in different categories, deed books and will books. Frederick County has only neatly bound volumes of photostats of these, and photostatic reproduction is made in Annapolis.

In the Land Office are more than thirty relevant Ohio Company items, including 15 or more warrants or renewals thereof, 8 or more surveys or resurveys thereof, and 7 or more patents. Photostats of these are obtainable and easily secured at Annapolis.

The central courts records in the Hall of Records are voluminous and contain much Ohio Company data. In point of both number of items and duration of litigation the contest for possession of *Pleasant Valley*, a three-hundred-acre tract near Old Town, Maryland, is most significant. As first a dispute in the provincial land court, 1761–80, and then in sequence, a suit in the Western Shore General Court, in the Allegany County Court, in the Court of Appeals, and again in the Allegany County Court, it ran on, under changing writs and titles, from 1780 to 1821, with judgment records of great length, containing, imbedded, copied records of early transactions and sometimes having significant boxed files of some of the original papers involved. The docket items number 57 and the depositions, either preserved in boxed files or copied in the extensive judgment records, number a score or more. As mentioned below in a footnote to an item calendared in Appendix D, the judgment records in connection with this case fill more than four hundred folio pages.

As indicated below in the narrative and in Appendix A, George Mason took two bonds in payment for two tracts of land. These two bonds with the signatures of Thomas Beall, son of Samuel, and three co-signers on each of the two bonds were not promptly paid and George Mason brought suit about the matter. In the suit which was initiated June 4, 1791 and was settled in 1799, there were issued 8 warrants, June 4; 8 declarations including copies of the bonds, June 15, 1791; 8 scire facias writs January 7, 1793; and 8 more scire facias (really fieri facias) writs of September 7, 1797, the originals of which are found in the boxed files of the case, along with sundry other items. In the docket books of the court are 78 items. The total of all items in this case number more than 116.

Thus, in all, there are, omitting the Land Office documents, about two hundred central government archival items relating to the Ohio Company in the Hall of Records.

At the courthouse in Winchester, Frederick County, Virginia, one finds most fortunately not only the court procedure and judgments preserved in the order books, but, remarkably preserved, files of original papers involved in the suits, neatly folded after the manner of lawyers files and arranged chronologically. This is not unique, for similar files have survived in Augusta County, Virginia, and in Allegany County, Maryland. Fires and war have done great damage to many such records elsewhere, but in places such as Winchester, Virginia, and Frederick, Maryland, much material, hitherto neglected but of great value, has survived.

Mercantile Items

The Ohio Company items found at Winchester, Frederick County, Virginia, and at Frederick, Frederick County, Maryland, are predominantly commercial and mercantile, recorded or filed in connection with litigation against those who bought goods from cargoes which were imported from Europe and jobbed or retailed along the upper Potomac, usually, probably, at the New Store. Since the related documents have been greatly neglected, emphasis is here put upon them as a new feature.

The mercantile trade of the Ohio Company was carried on partly with the Indians of the Ohio Valley, partly with military personnel using Ohio Company goods from its imported cargoes, and partly with settlers along the upper reaches of the Potomac River. At the time, these settlers who had accounts with the Ohio Company lived mainly in Frederick County, Virginia (of that day) or in Frederick County, Maryland. With few exceptions the surviving records of the commercial business of the Company are to be found in the archives of these two counties, areas each of great extent, 1750–55.

In the Darlington Library and in files of papers of suits in

Frederick County, Virginia, are 20 Frederick County commercial accounts, 13 promissory notes, and 6 commercial bonds. In connection with them there are 25 petitions, 14 declarations, 60 warrants, of which 2 are writs of attachment, and 135 trial records in the order books, as such volumes are there designated.

Of this total of 174, Frederick County, Virginia, items, it has seemed advisable, at present, to publish only type samples since there is much similarity and repetition within each of the 7 types above mentioned.

In the text and in a few footnotes will be found reference to about 40 Virginia commercial debtors of the Ohio Company against whom litigation, sometimes dragging out for a decade, had to be carried on in the county court.

Somewhat unfortunately the original trial papers once filed in Frederick County, Maryland, and now deposited in boxes at the Hall of Records at Annapolis, are few in number and irrelevant to the story of the Ohio Company. But fortunately the Maryland Courts often made inclusive judgment records, which furnish detail not only about legal processes but about transactions involved in a given case. An attempt has been made to summarize some of the data thus preserved.

The records of Ohio Company commercial transactions in Frederick County, Maryland, though different in recordation, are little less voluminous and significant than those in the Virginia county of the same name. In the Frederick County, Maryland, docket books now in the Hall of Records of Annapolis are found at least 108 items, all brief, but containing, nevertheless, valuable abbreviated notations about debt and property. Involved are the obligations of about 20 debtors and 2 or 3 others on the bail or among the executors of a debtor.

In the judgment records of Frederick County, Maryland, are 42 items in regard to suits against the debtors. Sixteen of the judgment records are, according to the Maryland policy, inclusive. Imbedded in the judgment records, are found 15 warrants, 11 declarations, 4 accounts, 2 promissory notes, and references to other accounts, promissory notes, and amounts of indebtedness. The consideration of these 150 items is essential to the true picture of the financial operations of the Ohio Company. Among other things, the existence of 108 trial items in regard to about a score of commercial transactions may well demonstrate that wealth and money were almost nonexistent along the upper Potomac. It would follow that probably most of the Ohio Company goods were sold on credit, that cash sales were possibly few and small, and that litigation had to be entered upon against an unusually large percentage of the debtors.

In summary, among the commercial or mercantile items relating to the Ohio Company, 1750–1763, are 256 items, of which 174 transactions are from Frederick County, Virginia and 182 (including 32 imbedded documents in the judgment records) from Frederick County, Maryland. The sheer bulk of these items, some of them of considerable length and within each type, very repetitive or similar, is, as said, responsible for the decision to publish in Appendix A, only samples of them. A table of the purely financial aspects of these mercantile items will be found in Appendix B.

Land Items

In the matter of land items there is much information not only in several state land offices but also in county courthouses among records of deeds, wills, and litigation.

On the Ohio Company landholding, known as the *New Store Tract,* opposite the mouth of Wills Creek, once Fairfax property, and, in turn, later in Frederick County, Hampshire County, and Mineral County, there is adequate information. The original entry records of 1748 have not been found, but there are as Ohio Company items 3 deeds including Lots 14, 15, and 16 dated October 25, 1754; a resurvey warrant of March 1, 1768; the resurvey of May 5, 1768; the patent to the resurvey, February 13, 1773; the indenture lease of the property, July 13, 1785; and the deed to the property on the same day. To these 8 title items must be added several descriptive advertisements in 1763 for the sale of the property.

On the Gist settlement of Ohio Company property along the Youghiogheny River, in what is now Fayette County, Pennsylvania, there are numerous certificates, surveys, deeds, etc., most of them in the Pennsylvania Land Office in Harrisburg but some of them in the Fayette County archives at Uniontown.

On Ohio Company landholding in Maryland there are more than 30 title items extant, including 6 warrants with 2 renewals, 6 surveys, 4 resurveys, 6 patents, 4 deeds, 2 bonds, a deposition, and a petition, all of which may be called legal title documents as contrasted with hundreds of litigation items found in connection with (1) a quarrel about one tract (*Pleasant Valley*) which under various suits ran on from 1751 to 1821; (2) a suit of George Mason against Charles Clinton for unpatented parts of the Walnut Bottom Resurvey of June 13, 1761; and the great suit of George Mason IV, George Mason V, and the latter's executors against the signers of the two bonds submitted in 1783 in payment for *Walnut Bottom* and *Limestone Rock*. A statistical table of the Virginia and Maryland landholdings of the Ohio Company, particularly of the finances of purchases and sales by the Company, is found in Appendix C.

On the important survey made by the Ohio Company of 400,000 acres in Kentucky, in 1775, there have not been found any original Ohio Company surveys, patents, or deeds, but the material relating to the great survey of 1775 is widely scattered in the Kentucky Land Office and in Virginia and Kentucky local archives.

A Depository of Ohio Company Documents and Transcripts

The University Library has organized the manuscripts and transcripts of this collection of Ohio Company historical data and items, some of them photostatic and others microfilm, in conveniently boxed files, arranged chronologically. These files are open to anyone wishing to consult or visit the Darlington Library at the University of Pittsburgh.

They are known as the A. P. James Collection, Collated Transcripts of Manuscripts Relating to the Ohio Company of Virginia.

Limited Content of this Volume

The items published in Appendix A are arranged in chronological order. Where the date is not at the top of the original manuscript it is bracketed herein. Some of the bracketed dating of items is approximation and as such cannot be fully guaranteed as to perfect accuracy. The use of the chronological order and the possible benefit of the reader seemed to call for such approximate dating.

Most of the documents published in the appendix are published in full, including also where found, addresses, endorsements, annotations, and so forth. In some cases, only extracts from documents otherwise largely irrelevant are utilized.

The total relevant items number more than 1,200, which made questionable the wisdom of including a list of them otherwise than in an Appendix, for the list in larger type if at the beginning of the volume in small type would fill about seventy pages, at a cost above value, and probably fatigue or antagonize the reader.

In a work of such scope and size, the bibliography and index are problems of proportion. It has seemed advisable to confine the bibliography to highly relevant items and to limit the index to the more significant names and subjects found in the narrative, the appendixes, and the bibliography.

Omitted here, as already in print, are materials fundamental to the history of the Ohio Company. Highly important items are the minutes, resolutions, orders, and instructions of the meetings whether of the Company as a whole or of the Committee of the Ohio Company. They are found almost entirely in the George Mercer Papers of the Darlington Memorial Library and are available in the ably edited and well printed *George Mercer Papers*. Hardly less important are the petitions, memorials, and other formal statements of the case or claims of the Ohio Company. Many of these are likewise found in the *George Mercer Papers*. Excellent service was rendered by Fernow in 1890 and Bailey in 1939 by printing, in appendixes, many of the materials of this second type. The thorough student of the subject should have in possession or for consultation the *George Mercer Papers* (Lois Mulkearn ed.) and the *Ohio Company of Virginia*, by Kenneth P. Bailey.

Acknowledgments

In research on the scale and in the proportions involved in this project it is virtually impossible to acknowledge fully and completely obligations to all who have rendered assistance of one kind or other. A general statement of genuine appreciation and gratitude must suffice. It may be of some value to testify that everywhere, without exception, archivists, librarians, public officials in charge of records, and private individuals in possession of documents were uniformly courteous, and extended all the aid which could be expected under the circumstances.

The obligation to each other of the editors of the two volumes of the Ohio Company are so obvious to anyone that they need not be stated.

For assistance in secretarial capacity, thanks must be given to Perra Rose, Lillian E. Holbrook, Phyllis Ayers, Helen K. Bole, Mable Williams James (my wife), Alice Linton, and others, some of whom as secretaries of various officials of the University gave service beyond their normal duties.

For support of this project, credit is here given to John G. Bowman, chancellor of the University at the inception of the work, to Rufus H. Fitzgerald, his successor, who re-established the project in 1948, and to Stanton C. Crawford who gave it much attention and encouragement. Also included in the category of supporters must be the successive University librarians, Leland D. Baldwin, A. L. Robinson, and Lorena A. Garloch, each of whom in turn manifested keen interest and gave requisite aid. Credit must particularly be amplified in the case of Dr. Robinson who long served as chairman of a supervisory committee, but whose credit must be shared with additional members of the committee, John W. Oliver, former head of the history department, and Agnes Starrett, University editor and director of the University of Pittsburgh Press.

The search for relevant material on the Ohio Company involved, as indicated above, much travel and extended correspondence. Indebtedness to the larger manuscript depositories is seen in reference to the locations of documents and is gratefully acknowledged. Among these may be mentioned the Darlington Memorial Library of the University of Pittsburgh; the library of Duke University; the Department of Archives of North Carolina; the Alderman Library of the University of Virginia; the library of William and Mary College; the files of the Colonial Williamsburg project; the archives of the Virginia State Library; the Virginia Historical Society; the manuscript division and the Division of Maps of the Library of Congress; the National Archives; the Peabody Institute; the Enoch Pratt Library and the Maryland Historical Society at Baltimore, Maryland; the archives of the Hall of Records and of the Land Office at Annapolis, Maryland; the Historical Society of Pennsylvania; the Ridgeway Branch of the Philadelphia Free Library; the library of the University of Pennsylvania; the Friends Historical Society and the American Philosophical Society in Philadelphia; the New York Public Library in New York City; the New York State archives at Albany; the libraries at Yale, Brown, and Harvard universities; the Massachusetts Historical Society; the state archives in the capitol at Boston; the Essex Institute at Salem; the American Antiquarian Society at Worcester; the small manuscript collection of Amherst College; manuscripts or archives of the Division of Archives, the Land Office and the Pennsylvania Historical Library and Museum, Harrisburg, Pennsylvania; the Mercer Museum and Library of Doylestown; the collections of the Ohio Archaelogical and Historical Society at Columbus; the manuscripts of the University of Chicago Library and the Chicago Historical Society; the Draper collection of the Wisconsin Historical Society at Madison; the materials of the William L. Clements Library at Ann Arbor, Michigan; the manuscripts of the Kentucky archives, particularly in the Land Office; materials at Charleston, West Virginia in the Land Office, the division of archives and the museum; the West Virginia Collection in the library of West Virginia University; the Henry C. Huntington Library of San Marino, California; and the Kentucky Collection of the Western State College of Bowling Green, Kentucky. Involved in the accumulation of data were notes taken in earlier years in the great historical depositories at Detroit, Ottawa, London, and Paris.

Unusually significant in the search for papers related to the Ohio Company were visits to county courthouses in counties such as Philadelphia, Lancaster, Cumberland, Bedford, Westmoreland, Fayette, and Allegheny in Pennsylvania; Ann Arundel, Prince Georges, Charles, Montgomery, Frederick, Washington, and Allegany in Maryland; Fairfax, Stafford, King George, King William, Spotsylvania, Westmoreland, Richmond, Lancaster, Northumberland, York, Augusta, Botetourt, and Montgomery, in Virginia; Brooke, Hampshire, Mineral, Monongalia, and Ohio in West Virginia; and Harrison, Scott, Mason, Fayette, Clark, Bourbon, Nicholas, and Bath in Kentucky. Of these county archives, those of the counties of Washington, Frederick, and Allegany in Maryland, and of Frederick in Virginia proved the greatest sources of unused Ohio Company material.

(The value and significance, in historical research, of local governmental archives and records is too frequently overlooked by general and broad regional historians. Only property title tracers and genealogists seem to pay full attention to this widespread and voluminous data.)

Since repeated visits were made to the four counties last named, the officials of these counties must be given special credit and appreciation. In more particular acknowledgment, the editor is indebted to Mr. Lee Whitacre, clerk of the Court of Frederick County (and his assistant, Mrs. Kathryn Lineweaver, deputy clerk), not only for uniform courtesy and aid in research but for permission to microfilm hundreds of items so fortunately preserved and duly under his supervision. Specific and particular appreciation must be extended to Morris L. Radoff, archivist, Roger Thomas, assistant archivist, and Gus Shordas, assistant archivist, of the Hall of Records of Maryland at Annapolis, the last of whom did, in research on the project, much work beyond his regular hours. The same special gratitude must be extended to Richard N. Williams II, director of the Historical Society of Pennsylvania, and to his assistants. Also to be mentioned personally are Lester Cappon, of the Colonial Williamsburg project, and Wilmer P. Hall, of the Virginia State Library, who furnished data which might otherwise not have been located.

It is often the complaint of those professionally engaged in the fields of the humanities and the social sciences that in comparison with those in the fields of the physical and biological sciences, they are inadequately financed. While there is much justification for such complaint there are notable cases of splendid promotion of research, writing, editorial work, and publication in the humanities and the social sciences. The promotion by the University of Pittsburgh and The Buhl Foundation of such projects as the Western Pennsylvania Historical Survey, 1931–1936, and subsidized research on Ohio Company Papers, 1941–1942 and 1948–1957, is a splendid example of such support. Mention has been made, above, of Chancellor John G. Bowman and his successor, Chancellor Rufus H. Fitzgerald. In thanks to The Buhl Foundation special mention should be made of Dr. Charles F. Lewis, its former director.

ALFRED P. JAMES

University of Pittsburgh

Contents

I

Background: Historical Antecedents and Forces

IMPORTANT HUMAN ORGANIZATIONS or institutions have two aspects in common. They develop out of past influences and they affect later times. No familiar metaphor describes later effects, but the slogan, "The roots of the present lie deep buried in the past," can be applied not only to all the present but also to any moment of the past.

The Ohio Company of Virginia had some roots buried deep in the history of civilized man. Human nature appears to have shown from the beginning certain definite traits, among them the desire for prestige, for power, and for economic security. These traits may not be instincts but they certainly have been factors.

In the centuries from the decay of the Roman Empire in the West to the discovery of the New World, the struggle for the acquisition of more land and greater territory was incessant, for the very good reason that the possession of landed estates was the road to distinction, power, and whatever economic security may be said to have existed.

The desire of the members of the Ohio Company of Virginia for

500,000 acres of land in the hitherto unsettled parts of North America was in keeping with the outlook of their ancestors for more than a thousand years. But more particularly it was completely in the traditions of Virginia and Maryland for more than a century. The Culpepers, the Fairfaxes, the Byrds, the Calverts, and numerous others were exemplars and possibly the inspiration for the gentlemen of the Ohio Company.

In the background of the Ohio Company was the Age of Discovery and European colonization and settlement of North America. The work of Columbus and Cabot and of the London Company was continued and carried farther west by the Ohio Company.

The colonial rivalries of European states from the fifteenth to the middle of the eighteenth century were instrumental in the formation of the Ohio Company. A significant part of these rivalries was what the famous English historian John R. Seeley aptly called "The Second Hundred Years War" between England and France, which he showed as beginning in 1689 and lasting until 1815. On this there are many thousands of documents in the public archives of Great Britain, France, the United States, and Canada.

These extensive materials embody information on many unusually complicated problems; the more important were ten questions:

1. Did the international law of the seventeenth century give the discoverer of the mouth of a river claim to the possession of the entire basin drained by it?

2. If so, did the discovery (and occupation) of the mouth of the St. Lawrence River give France claim to the St. Lawrence River drainage system, including the entire Great Lakes area?

3. Did the French in 1669 explore what is now called the Allegheny River?

4. Did the discovery of the mouth of the Ohio River by the French give them claim to the entire Ohio Valley?

5. Did the occupation of the mouth of the Mississippi by the French give them a valid claim to the entire Mississippi Basin?

6. Was La Belle Riviere (the Ohio and the Allegheny), as the French claimed, a tributary of the Wabash, or was the Wabash, as the English claimed, a tributary of the Ohio?

7. Were the Iroquois Indians territorial overlords of all Mississippi

Valley lands as far south as the Cumberland River and as far west as the Mississippi River?

8. Did the Iroquois Indians, therefore, and not the French nor the English, possess legal title to the lands controlled by them?

9. Did the Iroquois have the right to sell territory occupied by other Indians actually in physical possession of the territory?

10. Did the British by treaties with the French and the Iroquois establish overlordship of all the above mentioned area?

These, and other such problems of less significance, imbedded in diplomatic interchanges, pamphlets, maps, and letters, gravely affected the position and policies of the Ohio Company.

Five aspects of the background of the Ohio Company were particularly American, and little, if at all international:

1. the earlier exploration of the Piedmont, Appalachian, and trans-Appalachian frontier, the continuation of which exploration was a notable accomplishment of the Company; [1]

2. the land distribution systems of the American colonies, particularly those in vogue in New England, New York, Pennsylvania, Maryland, and above all in Virginia,[2] systems greatly affecting and affected by the desire for land possession and speculation in landed property as a traditional trait of civilized men;

3. trade with the Indians;

4. westward expansion of white settlement;

5. the conflicting territorial claims of various British American colonies.

The last three of these call for some elaboration.

Trade with the Indians antedated permanent white settlement in Virginia, New France, and New England. The famous fur trade began with white settlement and ran with shifts and changes but without serious breaks throughout two centuries. Competition with

[1] The literature on this earlier exploration is voluminous. Special mention should be made here of Clarence W. Alvord and Lee Bidgood, *The First Explorations of the Trans-Allegheny Region by the Virginians, 1650–1674.* An important purpose in the establishment of the Ohio Company is fully understood only through a knowledge of these earlier explorations.

[2] The imperial policy of land grants is a remote but important aspect of this problem.

the French appeared early in New England and New Netherland. Soon, by a shift, competition was mainly between New France and New York. Later the competition was mainly between French Canadians and Pennsylvanians. In the meantime Virginians and Marylanders began to trade, particularly with the Indians of the South and of the Ohio Valley. In the upper Ohio Valley the Ohio Company brought Virginians and Marylanders directly into fur trade competition not only with the French but also with New York and Pennsylvania.[3]

The story of the Ohio Company is an important item in the history of the westward expansion of the United States, which in turn is a feature of the Europeanization of the modern world. The history of American westward expansion, written by whites, neglects the retreat and retrenchment of Indians, a much neglected tragedy. Westward expansion of the whites of Virginia and Maryland was in stages, first to the headwaters of tidal navigation, then to the foothills of the Blue Ridge Mountains, next into the Great Valley, and finally, mainly in connection with the Ohio Company, over the Appalachian Mountain ridges into the valley of the Ohio River, a region hitherto visited only by Indians and rambling fur traders of New France, New York, and Pennsylvania, or by random adventurous explorers.

Many conflicting territorial claims grew out of colonial charters. The Ohio Company of Virginia found itself involved in matters highly complicated by charter provisions of Pennsylvania, Maryland, and Virginia.[4] With such matters the Company wrestled valiantly but vainly.

There were regional factors, almost local, in the more immediate background of the Ohio Company. The oldest of these was the land

---

[3] On this the records are voluminous and the bibliography of printed works very extensive. Not only were the financial aspects of the fur trade involved here, but also the whole question of Indian relations in other matters such as military diplomacy and land cessions.

[4] Alfred P. James, "The Role of Virginia and Virginians in the Early History of Southwestern Pennsylvania," *Western Pennsylvania Historical Magazine* (hereinafter cited as *W. Pa. Hist. Mag.*), XXXIV (1951), 51-63.

situation in the Northern Neck of Virginia lying between the Rappahannock and the Potomac rivers. To the dismay of earlier comers, Charles II granted in 1673 title to more than 5,000,000 acres of land between the two rivers to a few Cavalier friends who had lost estates in England during the Great Rebellion. In a relatively short time, Thomas Lord Culpeper bought out the other grantees and the territory became a Culpeper holding. By the marriage to Thomas Lord Fairfax of Catherine, granddaughter and sole heiress of the Culpeper estate, this vast landed estate in Virginia came into the possession of the Fairfax family.

An early Virginia manager of the estate was "King" Robert Carter, who lived at Weems, Virginia, in a mansion overlooking Carters Creek, the Corrotoman River, and the wider waters of the Rappahannock. From him are descended many distinguished Americans. His tombstone still survives at Old Christ Church at Tombs, Virginia. His position as land agent enabled him to amass vast landed estates for himself and his children.

But Catherine Fairfax became dissatisfied with the revenues sent her by "King" Carter and, in 1713, replaced him with Thomas Lee, nephew of Thomas Corbin, a rich tobacco merchant of London. To this appointment, as Fairfax land agent, Thomas Lee owed his rapid acquisition of property in Virginia and the high position he and his descendants were later to hold in Virginia affairs.

As manager of the Fairfax property in Virginia, 1713–47, Thomas Lee became interested in western expansion and familiar with western problems. Under him much surveying was done in the Piedmont region and extensive sales made on the quit rent plan. It was under him that settlement of the lower Shenandoah Valley began in the decade before the organization of the Ohio Company.

Among other things, Thomas Lee knew that Germans from Pennsylvania were on the move south and west along the valleys of the Appalachian Mountains. Probably he came to believe that with good land titles and adequate protection they could be relied upon to settle upon lands farther west, beyond the giant Fairfax estate. One explanation of the formation of the Ohio Company is the migration of Germans to the Shenandoah Valley, 1735–45.

Since the Germans and the Scotch-Irish of Pennsylvania crossed first from Pennsylvania into western Maryland, a similar westward movement north of the Potomac was natural. The history of Frederick County, Maryland, parallels in time that of Frederick County, Virginia, with great similarities in settlement and acquisition of lands.

Probably another highly immediate factor in the origin of the Ohio Company arose when Thomas, sixth Lord Fairfax, a bachelor, took up permanent residence in Virginia in 1747 and shortly afterwards appointed as his land agent, his cousin William Fairfax, father of George William Fairfax and ancestor of the Fairfaxes of later Virginia. Thomas Lee faced the end of his earlier role and the necessity of turning elsewhere for speculative activity.

The influence of the Fairfax property and family on Lawrence, Augustine, and George Washington is well known. Like Thomas Lee, the Washingtons looked westward with the Fairfaxes to the Allegheny Mountains, and were ready, if opportunity arose, to project themselves into the lands of the upper Ohio Valley.

Neighbors, and some of them relatives of the Fairfaxes, the Lees, and the Washingtons, were Presley Thornton, John Carlyle, Jacob Giles, Nathaniel Chapman, and James Scott. These men were the nucleus of those who promoted the Ohio Company in 1747. Other neighbors, acquaintances, and relatives later became members.[5]

Not to be disregarded among those who probably instigated the organization of the Ohio Company was the famous Maryland frontier figure, Thomas Cresap.[6] After much trouble elsewhere, he moved to western Maryland and finally settled at Old Town about 1741. Here an old Indian trail crossed the Potomac River, and with the passing Indians, Thomas Cresap carried on a lively trade. Rival Pennsylvania traders and high political authorities in Philadelphia believed that the very conception of the organization of the Ohio

---

[5] Elaborate detail concerning the gentlemen of the Northern Neck of Virginia in the eighteenth century is found in the first volume of Douglas Southall Freeman, *George Washington, A Biography*.

[6] See Kenneth P. Bailey, *Thomas Cresap, Maryland Frontiersman*.

Company originated in the restless disposition and fertile mind of Thomas Cresap.

Marylanders and Virginians in the 1740's were bent upon aggressive westward expansion. Thomas Bladen, Esquire, governor of Maryland, secured a warrant,[7] October 21, 1743, for 2,000 acres, of which about 1,000 acres were to be located "between the Lowest Old Town and the mouth of Savage river and Evetts creek and Wills creek. . . ." Thrice renewed, this warrant provided surveys of lands, title to which was later secured by George Mason for the Ohio Company. Almost simultaneously, in Virginia, James Patton and others put in a petition [8] for 200,000 acres on Woods River, and although not successful, claimed to have been granted preference in the future.

Of great significance was the Indian Conference at Lancaster, Pennsylvania, June 22 to July 4, 1744, and the resulting Indian Treaty.[9] Virginia was represented by Thomas Lee and William Beverley. The deed signed by the Indians, July 2, 1744, became vital in the Ohio Company's affairs. In it the Six Nations Indians "renounce and disclaim not only all the Right of the Six Nations, but also recognize and acknowledge the Right and Title of our Sovereign the King of Great Britain to all the Lands within the said Colony, as it is now or hereafter may be peopled and bounded by his said Majesty and Sovereign Lord the King his Heirs and Successors." [10]

A tempting bait dangled before the land speculators and politi-

---

[7] See a copy in Maryland Hall of Records, Court of Appeals Judgments, Liber T. H. No. 16 (1815), folio 138 and the record, *ibid.*, Land Office, Liber L. G. No. 2, folio 182.

[8] *Executive Journals of the Council of Colonial Virginia*, ed. Wilmer L. Hall, Vol. V; Etting Collection, Ohio Company Papers in Historical Society of Pennsylvania (hereinafter cited as H.S.P.), and printed in Kenneth P. Bailey, *The Ohio Company Papers*, p. 345.

[9] *Pennsylvania Colonial Records* (hereinafter cited as *Pa. Col. Recs.*), IV, 698-737; *Indian Treaties Printed by Benjamin Franklin, 1736–1762*, pp. 138-42.

[10] Copy in Public Record Office (London) Colonial Office Papers (hereinafter cited as P.R.O. C.O.) 5: 1330, Library of Congress transcript, pp. 138-42.

cians of Virginia. The language of the deed was vague and the right of the Six Nations to sell the territory appeared questionable, but the opportunity thus established proved irresistible. Direct action began within three months. On April 26, 1745, four petitions[11] totaling 300,000 acres were granted, with four years to fulfill the terms of the grants.

On November 4, 1745, John Blair, William Russell and Company petitioned for and received a grant of 100,000 acres westward of Lord Fairfax's line on the waters of the Potomac and Youghiogheny,[12] with four years to fulfill the terms of the grant. This vague general grant both anticipated and foreshadowed other petitions for land grants in that region, but for several years there was no real activity in carrying out the terms of the grant.

Marylanders, in 1745, more than matched the interest of Virginians in Western lands. In addition to the warrant of 1743, frequently renewed, Thomas Bladen secured a warrant, April 15, 1745, for 2,000 acres, and another warrant, April 16, 1745, for 3,000 acres.[13] Unlike in Virginia, the Maryland warrants were quickly followed by surveys[14] establishing named tracts of land, of which the Ohio Company in later years bought several, either from Bladen or from the Cresap family.

---

[11] Data on these and other Virginia grants are found in many places, notably in P.R.O. C.O. 5: 1423 and 1429; in Etting Collection, H.S.P.; in Draper Collection in Wisconsin Historical Society; in the Washington Papers in the Library of Congress; and in George Mercer Papers of the Darlington Memorial Library of the University of Pittsburgh (hereinafter cited as D.M.L. MS.), which are in print in *George Mercer Papers,* ed. Lois Mulkearn.

[12] The somewhat vague geographical language of this grant implies that it was intended to be located within rather than beyond the Appalachians.

[13] These two items are from the Maryland Land Office, Liber L. G. No. D., folios 396 and 397. The warrant of April 16, 1745 is printed below in Appendix A, p. 188. There is some indication that the warrant of April 15, 1745, was a replacement or further guarantee of the warrant of October 21, 1743.

[14] Two of these surveys are printed below in Appendix A, pp. 188-94, four of them are calendared in Appendix D, pp. 300-1, and many others are mentioned in land litigation documents.

II

Organization and Establishment

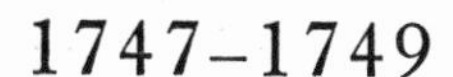

1747–1749

THOMAS LEE, as a result of his Fairfax lands experience and his service for Virginia at the Lancaster Indian conference of 1744, became a leader in the development of the West and probably initiated the organization of the Ohio Company. Great movements and important organizations, however, are usually complex. The Blair-Russell Company petition and grant of November 4, 1745,[1] antedated the first petition of the Ohio Company by nearly two full years. And, on April 22, 1747, William McMachon and Company, having put in a petition, were granted 60,000 acres adjoining the earlier Blair grant, "on the waters of Potomac W^t & N.W.^t of Ld Fairfax's Line & on the branches of Youghyoughgane & Monongahaly." [2] It was probably in connection with this petition of William McMachen and others that

[1] *Executive Journals, Council of Colonial Virginia,* V, 195; Record of Land Grants, Virginia, D.M.L. MS., printed in *George Mercer Papers,* p. 289.

[2] No particular explanation of this petition and grant has been found, but since it was only six months earlier than the petition of the Ohio Company of October 20, 1747, it may be that the organization of that company was under consideration, and that others knew about it and put out a petition in anticipation, a common matter in land speculation at all times and everywhere.

Monongahaly

Sir William Gooch, governor of Virginia, wrote his letter of June 10, 1747, to the Board of Trade and Plantations asking for instructions about such petitions,[3] thereby establishing for future colonial times an important imperial factor in the matter of Virginia's Western lands.

How early the gentlemen living in the Northern Neck of Virginia and nearby Maryland began to discuss the formation of a company to engage in Western land activities has not been indicated by records which have been found. These gentlemen generally worked slowly, as is well indicated by the surviving records of the Ohio Company of Virginia, and discussion about such a company may have extended over several years, at meetings of the legislature, at county courts, and on informal visits. Such discussions came to a head in the autumn of 1747 and the informal organization of the Ohio Company obviously took place before October 20, 1747, for on that date, "Thomas Lee, Esq. and eleven others" put in a petition to the Governor and Council of Virginia for a grant of "200,000 acres to be laid out from ye Branche called Kiskamanetts and Buffalo creeke,"[4] etc. Judged by eventualities this petition was not given a cordial reception by Governor Gooch and the members of his Council. As was demonstrated later, many of the members of the Council of Virginia were jealous of the gentlemen from the Northern Neck and had no intentions of supporting their plans. Governor Gooch, it is reasonable to suppose, had official scruples, and he played safe by entering into an extended correspondence about the matter with the authorities in London.

Comment will be made later on the "eleven others," who with Thomas Lee, Esq., entered this first petition, October 20, 1747. Some of them were probably assembled in Williamsburg for a meeting of the legislature. They evidently learned quickly of the unfavorable reaction of Governor Gooch and his Council, for on October 24, 1747, official instructions by the Company were handed to Thomas Lee, instructing him to offer a share in the partnership to John

[3] P.R.O. C.O. 5: 1326, L.C. transcript, pp. 465-70.

[4] P.R.O. C.O. 5: 1333/155. See the item in *Virginia Magazine of History and Biography* (hereinafter cited as *Va. Mag.*), V, 241.

Hanbury, a prominent London merchant,[5] an offer which may be considered the first recorded step in the formation of a policy to petition the Crown over the heads of Governor Gooch and his Council. Whether or not such a decision on the part of the Company was made known to Governor Gooch, he went ahead with his own program. On November 6, 1747, he wrote to the Lords of Trade, stating that he had received the petition and asking for more definite instructions.[6]

Probably in the winter months of 1747–48, Thomas Lee, in accordance with his instructions, wrote John Hanbury proposing that he become a member of the Ohio Company of Virginia,[7] though no such correspondence has been found.

About the same time Pennsylvania was promoting an Indian Conference to be held at Logstown in 1748 and requested Virginia to participate.[8] Virginia did not, as in 1744, send delegates, but she did appropriate funds for a gift which Conrad Weiser was expected to deliver at the Conference, an appropriation which the members of the Ohio Company of Virginia may have solicited and supported in the legislature.[9] Conrad Weiser carried out the program.[10] He divided the goods at Logstown into five heaps, "one heap whereof your brother Assaroque sent to you to remember his Friendship

[5] D.M.L. MS., printed in *George Mercer Papers*, p. 2. Tentative articles of agreement seem to have been established at some earlier time according to the Resolutions of the Ohio Company, Octobr 24, 1748, printed in *George Mercer Papers*, p. 167. Clearly an "Agreement in Company" antedated October 24, 1747.

[6] P.R.O. C.O. 5: 1326, L.C. transcript, p. 547, printed in full in Kenneth P. Bailey, *The Ohio Company in Virginia*, p. 297.

[7] See D.M.L. MS., as printed in *George Mercer Papers*, *passim*, but especially Part II, *Case of the Ohio Company* as reproduced there in facsimile.

[8] *Pa. Col. Recs.*, V, 120, 140, 145-52, 189, 190, 257.

[9] See Thomas Lee to Conrad Weiser, May 14, 1748, Peters Papers, II, 102, H.S.P.

[10] Note Lee's first letter to Weiser, February 13, 1748, Peters Papers, II, 89, a.l.s., H.S.P., printed below, p. 195, and his later letter of December 11, 1748, *ibid.*, folio 115, a.l.s., and see Conrad Weiser's Journal in *Early Western Travels*, ed. R. G. Thwaites, I, 21-44.

and Unity with you."[11] Conrad Weiser specifically mentioned "the President & Council & Assaraquoa."[12] As can be noted in surviving documents of the period, the Ohio Company of Virginia considered Conrad Weiser at this time a delegated agent of the Company, though they later complained that he sacrificed imperial and Virginia prestige to the advantage of the Penns and the Iroquois, an accusation often made later by others.

Action on Governor Gooch's letter of November 6, 1747, which had been received December 17, was taken by the Board of Trade and Plantations on January 19, 1748. In a letter[13] to the powerful minister, the Duke of Newcastle, the Board of Trade and Plantations requested him to lay the letter before His Majesty for consideration by the King in Council. The Board replied to Gooch on the same date, notifying him of the action being taken.[14]

A little more than a month later, the Privy Council Committee for Plantation Affairs, in reply to the request of the Board of Trade and Plantations, issued an "Order . . . to consider whether it is to His Majesty's advantage to give Governor Gooch power to grant lands to certain persons in partnership."[15] This action had reference to the Ohio Company of Virginia petition of October 20, 1747, and Governor Gooch's letter of November 6, 1747.

In answer to the letter of January 19, 1748, of the Board of

---

[11] *Early Western Travels*, I, 39. Assaraquoa, an Indian name for the governor of Virginia.

[12] *Ibid.*, p. 40.

[13] P.R.O. C.O. 5: 1366/410. It is mentioned in D.M.L. MS., printed in *George Mercer Papers*, p. 1, and in Gooch to the Board of Trade, June 16, 1748, P.R.O. C.O. 5: 1327/7-8.

[14] P.R.O. C.O. 5: 1366/408; mentioned in Gooch to the Board of Trade, June 16, 1748, *loc. cit.*, and in *Journal of the Commissioners for Trade and Plantations . . .*, 1741–1749 (hereinafter cited as *J.B.T.*), p. 265.

[15] P.R.O. C.O. 5: 1327/1-3, printed in full in Berthold Fernow, *The Ohio Valley in Colonial Days*, Appendix D, pp. 241 f.; mentioned in D.M.L. MS., printed in *George Mercer Papers*, p. 234; also mentioned in Bailey, *Ohio Company . . .*, p. 39. Royal action on the matter took place February 10, 1748, Public Record Office, Privy Council Register 2: 100/540 (hereinafter cited as P.R.O. P.C. Register), but further action was held up until February 23, 1748.

Trade and Plantations inquiring about his scruples and the difficulties in granting lands beyond the great mountains to the westward, Governor Gooch on June 16, 1748, replied that he thought that it might give umbrage to the French at a time when England was "in Hopes of entering into a Treaty for establishing a general peace." [16]

From its inception the Pennsylvanians kept a sharp watch on the Ohio Company of Virginia, which they saw as a threat to both Pennsylvania trade and Pennsylvania claims. George Croghan, "the king of the traders," of Pennsylvania, with heavy investments in packhorses and storehouses, wrote [17] (July 3, 1748) of "an alarm that Mr. Cresap and Mr. Parker spread amongst ye Indians Last fall that ye Virginians was going to Settle a Branch of Ohio Call'd Yougogain . . . ," which statement, though possibly mendacious or at least based on rumor, indicates that in late 1747 the Ohio Company was already loosely organized and had Cresap and Parker as its frontier representatives. That able and faithful individual, the Rev. Richard Peters, provincial secretary and clerk of the Council, 1743–76, kept Thomas Penn, the proprietor, closely in touch with developments. On July 28, 1748, he wrote to Penn about the Ohio Company of Virginia, calling Thomas Cresap, "that vile fellow Cresap who had suggested a scheme to Colonel Lee and other great men of Virginia to make trading houses at Allegheny" and commenting on Lee that he had "a plodding head" and that he had proposed a plan to the British ministry to erect forts on the Ohio River, "as if thereby all the country might be secured to his Majesty up to the Mississippi." [18]

At the very time the Indian Conference at Logstown was in

---

[16] P.R.O. C.O. 5: 1327/7-8, L.C. transcript, printed in part in Fernow, *op. cit.*, Appendix D, pp. 243 f.

[17] *Pennsylvania Archives* (hereinafter cited as *Pa. Arch.*), ed. Samuel Hazard, II, 31.

[18] Peters Letter Books, 1737–1750, IV, 143, H.S.P., cited by Lawrence H. Gipson, *Zones of International Friction in The British Empire Before the American Revolution*, V, 288 n., and quoted by Herbert L. Osgood, *The American Colonies in the Eighteenth Century*, IV, 78.

session, the prospects of the Ohio Company of Virginia were given a boost by the suspension of John Custis as president of the Council of Virginia, and the elevation of Thomas Lee to that position,[19] which on the proposed retirement and departure of Governor Gooch would make Lee, as president of the Council, the interim governor, a development which took place the following year.[20] This circumstance eventually for a period made the chief promoter and the largest stockholder of the Ohio Company the head of the government of Virginia.

In the meantime, in London the Board of Trade and Plantations in response to the order of February 23, 1748, made a report, September 2, 1748,[21] to the Privy Council favoring and approving the grant of the petition of the Ohio Company of October 20, 1747. The first official stamp of imperial approval of the grant was thus obtained a little more than ten months after the original petition. And it is on the first anniversary of the petition, October 20, 1748, that one finds the first surviving resolutions[22] of the Ohio Company of Virginia. Since these resolutions are those of the Committee of the Ohio Company, it is reasonable to suppose that other meetings, of which no record has survived, were held in 1747 and 1748 and that in one such meeting this Committee was appointed to transact business between the official meetings of the Company.

These resolutions of October 20, 1748, antedating the grant but indicating the spirit and activity of the Company, are so revealing that quotation here seems necessary. A carefully collated transcript of the original longhand material is as follows:

---

19 P.R.O. C.O. 5: 1328/1-3, Custis suspended August 26, 1748. Lee took oath as President of the Virginia Council, September 4, 1748.

20 Thomas Lee to the Board of Trade and Plantations, October 2, 1749, P.R.O. C.O. 5: 1327/113-15.

21 P.R.O. C.O. 5: 1366/411-17; Fernow, *op. cit.*, Appendix D, pp. 244 f. Mentioned in *J.B.T.*, 1741–49, p. 342. See the D.M.L. MS., printed in *George Mercer Papers*, p. 1.

22 D.M.L. MS., printed in *George Mercer Papers*, p. 167, and mentioned in résumé, p. 3. See the facsimile opposite p. 166.

Mount Vernon Octo.[r] the 20.th 1748.

Wee the Subscribers of the Committee of the Ohio Company having met at Major Lawrence Washington's this day by appointment.

1.st Have allow'd Col.[o] Thomas Cresaps Acco.[t] for Soliciting a Grant &c. at Williamsburgh £12.5

2.[d] Have allowed Lawrence Washington as paid the Clerk of the Counsel 1. . 1. 6

3.[d] Ordered that M.[r] James Wardrope pay Col.[o] Cresap in p.[t] of his Acco.[t] 10. . . . . .

4.[thly] It is the Opinion of the Committee that sending for a Cargo be Postponed ti'l a Grant shall be obtained at Williamsburgh or in England.

5.[thly] It the opinion that as soon as a Grant for the Lands is obtained and upon Notice thereof given to each member of the Comp.[a] they shall immediately furnish the Committee with Letters of Credit on M.[r] John Hanbury for One hundred pounds Sterling [23] or Bills of Exchange payable to M.[r] John Hanbury to be remitted by the Committee except what shall be adjudged necessary for wampum, &c.

6.[thly] It's the opinion of the Committee that as soon as a Grant is obtained that the Members which may be Assembled at Williamsburgh shall have power to give the Committee such Instructions as may be necessary for M.[r] Wardrope to send M.[r] Stedman in Rotterdam for procuring Foreign Protestants to settle the Land.

7.[thly] That M.[r] James Wardrope agrees to every Article the Company has agreed to [24] and will sign whenever the Articles of Agreement shall be brought to the Committee.

Signed. Law.[ce] Washington
James Wardrop
James Scott
John Carlyle

In these resolutions of October 20, 1748, adequate light is for the first time furnished on the activities and program of the Company in the first year of its existence. Summarized, they may be

[23] The first recorded levy. See also the Arthur Dobbs Account, D.M.L. MS., printed in *George Mercer Papers*, p. 183.

[24] Additional evidence of meetings and of "Articles" of Agreement antedating October 20, 1748.

stated briefly. Colonel Thomas Cresap solicited the grant at Williamsburg (probably in October, 1747) and was allowed twelve pounds and five shillings for his services. The Company had to pay the Clerk of the Council at Williamsburg a fee of one pound, one shilling and sixpence which was advanced by Lawrence Washington. James Wardrop was the first treasurer of the Company. Discussion of ordering a cargo of Indian goods had already taken place. Even before the grant was made, Mr. John Hanbury was looked upon as the London factor of the Company. A levy of one hundred pounds per member was provisionally voted. Wampum was sought for necessary and duly projected negotiations and treaties with the Indians. The Company early envisioned the settlement of its expected lands by German Protestants from the Rhineland, who would come probably by way of Rotterdam. Some Articles were agreed upon by the Company before October 20, 1748, and formal Articles of Agreement were under consideration. In many ways the Ohio Company of Virginia was already well established and very active, even if not officially and fully organized, on October 20, 1748.

Of this activity of the Ohio Company of Virginia in 1748, not only Virginians, but also Pennsylvanians, were aware. And in fact, knowledge of the program and its prospects was current in Quebec, London, and Paris. William Trent, at that time a Pennsylvania fur trader, in a letter to Richard Peters, October 20, 1748,[25] mentions the operations of the agents of the Ohio Company of Virginia, in the service of which somewhat ironically he was soon to participate actively himself. It was doubtless in response to the threat from the Ohio Company of Virginia that the French made ready in Quebec the expedition to the Ohio started early in 1749 [26] under Céloron de Blainville.

The interests of the Ohio Company of Virginia, meanwhile,

---

[25] Provincial Papers, Pennsylvania Archives, Harrisburg, a.l.s.; Peters Letter Books, H.S.P.; *Pa. Arch.*, II, 16-17; Charles A. Hanna, *The Wilderness Trail*, I, 346-47; and in part, Bailey, *Ohio Company . . .*, p. 71.

[26] P.R.O. C.O. 5: 1327/13-14, 37. Printed in full in Fernow, *op. cit.*, Appendix D, p. 248.

were being advanced in London. On November 24, 1748, nearly three months after the favorable report of the Board of Trade and Plantations of September 2, 1748, the Privy Council Committee for Plantations ordered that the Lords Commissioners prepare a draft of instructions for the Governor and Council of Virginia relative to granting lands west of the great mountains.[27]

The Board of Trade and Plantations, in accordance with this order of November 24, 1748, drew up "Additional Instruction," dated December 13, 1748, authorizing Governor Gooch and Council of Virginia to grant lands on the Ohio River to a partnership of grantees. Somewhat obviously this action referred to the Ohio Company of Virginia petitioners of October 20, 1747.[28]

Very important in the winter of 1748–49 was legislative action in Virginia, December 2, 1748,[29] revising the laws about surveyors and surveying, providing for the licensing of surveyors by the President and Masters of William and Mary College, and setting up the system of county surveyors, a tangled arrangement with which the Ohio Company of Virginia was to have difficulties and suffer disaster.

Shortly after December 13, 1748, an item of confusion entered into the case, one which was destined to delay final action for another five or six months. Thomas Lee, president of the Virginia Council and prominent figure in the Ohio Company of Virginia, who in 1748 was engaged in a lively correspondence with Conrad Weiser,[30] also probably carried on in late 1748 an extended correspondence with John Hanbury and must have suggested that

[27] P.R.O. C.O. 5: 1327/21-22. Printed in part in Fernow, *op. cit.*, Appendix D, p. 255. Dated and mentioned in *George Mercer Papers*, p. 679.

[28] P.R.O. C.O. 5: 1327/39-41. These Additional Instructions of December 13, 1748, being later replaced, were probably never sent to America.

[29] William Waller Hening, *The Statutes at Large . . .*, VI, 33-38. See also Charlton Palmer to George Mercer, December 27, 1769, D.M.L. MS., printed in *George Mercer Papers*, p. 310.

[30] Mentioned in *George Mercer Papers*, p. 409 and Gipson, *op. cit.*, IV, 241. Consult particularly Lee to Weiser, February 13, 1748 (printed below, p. 195) and Lee to Weiser, December 11, 1748, Peters Letter Books, II, 115, H.S.P.

Hanbury put in a petition for the Company directly to his Majesty in Council.[31]

Exactly when John Hanbury drew up his famous petition [32] and presented it to the Privy Council is not clearly discernible. Ostensibly it was later than December 13, 1748, and certainly antedated January 11, 1749, for after its presentation by the proper minister, "His Majesty was pleased by his Order in Council of the 11th of last month [January] to refer unto the Committee the humble Petition of John Hanbury of London Merchant." [33]

In his petition, John Hanbury, who had evidently agreed to become a member of the Ohio Company of Virginia, mentions as petitioners, in addition to himself, "Thomas Lee, Esqr., a member of His Majesty's Council and one of the Judges of the Supreme Court of Judicature in His Majesty's Colony of Virginia, Thomas Nelson Esqr., also a Member of His Majesty's Council in Virginia, Colonel Cressup, Colonel William Thornton, William Nimmo, Daniel Cressup, John Carlisle, Lawrence Washington, Augustus Washington, George Fairfax, Jacob Gyles, Nathaniel Chapman, and James Woodrop Esqrs., all of His Majesty's Colony of Virginia and others their Associates for settling the Countreys upon the Ohio and extending the British trade beyond the Mountains on the Western Confines of Virginia. . . ." Of the names mentioned, John Hanbury did not belong to the "several Persons in Partnership," mentioned by Governor Gooch on November 6, 1747. Thomas Nelson seems merely to have permitted the use of his name, for he told Colonel Thomas Lee "that he

---

[31] Most unfortunately the papers of John Hanbury have not been found. If perchance extant they would throw great light on the Ohio Company of Virginia, and probably upon many other aspects of American colonial history of the eighteenth century.

[32] In P.R.O. C.O. 5: 1327, L.C. transcript, p. 54, printed in Bailey, *Ohio Company . . .*, pp. 298-301 and found in the *Case of the Ohio Company*, pp. 2-3, reproduced in facsimile in *George Mercer Papers*, Part II.

[33] P.R.O. C.O. 5: 1327/51 f. Printed in Fernow, *op. cit.*, pp. 248-55, and in Bailey, *Ohio Company . . .*, pp. 302-3. See also D.M.L. MS., printed in *George Mercer Papers*, pp. 246-48, and Part II, the *Case . . .*, pp. 2-3. There is reason to believe that the undated petition, though composed earlier, was presented on January 10, 1749.

desired to be Excused and did not Intend to be one of the Ohio Company." [34] William Thornton's name was an error for Francis Thornton who resigned before his death in 1749. William Nimmo also died before June 21, 1749, but had told Colonel Thomas Lee that "he never Design'd to be one of the Comp.[a] and only lent his name to Major Lawrence Washington in the Petition never Designing to be concerned further." [35] Evidently Daniel Cresap merely permitted the use of his name, for George Mason in 1778, writing officially, said, "Daniel Cresap (whose name was inserted in the petition and Royal Instruction [never was] a member of the said Ohio Company, never advanced a Shilling, [or hath] had any manner of Concern, or Interest whatsoever, in the said Undertaking, or Copartnership." [36] John Carlisle (John Carlyle) sent in a written resignation in early 1749, which was agreed to at the meeting of the Ohio Company, June 21, 1749.[37] George [William] Fairfax also sent in a written resignation which was accepted on June 21, 1749.[38]

Thus, of the twelve names, that of Thomas Lee and eleven others, on the petition of October 20, 1747, and of the fourteen mentioned in the petition of John Hanbury, presented to the King in Council, January 11, 1748 (an addition of John Hanbury and one other not identified) six names were no longer available after June 21, 1749.[39]

---

[34] Resolutions of the Ohio Company, June 21, 1749, D.M.L. MS., printed in *George Mercer Papers*, pp. 141-42, 168-70. See the résumé, pp. 3-4.

[35] *Ibid.*

[36] Virginia State Library MS. (hereinafter cited as V.S.L. MS.), printed in Bailey, *Ohio Company* . . . , p. 321. It is now evident that, while not a member in 1778, Daniel Cresap became owner of a fortieth share April 19, 1783, by deed from his father Thomas Cresap. See the deed below, pp. 275-77.

[37] D.M.L. MS., printed in *George Mercer Papers*, pp. 141-42. See also V.S.L. MS., Memorial of the Ohio Company, November 20, 1778, as printed in Bailey, *Ohio Company* . . . , pp. 320-27.

[38] *Ibid.* None of these letters of resignation was found.

[39] For some unknown reason, the name of James Scott, who was appointed to the Committee in 1748 and remained a member of the Ohio Company until his death in 1782, was not on the list in the Hanbury petition. Probably he was not among the twelve who drew up the first petition of 1748. There was evidently, at the beginning, much uncertainty about memberships.

In his petition John Hanbury mentioned the two purposes of the Ohio Company of Virginia as land settlement and Indian trade. He made reference to the Indian deed to Virginia at the Lancaster Conference of 1744. He emphasized the possibility of promoting British trade; praised the possibilities on that frontier; and stated the terms of the petition and the desired grant. Doubtless he got most of his data from the petition of October 20, 1747, of which a copy was probably sent him, and from further letters of Thomas Lee and possibly of Lawrence Washington. In the lack of a copy of the earlier petition, it may be assumed, therefore, that much of its contents and some of its language are incorporated in the later petition of Hanbury.

The petition of John Hanbury, referred to the Committee of Council for Plantations on January 11, 1749, was by them referred on February 9, 1749, to the Lords Commissioners for Trade and Plantations (Board of Trade and Plantations) for their consideration thereof and a Report of "their Opinion thereupon. . . ."[40]

The last sentence (a long one) of this "order of the Lords of the Committee of Council" well indicates the confusion and explains the further delay. It bears quotation as follows:

> And Whereas there was likewise laid before the Lords of the Committee a Report made by the Lords Commissioners for Trade and Plantations dated the 13th of December last, together with a Draught of an Additional Instruction prepared by the said Lords Commissioners for Sir William Gooch Bart. His Majesty's Lieutenant Governor of the Colony of Virginia, impowering him to make Grants of Lands on the Western Side of the Great Mountains, to persons in Partnership, who have applied for the same, And their Lordships observing that the Lands proposed to be granted by the said Instruction, are Situated in the same place with those prayed for by the aforementioned Petition of John Hanbury and others, and may probably have some relation to each other, Do therefore, think it proper to refer back to the said Lords Commissioners for Trade and Plantations the said Report and Draught of Additional Instructions, for their further Consideration.

[40] P.R.O. C.O. 5: 1327/51-70, printed in Bailey, *Ohio Company . . .*, pp. 302 f. and in Fernow, *op. cit.*, pp. 348 f. For the date January 11, 1749, see P.R.O. P.C. Register 2: 101/145.

Between February 9, 1749, and February 23, 1749, the Board of Trade made further investigations and finally drew up another set of Additional Instructions[41] to Governor Gooch in which he was "directed and required forthwith to make a Grant or Grants to the said Petitioners and their Associates of 200,000 Acres of Land . . ." on certain conditions. And in reply to Gooch's letter of explanation of June 6, 1748, the Board of Trade, March 4, 1749, wrote him, fully informing him of developments.[42] All this activity in America and in London did not escape the attention of Thomas Penn, Lord Proprietary of Pennsylvania, who, on February 20, 1749, wrote Richard Peters on the matter and about the proposals "made by Coll Lee to the Ministry" and about his "Indian Trade Schemes."[43]

While the Board of Trade and Plantations were reconsidering the instructions to Governor Gooch, the Committee of the Ohio Company met at Cameron, February 23, 1748. Its main business was to order each member to pay Nathaniel "Chapman on Order the sum of One hundred pounds Sterling to be laid out in Goods, for carrying on the Indian Trade, the money to be paid out at or before the fifteenth day of April next. . . ." The money received was to be remitted to Thomas Lee "to be by him remitted to our correspondent in London along with the Invoice for this trade."[44] It was also ordered, "that the Letter of this date from the Committee to Thomas Lee, Esq.r & also a Copy of that to each Member be inserted in the Company Books."[45]

In London the business of sanctioning the grant to the Ohio

[41] P.R.O. C.O. 5: 1366/434-39. See *J.B.T.*, 1741-49.

[42] P.R.O. C.O. 5: 1366/439-44.

[43] Penn Papers, Saunders Coates, H.S.P., pp. 29-36, a.l.s.

[44] D.M.L. MS., printed in *George Mercer Papers*, pp. 167-68. See résumé, p. 3. Actually this order for the first cargo of goods for the Indian trade was deferred for four months, and the cargo arrived in the late winter of 1749–50.

[45] Letter in Emmet Collection, New York Public Library (hereinafter cited as N.Y.P.L.), printed below, p. 196. Some idea of the extent to which historical documents disappear is afforded by the fact that none of the copies mentioned has been found.

Company of Virginia speeded along in the spring of 1749. A letter of the Board of Trade to Governor Gooch, March 4, 1749, foreshadowed approval of the petition.[46] By March 16, 1749, the Board of Trade and Plantations had ready the draft of His Majesty's Instructions to the Governor of Virginia to make the requested grant of lands to the Ohio Company of Virginia.[47] On April 3, 1749, it received the Order of the Privy Council approving the Additional Instructions (of March 16, 1749) to be sent to Governor Gooch. Probably they had the royal signature.

John Hanbury was keeping in touch with the development of all this. Sometime between March 13, 1749, and April 3, 1749, he reported progress to Thomas Lee,[48] who probably received this report very late in May, for on June 1, 1749, Lee wrote a letter to Gentlemen of the Ohio Company, saying Mr. Hanbury advised him that the instructions to Governor Gooch to grant the lands to the Ohio Company were ready for the King's signature.[49] Lee said he expected the Governor would receive the instructions by the next ship, and agreed to take upon himself the matter of dealing with the Governor. As President of the Council and a Judge of the Supreme Court he was in a position to do it.

The chances are, though there is no positive proof, that the member to whom Thomas Lee wrote was Major Lawrence Washington, the next most important member in the Company at that time and the one most easily in touch with other members residing on the upper Potomac.

Notwithstanding the "Business of Importance Relating the

---

[46] P.R.O. C.O. 5: 1366/439-44.

[47] P.R.O. C.O. 5: 1327/93-96. Mentioned in D.M.L. MS., printed in *George Mercer Papers*, p. 2, Part II, the *Case* . . . , p. 3, and George Mason to James Mercer, January 13, 1772, pp. 315-18. See also Bailey, *Ohio Company* . . . , p. 31, Fernow, *op. cit.*, p. 268, and *Va. Mag.*, XII, 162-63.

[48] P.R.O. C.O. 5: 1327/57-58. Probably Hanbury wrote March 16, 1749, immediately after the approval of the grant by the Privy Council.

[49] Hanbury letter not found. It is mentioned in a letter of Thomas Lee to members of the Ohio Company, June 1, 1749, a N.Y.P.L. MS. printed below, p. 196.

Compy,"[50] the "General Meeting" for which the Committee had appointed the eighteenth day of May was postponed, very likely for the reason that the expected information from London had not arrived. And instead of at Cameron, the General Meeting was held at Stafford Court House on June 21, 1749.[51]

At this meeting only six of those named in the Hanbury Petition were present.[52] But those who attended, and especially Thomas Lee, were not to be deterred by any small difficulty. Seven new members of the Company had been secured in America. The "six of those named in the Petition and John Tayloe Esq.r Presley Thornton Esq.r James Scott Clk. Richard Lee, Philip Ludwell Lee,[53] Gawin Corbin & Hugh Parker, seven others of the Company met and proceeded to Business."[54] All but one of these, Hugh Parker, were relatives, neighbors, or close friends of Thomas Lee.

The first business of the meeting was the acceptance of withdrawals and resignations. Then George Mason "on his Desire and Paying his Share" was admitted as the sixteenth member. In spite of their limitation at the time to sixteen members they established the Capital Stock at four thousand pounds sterling. A long letter to John Hanbury[55] drawn up the previous day was approved, a letter in which they thanked him for his work in connection with the Petition, instructed him to offer the Duke of Bedford a Share

---

[50] N.Y.P.L. MS., Orders of the Committee of the Ohio Company, February 23, 1749, printed below, p. 196. See also D.M.L. MS., printed in *George Mercer Papers*, pp. 167-68.

[51] D.M.L. MS., printed in *George Mercer Papers*, pp. 141-42, 168-70, and in résumé, pp. 3-4.

[52] *Ibid.* John Hanbury was in London, Francis Thornton and William Nimmo were dead, Daniel Cresap was not then a member, and Thomas Nelson, John Carlyle, and George (William) Fairfax had requested their withdrawal.

[53] The eldest son of Thomas Lee, who before February 22, 1749, bought and gave his son a full two-fortieths share. See the excerpt from the Last Will and Testament of Thomas Lee, February 22, 1749, below, p. 197.

[54] D.M.L. MS., printed in *George Mercer Papers*, pp. 141-42, 168-70.

[55] Copies in D.M.L. MS., printed in *George Mercer Papers*, pp. 140-41, 168-70.

in the Company, sought through Hanbury a letter from the King to Governor Gooch instructing him to protect the Company, to permit it to have its own surveyor, and to permit a present out of the Virginia quitrents for the Indians on the Ohio.

And now at last, in this letter, they ordered a cargo of goods worth two thousand pounds to be sent over to Virginia by the last of November, and also a second cargo [56] to reach Virginia by the first of March, both of which cargoes they wished insured. The letter is signed by fourteen members, one of whom, James Wardrop, was not present on June 21, and it is not signed by George Mason, who was admitted after the letter was drafted. A curious annotation, in the way of postscript, said, "We consider you as one of our Comp.[a] & that your share 125£ sterling will be added to what we remit." [57]

Having bound themselves to bear in equal proportion all future charges, the Company next employed Hugh Parker to transport goods between the lower falls of the Potomac and the "General Factory on the River Ohio" for the consideration of "twelve shillings Current money for every hundred weight" and made him "their Factor at the Ohio." They also authorized Thomas Cresap and Hugh Parker to "cause the necessary Roads to be made and the Houses to be built for carrying on the said Trade to the best advantage." Due provisions were made for the Factor in regard to prices, credits, etc., and Nathaniel Chapman, the treasurer, was instructed to pay out the cash on hand for the construction of a road, etc. Steps were also taken to bring from England "a Good Gun Smith and a good white Smith and a set of Tools for each and a taylor."

Several provisions in these full minutes or resolution of this full meeting of the Company indicate that from the beginning

---

[56] This second cargo was later deferred to 1751, George Mason to Lawrence Washington, May 27, 1750, Moncure D. Conway, *Barons of the Potomac and Rappahannock*, pp. 280-81.

[57] The citation is from a George Mercer Paper, D.M.L. MS., a variant textual copy mentioned but not fully printed in *George Mercer Papers*, pp. 168-69.

the Ohio Company of Virginia hoped for and probably expected the support and cooperation of the government of the Colony of Virginia, regardless of the delay in granting the first petition of October 20, 1746. Set up in the Resolutions, these provisions are:

> And the said Comp[a] further desire that the Indians at the Ohio be invited to a Treaty and an Interpreter provided at the Expense of the Government and that a proper Application be accordingly made and that their factor be put in the Commission of peace for Augusta County.[58]
>
> That Legal Endeavours be used to prevent the Pensilvania and other Traders from Trading on the Branches of the River Mississippi without a Lycence from this Government.
>
> Also that Major Lawrence Washington apply to the Governor for a Dozen or two of Muskets which he is to send round by water to Potomack if obtained.

This meeting also ordered "that Col[o] Philip Lee and M[r] George Mason be added to the Committee."

Certainly the colonial gentlemen who gathered at this county seat in June, 1749, were not lacking in confidence and a sense of their importance. They cannot be accused of timidity and undue modesty. All present signed the minutes. Only the names of John Hanbury, in London, George Mason, who seems not to have been present, and James Wardrop, who left early, are missing.

In spite of the poor communications of the time, information two centuries ago spread with considerable rapidity. Within twelve days, George Croghan in Pennsylvania, writing on July 3, 1749, reported Hugh Parker and Thomas Cresap as agents of the Ohio

---

[58] See *Executive Journals, Council of Colonial Virginia*, V, *passim;* a Commissioner for Peace was another name for Justice of the Peace. Augusta County, at this time, included all the northwest territory lying beyond the Fairfax property line. Actually Frederick County, Virginia, was nearer and of easier approach to the upper Ohio Valley. Persons unfriendly to the Ohio Company were dominant in Augusta County and there has been found no record of an Ohio Company factor being on the Augusta County Commission of Peace. But Christopher Gist, after his settlement at Monongahela, was, August 17, 1753, appointed a Justice of the Peace of Augusta County, *Abstracts of the Records of Augusta County, Virginia,* ed. Lyman Chalkley, I, 69.

Company and asserted that the Indians would resist any settling on the Ohio River.[59] On both points his information was correct; on the second part it was highly prophetic of the future.

The instructions from London to issue the grant to the Ohio Company of Virginia appears to have reached Williamsburg in June and been submitted to the Council on July 12, 1749. An extraordinary reaction followed. On that day Virginia politicians and land speculators put in five petitions for Western lands which were duly granted.[60] These grants involved a total of 1,450,000 acres.

Since the fifth petition, that of John Tayloe, William Parks, and James Ford in behalf of themselves and company, "was a renewal of an older grant for one hundred thousand acres of land lying in Augusta County on the three branches of the Mississippi River the one known by the name of Woods River and the other two to the westward thereof . . . ," it is generally omitted in discussions, but the other four grants totaled 1,350,000 acres of land and contained seventy-four names.

In accordance with the instructions sent from London, the grant was made at this time to the Ohio Company of Virginia,[61] though in addition to the usual expense of surveys and payments of fees required in all such transactions, the Ohio Company, unlike the other companies, was put under binding terms about the settlement of families and the construction of a fort and storehouses, a burden and a risk voluntarily assumed by the promoters in 1747 and not imposed upon them by their opponents in Virginia or by imperial officials in England.

---

[59] *Pa. Arch.*, II, 31, Croghan to unknown person.

[60] *Executive Journals, Council of Colonial Virginia*, V, 296-97; D.M.L. MS., printed in *George Mercer Papers*, pp. 250-51. See also *Va. Mag.*, V, 177, and Bailey, *Ohio Company . . .*, p. 67.

[61] According to the "List of Early Land Patents and Grants petitioned for in Virginia to 1769," *Va. Mag.*, V, 177, and the "Record of Land Grants, Virginia," D.M.L. MS., printed in *George Mercer Papers*, pp. 289-91, the date was July 12, 1749. But according to P.R.O. C.O. 5: 1328/353, L.C. transcript, the date was July 13, 1749. See also *Executive Journals, Council of Colonial Virginia*, V, 295.

In the meantime, John Hanbury had not been idle in London. A letter [62] of Samuel Smith to John Hanbury, June 24, 1749, began, "As you have admitted me to be an Associate with you & the Gent^{m} of Virginia in the late Grant of Lands on the River Ohio . . . ," and proposed attracting German and French Protestants as settlers by waiving quitrents for ten years and sending "an Officer and a Company of men from Ireland" for their protection.

Thus in the middle of July, 1749, the Ohio Company of Virginia was well organized, its finances were in good shape, and it had after two years' delay received the formal grant of 200,000 acres of Western lands on terms suggested by itself. Much had been accomplished and, earlier obstacles and barriers having been cleared, the road of the future seemed open. But appearances belied the real future. The self-sought but restricting terms of the grant, the complications of foreign affairs, and the intricacies of imperial and colonial claims were destined to ruin everything save honor and distinction.

---

[62] From photostat in the Department of Archives of North Carolina, from the Arthur Dobbs Papers in the Public Record Office of Northern Ireland.

III

Early Procedure

1749–1750

Of the activities of the Ohio Company of Virginia from the middle of July, 1749 to late in September there is little record. Probably its members largely marked time while awaiting the cargo of goods ordered from John Hanbury and expected to arrive by the last of November. In the interim several items of indirect interest appear in the contemporary records.

There was no letup in the concern of Pennsylvania authorities about the plans of the Ohio Company. In a letter of July 31, 1749, the Proprietor wrote Governor James Hamilton to "give the greatest as well as the most speedy encouragement to Trade you can, that we may not be long after the Ohio Company." [1] Thomas Penn also wrote Richard Peters on August 2, 1749,[2] thanking Peters for his report on the Ohio Company of Virginia, stating that he thought their grant lay south of Pennsylvania, but requesting to be kept informed about the matter; all of which was an ominous forboding of the final outcome, in which virtually all of the 200,000 acres first granted to the Ohio Company of Virginia

[1] Penn Letter Books, II, 270-74, H.S.P.

[2] Penn Official Correspondence, IV, 219, H.S.P.

came under the permanent jurisdiction of Pennsylvania.[3] George Croghan, a Pennsylvanian, claimed to have purchased[4] from the Indians, August 3, 1749, a large tract of land lying between the Monongahela and the Ohio. This may have been an attempt to forestall the Ohio Company. Hugh Parker, on August 16, 1749, wrote to President Lee that the Indians were alarmed at hearing of a Fort which the Ohio Company intended to erect. This information, when presented to the Board, October 27, 1749, led the Executive Council to advise the President to write to Conrad Weiser for a full report on the matter.[5] The other item is that on September 4, 1749, Thomas Lee took oath as president of the Virginia Council.[6] On the departure of Governor Gooch,[7] he became the acting governor of the colony.

From the records which have survived it is clear that quarterly meetings of the Company were projected by its promoters and early members. The autumnal general meeting of 1749 was held September 25, at Potomack Falls, Fairfax County, Virginia,[8] with, however, only six members present: Thomas Lee, John Tayloe, Presley Thornton, Gawin Corbin, Richard Lee, and James Scott. The business done was slight. At his own request Nathaniel Chapman was succeeded by George Mason as "Cashier of the Company," in other words as treasurer and recorder.[9] Thanks were voted to Mr. Hanbury, and he and Samuel Smith (of London) were "Chairfully" accepted as partners. It was resolved that "Col° Cresap and Mr. Parker be employed to Survey our Land, and that this may be done as soon as possible. . . ." Probably more im-

[3] *Executive Journals, Council of Colonial Virginia*, V, 302-3.

[4] Colonial Papers, B. Gratz Book, V.S.L. See details of this alleged transaction in the Indenture of September 19, 1775, Etting Collection, Ohio Company Papers, H.S.P., printed in Bailey, *Ohio Company* . . . , pp. 403 f.

[5] *Executive Journals, Council of Colonial Virginia*, V, 302-3.

[6] P.R.O. C.O. 5: 1327/115; *Executive Journals, Council of Colonial Virginia*, V, 300.

[7] P.R.O. C.O. 5: 1327/113-14.

[8] D.M.L. MS., printed in *George Mercer Papers*, pp. 170-71.

[9] A position held by Mason until his death forty-two years later, in 1792. As the documents below, published or calendared, clearly show, this was the most responsible position in the Company.

portant were several resolutions impowering Mr. Hanbury to make proposals and agreements for bringing over "to seat on our Companys lands Germans or other protestants"; requesting him to solicit that the instructions be changed so as to omit the requirement of building a fort; asking him to endeavor to obtain an order from London to Virginia to make presents to the Indians; and also that he try to obtain an Order "to Run the Line between Virginia and Pensilvania on the same Terms as the Caroline line was Run. . . ." The final resolution was that the "Honble Thomas Lee Esq. do write to Mr. Hanbury in the name of the Company as to all matters before mentioned." [10]

From the meeting of September 25, 1749, until his death, November 14, 1750,[11] Thomas Lee was more than ever the mainspring in the Ohio Company of Virginia. During the larger part of this time he was acting governor of Virginia, and in the opinion of many would have been appointed governor had it not been for his untimely death. Any implications that he misused his position in the interest of the Ohio Company are without support in records now available. He seemed very careful to uphold the responsibilities of his new position. In his first official letter of October 2, 1749, he merely stated that he had taken office and asserted his allegiance.[12] A second letter to the Board of Trade and Plantations, October 18, 1749,[13] presented factually the case of the Ohio Company, reporting that it began action on the receipt of news of the Royal Instructions to Governor Gooch, that it ordered a shipment of goods from Mr. Hanbury, that it sent out explorers

---

[10] Presumably Thomas Lee did this shortly afterwards, but no copy of the letter has been located. Numerous and varied attempts to locate John Hanbury papers in England failed of any results.

[11] Burton J. Hendrick, *The Lees of Virginia; Biography of a Family*, p. 124. Bailey, *Ohio Company* . . . , p. 79, says he died February 12, 1751. Conrad Weiser in a letter to William Johnson (*The Papers of Sir William Johnson*, I, 318) says he died in October, 1750.

[12] P.R.O. C.O. 5: 1327/113-14.

[13] *Ibid.*, 195-200. Printed in part in Fernow, *op. cit.*, pp. 258 f. Referred to in Bailey, *Ohio Company* . . . , pp. 69, 111, 118.

(Hugh Parker and Thomas Cresap), that the Indians were hostile and a treaty with them necessary, that the settlement of the Virginia-Pennsylvania boundary line was essential, and that the construction of a regular military fort was too expensive for the Company. The chances are that by the same post he wrote John Hanbury [14] on the points outlined in the resolutions of September 25, 1749. In his new position he was in a situation to further the Company resolutions of June and September, seeking the support of the government of Virginia in calling an Indian treaty conference and providing presents for the Indians. What he did and how much he accomplished is not fully revealed by any documentary evidence. He did communicate to the Council, October 27,[15] the letter [16] of Hugh Parker of August 16, about Indian dislike of a fort on the Ohio, and secured an Order of the Council November 6, 1749, permitting surveys "beyond the great Mountains" and incorporating new directions and instructions for surveyors.[17] On November 7, 1749, Lawrence Washington, who had gone to England during the summer carrying samples of supplies wanted by the Ohio Company, wrote a long letter,[18] probably to John Hanbury, on the situation in the Ohio country in such matters as geography, Indians, the fur trade, and French competition. And Barney Curran, a hired man of Hugh Parker, about this time carried a message of Thomas Cresap to the Ohio Indians that he had cheap goods and wanted them to come to the Potomac region to get them.[19]

In the late autumn of 1749 preparations were made for the cargo of goods ordered to be in Virginia by the last of November. Hugh Parker and Thomas Cresap took some of the required steps. They

---

[14] Letter not found.

[15] *Executive Journals, Council of Colonial Virginia*, V, 302-3.

[16] Letter not found.

[17] *Executive Journals, Council of Colonial Virginia*, V, 306.

[18] Conway, *op. cit.*, pp. 272-77.

[19] Mentioned, *Pa. Col. Recs.*, V, 460.

made for the Ohio Company,[20] probably from an agent of Lord Fairfax, a purchase entry of land opposite the mouth of Wills Creek. It is possible that George Washington made the survey of some of the entry for his *Writings* contain an early item: "Mem. to survey the lands at the mouth of Little Cacepehon and the Mouth of Fifteen Mile Creek for the Gentlemen of the Ohio Com:"[21] On some of this land a small storehouse may have been constructed during the winter[22] of 1749–1750.

Just as, in his official capacity as acting governor of Virginia, he should have done, Thomas Lee on November 22, 1749, wrote a polite but firm letter[23] to Governor James Hamilton of Pennsylvania saying: "I am sorry that so soon I am obliged to complain to you of the insidious behavior of some traders from your province, tending to disturb the peace of this colony and to alienate the affections of the Indians for us." The cleverness and force of the letter can hardly be surpassed. Three additional parts of it bear quotation. "His Majesty has been graciously pleased to grant to some gentlemen and merchants of London and some of both sorts inhabitants of this colony, a large quantity of land west of the mountains" is a very neat official announcement. Complaints about Pennsylvania are followed by the statement: "yet these are the lands purchased of

---

[20] See the Resolutions of January 29, 1750, approving the purchase, D.M.L. MS., printed in the *George Mercer Papers*, p. 171. See also *William and Mary College Quarterly*, VI (April, 1888), p. 226 (hereinafter cited as *W. & M. Quarterly*). Record of this purchase (or entry) was not found in the Fairfax Land Papers in the Land Office archives at Richmond, Virginia, nor in the archives or records of the counties of Virginia along the upper Potomac.

[21] Fitzpatrick edition, I, 18.

[22] Maryland authorities on local history believe that the earliest post or store of the Ohio Company was in Maryland on the west bank of Wills Creek. Evidence to confirm this was not found. It is more likely that at first the Ohio Company used the property and facilities of Thomas Cresap at Old Town.

[23] Gratz Collection, Colonial Governors, Case 2, Box 30, a.l.s., H.S.P.; *Pa. Col. Recs.*, V, 422-24. Copies in P.R.O. C.O. 5: 1327/195-96 and in Pennsylvania Provincial Record, M, 1748–55 (Harrisburg), folios 51-53. It is quoted in part in Bailey, *Ohio Company . . .*, pp. 112-13.

the Six nations by the Treaty of Lancaster." As another point Lee wrote: "We are informed that there is (*sic*) measures designed by the court of France that will be mischievous to these colonys which will in prudence oblige us to unite, and not divide the interest of the king's subjects on the continent." As a judge, Thomas Lee had evidently listened to and profited by many excellent pleas by able lawyers. A second letter of Lee, December 20, 1749,[24] mainly about running the boundary line between Virginia and Pennsylvania was similar in spirit and cleverness. Thus early Thomas Lee brought into the open a fire which had been smouldering for several years, though as yet the Ohio Company had not begun its trade with the Indians.

In his letter of reply, January 2, 1750,[25] Governor Hamilton expressed his concern about the behaviour of the Pennsylvanians, promised his attention to the matter and, in reference to the Ohio Company group, shrewdly remarked, "I am induced to desire your opinion whether it may not be of use that the Western Bounds of the Province be run by Commissioners to be appointed by both Governments, in order to assure Ourselves that none of the Lands contained in that Grant are within the Limits of this Province." It must be said that this was a fair warning, and Governor Hamilton followed it up by a challenging offer to appoint Commissioners.[26] He, also, January 2, 1750, wrote similarly to Governor Samuel Ogle of Maryland.[27]

During the early months of 1750 the affairs of the Ohio Company of Virginia seemed to drag badly.[28] A winter meeting of the Committee of the Company, January 29, 1750, attended by "J. Scott, Mason, Wardrop," did a minimum of business. It approved the purchase entry of land before mentioned, "Resolved that the same

---

[24] *Pa. Col. Recs.*, V, 423-24.

[25] Penn Papers, Official Correspondence, H.S.P., IV, 177; *Pa. Arch.*, fourth series, II, 123-24.

[26] Penn Papers, Official Correspondence, H.S.P., IV, 177; copy in Pennsylvania Provincial Record, M, 1748–55, folios 53-54. In *Pa. Arch.*, fourth series, II, 123-24 and *Pa. Col. Recs.*, V, 422.

[27] Penn Papers, Official Correspondence, H.S.P., IV, 199.

[28] D.M.L. MS., printed in *George Mercer Papers*, p. 171.

is the most convenient place to settle the Factory and begin the Trade at," and "Ordered that Mr. Parker apply to Lord Fairfax to obtain a Grant in the Company's name for S.d Lands & that he do with all possible expedition build convenient houses & stores for the Reception of the Goods thereon," [29] the last, a resolution, indicating that the Ohio Company store and houses in Virginia had not yet been built, that the cargo [30] ordered from Hanbury had not yet reached the mouth of Wills Creek, and that the Ohio Company of Virginia had not entered into the fur trade before the early part of 1750. Literally and figuratively things were moving slowly. In the language of a later petition: the gentlemen employed "to discover the Lands beyond the mountains to know where" the Company "should make their Surveys" had not made "any considerable progress." [31] In a letter to Governor Hamilton of Pennsylvania during this winter, 1749–1750, Governor Ogle of Maryland expressed skepticism in regard to the Ohio Company.[32] In discussion of the extension of the temporary boundary line of Maryland, he said he did not see how the Company could proceed to settle the lands of their intended grant until the matter of boundary lines was settled.

Writing to Conrad Weiser, February 27, 1749, Thomas Lee, after an expression of confidence in him, mentioned the Lancaster conference of 1744, presents for the Indians, the royal grant to the Ohio Company, a proposed conference with Indians, and his good opinion of Hugh Parker, who was being sent as carrier of the letter.

Probably there was at this time more activity in London than in Virginia. Peter Collinson in a long letter to Arthur Dobbs, March 10, 1750, wrote "The Ohio Company goes on briskly I great Quantity of Good and fine Cloths for pts [presents] are gone to Engage our New Allies to be firm to our interest," [33] an indefinite statement

[29] D.M.L. MS., printed in *George Mercer Papers*, p. 171.

[30] It seems to have reached the lower Potomac sometime in March, 1750.

[31] P.R.O. C.O. 5: 1328/153-59; Bailey, *Ohio Company . . .*, pp. 304-9.

[32] Penn Papers, Official Correspondence, H.S.P., IV, 179, February 3, 1750; *Pa. Arch.*, II, 40-41; *Pa. Col. Recs.*, V, 422.

[33] Arthur Dobbs Papers, North Carolina State Department of Archives and History, Raleigh, North Carolina.

which may refer to official imperial or colonial presents, but possibly included the recently sent first cargo of the Ohio Company.

At a meeting of the Ohio Company, March 27, 1750, after the arrival of a cargo and letters from England, Capel Hanbury and Robert Dinwiddie were admitted as members.[34] Two days later, March 29, 1750, at a meeting of the Committee of the Ohio Company, Christopher Gist was employed to take a cargo to the Ohio country,[35] thus relieving Hugh Parker of some of the responsibilities [36] resting upon him as their "Factor."

---

[34] D.M.L. MS., printed in *George Mercer Papers*, p. 5.

[35] No records of such a trip were found. But Gist may well have transported a big load, not a ship's "cargo," of Ohio Company goods in April and May, 1750, and sold some of them in Maryland on the trip, for his headquarters at the time were seemingly at Old Town, Maryland. In 1755, the Ohio Company sued Gist in the Frederick County, Maryland, court. See the items, below, pp. 229 and 328.

[36] Hugh Parker, the factor or trade agent of the Ohio Company and himself a member, was in March, 1750, a courier between Thomas Lee and Conrad Weiser. Gist may have been in local control of Company affairs until Parker arrived and assumed control at the New Store in June, 1750.

IV

Trade and Exploration

1750–1752

As a series of documents[1] which have recently come to light clearly show, the Ohio Company began mercantile accounts with individuals as early as May 24, 1750.

Evidently the first cargo of goods, purchased for £2,000, reached the Potomac River in the winter of 1749–1750, probably in March 1750, rather than in November 1749, as ordered. As the account[2] of Zacheus Ruth shows, he bought two weeding hoes on May 24, 1750. And on the same day James Ross opened an account with a purchase of "1 half barrell of Gunpowder £5..0..0" and "100 lb of Lead £2..6..0."[3] A letter[4] of George Mason to Lawrence Washington, May 27, 1750, in regard to the qualifications and securities of Hugh Parker as factor of the Company, indicates that the goods of this cargo had, up to that date, "lain quite still" somewhere along the lower Potomac, below the Falls. Seemingly in June and July

[1] Some of the documents were purchased from a New York dealer by the Darlington Memorial Library; others were found in official archives and records at state capitals, in county courthouses, and in private possession.

[2] D.M.L. George Mason Papers.

[3] *Ibid.*, printed below, pp. 197-98.

[4] Conway, *op. cit.*, pp. 280-87.

1750,[5] Hugh Parker, the Ohio Company "Factor" transported the goods of the first cargo from the tidewater reaches of the Potomac to its upper waters, probably first overland to the mouth of the Conococheague (present day Williamsport) and later by water to the mouth of Wills Creek, where the Company built a storehouse on the *New Store Tract*.

Pennsylvania authorities, who were well informed, manifested much alarm concerning this activity. Governor Hamilton in his instructions to Lewis Evans, June 26, 1750, said, "Get informed of the Stock and scheme of the Virginia C.°, trading to Ohio, and what disadvantages they labour under, or advantages they now or hereafter may enjoy more than we from their situation."[6]

In late June goods were sold to Jeremiah Jack.[7] An account of £4:15:0 was opened with the Ohio Company by Evan Shelby of Maryland on June 3, 1750;[8] and another account of £3:11:16 opened by Joseph Volgamore[9] of Maryland on July 9.

An item in a suit of George Mason against Daniel Ashcraft, August 1751, indicates that a petition and warrant against the defendant was entered on September 19, 1750.[10] If so, this is the earliest litigation found recorded and the sale of goods must have been made in May or June. These accounts may well have been opened while the goods were in shipment up the Potomac in late June and early July. And on July 23, 1750, the account of Jeremiah Jack was further enlarged to a total of £12:5:6. On the following day the Company took a promissory note of William Richey for £4:15:0 current lawful money of Maryland.[11] One day later James Findley

---

[5] See the account of John Hammer, D.M.L. George Mason Papers, printed below, p. 199.

[6] Pennsylvania Provincial Papers, XI, 25, copy.

[7] D.M.L. George Mason Papers.

[8] Frederick County, Maryland, Judgment Record G, 1752–53, folios 713-15.

[9] *Ibid.*, H, 1754–59, folio 32.

[10] Frederick County, Maryland, Dockets, 1751, August Term, folio 154. Found in Hall of Records, Annapolis, Maryland.

[11] D.M.L. George Mason Papers, below, p. 200.

opened an account[12] of £2:19:1/2 with the Ohio Company. A promissory note of Jasper Sutton for £5:13:9, was taken in, July 27, 1751 and on July 28, 1750, accounts in Virginia were opened by Thomas Caton[13] and Remembrance Williams[14] and an account of £6:7:0 in Maryland by Van Swearingen.[15] On August 1, 1750 Caton's account was enlarged to £67:13:9. A day later began the account of John Johnson of Maryland for £7:3:0.[16] Bills of goods were sold on August 3-4, 1750 to Thomas Wood,[17] Peter Tostee,[18] and Samuel Taylor.[19] Another account was opened with Enoch Enochs[20] on August 10-11, 1750. A month later, September 11, 1750, Thomas Swearingen made out a promissory note of £3:0:0 to John Yeats, who possibly, in exchange for merchandise, assigned it to the Ohio Company.[21] Probably in the middle of September, 1750, the Ohio Company disposed of goods to two fur traders, Aaron Price and Barney Curran, to the enormous amount of £792:18:2½; for on September 14, 1750 these two gave their double indemnity penal bond for that amount, a bond fully paid in less than two years.[22] It is very likely that in the late summer and early autumn of 1750 the storehouse on the *New Tract* was completed. The account of Thomas Rutherford for £14:8:9 dates from October 28, 1750,[23] and a promissory note for £5:3:4½ from John Nicholls of Maryland is dated October 29, 1750.[24]

[12] D.M.L. George Mason Papers, calendared below, p. 305.

[13] *Ibid.*

[14] A completed transaction, at £ 2 . . 1 . . 10.

[15] Frederick County, Maryland, Judgment Record H, 1754–59, folio 30.

[16] *Ibid.*

[17] D.M.L. George Mason Papers. A completed transaction at £ 3 . . 11 . . 6 3/4.

[18] *Ibid.* A completed transaction at £ 6 . . 3 . . 9.

[19] *Ibid.* The beginning of a complex account involving transactions at different times.

[20] *Ibid.* The beginning of a complex account and continued transactions.

[21] Frederick County, Virginia, Court Docket Papers, commonly called "Loose Papers," and filed on final transaction in a suit.

[22] Frederick County, Maryland, Judgment Record H, folios 575-76, printed below, pp. 200-1.

[23] D.M.L. George Mason Papers.

[24] Frederick County, Maryland, Judgment Record G, 1752–53, folio 727.

Here we have sufficient evidence that the Ohio Company of Virginia had actively entered into trade and merchandising in the summer of 1750. Since only accounts which caused trouble and produced litigation are known to have survived, it is impossible to do more than estimate the volume of business and number of accounts, most of which were probably on credit.[25]

But the Ohio Company had a larger vision than that of selling imported goods to merchants, Indian traders, and farmers along the Potomac River in Virginia and Maryland. It certainly had in mind settlements and an extensive Indian trade in the Ohio Valley. Nevertheless, in its establishment and trade on the Potomac the Company had reasons for satisfaction with its operations of the first fifteen months following its grant of July 12, 1749. The sales thus recorded, though on credit, amounted in money to half of the London cost of the first cargo and probably to twenty percent of its contents.

Long before the death of Hugh Parker, which occurred during the late spring of 1751,[26] Thomas Lee appears to have become dissatisfied with him. Exploration, the laying out of roads, building construction, and surveying were being neglected, and probably not

---

[25] According to George Mason, the treasurer, writing in 1778, the Company was "Obliged to give large Credits to the Indian-Traders, most of whom were killed, captivated or ruined in the Course of the war, and the Debts due . . . thereby lost." Petition of November 20, 1778 as printed in Bailey, *Ohio Company* . . . , p. 323. The words, "large Credits" and "Indian-Traders," imply accounts, probably, not found in recorded litigation. George Croghan may have been one such "Indian-Trader." On consultation by the author and editor of this volume, a Frederick County, Virginia, lower court judge stated, in 1949, that while today less than 2 per cent of such mercantile transactions became a matter of litigation, he believed that earlier, before the coming of credit associations and credit ratings, the percentage of such accounts in litigation may have been as high as 10 per cent. If his opinion was sound the number of Ohio Company mercantile accounts found recorded in litigation may be multiplied many fold to get their total. Probably cash sales were few. And, as indicated elsewhere, the frontier was a debtor area, and the percentage of accounts unpaid and in litigation may have been very high.

[26] See the Indenture or Articles of Agreement, May 23, 1751, printed below, pp. 205-20.

in skillful and efficient hands. At some time in early 1750 he made a contact with Christopher Gist, a Marylander who had recently moved to North Carolina. Recognizing his worth, Thomas Lee promptly drew him into the service of the Ohio Company.

Looking backward, which is much easier for the historian than looking forward was for the Ohio Company, it may be said that the Company lost almost a year's time after receiving their grant before they began to make much headway on their Ohio Valley project, a loss which later circumstances were to make disastrous.

When, therefore, Thomas Lee and the Committee of the Ohio Company (Chapman, Scott, Mason and Richard Lee) met at Stafford Court House, September 11, 1750, they employed Gist as an explorer, gave him his well known instructions, agreed to pay him £150, current money, and authorized the Treasurer to advance Gist £30, current money, and instructed Hugh Parker (the Company's Factor) to supply him with arms, ammunition and such other things as were necessary.[27] With the long ago printed instructions to Christopher Gist on this occasion students of this field of history are very familiar.

In addition, a matter hitherto unknown, the Committee on the same day made an Agreement with Gist, "for the greater Encouragement of the first settlers upon the Company's Lands."[28] This agreement is so revealing that it is here cited in full, as follows:

> "Whereas M.r Christopher Guist proposes to remove one hundred and fifty or more Family's to the Ohio Company's Land on the Branches of the Mississippi to the Westward of the great Mountains. We hereby agree and oblige ourselves that all such persons as will remove themselves to, and settle upon the said Lands contiguous to each other, within two Years from the Date hereof, shall have a Fee simple in any Quantity of the Companys Land not exceeding fifty acres for every person they remove more than four, or one hundred Acres for every person less than four upon the following Terms.
>
> To pay to the Ohio Company after the Rate of four pounds Sterling for every hundred Acres within three years after seating upon the Land

[27] D.M.L. MS., printed in *George Mercer Papers*, pp. 171-73.
[28] *Ibid.*

to have their Title Deeds signd and acknowledged upon payment of the Consideration money. To hold their Lands five years Quit Rent free and then to pay the usual Quit Rent of Virginia. In Witness whereof We have hereunto set our Hands this 11.th day of September 1750."

Here, in a nutshell as it were, one has the main feature of the speculative land program of the Ohio Company. Owing to one or more variables, most notably the purchasing power of money, it is not easy to calculate how great would have been the profit to the Company if they had succeeded in disposing of 500,000 acres on such terms. Theoretically the profit would have been triple the costs, or money invested.

And Thomas Lee did not get this important work started any too soon, for in a little more than two months he was dead and his valuable leadership at an end. On September 29, 1750, he had sent in a long document to the Board of Trade and Plantations in answer to queries about the state of the colony.[29] In this he had mentioned the old matter of the Virginia-Pennsylvania boundary line, about which Governor Hamilton of Pennsylvania had written on January 2, 1750;[30] a matter which was taken up for consideration by the Board of Trade and Plantations, October 16, 1750.[31] But this was a matter which neither Thomas Lee nor most of the members of the Ohio Company of Virginia were to see finished before death. Lee's life and his role in the Ohio Company came to an end, November 14, 1750.

Very probably, on the death of Thomas Lee, leadership in the Ohio Company fell upon Lawrence Washington. The "unhappy state of" his "health"[32] really incapacitated him for the responsibility. Greatly interested in religious freedom for potential German settlers on the Ohio Company grant and knowing the situation in Virginia, he wrote to Hanbury,[33] probably in late 1750, suggesting imperial action in this matter.

---

[29] P.R.O. C.O. 5: 1327/231-46.

[30] *Pa. Col. Recs.*, V, 422, 425.

[31] *J.B.T.*, 1750–53, pp. 97-99; P.R.O. C.O. 5: 1366/463-65 and 1423, Council Journal. See Gipson, *op. cit.*, IV, 233.

[32] *The Writings of George Washington*, ed. Jared Sparks, II, 481.

[33] *Ibid.*

When the next meeting of the Committee of the Ohio Company was held at Occoquon Ferry, on December 3, 1750,[34] the first resolution took care of Lee's former work and the circumstances of his death, as follows:

> "Ordered that the said George Mason correspond with John Hanbury Esq.r concerning all matters that relate to the Company and that he apply to the Executors of the honble Thomas Lee Esq.r dec.d for all papers relating to the Companys Affairs which are in their hands." [35]

The remaining two resolutions are essential here as an introduction to the valuable document printed below [36] in its first full revelation to the public. They are:

> "Resolved that it is absolutely necessary the Company should enter into more regular Articles than they have hitherto done and that the members in England should Authorize some person in Virginia to sign such Articles in their Behalf
> "Ordered that M.r George Mason write to M.r Hanbury on that Head, and that the said George Mason, M.r James Scott and M.r Nathaniel Chapman or any two of them apply to M.r John Mercer to consider and draw up such Articles and desire him to attend the next general meeting of the Company." [37]

It was on this occasion that a Seal for the Company was proposed, with a design in accordance with the Company's program, "Three deer passant and regardant in a proper field—The crest—A Beaver —The Supporters—two Indians—one with a Bow and Arrows—the

---

[34] D.M.L. MS., printed in *George Mercer Papers*, p. 173.

[35] *Ibid.* If done this means that these papers went from Thomas Lee to George Mason. Some of them were later put in the hands of John Mercer, lawyer and attorney of the Ohio Company, who sent copies of them to George Mercer. After the death of John Mercer the papers were probably returned to George Mason and destroyed or damaged by fire.

[36] Pp. 205-20.

[37] This resolution of December 3, 1750, is the entry of John Mercer into the affairs of the Ohio Company, in which for nearly two decades he was to play a prominent role, particularly as compiler of much of the materials or archives now in the George Mercer Papers.

other with a Riffle gun—the Motto underneath—Pax et Commercium."[38]

While there is no later trace of the seal and no record that George Mason carried out his instructions to write to Mr. Hanbury about the Articles, we do know that John Mercer was quickly approached about drawing up the Articles of Agreement. Very fortunately we are able to publish a carefully collated transcript of a photostat of the original document, signed and sealed by many of the members. From internal evidence it is apparent that John Mercer began the actual copying of the Articles on the parchment before the end of December, 1750, though the document was not signed and sealed until the following May.

Evidences have also survived of considerable activity of the Ohio Company along the upper Potomac in mid-winter, 1750–1751. An account of £3:1:10½ with the Company was opened by David Cragge [Craig] and another of £7:15:3½ by Mark McDonough on January 15, 1751.[39]

Hugh Parker, the "Factor" of the Company, was active in the last few months of his life. On February 9, 1751, he received a Bill of Sale from Neal Ogullion in which the latter in consideration of "the sum of one hundred and eighty pounds current money," acknowledged the sale to the Ohio Company of "Three Red Cows and one brown Cow and two Brindled coloured steers...also two Horses and three Mares...also six sheep...also four hundred weight of Bacon... also...Title...to a Bond... [to] a certain Tract of Land...also Eleven Acres of Wheat and Rye...also one other Horse a Roan...." This Bill of sale was recorded March 19, 1751.[40] On March 1, 1751, he

---

[38] No trace of such a seal has been found. For the proposal, see D.M.L. MS., printed in the *George Mercer Papers*, p. 6. And in particular see the excellent delineation of such a seal, opposite the title page. It should be apparent that the emphasis in the provisions of the seal is upon Indian trade rather than upon land speculation.

[39] D.M.L. George Mason Papers. The items are duly calendared below, p. 307.

[40] Frederick County, Maryland, Deeds B, folios 347-48, printed below, pp. 203-4.

received a similar Bill of Sale [41] from Aaron Price for eighteen months service of a servant woman, four feather beds and their furniture, twelve chairs, a table, three iron pots, two kettles, a coffee mill, one Box Iron & Heater, a dozen plates, tubs, barrels, a spinning wheel, a trunk, a churn and a frying pan; along with four cows, one bull, three calves, three horses, twenty hogs and all his grain. These Bills of Sale to the Ohio Company [42] involved an outlay of £240. The records of them lay unnoticed for nearly two centuries before they were noticed by the editor in his research on this project.

The relation of Conrad Weiser with Virginia, Pennsylvania, and the Indians throws some light on the Ohio Company. Weiser, October 4, 1750 [43] sent Thomas Lee an account of his expenses. Lee's successor, President Lewis Burwell, wrote Weiser, February 11, 1751, "This serves to enclose to you a Sett of Bills of Exchange on Messrs John and Capel Hanbury, Merchants in London, for thirty pounds sterling, which was designed to have been sent long ago to you, by the President Thos Lee Esqr: but was unhappily prevented by his sudden death." [44]

Richard Peters, the watchdog of the Pennsylvania Proprietor, intercepted the correspondence of Burwell. He wrote Weiser, March 20, 1751, "the enclosed letter .... I was going to send by Express but Billy Logan judged that you would not take it amiss if I opened it to see whether it was worth while, & I accordingly did & so kept it till a good opportunity ......" Peters added, "You see what amazing neglegence there is in Indian affairs at Virginia & that they know nothing perhaps none of your letters to Col^{l} Lee have seen ye Light." [45]

---

[41] Frederick County, Maryland, Deeds B, folios 343-44, recorded March 19, 1751, and printed below, pp. 200-1.

[42] Apart from the bond on Sugar Bottom (the tract of land of Neil O'Gullion) and the possibility of Hugh Parker aiding old friends, these sales seem intended as a measure to provide, locally, supplies for the settlement at the New Store across the Potomac in Virginia.

[43] Weiser Correspondence, I, 28, H.S.P.

[44] Peters Papers, III, 27, H.S.P.

[45] *Ibid.*, p. 30.

Christopher Gist, setting out on October 31, 1750, on his first exploration, from which he returned about seven months later, needs no comment here. His journals, well annotated by William Darlington, have long been public property. Comment upon them is unnecessary.[46] It might escape notice that while on his exploration Gist was so removed from civilization that he did not learn Thomas Lee died two weeks after his departure, and six months later, in the middle of May 1751, wrote him from the frontier.[47] In the light of the commercial accounts of the Ohio Company in the summer and autumn of 1850, and of a bond of September 14, 1850, of Aaron Price and Barney Curran, with its endorsement of settlement of the bond by August 20, 1752, it is noteworthy that Christopher Gist's First Journal shows that Barney Curran with Ohio Company goods was travelling with him from November 26, 1750 to December 26, 1750 and possibly later, a fact of a significance clearly revealed by the bond and its endorsement.

One of the longest and most important meetings of the Ohio Company of Virginia was held at Stafford Court House, May 21-24, 1751.[48] As old members, Presley Thornton, Richard Lee, Augustine Washington, Lawrence Washington, Nathaniel Chapman, Jacob Giles, James Scott, Thomas Cresap and George Mason were present, and John Mercer, being admitted a member, made a total attendance of ten.[49] The adoption of measures to clear up the account with the Company of Hugh Parker, former member and first factor of its trade, was the earliest business transacted. Thomas Cresap, as his executor, reported that Parker's estate was much involved. Next in business done, John Mercer was admitted to membership. Then came a transaction now for the first time fully revealed to the public.

---

[46] They are reprinted in the *George Mercer Papers*, as an integral part of the George Mercer Papers considered as an archive.

[47] *Christopher Gist's Journals . . .*, ed. William M. Darlington, p. 65.

[48] D.M.L. MS., printed in *George Mercer Papers*, pp. 6-7, 142-43, 173-75.

[49] *Ibid.*, p. 174.

"John Mercer having by the Direction of the Company prepared an Indenture with divers Covenants and Agreements to be entered into and executed by the several Members thereof for the Settling and carrying on their Copartnership, the same was read and approved of and then duly executed by . . . the ten members present and resolved that a Counterpart thereof shall be with all convenient speed be transmitted to John Hanbury Esqr in order that the same may be executed by the several Members and Partners of the said Company in Great Britain and Ireland and that the other Members living in Virginia and Maryland be forthwith applied to in order that they may execute the same." [50]

An attached resolution continued:

"And the said John Hanbury is hereby requested to get a sufficient number thereof printed in London that every of the said partners may have a Counterpart thereof duly executed." [51]

The indenture itself [52] shows that in addition to the ten signatures mentioned, Robert Dinwiddie of the third Part, Philip Ludwell Lee, "of the Seventh Part," John Taylor "of the eighth Part," and Gawin Corbin "of the tenth Part," signed at a later time. But, so far as one can judge by the document in use, six out of twenty signatures were not obtained, including John Hanbury "of the first Part," Samuel Smith "of the fifth Part," Capel Hanbury "of the fourth Part," Arthur Dobbs "of the second Part," The Executors' of Thomas Lee "of the sixth Part," and James Wardrop "of the eighteenth Part." Of the foreign members only Robert Dinwiddie signed the document, as we have it.[53] The explanation of the failure

[50] D.M.L. MS., printed in *George Mercer Papers*, pp. 6-7, 142-43, 173-75.

[51] No trace of such an imprint has been found.

[52] From photostat in Virginia Historical Society. The original with its autograph signatures and accompanying seals was in the possession of Judge A. T. Embery of Fredericksburg, Virginia. Both Judge Embery and the Historical Society of Virginia generously consented to its publication herein. It is commonly supposed to be the copy once in the possession of John Tayloe. But the text, with its signature and seals, may well be the original draft.

[53] And he may have signed this copy after his arrival in Virginia in November, 1751.

of James Wardrop to attach his signature is that he had taken up residence in Great Britain.[54]

Several facts stand out from an examination of the Indenture. It styles the Company, the "Ohio Company," not the "Ohio Company of Virginia." While it repeatedly mentions a joint and common stock, it speaks of "The Ohio Company" as a "Copartnership." It reveals that Hugh Parker had handled imported goods, before his death, in 1751. It put a time limit of twenty years, 1751–1771, on the corporate life of the Company. It contained the usual legal provisions for transfer and inheritance of shares. It provided for a Committee, a Treasurer or Receiver, books of record, the liabilities of members, annual meetings, the final division of the assets of the Company and the means of altering, revising or changing the terms of the Indenture itself.

The history of the memberships, parts and shares requires some elaboration. According to the Articles of Agreement there were twenty partners. According to the Petition of 1778 this membership of twenty partners was uniformly upheld. But the Articles of Agreement mention "forty equal Parts or Shares." Each partner had "Two such Parts and Shares." And each partner was, if present at a meeting, "entitled to one Vote for every fortieth Part or share in the Lands and common Stock. . . ." An important clause states, "And where any Heirs Executors, Administrators or Assigns are or shall be entitled to any Share or Shares of the said Company's Lands and common Stock, they shall not have or be allowed any more than one Vote among them for every fortieth Part or Share. . . ."

The fate of the twenty partnerships, of two shares each was as follows: The first two fortieths were allotted to John Hanbury, London merchant who died in 1758. They were gone elsewhere by 1778, presumably either to Osgood Hanbury, London Merchant or, perhaps, to George Mercer.

The second two fortieths went to Arthur Dobbs of Ireland who

---

[54] His signature on the petition of April 2, 1754, shows him already returned to Great Britain, P.R.O. C.O. 5: 1328/153-59. See Bailey, *Ohio Company* . . . , p. 309.

died in 1765, and were held by his heirs in 1778. The third two fortieths were assigned to Robert Dinwiddie, who died in 1770, and were held by his heirs in 1778. The fourth two fortieths belonged to Capel Hanbury, London merchant who died in 1765 and whose two fortieths belonged to his heirs in 1778. The fifth two fortieth shares were assigned to Samuel Smith, London merchant, but taken over by the Hanburys in 1763 and probably assigned to Osgood Hanbury but, possibly, bought by George Mercer. The sixth two fortieth shares were taken by Thomas Lee and by his Last Will and Testament left to his second son, Thomas Ludwell Lee, with the proviso that all profits therefrom should be shared equally with Richard Henry Lee, third son, and Francis Lightfoot Lee, fourth son. The shares were held by the heirs of Thomas Ludwell Lee in 1778. The seventh two fortieths shares were bought by Thomas Lee for his oldest son, Philip Ludwell Lee, and given to him before June 21, 1749, and held in 1778, after his death in 1775, by his estate or heirs. The eighth two fortieths were taken by John Tayloe and held by him in 1778. The ninth two fortieths, intended for Francis Thornton, seems to have been taken over by his son Presley Thornton and on his death in 1769, inherited by his son Peter Presley Thornton who held them in 1778. The tenth two fortieths went to Gawin Corbin, who sold them to Robert Carter in July 1753, who in turn held them in 1778 and afterwards. The eleventh two fortieths belonged to Richard Lee who continued to hold them in 1778. The twelfth two fortieths were the property of Augustine Washington who disposed of them to Robert Carter who held them in 1778 and afterward. The thirteenth two fortieths were held by Lawrence Washington, from whose estate they were bought by Lunsford Lomax, on whose death they went to Thomas Lomax who held them in 1778. The fourteenth two fortieths were allotted to Nathaniel Chapman of Virginia and from 1760 to 1778 held by Pearson Chapman. The fifteenth two fortieths were held by James Scott, clergyman and planter, from 1749 to 1778 and beyond. The sixteenth two fortieths were bought by George Mason in 1749 and held by him in 1778. On his death they went, in 1792, to his oldest son, George Mason of Lexington, and by the latter were assigned to his children. The seventeenth two fortieths were bought by John Mercer in 1751, who in 1759 by deed nominally divided the two fortieths equally between himself and his two sons George and James, but who continued active as secretary and lawyer of the Ohio Company and whose estate still held the two fortieths in 1778. It is doubtful that either George Mercer or James Mercer acquired real ownership of one of the two fortieths and that James Mercer was ever a member. The latter probably served, like his father, as legal adviser.

The eighteenth two fortieths were held by James Wardrop of Maryland, who returned to Great Britain and whose heirs held the shares in 1778. The nineteenth two fortieths were continuously in the possession of Jacob Giles of Maryland from 1748 to 1778 and beyond. To Thomas Cresap was assigned in 1751 the twentieth two fortieths, who held them in 1778, but in 1783 divided them, in a deed, between his son Daniel Cresap and his grandsons James Cresap and Michael Cresap, sons of Michael Cresap.

Of about forty-five names mentioned anywhere as owners of shares or members of the Ohio Company, only thirty were actually, at any time after May 23, 1751, members holding two fortieth shares. Of the remaining fifteen, John Carlyle withdrew in 1748; Daniel Cresap was deeded one fortieth in 1783; James Cresap and Michael together had one fortieth in 1783; George William Fairfax withdrew in 1749; Richard Henry Lee and Francis Lightfoot Lee had each by the will of Thomas Lee, claim to two thirds of the profits of two fortieths willed to Thomas Ludwell Lee; James Mercer had by unrecorded deed from his father, joint claim with his brother George to one fortieth; Thomas Nelson withdrew in 1749; William Nimmo withdrew before his death in 1749; Hugh Parker died in 1751; Francis Thornton died in 1749; William Thornton was never a member; and George Washington had no share or shares.

However informally the Ohio Company may have begun and continued, after the adoption and signing of this Indenture in May 1752, it became for twenty years a legal entity recognizable as such by the law and the courts.

Having adopted the Articles of Agreement, the May meeting of 1751 appointed George Mason treasurer and receiver and appointed as a committee until the next general meeting, Lawrence Washington, Nathaniel Chapman, James Scott, George Mason, and John Mercer, with powers outlined in the Articles so adopted.[55]

It was also resolved that the Company write again to Mr. Hanbury and the "Heads" on which the letter should be written were outlined.[56] The second "Head" was merely another plea to the British government to be excused from building and garrisoning "a regular Fort" a requirement, they asserted, which was far beyond their limited resources. The first "Head," outlined for the letter, is in its audacity, little short of amazing. Condensation or paraphrase seems inadvisable.

> "To apply to the Earle of Granville for a Grant of fifty thousand or more Acres of Land upon the branches of the Ohio to the Westward of the great Mountains on or near the line dividing Virginia and Carolina, and to the Lord Baltimore for ten thousand or more Acres of Land in different tracts near the back line between Pensylvania and Maryland, and to Mr. Penn for ten thousand or more Acres of Land at or near a place called Rays town upon the Juniatta or the branches thereof, fifteen or twenty thousand Acres on Lowelhanning and Kiskamonito Creeks which empty into the Ohio, or as much thereof as belongs to Pensylvania, five thousand Acres upon a branch of the Ohio called Chomohonan and four thousand Acres at a place called the three forks of Youghogane being a branch of the Ohio, the Company being of Opinion that if the same can be obtained upon reasonable terms it will be much for their Advantage and greatly contribute to the security of their Settlements and encrease of their Trade."[57]

An examination of a topographical map of the upper Ohio Valley will reveal that the gentlemen of the Ohio Company sensed early

---

[55] D.M.L. MS., printed in *George Mercer Papers*, p. 174.

[56] *Ibid.*, p. 142.

[57] Since the journal of the first exploration of Christopher Gist had not yet been received, it is uncertain where the Ohio Company got its geographical information. Was it from contemporary maps by Lewis Evans, or by John Patton, or by others, or was it information widely known?

the strategical sites of the region. They may have exceeded the limits of probability, but their eventual failure was a matter of circumstance rather than of men and plans.

Further resolutions of the Ohio Company meeting, May, 1751, involved establishment of "a plantation and Quarter" at the mouth of Wills Creek with a few Negro slaves; a decision to get the road constructed from Wills Creek to the three forks of the Youghiogheny; the purchase from Thomas Bladen of five hundred acres of land on Wills Creek in Maryland; the provision of a licensed surveyor; a meeting of the Committee to examine Gist's "Journal Report" and submit it to members in America and abroad; and a redundant resolution giving to the Committee powers, already provided for in the Indenture.[58] Lawrence Washington, after the death of Thomas Lee, the leader of the Ohio Company and in 1751 probably the chairman of the Committee, seems to have taken care of the correspondence with Hanbury, Dinwiddie, and others.[59]

The death of Hugh Parker in the late spring of 1751 did not put an end to the mercantile transactions along the upper Potomac. The Company opened an account with Providence Mounts on June 8, 1751;[60] it took a promissory note of Jacob Wolff for £2:8:6 on July 9, 1751.[61] It is uncertain whether after Parker's death this business was conducted by Thomas Cresap, William Trent or some subordinate storekeeper at the New Store opposite the mouth of Wills Creek.

Christopher Gist wrote Thomas Lee, May 15, 1751, that he would arrive for a meeting with the Ohio Company by the 15th of June.[62] As stated immediately above, a resolution of the May meeting called for a special meeting of the Committee "upon the return of Christopher Gist." Evidently Mr. Gist was a full month late in handing in his report, for the meeting of the Committee, composed of Law-

[58] D.M.L. MS., printed in *George Mercer Papers*, pp. 143, 175.

[59] *Writings of George Washington*, ed. Sparks, II, 481-82.

[60] D.M.L. George Mason Papers.

[61] *Ibid.*

[62] See *Gist's Journals . . .*, of that date. See *George Mercer Papers*, pp. 31, 121, and Appendix to the *Case . . .*, p. 12.

rence Washington, James Scott, George Mason, and J. Mercer, was held on July 15, 1751 "at the Rev. Mr. James Scott's. . . ."[63] It was on this date that Gist "returned his plan and Journal."[64] The Committee were not satisfied with Gist's recommendation that their land be taken up along the two rivers of Miamis and decided to send him out again to "view and examine the lands between Monongahela and the Big Conway. . . ."[65] For this purpose they drew up a second set of Instructions.[66] But "in the meantime, conceiving it to be greatly for the company's interest, as well as the government's, to cultivate a friendship and correspondence with the Ohio Indians and that nothing could answer that end more effectually than procuring a commission for the said Gist to meet those Indians at the Logs town, at a grand council they were to hold there in the following month (and then they were to receive his majesty's present) and to engage Mr. Andrew Montour (one of the chiefs of the six nations) in the interest of the government of Virginia, and the company the said committee, recommended him to the president and council for that purpose. . . ."[67]

In this month of July, 1751, business seemed to have been as usual at the New Store. A Writing Obligatory for £80:5:6 was accepted from Robert Erwin of Maryland, July 4, 1751.[68] A promissory note of Abraham Teagarden for £4:1:6, Pennsylvania money, was taken July 17, 1751; and another, of John Tucker for £5:13:5, Pennsylvania money, on the same day; a bond of John Adam Long for £16:9:6 was taken July 26, 1751; and a promissory note for

---

[63] D.M.L. MS., printed in *George Mercer Papers*, p. 175, and Part II, the *Case* . . . , p. 5.

[64] *Ibid.*

[65] *Ibid.*

[66] Printed in *Gist's Journals* . . . , p. 67, and in *George Mercer Papers*, pp. 31-32, 252.

[67] D.M.L. MS., printed in *George Mercer Papers*, pp. 50, 237, and Part II, the *Case* . . . , p. 5. See also, *Executive Journals, Council of Colonial Virginia*, V, *passim.*

[68] Mentioned in Frederick County, Maryland, Judgment Record G, 1752–53, folio 443.

£5:13:9 of Jasper Sutton on July 27, 1751. A promissory note of William Patterson for £7:0:0 Pennsylvania currency was taken August 24, 1751.[69]

The conception of having Gist and Montour at the forthcoming Indian Council was a good one but the plan did not work. "The Indians for some reasons (the certain grounds of which cannot be assigned), failed to meet at Logs town in August one thousand seven hundred and fifty one according to their appointment tho' Col.° Patton beforementioned went there as a Commissioner from Virginia. . . ."[70] But Lewis Burwell, now president of the Council of Virginia, was no friend of the Ohio Company, and Colonel James Patton was a leading founder of rival land companies; and so it may have been just as well for the Ohio Company that the Indians did not assemble.

In long lost documents of the Ohio Company now in the Darlington Memorial Library and printed in the *George Mercer Papers*, we see for the first time what happened to the plan and journal submitted by Gist, July 14, 1751. The Committee "ordered a copy of his journal and plan to be transmitted to Mr. Hanbury expecting he would have had them printed." John Mercer later wrote, "That M.r Hanbury communicated the plan is apparent not only from those parts (of which there never had been any thorough discovery made before) being laid down according to his plan in all the Maps of those parts published since but from his journey being pricked off in the map of Virginia and some other maps published in England since that time. . . ."[71] Nor, according to John Mercer, was the journal printed as expected.[72] In addition to Gist's "plan map and Journal" thus sent to John Hanbury, John Mercer, writing to George Mercer, March 9, 1768, says that he himself "made

[69] The five items are from the D.M.L. George Mason Papers.

[70] D.M.L. MS., printed in *George Mercer Papers*, pp. 51, 237. Patton went only as a messenger. See *Executive Journals, Council of Colonial Virginia*, V, *passim*.

[71] *Ibid.*

[72] No copy has been found.

off" a map from Gist's *Journal* and sent a copy to Mr. Hanbury earlier than Lewis Evans' first map of the region.[73]

As already stated, the proposed Indian Conference of August 1751, never assembled. Very probably the Ohio Company was more concerned about the conference than either the Indians or the government of Virginia. The old hostility of the latter to the Ohio Company was meanwhile in full swing. A Lieutenant-Governor of Virginia, Robert Dinwiddie, had been appointed on July 4, 1751, by the imperial government;[74] and news of this eventuality had reached Virginia by July 18, 1751, with information that the appointee was making ready for his voyage to America.[75] It was probably widely known that he was affiliated with the Ohio Company, for he had been included in the Articles of Agreement adopted at the May meeting two months earlier. Rivals and opponents of the Ohio Company made use of the intervening time. Lewis Burwell, President of the Council of Virginia, writing August 21, 1751, to the Board of Trade and Plantations,[76] proposed that an Indian Conference be held in May 1752, a date involving a probably necessary delay of nearly a year.

It may be that some of the first cargo of goods remained unsold in the late summer of 1751, or that a second cargo had arrived, for from Virginians on October 4 the Company took a bond of John and Isaac Pearis for £25..12..6, Maryland money; on October 8, 1751, a promissory note of Jacob Hood for £3..8..7; on October 25, a promissory note of Jonathan Coburn for £5..6..0; and on October 28, 1751, a promissory note of William Castleman for £3..7..2.[77] And from Marylanders the Company took on October 5 a promissory note from Jacob Houghland for £10..16..0, on October 7 a "certain Bill Obligatory" from William Erwin for £9..10..7, and on

---

[73] D.M.L. MS., printed in *George Mercer Papers*, p. 225; a copy of the original is reproduced in facsimile, opposite p. 72.

[74] P.R.O. C.O. 5: 234/50, 211-12; *Virginia Gazette*, November 21, 1751. See Louis F. Koontz, *Robert Dinwiddie . . .*, pp. 95-100.

[75] *Virginia Gazette*, July 18, 1751.

[76] P.R.O. C.O. 5: 1327/355-60.

[77] All three in D.M.L. George Mason Papers.

October 9 a "Bill Obligatory" from Richard Chapman for £5..6..11, Maryland Currency.[78]

More significantly, in the language of the record, at a council held October 26, 1751, "Both the Orders of John Blair Esq. William Russell and Company and William McMahan, John McMahan, Richard McMahan, Lewis Neal, John Neal, Mark Calmees and Company were renewed. . . ." The former company was allowed four years further time to "Survey &c" and the latter company was allowed five years further time and given the right to add other partners.[79] To fully appreciate this, it is necessary to recall that the Blair-Russell grant called for 100,000 acres of land lying to the westward of the line of Lord Fairfax on the "Waters of Potomack and Youghyoughgane,"[80] and that McMahan's grant was for "60,000 acres of Land adjoining to the Grant of John Blair Esq. and others. . ."[81] The later activities of the Blair-Russell Company were to prove that these rivals of the Ohio Company were not bluffing.

New comment on these renewals is not necessary for some member of the Ohio Company, probably John Mercer, made, many years after the renewals, the requisite remarks:

> "Note the Order of John Blair Esq. and Company pretended to be renewed by this last recited Order had expired November 4, 1749.[82] Mr. McMahan's would not have expired till April 22nd, 1752, but it is very remarkable that his was the single order that ever was granted for any longer term than four years according to which time it would have expired the April before . . ." etc.[83]

---

[78] All cited in law suits, in Frederick County, Maryland, Judgment Record G, 1752–53.

[79] D.M.L. MS., printed in *George Mercer Papers*, pp. 51, 251.

[80] *Ibid.*

[81] *Ibid.*

[82] It is somewhat obvious that the renewal was extra-legal or unconstitutional.

[83] D.M.L. MS., printed in *George Mercer Papers*, Part II, the *Case . . .*, p. 6. An examination of the terms of the original orders shows that the McMahon grant was dependent upon the prior location of the Blair-Russell surveys.

Lieutenant-Governor Robert Dinwiddie reached Virginia in the third week of November, 1751.[84] On board the ship in which he arrived was a cargo of goods for Colonel Mason and the Ohio Company which could not be delivered because of the severity of the winter weather.[85] This joint arrival of Governor Dinwiddie and the Ohio Company cargo was probably a coincidence, though Governor Dinwiddie did "have the success and prosperity of the Ohio Company much at heart.[86]

As is well known to advanced students of American history, Governor Dinwiddie was an energetic official.[87] Shortly after the ceremonies of his reception, Governor Dinwiddie plunged into the affairs of the Ohio Company and of the West. On December 12, 1751, pursuing the courses begun earlier by Thomas Lee, he wrote [88] to Conrad Weiser, the Indian interpreter who had already served Virginia in the Logstown Conference in 1748. Sanctioning the earlier proposal of Lewis Burwell, he spoke of the Indian conference to be held at Logstown in May 1752, promising to send commissioners and asking Weiser to "join and assist them." [89]

Probably on December 12, 1751, Governor Dinwiddie had not received the letter of Thomas Cresap,[90] recommending that the services of Andrew Montour be employed and that Montour be sent to the various Indian towns in the Ohio Valley. And when the new Governor wrote [91] on December 12, 1751, to Professor Joshua Fry of William and Mary College to serve as a commissioner at

---

[84] *Virginia Gazette*, November 21, 1751.

[85] Dinwiddie to Cresap, January 23, 1752 (Robert Dinwiddie, *The Official Records of . . .*, with an Introduction and Notes by R. A. Brock, often cited as *Dinwiddie Papers* and printed in *Virginia Historical Collections*, vols. III and IV, hereinafter cited as *Va. Hist. Colls.*), III, 17-18. Possibly this was the second cargo, but it may have been a third cargo, for it is doubtful that the second cargo was delayed twenty months.

[86] *Ibid.*

[87] See Koontz, *op. cit.*

[88] *Va. Hist. Colls.*, III, 6.

[89] *Ibid.*

[90] *Calendar of Virginia State Papers and Other Manuscripts . . .*, ed. William P. Palmer (hereinafter cited as *Cal. of Va. St. Papers*), I, 245-47.

[91] *Va. Hist. Colls.*, III, 79.

Logstown in May and on the following day to Colonel James Patton with the same proposal,[92] he merely accepted nominations already made by the Council, many members of which were competitors and secret enemies of the Ohio Company, a fact particularly true of Patton, who had been pushing western grants for himself and his friends for more than six years. The tone of Dinwiddie's letter to Patton would seem to indicate that he was not unaware of the personal situation.

On the day of his letter to Colonel James Patton, December 13, 1751, Dinwiddie also wrote to his personal friend, Governor Samuel Ogle of Maryland,[93] asking his cooperation in the forthcoming Indian Conference. Five days later in a similar letter[94] to Governor James Hamilton of Pennsylvania he likewise mentioned the proposed conference at Logstown in May. Then on January 20, 1752, exactly one month after his arrival in Williamsburg as Governor, he reported to the Board of Trade and Plantations,[95] mentioning that the royal presents to the Indians had not yet been delivered but saying two commissioners had been appointed to deliver them at Logstown in May. He did not conceal the fact that the Ohio Indians were making complaints about Virginia's claims in regard to lands ceded by the Indians in the deed at Lancaster in 1744. And he complained himself about the "irregularities" of the traders most of whom "belong to the Colonies to the Northward of us." In hope that order might be established on the Ohio, he urged that the "Line between this Dominion and that of Pennsylvania be run. . . ." Certainly as much as to anything else, Governor Dinwiddie spent his first month in attention to the interest and welfare of the Ohio Company.[96]

---

[92] *Ibid.*, pp. 9-10.

[93] *Ibid.*, pp. 11-13.

[94] *Ibid.*

[95] P.R.O. C.O. 5: 1327/453, printed in *Va. Hist. Colls.*, III, 17-18.

[96] It is apparent that like Thomas Lee earlier, Robert Dinwiddie maintained a high code of official honor and gave prior attention to matters such as the welfare of the British Empire and the prerogatives of the Crown. See Koontz, *op. cit.*, *passim.*

In his letter[97] to Thomas Cresap, January 23, 1752, in reply to Cresap's letter of an earlier date, Governor Dinwiddie discussed the proposed Indian Conference in May, commented upon persons restraining the Ohio Company from making settlements, mentioned the cargo of goods on board ship in the lower Chesapeake, stated that Cresap's letter was the first from any member of the Ohio Company, sanctioned the employment of Andrew Montour, but refused to take any hurried and rash steps about the activities of the French among the Indians of the Ohio Valley.

During this period after the arrival of Dinwiddie in America, Christopher Gist was on his second journey of exploration. So far as is known, Gist may not have received the Commission of the President and Council as projected, July 16, 1751, by the Committee of the Ohio Company, but he did have instructions from Colonel Patton to invite the Indians to the Conference in May.[98] Early in December Gist met Nemacolin, the Indian who was later employed to blaze the trail to the Ohio.[99] During the winter Gist explored much of the region lying between the valleys of the Youghiogheny and Monongahela and the Ohio River on the west. He was sharply questioned by the Indians in regard to the purpose of his trip. Gist's very tactful reply secured for him Indian consent "to come and live upon the River" where he pleased.[100] On the trip Gist had killed a large number of animals, and on the end of his trip, March 29, 1752, he arrived at the Company's Factory at Wills Creek with "a good many skins." [101] It was in this Monongahela country, ex-

---

[97] *Va. Hist. Colls.*, III, 17. See Bailey, *Ohio Company* . . . , p. 77, and Koontz, *op. cit.*, p. 139.

[98] Second Journal, under date November 24, 1751. Evidently Patton had been named as commissioner before the arrival of Dinwiddie, and had assumed fully the confirmation of his nomination.

[99] *Ibid.*

[100] *Ibid.*

[101] These "good many skins" came up for consideration later. Without some unknown understanding, they belonged to the Ohio Company. Gist may have sold some skins to one Wafer, who may have sold them, on a bond, to George Croghan, which bond was taken by the Ohio Company. There is, elsewhere, a hint that Gist himself shipped "skins" to England.

plored by Christopher Gist and his son in the winter of 1751–52, that the activities of the Ohio Company on the frontier were to be concentrated during the following two years.[102]

---

[102] Thus the Monongahela Country was destined to be "The First English-Speaking Trans-Appalachian Frontier," article by Alfred P. James, *Mississippi Valley Historical Review*, XVII (1930), 55-71.

V

Climax of Activity

1752–1753

FOR THE TIME BEING, however, the members of the Company were very inactive. Thomas Lee was missed. Lawrence Washington was ill. George Mason and John Mercer had not assumed active leadership. Robert Dinwiddie was cautious about matters which were not of more than personal interest and all the members were very busy with many other responsibilities and interests. Probably, in the first half of 1752, things were quiet by reason of awaited developments from Gist's second journey and from the Indian Conference supposed to be assembled at Logstown in May.

Things, however were not completely lifeless. George Mason, as treasurer of the Company, took legal steps to collect outstanding unpaid accounts and promissory notes. In Frederick County, Virginia, he took out a warrant for the arrest of John Tucker, February 23, 1752.[1] On the following day he put in a petition and a warrant for £3:7:2, against William Castleman; and a warrant for £8:3:0 against Abraham Teagarden.[2] A day later he acted likewise against Jacob Wolf.[3]

[1] Frederick County, Virginia, Court Docket Papers, printed below, pp. 221-22.

[2] *Ibid.*

[3] *Ibid.*

On March 14, a promissory note for £2:5:10 was accepted from Amos Thacker and James Mayors of Maryland.[4] In the March Court, 1752, in Frederick County, Maryland, suits were brought against Van Swearingen, John Johnson, John Williams, and Joseph Volgemore.[5] On March 20, 1752 the suit against John Williams was settled, and a promissory note[6] for £7:11:2 with double indemnity bond was accepted from Nathaniel Tomlinson of Maryland. Probably on March 28, 1752, John Cunningham signed a promissory note for £2:9:6. A transaction involving £160:11:3 was featured by a double indemnity bond of James Martin, March 31, 1752.[7]

But though the mercantile interests of the Company were lively, political matters dragged badly. In London, John Mitchell, April 14, 1752, furnished the government an elaborate report on the boundaries of Virginia and encroachments upon it, a report in which he mentions the Ohio Company and its extensive grant.[8] In America measures were taken for the conduct of the negotiations with the Indians. Someone, probably either Thomas Cresap or Christopher Gist according to instructions, made a contact with Andrew Montour and drew him into the service of the Ohio Company and Virginia.

As early as April 18, 1752, Governor Hamilton knew about this and wrote Montour a friendly letter,[9] assuring him that he could announce to the Indians that Pennsylvania was in accord with the establishment of friendly relations between them and Virginia. On April 25, 1752, Governor Dinwiddie issued instructions[10] to Joshua Fry, Lunsford Lomax, and James Patton, the Commissioners to the Indian Conference at Logstown, which was expected to assemble late in April but did not begin until early

[4] Frederick County, Maryland, Judgment Record G, 1752-53, folio 715.

[5] Frederick County, Maryland, Dockets, March Term, 1752, folios 36, 40, 41, found in Maryland Hall of Records.

[6] Frederick County, Maryland, Judgment Record G, 1752–53, folios 65, 87.

[7] D.M.L. George Mason Papers, printed below, pp. 222-24.

[8] P.R.O. C.O. 5: 1327/429-30.

[9] *Pa. Col. Recs.*, V, 568.

[10] *Va. Mag.*, XIII, 148.

June. At the Governor's approval, Christopher Gist was allowed to appear at the Indian Conference but only as an agent for the Ohio Company,[11] not as a Commissioner of Virginia. Additional instructions to Gist were drawn up by George Mason, as spokesman for the Ohio Company.[12] A comparison of the two sets of instructions, presuming they are independent of each other, is a matter of interest and importance.

Governor Dinwiddie's instructions to Fry, Lomax, and Patton mentioned the gift of goods, the Lancaster Treaty and Deed of 1744, and enjoined that the Indians should be assured no fort to control them was desired or planned by the Ohio Company, that the old Pennsylvania tales about Virginians were to be discredited, that they were to agree with the Indians upon a permanent Virginia representative, that French plans should be emphasized, that Indian acts of violence should be stopped at once, and that the English desired to send a missionary among the Indians.

The Ohio Company instructions to Christopher Gist, enjoined upon him: acquainting the Indians with the facts of the establishment of the Ohio Company; an assurance of its benefit as regards cheaper goods for the Indians; that, to carry on the trade, settlements in accordance with the Lancaster Treaty of 1744 were necessary; that the Delawares would be given compensation for the loss of their hunting grounds; that the Ohio Company expected "to build Factorys and Storehouses . . . and send out large Cargoes of Goods"; that the Indians might settle like others on the Company lands on the same terms; that Andrew Montour would be utilized and given recompense; that the Indians should specify the kinds of goods desired; and that a report of Proceedings[13] must be furnished. Additional instructions to Gist authorized him, in case of failure of the three Virginia Commissioners to secure

[11] D.M.L. MS., printed in *George Mercer Papers*, pp. 176-77.

[12] *Ibid.* Also found in *Gist's Journals* . . . , pp. 234-36.

[13] The Proceedings (or minutes) of the Logstown Treaty of June 1-13, 1752, D.M.L. MS., printed in the *George Mercer Papers*, pp. 127-38, 273-84, seem to be the report of Lunsford Lomax and the text should be compared with variant texts published elsewhere, e.g., *Va. Mag.*, V, 143-74.

an agreement for the settlement of the Western lands, to endeavor himself to purchase it "upon the best terms you can for a quantity of Goods," with the deed in the names of the members of the Ohio Company. Gist also, and this late, April 1752, was instructed to see that the road was cleared "from Wills Creek to the Fork of Monongly."

The relative laxity of the Ohio Company in the first part of 1752 seems apparent from the fact that George Mason, the Treasurer, alone made out and signed Gist's instructions as above; from the probability that, though in the *Virginia Gazette* of April 10, 1752, a meeting of the Ohio Company was set for May 7, 1752,[14] the general meeting was not held until September 19, 1752; [15] and from the additional fact that even that late Gist had not finished "his plan & Report" of his second exploration which was not ready until the following month.[16] It is noteworthy that the account of his expenses at the Treaty of Logstown May-June, 1752, was not submitted until April 8, 1754.[17]

But the month of May 1752 was a time of great activity on the part of George Mason in suing negligent or recalcitrant debtors of the Ohio Company. Probably the legal measures were actually carried through by lawyers such as Gabriel Jones in Frederick County, Virginia, and Daniel Dulany, Junior, in Frederick County, Maryland. And Thomas Cresap who lived at Old Town, Maryland, seems sometimes to have served as an intermediary between George Mason, at *Gunston Hall*, and the lawyers practicing before the respective courts.

Surviving records show a petition against Jacob Hood, May 3, 1752; and a petition and warrant against Remembrance Williams, May 4, 1752. On May 5, 1752 a petition and a warrant were entered against John Cunningham for £2..9s..6d, Maryland

---

[14] Extract in *W. & M. Quarterly*, XII, 212.

[15] D.M.L. MS., printed in *George Mercer Papers, pp.* 175-76.

[16] There are many references. See P.R.O. C.O. 5: 1328/153-59, the petition of April 2, 1754, and Bailey, *Ohio Company* . . . , p. 307.

[17] Colonial Papers, 1740-49, Department of Archives and History, Virginia State Library.

money; a petition and warrant against Jasper Sutton, for £5..13..0; a petition and a warrant against William Richey for £4..15s, Maryland money;[18] and on May 18, 1752, a petition, containing the account, for a balance of £1..8s..8d, Maryland money and also a warrant were taken out against Samuel Taylor.[19]

The Logstown Indian Conference and Treaty of June 1-13, 1752[20] was primarily an Ohio Company enterprise, though it was conducted by the Commissioners of Virginia in the name of the King. A private conference held with Indian chiefs on June 9, 1752, revealed a wide open misunderstanding about the extent of land ceded by the Indians at Lancaster in 1744, a misunderstanding promptly taken up by the Commissioners of Virginia on June 10, 1752, who in exchange for the gift of goods asked confirmation of the Lancaster agreement, promising if settlement south of the Ohio were sanctioned by the Indians they would in the future have cheaper goods and greater security against the French. Minor matters about violence, crimes, travel, and wars between Indians were mentioned. In reply the Indian chiefs dealt with the relations of Indians to each other, the evil of the rum trade and, finally, with the all important land cession of 1744, which they avowed they understood to extend no farther than "the hill on the other side of the Allagany hill," though they consented to the construction of "a strong house at the fork of the Monogahela" while protesting against wicked traders. On June 12, 1752, agreement was still withheld by the Indians, who nevertheless asked for a good gunsmith to replace John Fraser, who aware of danger from the French and from hostile Indians threatened to remove from Venango. On the final day, June 13, 1752, the Indians took up the matter of the agreement of 1744, commented upon a murder committed by an Indian and asserted the necessity

[18] All nine items in Frederick County, Virginia, Court Docket Papers, and calendared below, p. 310.

[19] *Ibid.*

[20] There are many references. See P.R.O. C.O. 5: 1327/575-600; *Pa. Col. Recs.*, V, 532-39; *George Mercer Papers*, pp. 54-66, 127-38, 273-84 and Appendix to the *Case . . .*, pp. 17-22.

of referring the confirmation of the land cession to the Onondaga Council. But Andrew Montour in a private conference with the Indians secured the signing and sealing of a confirmation of the deed made at Lancaster. The conference closed with a discussion of English education of Indian children.

The confirmation of the deed of 1744, made June 13, 1752, not at Logstown but at Shannopins Town, and not incorporated in the official Proceedings of the Conference, is a vital Ohio Company document.[21] It should be specifically noted that the last half of the document of confirmation, allowed unmolested settlement "on the Southern or Eastern Parts of the River Ohio, called otherwise Allegany." Here was clear permission, so far as the Ohio Indians were concerned, for the Ohio Company to make settlements on its grant south and east of the Allegheny and Ohio rivers, anywhere from the Kiskiminetas to the Kanawha. As was natural, Governor Dinwiddie kept the imperial officials in touch with the course of affairs.[22]

The months June, July and August of 1752 likewise saw much legal action against the debtors of the Ohio Company. Early in June (or possibly late in May) there was in Frederick County, Virginia, declaration of claims for £8:3:10 against Abraham Teagarden;[23] and another for £11:6:10 against John Tucker.[24]

At Court, June 5, suits appeared against nine such debtors,[25] William Castleman, Jacob Wolf, Thomas Wood, Jacob Hood, James Findley, Peter Tostee, Thomas Swearingen, Abraham Teagarden and John Tucker. A petition and a warrant were issued June 8, 1752, respectively, against James Findley, Thomas Swear-

[21] P.R.O. C.O. 5: 1330/201-4. The diplomatic and legal aspects of the dependency of the Ohio Valley Indians upon the Six Nations Indians presented a difficulty, one familiar to American colonial historians.

[22] See his letters to the Board of Trade and Plantations, June 5, 1752, P.R.O. C.O. 5: 1327/461-66; to the Secretary of State, July 20, 1752, *ibid.*, 475; and to the Board of Trade and Plantations, October 6, 1752, *ibid.*, 383.

[23] Frederick County, Virginia, Court Docket Papers, below, pp. 223-24.

[24] *Ibid.*

[25] See the items calendared below, in Appendix D, and the table of such accounts, below, Appendix B.

ingen, Peter Tostee and Thomas Wood.[26] On June 15, a petition and warrant were issued against David Craig and warrants against Zacheus Ruth and Thomas Rutherford, and, one day later, against John Tucker.[27]

In Frederick County, Maryland, June 16, a suit, based on an earlier warrant and writ of attachment, was issued against Conrad Waltaker,[28] and suits [29] were entered against Richard Chapman, John Macfaddin, James Fowler, William Erwin, Jacobus Houghland, John Nicholas, Van Swearengen, John Johnson, Joseph Volgemore, Philip McGuire and Robert Erwin.

From the month of July, 1752, has survived a double indemnity bond [30] of £150:17:6 by Robert Lemen and a warrant against Zacheus Ruth.[31] The Ohio Company legal documents of August, 1752 total more than thirty. In Frederick County, Virginia, suits against Thomas Swearengen, Peter Tostee, James Finley, Thomas Wood, Jacob Hood, Enoch Enochs, and David Craig, were continued before the Court, August 6, 1752.[32] On August 8, a petition and warrant was issued against Jacob Hood.[33] Three days later a warrant was issued against Providence Mounts; [34] a declaration and a warrant against John Adam Long; [35] and a declaration and a warrant [36] against Thomas Caton. August 14, saw a petition and a warrant against Enoch Enochs, while August 18, brought a petition and a warrant against Frederick Ice.[37] In the

[26] Frederick County, Virginia, Court Docket Papers.

[27] *Ibid.*

[28] Judgment Record G, 1752–53, folios 212-15.

[29] Frederick County Court Docket, July Court, 1752, folios 76-98, Maryland Hall of Records.

[30] D.M.L. George Mason Papers.

[31] Frederick County, Virginia, Court Docket Papers.

[32] All in Frederick County, Virginia, Order Book, No. 4, 1751–53, folios 249-50.

[33] Frederick County, Virginia, Court Docket Papers.

[34] *Ibid.*

[35] *Ibid.*

[36] D.M.L. George Mason Papers.

[37] Frederick County, Virginia, Court Docket Papers.

Frederick County, Maryland, August Court suits[38] were further prosecuted against Van Swearingen, John Johnson, Joseph Volgemore, Richard Chapman, William Erwin, John Macfaddin, James Fowler, Jacobus Houghland, John Nicholas, Philip McGuire, Robert Erwin and Joseph Mounts, Senior, with a Maryland writ of attachment and a court judgment against Robert Erwin.[39]

It will be recalled that on September 11, 1750, the Ohio Company had made an agreement with Christopher Gist to secure one hundred and fifty or more families to settle upon the Company's lands.[40] In the language of the *Case of the Ohio Company*,[41] "The company were no sooner informed of the Indians resolution than they dispatched Mr. Gist to the northward to give notice to the persons he had there contracted with in the companies behalf that they might remove as soon as they would, to settle the land pursuant to their Agreement . . .[42] on his return he assured the Company that fifty of those familys would remove that fall or the next spring it being judged improper that the whole number should settle at once as they could not be conveniently supplied with provisions and proper necessaries for so many people." These families were, of course, German Protestant families, probably Moravians from Pennsylvania.

The death of Lawrence Washington, July 26, 1752, while not unexpected, was nevertheless a severe loss to the Ohio Company, in prestige if not in leadership. Within five years of its organization the Company had lost its two leading promotors and most substantial members.

---

[38] Frederick County, Maryland, Docket, August Term, 1752, folios 119-43.

[39] Frederick County, Maryland, Judgment Record G, 1752–53, folios 442-43.

[40] Above, pp. 40-46.

[41] Page 7. This sole known imprint is reproduced in facsimile in the *George Mercer Papers*, Part II. The item cited is based on an earlier manuscript.

[42] D.M.L. MS., printed in *George Mercer Papers*, pp. 238-39. Nowhere else was information found as to Gist's earlier contacts with these people, the agreement made, the order dispatching Gist, and this trip of the summer of 1752. Gist's trip was probably made in July and August, for he was at Logstown in June, 1752.

The regular autumn meeting of the Ohio Company was held at Alexandria, Virginia, September 19, 1752.[43] According to the minutes,[44] its sole business was the resolution, "Ordered that the Committee shall make an Entery for our first two hundred thousand Acres of Land from Kiskamonetas down the South East side of Ohio to the mouth of the big Conoway including the Land on all branches between the above-mentioned Rivers." [45] In a document written two years later, probably by John Mercer or his clerks, and printed eighteen years later by George Mercer, this resolution is elaborated. The document also mentions the allocation of "£400 towards building the Fort which was to be set about with the utmost Expedition. . . ." [46]

From the month of September 1752 documents or records of sixteen or more legal papers of the Ohio Company have been found. They begin September 1, with declarations [47] against Jonathan Coburn, Zacheus Ruth, and Thomas Rutherford; [48] a warrant for £10 against Providence Mounts; and an account, a petition and a warrant against Frederick Ice.[49] These are followed on the same day by suits [50] against Jonathan Coburn and Zacheus Ruth respectively, and on September 2, by suits respectively against

[43] D.M.L. MS., printed in *George Mercer Papers*, pp. 175-76, and Part II, the *Case* . . . , p. 7.

[44] *Ibid.*

[45] The inconsistency of this with the resolution of May, 1751, to take steps to buy some of this land from "Mr. Penn" is somewhat startling. It might seem that with the deaths of Thomas Lee and Lawrence Washington something more than leadership and prestige was lost. It is, however, probable that both in May, 1751 and in September, 1752, the members of the Ohio Company believed Pennsylvania to extend only to the westernmost ridge of the Appalachians, and while willing to buy Pennsylvania land east of the ridge, were unwilling to recognize Pennsylvania claims to land west of the ridge.

[46] D.M.L. MS., printed in *George Mercer Papers*, p. 239. Preliminary steps may have been made in the late autumn of 1752 and continued in early 1753.

[47] Frederick County, Virginia, Court Docket Papers.

[48] D.M.L. George Mason Papers.

[49] Frederick County, Virginia, Court Docket Papers.

[50] Frederick County, Virginia, Order Book, No. 4, 1751–53, folio 270.

Thomas Caton[51] (along with the jury list),[52] Providence Mounts,[53] and John Adam Long.[54] On September 14, there were suits,[55] respectively, against Enoch Enochs, Jacob Hood and Frederick Ice; and on September 19, a warrant against Thomas Caton, and, October 5, 1752, a suit against Thomas Caton,[56] and a suit[57] against Providence Mounts, with a jury list.[58]

An ominous spectre of future trouble for the Ohio Company appeared on the scene in the summer of 1752. Since 1748 the French had been greatly concerned about the rival English fur trade and the activities of the Ohio Company. The famous expedition of Céloron de Blainville in 1749 had been followed by attacks on English traders in the Ohio Valley in the years immediately following. Thomas Cresap wrote a long letter on the matter in the late months of 1751.[59] At the end of the Logstown Conference in mid June 1752, William Trent, an old fur trader, was employed by the Virginia Commissioners, Fry, Lomax, and Patton, to deliver a share of the treaty goods to the Twightwees on the Miami rivers. Andrew Montour accompanied Trent as interpreter. This work occupied Trent and Montour from June 13, until late summer. Trent's *Journal* of this trip is one of the important documents of the year.[60] It was not turned in to Dinwiddie until late autumn, but it revealed a troubled situation north and west of the Ohio River.

In the summer of 1752 the French finally carried out earlier threats against the Indians who traded with the English. A group

---

[51] *Ibid.*, folio 283.

[52] D.M.L. George Mason Papers.

[53] Frederick County, Virginia, Order Book, No. 4, 1751–53, folio 283.

[54] *Ibid.*, folio 284.

[55] *Ibid.*, folio 302.

[56] *Ibid.*, folio 332.

[57] *Ibid.*, folio 333.

[58] Frederick County, Virginia, Court Docket Papers.

[59] *Cal. of Va. St. Papers*, I, 245-47.

[60] *The Journal of William Trent*, ed. Alfred T. Goodman. See Dinwiddie to the Board of Trade and Plantations, July 6, 1752; P.R.O. C.O. 5: 1327/447-502.

of Wisconsin Indians, mainly Ottawas under the leadership of Charles de Langlade, fell upon the trading post at Picawillany,[61] drove off the white traders, and burned the post shortly before the arrival of Trent with the goods carried by him from Logstown.[62] In all reality this attack in 1752, and not the famous episode at Junonville's Glen two years later, was the actual beginning of the French and Indian war which was to continue until 1763 and virtually ruin the plans and expectations of the Ohio Company of Virginia.

But the gentlemen of the Ohio Company did not foresee the future and went ahead with their activities and plans. There is good reason to believe that Nemacolin's Path, the road from Wills Creek to the Monongahela at its junction with the Youghiogheny, was blazed and possibly partly cleared in the late summer of 1752.[63] After the final receipt from Christopher Gist of the plan and Journal of his second trip of exploration, which was probably delivered early in October, an announcement was made in the *Virginia Gazette*, October 6 and 12, 1752, of a meeting of the Ohio Company to be held November 20, 1752.[64]

In the meantime the members of the Company decided to submit another petition to the Governor and Council of Virginia.[65] Since the petition has hitherto not been known, its contents may with special profit be analyzed. It mentions the previous work of the Company and employment for the two preceding years of persons to explore the west and cultivate trade and friendship with the Indians, and the clearing of the road from Wills Creek to one of the branches of the Ohio. It petitions for leave to survey and take up their first two hundred thousand acres in as many surveys as they shall think fit. It expresses confidence in the ability of the Company to meet the terms of the grant, suggests addi-

---

[61] Wisconsin Historical Society *Collections*, VIII (1879), 209-23.

[62] *Journal of William Trent, loc. cit.*

[63] *Pa. Col. Recs.*, II, 36; *Pa. Arch.*, II, 239-66; *George Mercer Papers, passim.*

[64] *W. & M. Quarterly*, XV, 11.

[65] P.R.O. C.O. 5: 1328/153-64; D.M.L. MS., printed in *George Mercer Papers*, pp. 66-68, 271-73, and Part II, the *Case . . .*, pp. 7-8.

tional grants to settlers beyond those of the Company, makes reference to the fort built by the French on the west end of Lake Erie, asserts that the members of the Ohio Company are not mere landmongers, protests the nature of some other grants, and petitions specifically against private persons being permitted to take up large grants in regions explored by the Ohio Company and ends with an offer to admit others as members on the same terms.

This somewhat moderate and yet somewhat bitter petition seems to have been disregarded if not rejected.[66] And strangely enough, at this very time, November 6, 1752, on petitions duly made, there were granted, to Lunsford Lomax, 200,000 acres, William Trent, 200,000 acres, Andrew Montour, 80,000 acres and John Mercer and thirteen partners, 140,000 acres.[67]

The autumn meeting of the Ohio Company called for November 20, 1752, was actually held on November 22-23, 1752, at Stafford Court House. Of the resolutions or minutes of this important meeting there are two manuscripts which are not wholly identical in contents.[68]

The first resolution appointed a Committee to serve until the next general meeting and instructed it to employ a factor, order goods from Hanbury and transact all necessary business.[69] The second resolution awarded Andrew Montour thirty pistols for his service at Logstown in May and made him an offer of 1000 acres of land for moving to Virginia.[70] The third resolution was "Resolved that the two shares of M.r Dobbs and M.r Smith be disposed of and not sunk in the Company, the Company being of Opinion that the Shares of the Company shall be kept up

---

[66] D.M.L. MS., printed in *George Mercer Papers*, pp. 66-68. There is nothing about it in the *Executive Journals, Council of Colonial Virginia*, V.

[67] D.M.L. MS., printed in *George Mercer Papers*, p. 290. The only reasonable explanation of all this is that these grants were expected to be south of the Great Kanawha in present West Virginia and Kentucky. It is, however, not impossible that they were acting in accord with the Ohio Company.

[68] *Ibid.*, pp. 143-44, 176.

[69] Identical in both manuscripts.

[70] Identical in both manuscripts.

twenty."[71] The fourth resolution instructed the Committee to employ surveyors and encourage settlement, reserving tracts every twenty miles for the Company's storehouses, and desired the Committee to draw up and transmit to Mr. Hanbury "a Representation of the Case."[72] A fifth resolution provided for supplying the Emperor of the Cherokees and his party with goods from the Company's Store at wholesale prices to be paid by the Government. The last resolution was: "Col.° Lunsford Lomax having purchased of the Executors of Lawrence Washington dec'ed the said Lawrence Washington's Share of the Company's Lands and Stock, Resolved that the said Lunsford Lomax be admitted and received as a partner and be entitled to his two fortieth parts."[73]

In the meantime, in November, 1753, the Ohio Company continued its legal activities against its debtors. In Virginia, these included a suit against Enoch Enochs, and another against Frederick Ice, on November 9, 1752.[74] Also tried this month, in Maryland, were eleven continuations of earlier suits and six new suits respectively against Nathaniel Tomlinson, John Jones, Evan

---

[71] In one manuscript only. It was probably purposely omitted in the other. The latter manuscript was probably taken to Europe in July, 1763, by George Mercer. That Smith desired to dispose of his share was well known. Dobbs's share seems to have been paid in interest bearing notes or bonds. Probably he wished to sell, but he held the share at the time of his death in 1765.

[72] Identical in both manuscripts. The "Representation of the Case" here mentioned is probably incorporated in the petition of April 2, 1754, put out in London. It may have embodied material found in the George Mercer Papers, and printed in the *Case of the Ohio Company*, Part II of the *George Mercer Papers*. It is not impossible that the fragmentary "Case of the Ohio Company" in the George Mercer Papers is this "Case" above mentioned of November 22-23, 1753, which may have been sent to John Hanbury in February, 1754. There is some slight indication in the variant text, that the "Case" sent to Charlton Palmer in July, 1762, was a revised edition of this fragment.

[73] George Washington was not one of the Executors of Lawrence Washington. He did not participate in the sale of his two-fortieths share in the Ohio Company. The proceeds of the sale did not go to George Washington. See the last will and testament of Lawrence Washington in *Letters to Washington*, ed. S. M. Hamilton, VI, 398. The fifth resolution is identical in both manuscripts, but the sixth resolution is found only in the second manuscript.

[74] Frederick County, Virginia, Order Book, No. 4, 1751–53, folio 352.

Shelby, Amos Thacker and James Mayors, Catherine and Evan Shelby Jr. and Joseph Mounts.[75] Judgments were recorded in a suit against Amos Thacker and James Mayors, November 21, 1752, on a promissory note of March 14, 1752 for £2 .. 5s .. 10d, Pennsylvania money; [76] a suit against John Nicholls on a promissory note of October 9, 1751, for £5 .. 3s .. 4½d; [77] and a suit against Jacobus Houghland for £10 .. 16s, Maryland money on a bill obligatory of October 5, 1751; [78] and November 24, 1752, a suit against Evan Shelby for £3 Maryland money.[79]

Late in November 1752 the Board of Trade replied [80] to a Memorial [81] of Dinwiddie about the alteration of his instructions. In their "Thoughts & Opinion upon each Point in Order" they approved annual Indian presents, fair dealing with them, a relaxation of Virginia religious restrictions on dissent, a revision of the Virginia land laws and the future delineation of the provincial boundaries of Virginia, Pennsylvania and Maryland.

A minor but nevertheless important historical item of December 5, 1752, was Gawin Corbin's [82] assignment of his shares in the Ohio Company to Robert Carter.

Presumably before the end of the year 1752, the Representation of the Case was sent to Mr. Hanbury along with an order of a third cargo of £2,000 of goods for the Indian trade. It was probably done on or soon after December 10, 1752, for on that date Governor Dinwiddie (a member of the Ohio Company) wrote to the Board of Trade and Plantations suggesting the desirability of a present of £1,000 of goods to the Indians out of the royal quit

---

[75] Frederick County, Maryland, Dockets, November Court, 1752, folios 135-59.

[76] Frederick County, Maryland, Judgment Record G, 1752–53, folios 715-17.

[77] *Ibid.*, folio 726.

[78] *Ibid.*, folios 737-39.

[79] *Ibid.*, folios 713-15.

[80] P.R.O. C.O. 5: 1366/516-33.

[81] *Ibid.*

[82] Gunther Collection MS., a.l.s., Chicago Historical Society.

rents of Virginia and enclosing a list of the goods, a copy having been sent to Mr. Hanbury.[83]

The full course of events in the winter of 1752–53 is not revealed in the new documents herein published. A statement in a manuscript of the Ohio Company (written probably ten years later) is however, of particular value, as follows:

> "However the Company (resolved to do everything in their power) in the same month of Nov. 1752 employed one Trent hereinafter mentioned as a Factor to carry on their trade and pressed M.r Gist to proceed in the settlement and Survey as fast as possible and he in that fall and the next spring not only removed his own family but procured William Cromwell, his Son in Law, and eleven other families to settle between Yaughyaughgane and Monongahela . . ." [84]

Four warrants [85] were taken out in Virginia, by the Ohio Company against debtors on December 11, 1752, the first, alphabetically, against Jeremiah Jack for £11; the second against Richard Leans for £11; the third against Robert Lemen for £150 . . 17 . . 8d, and the fourth against William Patterson, for £7, Pennsylvania money. The total of the four claims, £179 . . 17 . . 8, was a significant sum, at the time.

In 1752 and 1753 the Ohio Company was seriously threatened by the activities of other land companies. Colonel James Patton, who had been granted 100,000 acres, mainly along the Great

---

[83] P.R.O. C.O. 5: 1327/531-36. Printed in *Journal of William Trent*, pp. 73-81. The list of goods is found in P.R.O. C.O. 5: 1327/565-67.

[84] D.M.L. MS., printed in *George Mercer Papers*, pp. 68-69, 240-41. The statement is specific about "1752" and about "in that fall and the next spring." It was, however, in the month of January, 1754, that George Washington, on his return from Fort LeBoeuf, met eleven families going out to settle. There may well have been two groups of eleven families each, one of late 1752 or early 1753 and another of January, 1754. George Mercer in 1753 mentions twenty families. The chance of a chronological error in Washington's account is remote and the chronology of the "case" may be defective. The first draught of the case may have been made in 1754, but it was rewritten, or recopied in 1762, a decade after the events.

[85] All found in the Frederick County, Virginia, Court Docket Papers and calendared below in Appendix D, p. 315.

Kanawha, a grant which had expired April 26, 1749, but nevertheless, July 12, 1749, been renewed in the name of John Tayloe, became very active in the last half of 1752 in making settlements, with the result that John Mercer in behalf of the Ohio Company and James Powers in behalf of John Lewis and others (The Loyal Land Company) entered caveats [86] against him.

In a long letter [87] to John Blair, January 1753, James Patton claimed to have been in 1743 the first petitioner for Western lands, to have "Discovered at Vast Expence" the land on three branches of the Mississippi, and to have been given first option on such land by Virginia Council. He asserted that he had settled 100 families on the land and returned the "Plans to the Secretaries Office before the Day prefixed." He appealed hotly against the "Caveateers." His statement of particular relevance was, "As to the Ohio Company who I understand Intends to survey their Lands to the Norward of the Waters of Woods River, if so it cannot Interfere with Mine."

That the activities of Cresap, Gist, and Trent in early 1753 were not without difficulties is more fully shown in two maps, one by George Mercer [88] and another of the Russell Survey, also shown on George Mercer's map. Notations on George Mercer's map furnish much detail about the Russell Survey. The map of the Blair Company invalidates none of the statements made by representatives of the Ohio Company.

John Blair, William Russell and Company, whose grant of 100,000 acres, made November 4, 1745, had expired November 4, 1749 and then been renewed October 26, 1751, for another four year period, began surveying in early 1753. John Blair was a very influential figure in Virginia politics and William Russell was an aggressive field agent. According to a surviving document [89]

[86] Not found. Probably burned either in 1781 at Williamsburg or in 1865 at Richmond.

[87] Draper MS., 1QQ75, Wisconsin Historical Society.

[88] Copy by a later draughtsman, reproduced in *George Mercer Papers*, opposite p. 226.

[89] D.M.L. MS., printed in *George Mercer Papers*, pp. 69, 241, and Part II, the *Case* . . . , p. 8.

of the Ohio Company and the *Case of the Ohio Company*,[90] Christopher Gist and his group "were no sooner seated than William Russell under colour of the order of council of November the fourth one thousand seven hundred and forty-five granting leave to John Blair Esq.r the said Russell himself and Company to take up one hundred thousand acres of land lying to the westward of the line of Lord Fairfax on the waters of Potomack and Youghyanghgane surveyed those very lands in February one thousand seven hundred and fifty-three. . . ." [91] A nice episode resulted.

According to the documents, Colonel Cresap was "then out with several persons to lay off a town [92] contiguous to the fort (which the company had agreed to build on Shurtees creek and raised four hundred pounds for that purpose)." Cresap ordered Russell to desist and had force sufficient to drive Russell away if he had wished, but refrained, under the impression that the law would take care of the matter. The Ohio Company entered a caveat [93] against Russell at the April General Court expecting the case to come up in June 1753, when to their surprise the case was made returnable in June 1754, "before which time the French got possession." Thus the Virginia land companies somewhat stymied each other, while the French carried on preparations and activities intended to thrust all of them out of the entire Ohio Valley.

But that the Ohio Company seriously intended to settle on its lands as quickly as possible is shown by the extended minutes of a meeting of the Committee, James Scott, George Mason, and John Mercer, at the home of John Mercer on February 6, 1753,

---

[90] *Case of the Ohio Company*, p. 8, in *George Mercer Papers*, Part II.

[91] Presumably, regardless of the grammar, "those very lands" means the lands along the Youghiogheny already settled by Christopher Gist, his relatives and associates, or in other words, by the Ohio Company. A copy of this survey, provenance unknown, is printed in F. B. Kegley, *Virginia Frontier . . .*, and shows the overlapping of the two claims.

[92] New information, not hitherto known. Note that Cresap was with Trent and with him wrote a joint letter to Dinwiddie January 23, 1753, as mentioned in Dinwiddie to Cresap, February 10, 1753, *Va. Hist. Colls.*, III, 22. The letter of Cresap and Trent could not be found.

[93] Not found.

minutes which throw valuable light also on the church history of Virginia. Mr. John Pagan, a merchant of Alexandria, Fairfax County, Virginia, had applied [94] to the Ohio Company to know what encouragement the Company would give to German Protestants to settle on their lands. Pagan expected to go to Germany and wanted to engage such immigrant settlers. The Committee, in reply, mentioned religious liberty under the Acts of Toleration of England; the civil rights of "English natural born Subjects"; the moderate taxes of Virginia not amounting to "above the Value of 8. "Sterl per poll"; [95] the absence of regular troops and of ecclesiastical courts; ten years freedom from all taxes to settlers beyond the Great Mountains, land at "£5 Sterl" for every hundred acres; the use of warehouses; purchase of goods at wholesale price, and credit for two years at five per cent interest.

Most certainly these were attractive terms; but not satisfied with terms only, the Committee elaborated upon the country as to navigation, roads, fish, fowl, game, good land, lumber, Indian peace, etc. Important historical detail is contained in these minutes. They mention a storehouse at Rock Creek,[96] a fine road [97] from Rock Creek to Conococheague, a boat [98] used by the Company for transportation from the mouth of the Conococheague to Wills Creek, the sixty mile cleared road [99] to Monongahela, and the expectation of building storehouses on the Monongahela. They also foreshadow the possible future navigation of the Ohio and Mississippi rivers, and promise to "lay off 200 Acres of Land for a Town to be called Saltzburg in the best and most convenient place to their Settlement. . . ." The two hundred acres of the town the Com-

[94] Application not found.

[95] D.M.L. MS., printed in *George Mercer Papers*, pp. 145, 176.

[96] See the list of Ohio Company Goods at Rock Creek, September, 1756, *Letters to Washington*, I, 362-64. These goods may have been stored on neighborhood property of George Mason or of Nathaniel Chapman, but they may have been in the well-known commercial warehouse of John Pimmett.

[97] Later used by Braddock in 1755.

[98] Mentioned by John Hammer in his account against Hugh Parker and the Ohio Company, July, 1750, below, pp. 199-200.

[99] Evidence that Nemacolin's Path was first cleared in 1752.

mittee proposed should "be divided into Lotts of one Acre each. Eight of which to be appropriated for a Fort Church and other public Buildings and Every Tradesman or other person settling and living three years in the said town to have one Lot forever paying the Quit rent of one farthing a year."

As has been already noticed,[100] Thomas Cresap with adequate help was in this month, February 1753, "out . . . to lay off a town contiguous to the fort . . ." showing that the Committee of the Ohio Company was not merely engaging in idle promises to induce foreign immigrants.

And George Mason, the Treasurer, through his lawyer continued to carry out legal measures in Virginia against delinquent debtors to the Company. A warrant against James Martin for £162 .. 11s .. 6d, Virginia money,[101] was taken out January 11, 1753. Five suits[102] were entered February 8, 1753, respectively against James Martin, Thomas Caton, William Patterson, Richard Lane, and Robert Lemen. At least ten declarations or warrants were entered on February 9,[103] seemingly after the earlier dismissal of suits on February 8. These include a declaration and a warrant, respectively, against Richard Leans, Jeremiah Jack, Robert Lemen, James Martin, and William Patterson, and probably a declaration against Thomas Caton.

Legal action of this type was continued in Virginia in March 1753 with five suits,[104] March 9, respectively, against John Cunningham, John Hammer, William Richey, Samuel Taylor, and Remembrance Williams. On March 14 appeared a declaration and a warrant against John and Isaac Pearis;[105] a petition and two

[100] Above, p. 76.

[101] Frederick County, Virginia, Court Docket Papers.

[102] Frederick County, Virginia, Order Book, No. 4, 1751–53, folios 392-93.

[103] All located in Frederick County, Virginia, Court Docket Papers, and calendared below in Appendix D.

[104] All found in Frederick County, Virginia, Order Book, No. 4, 1751–53, folio 438, and all five dismissed by reason of the summons not being executed by the sheriff's office.

[105] Frederick County, Virginia, Court Docket Papers.

warrants against Mark McDonough;[106] and, March 18, a petition and a warrant against John Hammer.[107]

In Frederick County, Maryland, March Court 1753, thirteen old suits[108] were presented and a fourteenth entered against Isaac Baker. Judgments were secured and recorded against Van Swearingen, Richard Chapman, William Erwin, Robert Erwin, John Jones, and John Nicholas.[109]

In April 1753 such legal action was actively continued. There was a suit against John and Isaac Pearis, April 3,[110] and on April 4 seven suits[111] respectively against John Cunningham, William Richey, Remembrance Williams, Samuel Taylor, George Park, Mark McDonough, and John Hammer. A warrant was entered against John and Isaac Pearis, April 5, and another warrant against Thomas Caton on April 12. The months of May and June saw the greatest activity in such proceedings. Thirteen suits,[112] in Frederick County, Virginia, featured the day at court, May 2, 1753, respectively against Thomas Caton, Richard Leans, Robert Lemen, James Martin, Jeremiah Jack, William Patterson, John and Isaac Pearis, Remembrance Williams, John Cunningham, William Richey, Samuel Taylor, Jasper Sutton, and George Park. Within ten days further warrants were entered against Caton, Jack, Leans, Lemen, Martin, Patterson, John and Isaac Pearis, Williams, and Sutton.[113] The court days of June 6-8, Frederick County, Virginia, saw fourteen Ohio Company items[114] including suits, respectively, against Jeremiah Jack, James Martin, Edward Lane, Robert Lemen, Daniel McCrory and John Collins, William Pat-

---

[106] *Ibid.*

[107] *Ibid.*

[108] All in the Docket, March Court, 1753, Trials, folios 4-7, Original Writs, folios 7-8.

[109] All six recorded in Judgment Record G, 1752–53, folios 760-869.

[110] Frederick County, Virginia, Order Book, No. 4, 1751–53, folio 454.

[111] All found, *ibid.*, folios 463-66.

[112] All found, *ibid.*, folios 476-95.

[113] All found in Frederick County, Virginia, Court Docket Papers.

[114] Frederick County, Virginia, Order Book, No. 5, 1753–54, folios 10, 11, 13, 41, 58, 59.

terson, John and Isaac Pearis, Enoch Enochs, John Cunningham, Remembrance Williams, Jasper Sutton, Samuel Taylor, William Richey, and George Park. Further warrants respectively against Patterson and against John and Isaac Pearis were entered June 11, 1753. In Frederick County, Maryland, on June 18, 1753, eight suits [115] were further prosecuted and judgments reached and recorded [116] against James Fowler, John McFaddin, Evan Shelby, and Joseph Mounts.

Another financial item of a very different type, which has survived, is an autograph draft signed by Augustine Washington, selling "My Part of the Ohio Company to Robert Carter," on June 2 for "three hundred and sixty Pounds Current Money." [117]

---

[115] Frederick County, Maryland, Docket, June Court, 1753, folios 53-80, Maryland Hall of Records.

[116] Frederick County, Maryland, Judgment Record G, 1752–53, folios 930, 1,007, 1,027.

[117] Washington Collection, MS., Chicago Historical Society, 1753.

VI

Facing Trouble

1753–1754

IN MATTERS of trade and legal action against those of its debtors who were remiss in payment of their obligations, the Ohio Company at this stage was obviously far from inactive or negligent. But for the unfortunate loss by fire of the papers of George Mason, posterity might have had a complete picture of the trade of this important eighteenth-century company, and also an important revelation of social and economic conditions along the upper Potomac, 1750–60.

A member of the Ohio Company,[1] writing about ten years later, in retrospect it is true, but in touch with the papers of the Company, expressed much bitterness at the failure, in 1753, of the Virginia government to support the Ohio Company and its legitimate claims and enterprises and asserted that Governor Dinwiddie had adequate information about the treacherous situation in the Ohio Valley but failed to act upon it. The member cited a letter of Governor Dinwiddie to the Committee of the Ohio Company dated February 15, 1753, as follows:

[1] John Mercer MS., Case of the Ohio Company, 1762. See *George Mercer Papers*, p. 72.

"I am sorry to hear by a (letter from Mr. Trent [2]) that some of the Twightwees are gone over to the French and that some French officers &c are at Logstown building of houses &c and that there are many others at their Forts on the Lakes which he calls an Army but hope they are only Traders from Canada." [3]

In an explanatory last sentence, Governor Dinwiddie added, "This information I had last week by Express which I returned and desired him to get what further Intelligence he possibly could between [now] and May, when I shall send some powder, Arms &c [4] to Winchester a present to the Indians." Governor Dinwiddie it was alleged had from excerpts and other data in the newspapers adequate information about the threatening situation, one full year before the crisis of 1754.

Probably the policies and actions of Governor Dinwiddie were discussed in a meeting of the Committee of the Ohio Company, April 4-6, 1753, of which no minutes have survived, but which is mentioned both in general documents [5] and in the financial account, with the Company, of Arthur Dobbs.[6]

Even more invidious and distasteful was the fact that at the General Court, on June 15, 1753, the Governor and Council made three separate grants of lands to Richard Corbin totaling 190,000 acres, on the Great Kanawha and Buffalo Creek territory lying within the Ohio Company grant, and based on an Ohio Company Map confidentially submitted to the Governor.[7]

[2] Obviously, the letter of January 23, 1753 by Cresap and Trent, mentioned in Dinwiddie to Cresap and Trent, February 10, 1753, *Va. Hist. Colls.*, III, 22. Trent, an elegant penman, probably wrote the letter.

[3] D.M.L. MS., printed in *George Mercer Papers*, p. 72. This letter of Dinwiddie was not found elsewhere.

[4] The expense account of William Trent, April 8, 1754, at the time the factor of the Ohio Company, shows that he carried this material from Winchester to the Indians, H.S.P. MS.

[5] D.M.L. MS., printed in *George Mercer Papers*, pp. 72, 225, 242, and Part II, the *Case* . . . , p. 10.

[6] *Ibid.*, p. 183.

[7] *Ibid.*, pp. 72, 225, 242. The Corbin land grants are found in several places, notably *Executive Journals, Council of Colonial Virginia*, V, 436-37, and in the Etting Collection, Ohio Company Papers, H.S.P., printed in Bailey, *Ohio Company Papers*, p. 240, and in *George Mercer Papers*, p. 251.

All this land company rivalry and activity was in the face of very threatening circumstances. By more than a coincidence, while these rival land companies were reaching out into the Ohio Valley, the French started, in early 1753, an expedition to the same region, to drive out the British Americans and build a string of forts from Lake Erie down the Allegheny River and the Ohio River to its mouth.

That story lies in large part outside the inner history of the Ohio Company, but the reader should have in mind that this French expedition left Montreal early, arrived in the early summer at Presque Isle Bay, constructed a fort there, built a road to the French Creek at Fort LeBoeuf (Waterford) and occupied Venango (Franklin, Pennsylvania) before winter. Circumstances prevented the fulfillment of their plan to seize the Forks of the Ohio in 1753 but everyone knew they hoped to do it early in 1754.[8]

That in the face of difficulties of so many kinds the Ohio Company continued its work is seen in the Statement of the Account of Arthur Dobbs,[9] showing that each share was on April 7, 1753, charged with a levy of £50. It was doubtless wanted to pay Trent, Montour, and Gist, build the storehouses at Redstone Creek, lay out the town and build the fort on "Shurtees" Creek.

The early summer of 1753 was featured by feverish preparations by the Ohio Company and the Colony of Virginia for a conference with the Indians at Winchester. These preparations involved an extensive correspondence, some of which now appears for the first time. A letter from William Trent, probably of April 10, 1753, an extract of which appeared in the newspapers, told of French attacks on British-American traders in the west and the arrival of French forces in the region.[10] A letter of May 6, 1753, from Governor Hamilton of Pennsylvania inquired about the fort to be built by the Ohio Company saying the Proprietor had

---

[8] In addition to older historical accounts, see especially Donald H. Kent, *The French Invasion of Western Pennsylvania*, a scholarly study based on newly available material from Quebec.

[9] D.M.L. MS., printed in *George Mercer Papers*, p. 183.

[10] Extract in D.M.L. MS., printed in *George Mercer Papers*, pp. 242-43.

expressed sympathy but demanded that Pennsylvania's claims should not be prejudiced.[11] Hamilton added that he was directed to assure "the Settlers, they Shall enjoy the Lands they bona fide Settle on the Common Quit Rent . . . ," a significant innuendo. Dinwiddie's reply, May 21, 1753, was merely that he had often spoken to members of the Ohio Company about the matter of the attitude of Pennsylvania.[12] In reply to a letter of William Trent from Winchester, Virginia, May 21, 1753,[13] Governor Dinwiddie, May 31, 1753,[14] deplored the bad situation of the Ohio Indians; ordered a present to be given to them; sent a message to them assuring them of his friendship and aid and asked for more information on the situation.

Governor Dinwiddie, June 16, 1753, in a long letter to the Board of Trade mentioned the possibility of religious toleration for "Foreign Protestants" in the "remote Parts of this Dominion," commented on "Exorbitant Grants of Land," said he would be glad to see the Pennsylvania-Virginia boundary line ascertained, reported, "All the English Traders have left the Ohio in a great Panick . . . ," mentioned the Winchester Conference and proposed two forts on the Ohio to be supplied with "twenty cannon, three Pounders, with Powder, Shott, &c." [15] He inclosed a statement on "The Method of taking up Lands in Virginia." [16]

In connection with plans for the Indian Conference at Winchester in 1753, Governor Dinwiddie drew the venerable William Fairfax into the picture. This elderly gentleman, cousin of Thomas, sixth Lord Fairfax and father of George William Fairfax and of

---

[11] P.R.O. C.O. 5: 13/625-28; *Pa. Col. Recs.*, V, 628-30; and in *Pa. Arch.*, fourth series, II, 182-85.

[12] MS. in N.Y.P.L. Copy in P.R.O. C.O. 5: 1327/555-59; and in *Pa. Col Recs.*, V, 630-32.

[13] Letter not found, but mentioned in Dinwiddie to Trent, May 31, 1753.

[14] D.M.L. MS., printed in *George Mercer Papers*, pp. 73-74, 284-85. Not published hitherto.

[15] P.R.O. C.O. 5: 1327/637-40.

[16] *Ibid.*, 657-72.

Anne the wife of Lawrence Washington, assumed great responsibility in public affairs in the summer of 1753. William Trent, at this period the factor and the active agent of the Ohio Company in the Ohio Valley, wrote Fairfax, May 22, 1753,[17] and again reported to him at Winchester in a letter of mid-June. In reply,[18] from Winchester, May 26, 1753, William Fairfax said Andrew Montour had informed him about the French forces moving toward the Ohio, that accompanied by his son George William Fairfax, Carlyle, and George Washington, he was at Winchester with arms for the Indians and awaited the Governor's instructions about them. The Governor did write to Colonel Fairfax on May 31, 1753.[19]

Yet when writing to William Trent on June 9, 1753, William Fairfax was still worried about getting arms and ammunition to the Indians on the Ohio, but on instructions from Governor Dinwiddie was ready to turn them over to Trent for their delivery.[20] On July 10, 1753, Governor Dinwiddie sent a message to the Half King, Shingas, and the Sachems of the Six Nations on the Ohio condoling them for the attacks of the French, and assuring the Indians of all assistance in his power.[21]

The effect of this trouble with rival land companies and the French upon the prospects of the Ohio Company in the first half of 1753 is well expressed in the Case of the Ohio Company[22] drawn up about a year later. It says, "Some of the persons who removed from the Northward to settle the companies' land finding the company was not able to obtain any immediate redress, not only returned back to their former habitation but stopped the other

[17] Not found, but mentioned in William Fairfax to William Trent, date cited, D.M.L. MS., printed in *George Mercer Papers*, pp. 78-79 and Part II, the *Case* . . . , p. 10.

[18] *Ibid.*

[19] Not found, but mentioned in D.M.L. MS., printed in *George Mercer Papers*, pp. 73-74, 284-85.

[20] *Ibid.*, pp. 79-80 and Part II, the *Case* . . . , p. 4.

[21] *Ibid.*, p. 286 and Part II, the *Case* . . . , pp. 11-12.

[22] *Ibid.*, p. 245.

families that were about to remove. . . ."[23] Further comment is, "this step with some other instances of the same prejudiced the Northward people to that degree that it is feared no promises or offers that the government of Virginia can make will ever be able to remove their prejudice or engage their confidence. . . ." Another point made is that "hence it is that some thousands from the Northern provinces have since passed through this colony to procure worse lands and on much worse terms to the Southward,"[24] a statement invalidated only by gross exaggeration of numbers.

The statements quoted above may be said to have reflected sober afterthought. In the summer of 1753 things obviously did not seem entirely unfavorable. Of this fact the minutes or resolutions of the meeting of the Committee of the Ohio Company at Stratford in Westmoreland County, July 25-27, 1753[25] are adequate proof. Having purchased the shares of Gawin Corbin and Augustine Washington, Robert Carter was admitted as a member entitled to two shares or four fortieth parts. Lunsford Lomax having purchased a share from the executors of Lawrence Washington was similarily admitted to membership. A resolution approved a Letter and State of the Company's Case[26] drawn up by John Mercer asking for an enlargement of their original grant from the Crown through the agency of Mr. Hanbury. Another resolution provided for the immediate erection of the fort on "Shertees" Creek and stated its features, while providing for laying out the

[23] This item is historically valuable. It may account for the eleven families above mentioned. These families may have gone out in early 1753 and returned east in the autumn. It should be recalled that George Mercer in 1753 found, or at least reported, twenty settlers. See his map notations, printed in *George Mercer Papers*, opposite p. 226.

[24] D.M.L. MS., printed in *George Mercer Papers*, p. 245. This is probably a reference to the Moravians, who after a preliminary exploration, began in 1753 settlement near present Winston-Salem, North Carolina.

[25] *Ibid.*, pp. 147-49, 178-79.

[26] *Ibid.* The document itself has not been found, though it was entered in the Company's books and probably copied for later such cases sent to Europe in 1762. It has been suggested, above, that the fragment in the D.M.L. MS. may be a 1754 copy of this 1753 case, sent to Hanbury in 1754 and that its contents are possibly incorporated in the petition of April 2, 1754.

adjoining town and mentioning a school for Indian children. A resolution approved a letter to Mr. Hanbury by George Mason asking for twenty swivel guns and other arms.[27]

The last recorded resolution of this conference of late July, 1753, is compactly filled with valuable historical information, "Ordered that the Treasurer pay unto Mr. Gist the sum of forty four pounds sixteen shillings current money of Virginia Currency paid by him for making a Road from Wills Creek to Mohongaly, and also the sum of Twenty pounds current money on Account of his journey to the Treaty at Loggs Town in May and July 1752. The Committee being of Opinion that the Allowance[28] made him by the Governor was not a sufficient satisfaction for his trouble and expence on the said journey."

Treated thus generously, Christopher Gist could accept with better will the additional responsibilities placed upon him in new instructions of the Ohio Company, July 27, 1753. Already published by Darlington and long known, the instructions will bear very close reading. They show that Gist had obtained a commission from William and Mary College as surveyor of the Ohio Company lands.[29] They mention the use of a measuring wheel to calculate distance; they confirm other evidences of the Russell survey of early 1753; they mention people who have settled already on the Company's lands. More particularly they enjoin the laying out of the town on "Shertees" Creek, and, after careful explorations, the making of extensive surveys totaling 200,000 acres.[30]

All this activity was counter to the ideas of Thomas Penn, who on August 16, 1753, wrote to Richard Peters, ". . . I have always been of opinion that the Land granted to the Ohio Company is within the bounds of Pennsylvania,[31] . . . else M.r Hanbury would

---

[27] A matter duly taken care of in London.

[28] Evidence that Gist at Logstown in 1752 was something more than merely an Ohio Company representative and observer.

[29] No other documentation of this has been located. The William and Mary College archives were largely destroyed by fire in 1859.

[30] D.M.L. MS., printed in *George Mercer Papers*, pp. 147-49, 178-79.

[31] Penn was not mistaken and, indeed, he was truly prophetic.

not have applyed to me to secure the Grant to them, in case it should prove to be within our Province."[32]

The Case of the Ohio Company probably written by the lawyer, John Mercer, 1759–60, is now for the first time available for historical use. It is a long, elaborate, and closely reasoned document of about six thousand words, supplemented by an Appendix of about twenty thousand words, dealing with seven different aspects of the history. The Case covers the Treaty of Lancaster of 1744, the Virginia land grants of 1745, the beginnings of the Ohio Company, the early activities of the Company in ordering cargoes and building storehouses and roads, the explorations of Christopher Gist, and troubles with the Indians and the French. The Appendix includes the Hanbury petition, the Virginia land grants of 1745, 1747, 1749, and 1751, extracts from Christopher Gist's journal of his explorations of 1750–51 and of 1751–52, Gist's Instructions of 1752, the second Ohio Company petition of 1754, minutes of the Logstown Indian Conference of June, 1752, and some letters of Governor Dinwiddie of 1753. Parts of the material included in the Case and the Appendix have long been in print but much of it is a recent find and throws valuable new light on the history of Virginia and the West from 1743 to 1753 and is thereby a distinct contribution to knowledge.

From internal evidence, mainly the comparison of documents, it is evident that the Letter and State of the Company's Case, drawn up by John Mercer, adopted by the Committee of the Ohio Company in July and transmitted to John Hanbury, was transformed into a petition, presented by Dobbs, Hanbury, Smith, and Wardrop to the Crown and referred by the King to the Lords of the Committee of Council for Plantation Affairs on March 28, 1754, and by this Committee to the Lords Commissioners for Trade and Plantations, April 2, 1754.[33] This final document, the petition of 1754, mentions the cession of 1744, the formation of the Ohio Company in 1748, the petition to the Crown of early

---

[32] See the items of July 1-6, 1753, in the expense account of Thomas and Richard Penn, Large Folio II, H.S.P., printed below, pp. 228-29.

[33] P.R.O. C.O. 5: 1328/153-59, 164.

1749, the royal instructions to the Governor of Virginia of March, 1749, the grant to the Ohio Company of 200,000 acres on July 12, 1749, the ordering of a cargo of goods, the purchase of lands on the Potomac, the sending out of explorers, the attempt to purchase lands from the Proprietors of Maryland and Pennsylvania, the construction of a wagon road, and an application for a commission for their Company surveyor. Mentioned also are a chart of the West, Gist's second expedition, the petition to the Governor and Council of Virginia in 1752, its rejection, the rejection by William and Mary of the Company's surveyor, the great land grants to others in July, 1749, and the resulting risk to the Ohio Company. The Case, thus seen, was followed by a new petition. Apart from possible minor inaccuracies the statements therein correspond entirely with the narrative herein.

Since so obviously the petition of early 1754 is that sent to Mr. Hanbury by the Committee of the Ohio Company in late July, 1753, it reflects the situation of the Company at that time. Troubled by rival land claims and by French threats they signify their willingness to seat 300 families and build two forts, one on "Shertees" Creek and another on the Ohio at the mouth of the Great Kanawha in return for a royal grant for the lands west of the great mountain and east of the Ohio River, extending from the Kiskiminetas to the Great Kanawha, urging that speed is necessary in order to anticipate the French and secure the region for the British. It cannot be said that the members of the Company tamely submitted to the dangers which threatened their investment and prospects.

Meanwhile the active correspondence of the first half of 1753 continued. William Trent wrote to Governor Dinwiddie, August 11, 1753, depicting the critical situation in the Ohio Valley and saying that immediate aid to the friendly Indians was vitally necessary.[34] He also kept William Fairfax at Winchester informed

[34] Etting Collection, Ohio Company Papers, H.S.P. printed in Bailey, *Ohio Company Papers*, pp. 22-24. Trent, the "factor" of the Ohio Company, was engaged in carrying Dinwiddie's military supplies from Winchester to the Indians on the Ohio and its tributaries.

about matters among the Indians.[35] In reply, Fairfax notified Trent that he was waiting to receive the Indians at Winchester and announced assistance from the southern Indians. The whole situation was destined to be convassed at the Indian Conference at Winchester, Virginia, September 11-15, 1753.

The critical situation in the Ohio Valley in midsummer 1753 may have curtailed Indian trade there, but on the other hand have hastened efforts of the Ohio Company to collect amounts due from traders and others in residence along the Potomac in Frederick County, Virginia, and Frederick County, Maryland. The Frederick County, Virginia, Court of August 8-10, 1753, saw suits against William Patterson, Jeremiah Jack, Richard Leans, John and Isaac Pearis, and Enoch Enochs.[36] On August 14, 1753,[37] a warrant was issued against Richard Leans and another warrant against Daniel McCrory and John Collins in connection with the James Ross estate. In the Frederick County, Maryland, Court, August 21, 1753, six old cases were prosecuted and suits were won against John Johnson,[38] Joseph Volgemore,[39] Nathaniel Tomlinson,[40] and Joseph Mounts, Sr.[41] In Frederick County, Virginia, thirteen suits were entered September 5, respectively, against Richard Leans, Jeremiah Jack (a second record), William Patterson (a second record), Richard Leans (a second record), Abraham Teagarden, John Tucker, John Adam Long, and Thomas Caton.[42] Another warrant was taken out against Jeremiah Jack on September 7, and a bond secured from him on September 21, 1753.[43]

---

[35] See Fairfax to (Trent), September, 1753, D.M.L. MS., printed in *George Mercer Papers*, p. 80, and Part II, the *Case* . . . , p. 12.

[36] Frederick County, Virginia, Order Book, No. 5, 1753–54, folios 91-115.

[37] Frederick County, Virginia, Court Docket Papers.

[38] Frederick County, Maryland, Judgment Record H, 1754–59, folios 30-32.

[39] *Ibid.*, folios 32-35.

[40] *Ibid.*, folios 87-88.

[41] *Ibid.*, folio 117.

[42] All found in Frederick County, Virginia, Order Book, No. 5, 1753–54, folios 138-77.

[43] Frederick County, Virginia, Court Docket Papers.

The Ohio Company in fact had not abandoned hope along the Ohio and its main upper tributaries, for John Fraser, who had removed from Venago and taken up residence on Turtle Creek just east of the Forks of the Ohio, wrote Mr. Young, August 27, 1753, "Cap.t Trent was here the night before last and viewed the Ground the Fort is to be built upon, which they will begin in less than a month's time. The money has been laid out for the building of it already, and the Great Guns are lying at Williamsburg ready to bring up." [44]

It is necessary to keep in mind that Governor Dinwiddie in the summer of 1753 was keeping the imperial government at London in the closest possible touch with the unhappy situation and relations which existed with the French in occupation of Erie Bay and of the upper waters of the Allegheny River, and threatening to move south and drive the British-Americans out of the Ohio Country.

The Winchester Indian Conference, an affair of Virginia only, began with the arrival of 98 Indians, men, women, and children, late in the day of September 10, 1753.[45] Andrew Montour that evening delivered a message from Governor Dinwiddie recalling French attacks upon them and preparing them for the conference. Monacatootha replied, asking that nothing be concealed. Drinks, smokes, and a good supper ended the day. The white and Indian personnel present when the conference was formally opened September 11, 1753, though small was significant, including no less than a dozen prominent Indian sachems or chiefs. In a message to the Indians, Governor Dinwiddie acknowledged the reception of a message from the Onondago Council saying they would drive out the French and asking the English to leave also, as the country belonged to the Indians. This acknowledgement was followed up by reference to the Logstown Conference of May, 1752, with its provisions for a strong house and the provision of military supplies, saying this would be done and adding that Southern Indians would

[44] *Pa. Col. Recs.*, V, 660. Probably, as yet, "the Ground the Fort is to be built upon" was considered the location at the mouth of Chartiers Creek.

[45] P.R.O. C.O. 5: 1328/48-86.

send aid and Virginia would furnish a retreat for the Indian women and children.

On September 12, 1753, Monacatootha replied for the Indians. Mildly proclaiming friendship with the English, he boldly stated the lands belonged to the Indians, repudiating both settlement and the building of the strong house. On the next day, September 13, 1753, Montour opened the meeting with a message of the Governor of Virginia to the Twightwees, the Wyandots, and Shawnees, warning them against the French and emphasizing the necessity of friendship among the Indians and between them and the English. Chiefs of the three Indian nations, in reply, gave the desired assurance of friendship. In the evening a private conference was held at which Monacatootha asked the aid of Virginia in securing help from Pennsylvania, a request which was quickly approved.

There was no meeting during the day of Friday, September 14, 1753, for the Indians had become too intoxicated, but at an evening meeting Montour delivered another message from Governor Dinwiddie to the Indians, asking for peace between northern and southern Indians and proposing a joint conference of them at Winchester the following year, apologizing for the small present and promising a large one later. The thanks of the Indians promptly followed.

On the last day of the Conference, the Turtle, a Twightwee chief, confirmed the friendship, gave the pipe of peace, and presented two beaver skins for Governor Dinwiddie. Monacatootha in behalf of all the Indians, spoke at length. He mentioned the lands, and the strong house, and desired to transact all business with Montour, Trent, and Gist and have military supplies brought out by them. He wanted trade to be controlled by the Indians rather than haphazardly carried on and asked for an agreement to this. In his opinion the rum trade was greatly in need of control. The Beaver then spoke for the Delawares, mentioning particularly Shawnees in captivity in South Carolina.

The Shawnees, at a private Sunday meeting, September 16, 1753, mentioned their agreement with Pennsylvania and promised friendship to all the English, a message gladly accepted by the Commissioner of Virginia. Monacatootha put in a special plea for the Shawnee captives, and several chiefs sought rum, five gallons of which were delivered to them. On this same Sunday a religious ceremony was held at the Court House with the baptizing of a number of Indians. The letter to the Governor of Pennsylvania was duly dispatched.[46]

In the final paragraph of his report to Governor Dinwiddie, William Fairfax euphemistically admits that the Conference was a failure and that confirmation of the Indian concession of the lands on the Ohio must await the anticipated conference of Dinwiddie with the Indians in May, 1754. Obviously the Indians were unwilling to get out of the Ohio Valley.

Moreover, the Indians were not fully satisfied with the war supplies furnished them at Winchester. They complained to William Trent who reported to Colonel William Fairfax who in turn promptly passed the information on to Governor Dinwiddie. A letter from N. Walthoe, secretary, to Trent announced the dispatch from Virginia of ten barrels of powder and four hundred flints.[47]

While relative failure characterized the Winchester Conference of September, it did not stop continued legal activity against the mercantile debtors of the Company. A double indemnity bond for £22 was secured, September 1, 1753, from Jeremiah Jack, Sr. and Jeremiah Jack, Jr.[48] On October 2, suits were continued against John Adam Long[49] and Thomas Caton.[50] On October 3, a suit was brought against Jeremiah Jack;[51] on October 10, a warrant of attachment was issued against John Adam Long.[52] These actions in Virginia were followed by prosecution, in Frederick County, Maryland, November Court, of seven old cases and judgments against John Johnson, Richard Chapman, William Erwin, Nathan-

[46] In *Pa. Col. Recs.*, V, 657.

[47] D.M.L. MS., printed in *George Mercer Papers*, p. 81, and Part II, the *Case* . . . , p. 13.

[48] Frederick County, Virginia, Court Docket Papers.

[49] Frederick County, Virginia, Order Book, No. 5, 1753–54, folio 190.

[50] *Ibid.*, folio 193.

[51] *Ibid.*, folio 204.

[52] *Ibid.*, Court Docket Papers.

iel Tomlinson, and Joseph Mounts, Senior. December 18, 1753, saw a warrant in Frederick County,[53] Virginia, against Francis Ross. And it should be here remembered that in November, 1753, George Washington was at the Forks of the Ohio and made a famous notation about the intended Ohio Company Fort.

---

[53] Frederick County, Maryland, Judgment Record, No. 6, 1754–59, folio 226.

VII

Disaster and Hiatus

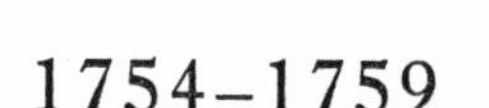

1754–1759

Governor Dinwiddie had not been present at the Winchester Indian Conference for a very good reason. He was preoccupied with the threat to the English claims in the West by the activity of the French south of Lake Erie. Already, December 10, 1752,[1] he had passed on to the Board of Trade and Plantations some of the information furnished him by Trent, Montour, Gist and others. On June 16, 1753, he was able to report the enlarged operations of the French and asked for instructions.[2] Such instructions drawn up in London, August 28, 1753,[3] he probably received in October. The contents of these instructions are very well known to students of American history. It was in accordance with them and with information from a letter of Trent of October 5, 1753, about fur traders and Ohio Company settlers being faced with the necessity of flight from the Ohio Valley, that Governor Dinwiddie sought some one to deliver a message of warning to the French upon the upper Allegheny River and, October 31, 1753, gave in-

[1] P.R.O. C.O. 5: 1327/531-36.

[2] *Ibid.*, 637-42.

[3] *Ibid.*, 211/31-32. They enjoined completion of the proposed fort on or near the Ohio.

structions to young George Washington to perform the hazardous trip. Anxiety about the Ohio Valley is seen in the "Act for Further Encouraging Persons to Settle on the Waters of the Mississippi," which was passed by the Virginia Assembly, December 19, 1753.[4]

To a considerable extent, therefore, matters were already beyond the future control of the Ohio Company when the Committee, November 2, 1753, met to transact business. It, nevertheless, ordered a levy of twenty pounds current money on each member to pay for building and finishing the fort at Chartiers Creek and clearing the road from Wills Creek to the Monongahela. It also ordered the Company's attorneys to enter caveats against the grants of June 15, 1753, to Richard Corbin.[5] Probably the members present had no idea that for more than four years to come there would be, so far as the records now indicate, no regular meeting of either the Committee or the Company.

The affairs of the Ohio Company, however, in some degree of importance, continued in the picture from November 1753 to October 1754. The agents of the Company were active, the property of the Company played a notable role, and things started in Virginia continued in motion in London. As an agent both of the Ohio Company and of Virginia, William Trent carried on discussions with the Indians in November 1753.[6] George Washington on his famous mission of the winter of 1753–54 stopped, November 14, 1753, at the Ohio Company's storehouse at the mouth of Wills Creek. As a guide, he employed Christopher Gist, then an agent of the Ohio Company. Washington travelled over the road cut by the Ohio Company earlier in the previous year. He stopped at Gist's Place both on his way out and on his way home. He reported meeting people in January 1754, some going to build a fort at the Forks of the Ohio, and some moving out to settle around Gist's Place. Washington carried back to Governor Din-

[4] Hening, *Statutes at Large . . .* , VI, 355-56.

[5] D.M.L. MS., printed in *George Mercer Papers*, pp. 150, 179.

[6] P.R.O. C.O. 5: 1328/27-44.

widdie a letter of January 6 from Trent,[7] saying among other things that if properly "impowered so to do," Trent could stop the French advance during the winter. On the receipt of this letter Governor Dinwiddie wasted no time in issuing a commission, January 26, 1754, to Trent as Commander and Captain to raise a maximum of 100 men to assist the friendly Indians, keep possession of the Ohio Valley and repel the French.[8] The commission was accompanied by a long letter[9] and a speech to the Half King.[10] A similar letter[11] to Lord Fairfax in January, 1754, urged him to collect and send out men to protect those already sent out by the Ohio Company to build a fort on the Ohio. Trent before April 12, 1754, raised 52 men and drew heavily upon the Ohio Company's store to outfit and maintain them.[12] George Washington likewise was directed to raise 100 men from Frederick and Augusta counties, and a letter of Dinwiddie to Lord Fairfax, lieutenant of Frederick County, stated the troops were sent "to protect those already sent by the Ohio Company to build a fort. . . ."[13]

Information about Washington's report of his trip and the colonial measures taken thereafter by himself was sent by Dinwiddie to the Board of Trade and Plantations[14] and probably, in due time, to John Hanbury.[15] But more important, so far as the inner

[7] *Va. Hist. Colls.*, I, 55. Mentioned in Dinwiddie to Trent, January 27, 1754, D.M.L. MS., printed in *George Mercer Papers*, pp. 81-82, and Part II, the *Case* . . . , p. 15. The letter of Trent was not found.

[8] *Va. Hist. Colls.*, III, 54; D.M.L. MS., printed in *George Mercer Papers*, pp. 82-83.

[9] *Va. Hist. Colls.*, III, 56; *George Mercer Papers*, pp. 81-82; P.R.O. C.O. 5: 14/146-50.

[10] Copy in D.M.L. MS., printed in *George Mercer Papers*, p. 286, and Part II, the *Case* . . . , pp. 11-12.

[11] *Va. Hist. Colls.*, III, 49.

[12] D.M.L. MS., printed in *George Mercer Papers*, p. 83.

[13] *Va. Hist. Colls.*, III, 48-50. Washington's instructions, p. 59, are dated merely January, 1754, but presumably were given him January 26, 1754.

[14] P.R.O. C.O. 5: 1328/99-105.

[15] A letter of Dinwiddie to Hanbury, February 12, 1754, is mentioned, but was not found.

history of the Ohio Company of Virginia in the first weeks of 1754 is concerned, William Trent was at the mouth of Redstone Creek, with about twenty men, building a storehouse or hangard for the Ohio Company.[16] Presumably Christopher Gist and his settlers were in residence at Gist's Place, to which he had given the name Monongahela. John Fraser probably was at his new post near the mouth of Turtle Creek, while others whom Washington had met on his return journey over the mountains were getting ready to build a fortified post on the point at the junction of the Monongahela and the Allegheny rivers. At this date it was the Ohio Company which was in the field, in disregard of the threat from the French on the upper Allegheny, accurate information about which was personally known to Gist and Fraser and doubtless had been fully revealed to Trent.

The receipt in the middle of February of the commissions and instructions of Governor Dinwiddie somewhat altered the status of things. These field agents of the Ohio Company became, by a subtle and indefinite transformation, the military agents of the colony of Virginia and of the British Empire. Trent, temporarily in chief command, proceeded quickly from the mouth of Redstone Creek to the Forks of the Ohio. There he met Gist and others. Two days later, February 19, 1754, Trent and Gist wrote letters to George Washington,[17] announcing an expected attack by the French and urging him to hurry up his reinforcements. Strangely enough on this same day, when Trent, Gist, Fraser, and Ensign Ward were on the frontier preparing to build the fortified post,

---

[16] *Documents Relating to the Colonial History of the State of New York* (hereinafter cited as *N.Y.C.D.*), VII, 269. See Croghan to James Hamilton, February 3, 1754, in Pennsylvania Provincial Papers, XII, 46, saying, "Mr. Trent is Just Come outt with ye Virginia goods, and has brought a quantity of Toules and workmen to begin a fort." If so, the goods seem to have been taken first to the mouth of Redstone Creek.

[17] Not found in the Washington papers. See *Maryland Gazette*, March 14, 1754, and the *Virginia Gazette*, March 29, 1754, and Draper MS. I JJ 23-25, Wisconsin Historical Society.

Governor Dinwiddie put out his famous proclamation [18] promising 200,000 acres of land in the West to volunteers who would serve in the military forces of the colony; thereby, whether wittingly or unwittingly, undermining eventually the claims of the Ohio Company to much of the region. Dinwiddie and the Virginia Council, as recorded,[19] may have been "satisfy'd that there are other Lands sufficient to answer the Quantity granted to the Ohio Company . . . ," but circumstances were to prove otherwise. And the Company might disclaim, as it did later, that it made any objection to the proclamation;[20] but the results were that the proclamation lands were later validated, while the Ohio Company, an earlier claimant, saw its claim unfulfilled. It is noteworthy that, on March 13, 1754, less than a month after the Dinwiddie Proclamation, Governor Hamilton of Pennsylvania wrote Dinwiddie that both the anticipated Ohio Company lands and the anticipated 200,000 acres of the Dinwiddie Proclamation were "really within the limits of Pennsylvania." [21]

The course of events in the Ohio Valley in the first half of 1754 is a famous part of the history of the French and Indian war, but it is also a part of the history of the Ohio Company. Its post at the Forks of the Ohio was captured, its settlements at Gist's Place were destroyed, its storehouse and goods at the mouth of Redstone Creek were burned. The hostilities postponed and in fact ruined its establishment of land claims and Indian trade in the region. It might be said that the Ohio Company was the greatest loser in the untoward events of this period.

But before the tragedy along the Ohio and the Monongahela is depicted, it may be noted that, contemporaneously, the second

---

[18] *Executive Journals, Council of Colonial Virginia*, V, 499-500; D.M.L. MS., printed in *George Mercer Papers*, p. 77. In Draper MS. I JJ 20-I JJ 22. See also the *Maryland Gazette*, March 7, 1754.

[19] *Executive Journals, Council of Colonial Virginia*, V, 462.

[20] D.M.L. MS., printed in *George Mercer Papers*, pp. 77-78, and Part II, the *Case* . . . , p. 17.

[21] *Pa. Arch.*, fourth series, II, 264-65. Copy in Pennsylvania Provincial Records M, 1748–55, folios 299-301.

petition to the Crown, as projected in November 1752 and submitted after July 27, 1753, was before the imperial authorities in London during this crisis in America. On March 28, 1754, it was referred by the King to the Committee of the Privy Council for Plantation Affairs.[22] On April 2, 1754, it was referred by this Committee to the Board of Trade and Plantations for their consideration and report.[23] It remained in their hands and under consideration for nearly three months.[24] Finally on June 25, 1754 [25] it was unfavorably reported upon, but it was then too late, anyhow. Events on the Ohio had already rendered the grant temporarily vain and it was therefore not made. Both in the New World and in the Old, the Ohio Company saw defeat and disaster in 1754.

In the new world, Trent, Gist, Fraser, and Edward Ward were busily at work, from the middle of February, upon the problem of assembling men and materials for construction of the fort planned in the earliest days of the Company. They naturally began by felling trees, hewing timbers, sawing planks, making shingles, and constructing a store house for themselves and their equipment.[26] As rapidly as possible with the men and supplies available, but with exasperating difficulties and delays, they carried forward the work of constructing a rude palisaded post. Trent, for very good reasons, it may be said, went back to Wills Creek.[27] He needed more men and more supplies. John Fraser, in accordance with his commission, was often absent on private business. Temporary command fell to Ensign Ward. In the absence of his superiors, Ward in mid-April was alarmed by the rapid approach from the North of a large French expedition under the command of M. de Contrecoeur. His meager force of thirty-three men was in no position to offer effective resistance.

---

[22] P.R.O. C.O. 5: 1328/153.

[23] *Ibid.*

[24] *J.B.T.*, 1754–58, pp. 32, 44, 45.

[25] P.R.O. C.O. 5: 1367/76-87.

[26] *N.Y.C.D.*, VII, 269.

[27] See the depositions of Ensign Edward Ward, May 7, 1754, P.R.O. C.O. 5: 14/293, and June 30, 1756, Etting Collection, Ohio Company Papers, H.S.P.

The details of Ward's parley with Contrecoeur and his final surrender and retreat to Redstone Old Fort need not be reported. The palpable result was that the long meditated fort of the Ohio Company was now lost, captured by an alien enemy, while in course of construction. Fort Duquesne, built on the site by the French and held by them for four and a half years, was in some ways a sign of the failure beyond the mountains of the great dream of the gentlemen of the Ohio Company, a marker of the beginning of virtually complete elimination of their actual operations in the region.[28] The steps of this elimination are well known. Washington, at the mouth of Wills Creek, on learning of Ward's retreat, courageously but foolishly decided to march to the Monongahela with only a few hundred men as against nearly a thousand under Contrecoeur. In May he reached Laurel Ridge and had his unfortunate encounter[29] with Jumonville. On June 28, 1754, he reached Gist's Place, expecting to go on to the mouth of Redstone Creek. In justified uncertainty, he stayed a day or two at this spot. Then learning of the rapid approach of the French under de Villiers, the avenging brother of Jumonville, he began, June 30, 1754, the laborious return up the mountain road. His wearied forces were attacked at Fort Necessity on July 3-4, 1754, and he was compelled to capitulate and return to Wills Creek.[30]

De Villiers on his way back to Fort Duquesne destroyed, July 5-6, 1754, not only Gist's settlement but also the storehouses and goods of the Ohio Company at Redstone Old Fort. The Ohio Company lost thereby not only its property but the last vestige of its painfully established hold beyond the mountains.

[28] As is stated in the context below, and evidenced by documents printed below in Appendix A, some of the relatives and associates of Christopher Gist returned to the area and easily established title to their old holdings, by both Virginia authority and Pennsylvania sanction.

[29] An episode about which governmental officials, diplomats, antiquarians, and historians have disagreed for two centuries and may never fully agree.

[30] The account of this campaign, Freeman, *op. cit.*, I, 354-411, is full and lucid, though featured by uncritical approval of Washington's policies and procedure. On the activities of De Villiers, see J.C.B., *Travels in New France* and the documents in Pierre Margry, *Decouvertes et Etablissements des Francais.*

In connection with this campaign of early 1754, there is found in the Darlington manuscripts a mutilated but hitherto unknown letter of George Washington to Thomas Cresap, April 28, 1754, written from Winchester, Virginia.[31] In it he complains of the lack of wagons, proposes to use packhorses, and takes measures to assure his forces sundry provisions, some of them from the Ohio Company's goods.

In the very midst of these disasters George Mason and his lawyers pushed the claims of the Company against its debtors. Probably in March a petition for £14 . . 17 . . 5, Maryland money, and a warrant were issued in Frederick County, Virginia, against George Parker, Jr.[32] A suit against Francis Ross was continued, March 5, and a declaration and warrant entered against him, March 11, 1754. In Frederick County, Maryland, five old cases[33] were prosecuted and entries recorded in the Judgment Record on March 19, 1754, against Catherine and Evan Shelby for an old debt of the late Evan Shelby for £14 . . 5 due since July 3, 1750;[34] against Isaac Baker, against Evan Shelby, Bail of John Johnson, for £17 . . 3;[35] against Joseph Volgamore for £13 . . 11 . . 6,[36] and against Joseph Mounts, Senior, for £9 . . 7 . . 11½.[37] In Frederick County, Virginia, the suit against Francis Ross was further prosecuted April 2, 1754, the suit against George Parker, Jr., won on April 4, 1754,[38] the suit against Francis Ross further prosecuted June 5, 1754, a warrant taken out against Jonathan Coburn for £12 . . 1, Maryland money, June 15, 1754[39] and a warrant entered

---

[31] D.M.L. MS., printed in *George Mercer Papers*, p. 85, and Part II, the *Case* . . . , pp. 17-18.

[32] Frederick County, Virginia, Court Docket Papers.

[33] Frederick County, Maryland, Dockets, March, 1754, folios 7-27, Hall of Records, Annapolis.

[34] Frederick County, Maryland, Judgment Record H, 1754–59, folios 324-26.

[35] *Ibid.*, folios 416-17.

[36] *Ibid.*, folio 421.

[37] *Ibid.*, folio 429.

[38] Frederick County, Virginia, Order Book, No. 5, folio 392.

[39] Frederick County, Virginia, Court Docket Papers.

against John Adam Long for £16 . . 9s . . 10d, Virginia money, September 16, 1754.[40] At the June Court, Frederick County, Maryland, 1754, the respective suits, against Joseph Crecroft and against Joseph Mounts, Sr., were both docketed and entered upon the Judgment Record.

The possessions controlled after July 6, 1754 by the Ohio Company were centered at the mouth of Wills Creek. They figured greatly in the campaign and correspondence of the last half of 1754. Washington mentions the Company's storehouse at Wills Creek, in letters respectively to Governor Sharpe of Maryland[41] and Governor Hamilton of Pennsylvania.[42] He proposed to use it as a military magazine or arsenal. Governor Dinwiddie mentions it in a letter to Colonel Hunter, May 4, 1754,[43] and in a letter of August (1754) to Colonel Innes, speaks of the possible use of six swivel guns at Wills Creek belonging to the Ohio Company. An order to Colonel Innes definitely instructed him to take possession of the Ohio Company's warehouse at Wills Creek.[44] Colonel Innes and George Washington had instructions to fit out the Ohio Company's store at Wills Creek as a magazine and to erect on its lands there "other Works."[45] According to a later statement of George Mason the houses and property of the Ohio Company at Wills Creek were destroyed by such military occupation and no compensation for such damages was granted later.[46]

The final repercussion of the Ohio Company troubles before the paralysis of the French and Indian War settled upon their immediate prospects appears in a series of petitions by Christopher Gist October 30, 1754, and May 7, 1755, to the Virginia legislature

---

40 *Ibid.*

41 April 27, 1754. *Writings of Washington*, ed. Fitzpatrick, I, 43.

42 *Pa. Col. Recs.*, V, 6, 29.

43 *Va. Hist. Colls.*, III, 150-51.

44 *Ibid.*, p. 297. See the confirmation of this, Dinwiddie to Sharpe, September 6, 1754, *ibid.*, pp. 304-5.

45 Dinwiddie to Fairfax, September 10 (1754), *ibid.*, p. 312.

46 See Toner Collection of Ohio Company Papers, VI, 395 f., and V.S.L. MS. Petition of the Ohio Company, November 20, 1778, printed in Bailey, *Ohio Company . . .*, pp. 320-27.

asking payment for his personal losses due to surveys by rival land companies and damage by warfare and the French.[47] Somewhat to the astonishment of any one unfamiliar with other similar cases, all his petitions were rejected.[48] His reward for his great work, 1750–1754, was not to be financial, but historical. He earned an imperishable name in the history of the American frontier.

The dire events of the summer of 1754 and the cessation of all trade with the Indians of the Ohio Valley did not completely destroy hopes for the future of the Ohio Company. On October 25, 1754, George Mason finally secured patents from Lord Fairfax for the lands of the *New Store Tract* upon which entry had probably been made by Hugh Parker in 1749 and a storehouse built in 1750. This part of the Fairfax lands had earlier been subdivided into lots. Patents for Lots 14, 15 and 16 were granted [49] to George Mason for the Ohio Company. Lot No. 1 of 237 acres and No. 5 of 329 acres became a part of the private estate of George Mason,[50] but Lots No. 14 of 220 acres, No. 15 of 334 acres, and No. 16 of 315 were later resurveyed along with 214 acres of additional waste land and held about thirty years for the Company, by George Mason.

Meanwhile, in August, 1754, Daniel Dulany, the attorney of George Mason, prosecuted old cases in Frederick County, Maryland, against Joseph Mounts, Sr., Nathaniel Tomlinson, and John Nicholas,[51] and in the month of November brought further suit against them, with a judgment, of record, against Joseph Mounts.[52] The docket for the March Court, 1755, contained not only items relating to these three cases, but also an item of a suit by the Ohio

---

47 *Journal of the House of Burgesses of Virginia*, 1754–55 and 1756–58, pp. 223, 244.

48 *Ibid.*, p. 247.

49 Northern Neck Land Grants H, 1751–56, Virginia State Library.

50 As shown in the Hampshire County records, at Romney, West Virginia.

51 Frederick County, Maryland, Dockets, August Term, 1754, folios 89, 93. Now in Hall of Records, Annapolis.

52 Frederick County, Maryland, Judgment Record H, 1754–59, folios 709-10. Spaces in the record are blank and make impossible an exact statement of the account.

Company against Christopher Gist. While the judgment entries against Nathaniel Tomlinson and Joseph Mounts are marked "nulla bona," the entry against Gist is recorded "Non Est Inventus."

From March 20, 1755 to June 5, 1755, the period of Braddock's expedition, there have survived no highly relevant papers concerning the Ohio Company except the few random references to the roads, storehouses, and goods of the Ohio Company. It was a period of frontier alarm followed by the arrival of Braddock's regiments and the preparation for his march against Fort Duquesne.

But by June, with Braddock's army at or beyond Wills Creek, legal processes against debtors could be resumed in Frederick County, Virginia. Eight suits [53] were entered on June 5-6, 1755, respectively, against Abraham Teagarden, Jonathan Coburn, William Patterson, John and Isaac Pearis, John Tucker, John Adam Long, Thomas Caton, and Francis Ross. In connection with these suits have survived jury lists of the Teagarden case, the Coburn case, the Pearis case and mention of the same jury in jury items of the Tucker case and the Long case.[54] The additional items of 1755, are three June items in Frederick County, Maryland, consisting of a docket item against Joseph Mounts, with a judgment record item, and two docket items [55] against John Nicholas. The docket, March Court, 1756, Trial No. 22, shows another item against Nicholas. And dating from September, 1756, in all probability, though it may have been projected by George Washington, a year earlier, is a list of Indian goods at Rock Creek belonging to the Ohio Company, with the prices at first cost in London.[56] Unfortunately the amount of each item is not given, but the prices

[53] All found in the Frederick County, Virginia, Order Book, No. 6, 1754–55, folios 283-305.

[54] All found in the Frederick County, Virginia, Court Docket Papers.

[55] Frederick County, Maryland, Dockets, June Term, 1755, folios 58-130. For the judgment record, see Frederick County, Maryland, Judgment Record H, 1753–59, folio 856.

[56] George Washington MS., L.C., printed in *Letters to Washington*, I, 362-64.

given enable one to estimate that the Ohio Company sold such goods on the frontier at about 2½ times the price paid in London.

In the midst of the distresses of the frontier from 1754 to 1756, George Mason, March 25, 1756, secured from Frederick Calvert, Proprietor of Maryland, through Horatio Sharpe, Governor, the patent[57] to 500 acres of land, a tract called *Walnut Bottom*, on Wills Creek, first surveyed in 1745 for Thomas Bladen and assigned September 11, 1753 to George Mason. A quit rent of one pound sterling was attached to the patent. Very probably the Ohio Company had taken possession of *Walnut Bottom* in late 1753, and thus held lands on both sides of the Potomac River near where Cumberland, Maryland, is now located.[58] It was property, whether in land, crops, timber, houses, or traders goods, utilized by Trent, Innes, Washington and others in 1754 and by Braddock and others in 1755.

Notwithstanding the deposition of Edward Ward, made, May 7, 1754, before the Governor and Council of Virginia,[59] the absence of William Trent from the construction of the fort at the forks of the Ohio in mid-April 1754 continued to be criticized. Probably Trent was instrumental in securing in Cumberland County, Pennsylvania, a second and fuller deposition of Ensign Ward duly sworn before one of the justices of the peace, June 30, 1756.[60] This deposition contains much interesting historical information. It stated that "a strong Square Log House with Loop Holes," was constructed by Trent at Redstone Creek, at the expense of the Ohio Company; that Trent's flour and meal which he had brought over the Mountain in mid-winter, was soon consumed by the "great

[57] Liber G.S. No. 2, folios 400-2, Maryland Land Office, Annapolis.

[58] The Ohio Company attempted to subdivide *Walnut Bottom* in the first half of 1763 and thus start a town which it proposed to name Charlottesburg, but was stopped by military authority. As will be observed below, it was sold in 1783 to Thomas Beall, later to be the founder of Cumberland, Maryland.

[59] P.R.O. C.O. 5: 14/193-96.

[60] Photostat in H.S.P., printed in Bailey, *Ohio Company Papers*, pp. 26-31. The original manuscript, or its record, should be in the Cumberland County Courthouse at Carlisle, Pennsylvania, but, if so, it is boxed, stored, and inaccessible.

Concourse of Indians" at the Forks of the Ohio, February 17 to April 17, 1754; that scarcity of provisions and Indian advice caused Trent to return to the Potomac for additional supplies and troops, that George Washington's men in the early summer were inadequately supplied with provisions and ammunition; that not only the supplies and the ammunition of Trent's men at the forks in April, 1754, but their pay for work came from the Ohio Company; and that on April 17, 1754, his only "Defence" was a few "Pallisadoes which he had order'd to be put up four Days before. . . ." Whether by collusion or otherwise, the allegations in this deposition are confirmed by statements in George Croghan's Journal, extracts of which were received by Sir William Johnson, June 25, 1757.[61]

In Frederick County, Virginia, George Mason continued litigation against Ohio Company debtors. The suit against Thomas Caton came up again August 6, 1756;[62] the Maryland suit against John Nicholas was docketed for August 17, 1756[63] and on September 7, 1756 George Mason entered a writ of attachment against Richard Pearis for £400.[64] The suit against Richard Pearis was again brought up February 2, 1757 but discontinued[65] on the motion of the plaintiffs. A month later, March 4, 1757, the old suit against Thomas Caton, often dismissed, came up again.[66] Caton, in the custody of the sheriff, brought suit, April 7, 1757, for his discharge.[67] In early 1758 at the January and February Courts of

[61] *N.Y.C.D.*, VII, 269.

[62] Frederick County, Virginia, Order Book, No. 7, 1755–59, folio 116.

[63] Frederick County, Maryland, Dockets, Autumn Court, 1756, folios 90-91, Maryland Hall of Records, Annapolis.

[64] D.M.L. George Mason Papers, printed below, Appendix A, pp. 229-31.

[65] Frederick County, Virginia, Order Book, No. 7, 1755–57, folio 181, printed below, p. 231. In all probability this was double indemnity penal bond damages, for Ohio Company goods used by Richard Pearis to supply his troops at Fort Frederick, Maryland, or as gifts to Cherokee Indians. The fact that Richard Pearis later held extensive property in Frederick County, Virginia, indicates settlement of the claim.

[66] *Ibid.*, folio 216.

[67] *Ibid.*, folio 232.

Frederick County, Virginia, cases came up, January 3, against Thomas Rutherford and, February 4, against Jeremiah Jack.[68] In each case the suits were abated by reason of the prior death of the defendant. And probably a declaration against Providence Mounts dates from April 1758.[69] The Frederick County, Virginia, Court of July 6, 1758 took up suits against Providence Mounts, Thomas Caton, the Executors of James Ross, and Robert Lemen.[70] On September 8, 1758, it secured a judgment against Robert Lemen for £75:8:10.[71]

In November 1757 the Ohio Company had trouble with Governor Robert Dinwiddie. He had been displaced and was on the point of departure from Yorktown when John Mercer, the Company's lawyer, realized that it had claims against William Trent for many hundreds of pounds of goods secured from the storehouses along the Potomac in 1753–54, on the credit of Governor Dinwiddie. At Trent's suggestion a warrant was sued out against Dinwiddie and in a long drawn out trial Trent eventually secured a verdict for the amount claimed and the costs of the suit. Correspondence of George Mason and John Mercer of a later date brought to light the account and the fact of its payment to the Ohio Company.[72] Owing to the destruction by fire of so many Virginia Court records, this case has largely escaped historians.

During the years from 1755 to 1758 the activities and prospects of the Ohio Company of Virginia were at a minimum. Its members turned their attention to other matters and its agents took

[68] Frederick County, Virginia, Order Book, No. 7, 1755–57, folios 352, 354.

[69] Frederick County, Virginia, Court Docket Papers.

[70] Frederick County, Virginia, Order Book, No. 8, 1758–60, folios 72-73, 80-91.

[71] *Ibid.*, folio 119.

[72] See the expense account of William Trent, April 8, 1754, Colonial Papers, 1740–1759, folios 72-73, V.S.L.; the account of Trent and Croghan with the Ohio Company, June 2, 1753–September 7, 1755, H.S.P. MS.; the letters of George Mason and John Mercer of early 1767, H.S.P. MS. printed below, pp. 239-41; and the List of Papers sent by William Trent to John Mercer, April 11, 1759, H.S.P., printed below, Appendix A, pp. 231-32.

other positions. A letter [73] of September 15, 1757 from Edmund Atkins, superintendent of Indian Affairs in the Southern Colonies, says, "I have appointed Christopher Gist, Esquire my Deputy in this Colony (Virginia) being well recommended for his fair Character; and he is the best acquainted here with the Indians." Apart from legal actions in regard to trade accounts the historical item of greatest significance is that of a meeting of the Committee of the Ohio Company December 20-22, 1757 at *Marlborough*, the home of John Mercer.[74] Frontier defense and military matters overshadowed these years. So far as Virginia was concerned it was, until 1758, the period of construction of frontier forts extending from the Potomac on the north to the North Carolina boundary on the south. In the writings of George Washington are many documents on this aspect of affairs. Fort Duquesne was the center from which radiated spasmodic yet incessant raids against the frontiersmen of Pennsylvania, Maryland, and Virginia. In the graphic language of Colonel Henry Bouquet it was a "nest of robbers." [75]

But with the advance of Forbes' troops to Rays Town and Loyalhannan and of Virginia regiments to Cumberland, normal conditions returned along the upper Potomac. At the Frederick County, Virginia, Court on September 8, 1758, a suit was won against Robert Lemen.[76] A jury list presumably of this trial has survived.[77] And with the continuation of the Forbes campaign

---

[73] Pennsylvania Provincial Papers, II, 81, Harrisburg, Pennsylvania.

[74] D.M.L. MS., printed in *George Mercer Papers*, p. 179. Its sole recorded business was: "Ordered that a Letter be wrote to Mr. John Hanbury desiring him to send the Company an Account of Sales of all Skins and Furrs in his Hands unaccounted for and also of the Skins and Furrs shipped by M.r Christopher Gist and ordered by him to be placed to the Companys Credit." Here it should be observed that the Company, in March, 1755, sued Christopher Gist, probably about goods and supplies used in 1752–1754, but not impossibly about these "Skins and Furrs."

[75] Alfred P. James, "The Nest of Robbers, Fort Duquesne, 1755–1758," *W. Pa. Hist. Mag.*, XXI (1938), 165-78.

[76] Frederick County, Virginia, Order Book, No. 8, 1758–60, folio 119.

[77] Frederick County, Virginia, Court Docket Papers.

against Fort Duquesne in late 1758, a profound change occurred. Defensive warfare was replaced with offensive measures which came to a climax in the Ohio region with the capture of Fort Duquesne on November 25, 1758. Full information about this soon reached the Atlantic Coast.

VIII

Renewed Activity

1759–1762

THE SITUATION in the Ohio Valley remained critical until the summer of 1759. The defeat of the French at Niagara in 1759 rendered the region relatively safe. Military matters, however, remained supreme for five more years. The war did not end until 1763. The Great Lakes area was occupied in the interim. The occupation of Illinois proved impossible before 1763 and difficult for another two years. And, in 1763, the year of the treaty of peace with France, an equally serious situation arose with the Indian revolt under the leadership of Pontiac. The frontiers in the years 1763 and 1764 were largely taken up with the Indian problems. Not until 1765 was the Ohio Valley ready for the rapid settlement by people from more eastern areas.

Governor Francis Fauquier of Virginia, who replaced Governor Dinwiddie, was no friend of the Ohio Company. In a letter to the Board of Trade,[1] January 30, 1759, Fauquier devoted the last paragraph to the matter of Western lands. In it he indulged in a "few Reflexions" of which one sentence was highly significant. "It is supposed" he wrote, "that all the Great Grants are actually forfeited, if so, and the Crown should think proper to resume

[1] P.R.O. C.O. 5: 1329/247-50.

them, I apprehend it will be best not to renew them, for great and extensive Grants are destructive to the well settling and peopling a Colony." He added in the next sentence, "This is the opinion of all the Gentlemen who are themselves concerned in some of these Grants, they acknowledge them to be detrimental; but as they expect some Proffit may be made by them they desire to have their Share." Fauquier thought that if such grants were to be resumed, surveys should be demanded early, the lands secured should be contiguous and "as near a Square as possible."

With relative security established on the Virginia frontier, George Mason, February 7, 1759, engaged in a series of suits in Frederick County, Virginia, respectively, against William Harrell, the Executors of James Ross, Peter Mounts, and Francis Ross.[2] He recovered £10 .. 2s .. 5d in the first suit; £28 .. 8s .. 3d in the second, £5 .. 7s .. 8½d in the suit against Mounts, and had the third suit abated by reason of the death of the defendant. And the old suit of 1757 against Dinwiddie was being prosecuted at Williamsburg, for on April 11, 1759, William Trent sent about a dozen documents to the prosecuting lawyer, John Mercer, while preserving for himself, and thereby for posterity, a list of the documents, the list annotated and endorsed.[3]

In the meantime profound changes had taken place in the general situation. First of all, the British imperial government, through the agency of the commander-in-chief[4] of his majesty's forces in North America, had assumed realistic control over the entire Ohio Valley. Military posts and garrisons were stationed in the area at Fort Bedford, Fort Ligonier, Fort Pitt, Fort Redstone, and elsewhere. These military settlements were the springboards of a permanent occupation by people wholly unrelated to the claims and expectations of the Ohio Company ten years earlier.

---

[2] Frederick County, Virginia, Order Book, No. 8, 1758–60, folios 195-99.

[3] H.S.P. MS.

[4] The great significance of this position, held in turn by Braddock, Shirley, Loudoun, Abercromby, Amherst, and Gage, is a twentieth-century revelation, the product of research and publication of such scholars as Clarence W. Alvord, Clarence Carter, J. C. Long, Lawrence Gipson, and others.

The British government, in disregard of the terms of old colonial charters, seemed to assume that it now had title to the distribution of the lands, an assumption which was fortified by the activities in London of numerous land speculators both from Virginia and from Pennsylvania.

Private individuals also began to stake out farm homesteads in the region during the years from 1761 to 1769. Virtually all of these settlers along the Youghiogheny and the Monongahela, the Loyalhanna and the Allegheny were utterly neglectful of the prior claims of the Ohio Company of Virginia.

Nevertheless, the members of the Ohio Company of Virginia renewed their activities in 1759. On July 6, 1759, a meeting of the Committee of the Ohio Company was held at Stafford Court House. Its most important work was an instruction to John Mercer to draw up "a full State of the Company's Case"[5] to be transmitted to Messrs. Hanbury in London. Probably the papers of the Company, earlier in the possession of Thomas Lee, and turned over in 1750 to George Mason, were placed for some time in John Mercer's possession in the latter half of 1759. The financial situation of the family of John Mercer seems to have been troublesome at this period. On November 25, 1759, partly to cover the obligations of their father, George Mercer and James Mercer signed a release indenture of 32,853 acres of land to John Tayloe and Presley Thornton.[6] It was on December 10, 1759 that George Mercer, son of John, was appointed to survey the lands on the

[5] D.M.L. MS., printed in *George Mercer Papers*. This full "State of the Company's Case," is found, so far as it has survived, on pp. 233-86.

[6] *Ibid.*, pp. 40-45. Efforts to locate the official record of this indenture were unsuccessful. The absence from the George Mercer Papers of the deed indenture, the retention of the frontier lands by George Mercer and James Mercer, and some financial data, may well indicate that the final step of a deed was never taken, and so the transfer of John Mercer's one-fortieth share may have been nominal rather than real. The language of the release embraces only one half of John Mercer's two-fortieths share in the Ohio Company. By the terms stated neither George Mercer nor James Mercer had as a result of the transaction a vote in the Company. It should be noted, however, that the destruction or loss of most of the early records of Stafford County has made these matters highly speculative.

Ohio.[7] In keeping with the instructions of July, John Mercer probably wrote to Messrs. Hanbury and began drawing up the "Case" as requested.

Probably in November, members of the Ohio Company had the information found in a letter of Colonel Adam Stephen from Pittsburgh, October 29, 1759, in which he said Pennsylvanians had engrossed the Indian fur trade and were pushing "all possible measures" to keep it, claiming the region as "within their Limits." [8] Stephen estimated that "About twenty Tuns of Skins & Fur had been brought to Pittsburgh in the last three months."

Probably it was not unknown to the members of the Company that political circumstances in Virginia, in the Ohio Valley, and possibly in London were none too favorable. Francis Fauquier, the recently arrived Lieutenant Governor of Virginia, clearly did not favor large grants of land to individuals and companies.[9] John Mercer wrote to Fauquier late in the autumn of 1759,[10] and on December 1, 1759, Lieutenant Governor Fauquier wrote a long letter to the Lords Commissioners of Trade, in which he touched upon the fur trade rivalry of Pennsylvania and Virginia, the necessity of completing boundary lines, the impact of the promises of Dinwiddie's Proclamation of land grants to soldiers, and the possibility of a separate new colony being established in the West.[11] The discussion of the probability of the Crown renewing the grant of the Ohio Company was carried on in political circles at Williamsburg in this same month of December, 1759.[12]

The uncertainty of the situation is clearly revealed in some of the correspondence of 1760. George Mercer (son of John Mercer, now a dominant figure in the Ohio Company) wrote on February 17, 1760, to George Washington asking his employment as a

---

[7] *W. & M. Quarterly*, III (1894), 129.

[8] P.R.O. C.O. 5: 1330/55-58; *Journal of the House of Burgesses . . .*, 1758–61, pp. 280-81.

[9] P.R.O. C.O. 5: 1329/183-86, L.C. transcript.

[10] D.M.L. MS., printed in *George Mercer Papers*, pp. 93-95, and Part II, the *Case . . .*, pp. 21-22.

[11] P.R.O. C.O. 5: 1330/51-54.

[12] *Journal of the House of Burgesses . . .*, 1758–61, pp. 281-82.

surveyor of Ohio lands, presumably for soldiers under the Dinwiddie Proclamation, for he makes no mention of the Ohio Company.[13] Governor Fauquier wrote to the Lords Commissioners of Trade and Plantations, March 13, 1760,[14] and again to the Board of Trade, May 12, 1760.[15]

Representatives of the Ohio Company in this year made approaches to Colonel Henry Bouquet, commandant at Fort Pitt, who owned a tract of land on the Conococheague Creek in Maryland and was much interested in the settlement of the frontier. Colonel Thomas Cresap, who as a Frederick County official must have known this, and may have acted on instructions of the Ohio Company, of which he was an old member, wrote offering him a share in the Ohio Company, July 24, 1760,[16] a letter to which Colonel Bouquet replied, September 12, 1760.[17] George Mercer made a similar offer to Bouquet, December 27, 1760,[18] in a letter in which, whether accurately or not, he mentioned considerable outstanding obligations of individuals to the Ohio Company for goods, stating that adding these to cash on hand the total amounted to, so he imagined, "£2,000 or £2,500." This solicitation, which he declined, Bouquet reported to General Amherst, the commander-in-chief, April 1, 1762.[19] Meanwhile, in the Frederick County, Virginia, Court, a suit entered by Thomas Caton against George Mason and Company, August 6, 1760, was continued, as was also the old suit against Caton, which was again continued, September 4, 1760.[20]

Nor was the Ohio Company inactive in Virginia and in London. On October 17, 1760, at a meeting of the Committee of the Ohio

---

13 MS., Washington Papers, L.C., printed in *Letters to Washington,* III, 172.

14 P.R.O. C.O. 5: 1329/199.

15 *Ibid.,* 1330/9-12.

16 Bouquet Papers, British Museum, Additional Manuscripts (hereinafter cited as B.M. Add. MSS.), 21645, folio 163, a.l.s.

17 *Ibid.,* 21653, folios 24-25, a.c.s.

18 *Ibid.,* 21645, folios 340-51, a.l.s.

19 *Ibid.,* 21634, folios 112-13, copy.

20 Frederick County, Order Book, No. 9, 1760–62, folios 86, 106, 168.

Company, the State of the Company's Case, as drawn up by John Mercer, the lawyer of the Company, was read, signed, and ordered to be transmitted to Mr. Hanbury.[21] John Mercer was also ordered to send a memorial and instructions to Charlton Palmer, a London lawyer.[22] And Thomas Cresap was again ordered to repair the storehouse at Wills Creek. At this time also, Thomas Ludwell Lee, second son of Thomas Lee, was appointed one of the Committee of the Ohio Company in replacement of Nathaniel Chapman.[23] George Mason, cashier or treasurer of the Company, also wrote shortly to Edward Athawes, merchant of London, authorizing him to pay the fee of Charlton Palmer when presented.[24] Mason also doubtless authorized Thomas Cresap, at this time, to furnish lumber for a storehouse to be constructed by the Company.[25] A valuable and interesting item, of November 8, 1760, is a letter of George Mercer to William Trent.[26] In it he wrote, "I am just returned from Williamsburg, where I had the pleasure to be present at your Trial with Governor Dinwiddie . . . they have brought you in a Verdict of £800 besides your Costs—" George Mercer may well have been in touch with the late October meeting of the Committee of the Ohio Company though no evidence of this was found, and it is not impossible that as the agent of his father, the attorney of the Ohio Company, he collected the verdict money, probably a bond or some other security deposit, and carried it to John Mercer at *Marlborough*, the family home.

Directly related to the above case, and indeed a sequel to the

[21] D.M.L. MS., printed in *George Mercer Papers*, pp. 150-51, 179-80.

[22] Instructions in D.M.L. MS., printed in *George Mercer Papers*, pp. 150-51, 179-80. Enclosed in the letter was the "Case of the Ohio Company," recently compiled, containing, imbedded, many Ohio Company matters. Enclosed also were a copy of the orders and resolutions of earlier years and a copy of a Pennsylvania Indian Act.

[23] *Ibid.*, p. 180. Chapman died intestate in 1760.

[24] Mentioned, *ibid.*, pp. 151, 185.

[25] *Ibid.*, p. 180.

[26] Etting Collection, Ohio Company Papers, a.l.s., H.S.P., printed in Bailey, *Ohio Company Papers*, pp. 347-48.

verdict, are items in the *Journals of the House of Burgesses of Virginia* . . . 1758–61. On March 1, 1761, it was "Ordered That a Committee be appointed to enquire whether any and What Part of a Judgment obtained in the General Court by William Trent against *Robert Dinwiddie* Esp., late Lieutenant-Governor of this Dommion ought to be paid by the Public. . . ." [27] A committee of four was appointed. On April 8, 1861, it made its report,[28] a compromise one, and submitted, for adoption, a resolution which "being read the second time, and the Question put that the House agree thereto, it passed in the Negative." [29]

Another of the Darlington Ohio Company manuscripts, apparently based in part on the Case and Appendix of 1754 probably dates from the winter of 1761–1762.[30] A document of more than twenty thousand words, it lacks about thirty-five hundred words in missing manuscript sheets at the beginning and about a thousand words in two pages missing later on, but the remainder of the pages, as in the Case of 1754, deal with Gist's instructions, expeditions, and journals, with Virginia land grants, with the Logstown Conference of 1752, with Trent's activities in 1753, with Washington's journey of 1753–54, with the Winchester Indian Conference of 1753, with incidents and documents of 1754, and with the situation after the capture of Fort Duquesne in late November 1758. The later material in the manuscript is, of course, not in the earlier Case and it contains important new data.

In the second week of September, 1761, a meeting of the Committee of the Ohio Company was held.[31] Philip Ludwell Lee was instructed to write to his friend, the Duke of Bedford,[32] soliciting his support; letters to the Hanburys [33] and to Dinwiddie were

---

[27] *Journal of the House of Burgesses* . . . , 1758–61, p. 236.

[28] *Ibid.*, p. 255.

[29] *Ibid.*

[30] D.M.L. MS., printed in *George Mercer Papers,* pp. 49-139.

[31] *Ibid.*, pp. 151-53, 180, 287-88.

[32] Letter not found.

[33] D.M.L. MS., printed in *George Mercer Papers,* pp. 152-53, and Part II, the *Case* . . . , p. 26; another copy is calendared on p. 181.

drawn up,[34] and the Humble Petition of the Ohio Company to His Majesty was planned to be presented by the London lawyer, Charlton Palmer.[35]

Such action on the part of the Company was in order, for on October 30, 1761, Colonel Bouquet put out a Proclamation against settlement on Indian lands; [36] while on November 11, 1761 the Earl of Egremont officially proclaimed a British policy of restraining all land grants in the Indian country.[37] In turn, the Virginia Council, January 21, 1762, "Ordered That an Advertizement be inserted in the Gazette, prohibiting Surveyors from admitting any Entries to be made with them for lands lying to the West of the Allegany Mountains till further orders shall be made thereon." [38] The correspondence of Lieutenant-Governor Fauquier with the Lords Commissioners of Trade,[39] and with Colonel Bouquet at Pittsburgh,[40] promised little governmental support for the plans of the Company.

A bad situation in regard to lands in Maryland along the upper Potomac arose in 1761, the beginning of troubles which bothered George Mason for the rest of his life, and his children and grandchildren for nearly a quarter of a century after his death.

Old land warrants and surveys of Thomas Bladen and of the

---

[34] Printed in Kate M. Rowland, *The Life of George Mason, 1725–1792*, I, 78; Samuel Wharton, *Plain Facts . . .*, pp. 120-21; and as D.M.L. MS., copy, in *George Mercer Papers*, pp. 151-52, and Part II, the *Case . . .*, p. 26. No more specific statement could be expected than that in the letter of September 9, 1761 to Dinwiddie. This letter, long ago in print, indicates that despite untoward developments the Ohio Company was not easily deterred from its aims.

[35] *The Case of the Ohio Company*, N.Y.H.S. imprint, pp. 25-26. See *George Mercer Papers*, Part II.

[36] B.M. Add. MSS., 21656, folios 720-28. See also *Pa. Arch.*, III, 571-74, and Wharton, *op. cit.*, p. 50.

[37] *N.Y.C.D.*, VII, 472-76. While this may have been a war measure and only for the duration of the war, it was ominous for the Ohio Company.

[38] Executive Journals, Council of Colonial Virginia, hitherto unpublished photostat in Virginia State Library.

[39] See the letter of Fauquier, November 30, 1761, P.R.O. C.O. 5: 1330/130-32, L.C. transcript.

[40] E.g., letter of March 12, 1762, B.M. Add. MSS., 21648, folios 60-61.

Cresaps were often not patented for many years, possibly partly as a result of almost continuous Indian trouble. Some of the tracts were at one time or another assigned to George Mason for the use of the Ohio Company. A frontiersman, Joseph Tomlinson, was informed in February 1759 that several of the Bladen tracts were for sale. Not satisfied with the situation revealed in Cresap's books, Tomlinson went in 1759 to Annapolis and consulted the Land Office of the Proprietary. He found that no caution money had been paid. This information he passed on to Mr. John Ross.[41] It obviously attracted attention, for about a year later Doctor David Ross of Bladensburg, Maryland, who, as a result of his position as commissary of the Maryland Regiment in 1755, may have been very familiar with the Wills Creek area, petitioned for a special warrant to secure much of this unpatented land.[42] On January 16, 1761, he secured warrants to that effect.[43] A dispute between Bladen's representatives and Ross quickly came before the Land Office Judges. The Tomlinson deposition made August 16, 1761, was part of the proceedings in the affair. But Doctor Ross with the renewment of his warrant, February 4, 1762, went ahead with the matter of surveys and patents for the disputed tracts.[44] The resurvey of *Walnut Bottom*, June 30, 1762, may have been induced by this quarrel to which George Mason as the result of assignment became a party. The "dispute in the land office" continued. The Land Office Judges wrote[45] on the matter to Governor Horatio Sharpe, November 11, 1762, and received from him an elaborate reply.[46]

Some of the surveys for Doctor Ross, hardly more than resur-

---

[41] Allegany County, Maryland, Judgment Record F, folios 326-31, copy.

[42] Maryland Court of Appeals Judgments, Liber T. H. No. 16 (1815), folios 69-72, Maryland Hall of Records.

[43] Liber W. S. No. 2, folio 170, Maryland Land Office, Annapolis.

[44] *Ibid.*, folios 164-69.

[45] *Ibid.*, Liber B. C. and G. S. No. 15, folios 814-18. Printed in Thomas Harris, clerk of the court of appeals, and Reverdy Johnson, attorney at law, *Reports of Cases Argued and Determined in the Court of Appeals of Maryland*. In 1810, 1811, 1812, 1813, 1814, and 1815. III, 516-21.

[46] *Ibid.*, folios 818-19; also printed as in preceding footnote, pp. 521-23.

veys of older surveys made by Thomas Cresap and his assistants for Bladen, were patented by Dr. Ross.[47] Probably the attempt of the Ohio Company to subdivide some of its claimed holdings in early 1763,[48] was motivated by the desire to establish a fait accompli in this dispute of 1761–1762.

But the members of the Company kept up their activities and possibly their expectations, for on June 30, 1762, John Murdock made a resurvey of the *Walnut Bottom* tract on Wills Creek, Maryland, along with 1,250 acres of vacant land for George Mason and the Ohio Company, a resurvey which was not duly patented and thereby the 1,250 acres eventually lost to the Company; and in the last week of July 1762 John Mercer, the lawyer and secretary of the Company, sent to Charlton Palmer a copy of an agreement entered into by a Virginia Company to take up 200,000 acres of land,[49] and the Orders of the Ohio Company,[50] duly attested as a true copy by Richard Rogers,[51] probably a copy of the Resolutions on the Company's books, then in the possession of John Mercer. He enclosed to Palmer two printed Acts of Assembly of Pennsylvania supporting the Facts in the Case of the Ohio Company.[52] Copies or duplicates, of the letters, of September 10, 1761, dispatched by the Committee of the Ohio Company respectively to Dinwiddie and to Messrs. Hanbury in London, are mentioned as already in the hands of Palmer.[53] Unfortunately some half a dozen letters of the last half of 1762 referred to in the Darlington manuscripts [54] have not been found.

As late as 1762, George Mason was pushing the prosecution of

---

[47] Maryland Court of Appeals Judgments, Liber B.C. and G.S., No. 15, folios 479-81.

[48] See the advertisements in the *Maryland Gazette*, February 17, 1763 and June 16, 1763. The attempt met with a virtual veto from military commandants, but particularly from General Amherst who in the light of Indian threats considered the site of Walnut Bottom as of vital imperial importance.

[49] D.M.L. MS., printed in *George Mercer Papers*, pp. 46-48.

[50] *Ibid.*

[51] *Ibid.*, p. 153.

[52] *Ibid.*, pp. 153-65.

[53] *Ibid.*, pp. 46-48.

[54] *Ibid.*

Thomas Caton, the old Ohio Company debtor, in a suit which came before the court March 3, August 4, September 9, and November 4, only to be continued to later courts.[55]

---

[55] Frederick County, Virginia, Order Book, No. 10, 1760–62, folio 373 and 1762–63, folios 84, 181, 332.

IX

Lands, Petitions, and Memorials

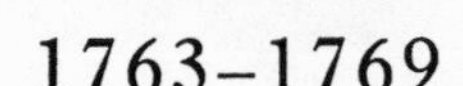

1763–1769

THE YEAR 1763 was in several ways important for the Ohio Company. The old litigation with Thomas Caton dragged on. The suit against him in the Frederick County, Virginia, Court was further continued March 3, 1763; the strange suit of Caton against George Mason was dismissed, March 24, 1763, on "Complainant failing to prosecute"; and on May 4, 1763, the old suit against Caton with damages of £132 . . 12 . . 9¾ was won, bringing to a close a litigation of more than twelve years, involving thirty recorded items.[1] It was the Ohio Company's last mercantile litigation of which record has been found.

This year seems to have seen a strange move by Thomas Cresap, himself a member of the Ohio Company, in which he made a private treaty [2] with the Six Nations Indians, giving him a large grant of land in the vicinity of Redstone Creek, a region still claimed by the Ohio Company. His activities there aroused the op-

[1] Frederick County, Virginia, Order Book, No. 10, 1760–62 and 1762–63, folio 430; No. 11, 1763–64, folios 2, 92.

[2] Clarence W. Alvord and Clarence Carter, *The New Regime, 1765–1744*, pp. 464-65; Bailey, *Thomas Cresap . . .*, p. 115.

position of Colonel Henry Bouquet.[3] In the absence of records of events, many of which may have gone unrecorded, the affair has the air of mysterious scheming.

But much more important matters were taken up by the Company. On February 19, 1763, "By Order of the Committee of the Ohio Company" an advertisement appeared [4] calling for a meeting "Tuesday the first of March next," stating "the Company has suffered very much from their neglecting to meet for so long a Time." The third and last sentence says, "To prevent the Trouble of Law Suits . . . those who have any Accounts to settle with the Company, are also requested to attend." In the same column of the same issue of the *Maryland Gazette* appeared also an advertisement, signed by George Mercer, offering for sale "on Friday the 15th of April next" a "Number of Lots for a Town at Fort Cumberland." The advertisement furnishes a most valuable description of the Ohio Company property in Virginia, immediately across the Potomac River from the mouth of Wills Creek. This was offered for lease. It mentions "Two very good Store-Houses . . . one 45 by 25, with a Counting-Room and Lodging-Room at one End, the other 44 by 20, with proper conveniences for a Family to live in, two Stories high each, besides Garrets, with good dry Cellars fit for storing Skins, the whole Size of the Houses; and a Kitchin, Stable for 12 Horses, Meat-House and Dairy." The buildings are described as "entirely new, and will be compleatly finished, and fit to enter upon immediately." George Mercer, whose name was subscribed to the advertisement, was to deliver deeds to purchasers.

As advertised, the meeting of the Committee of the Ohio Company was held "at Stafford Court house on Wednesday the 2d day of March 1763." Its sole recorded business was a resolution [5] about the proposed town at the mouth of Wills Creek.

The advertisement of February 17, 1763 stated in general

[3] Bouquet to Amherst, April 1, 1762, B.M. Add. MSS., 21634, folios 81-83.

[4] *Maryland Gazette*, No. 928, February 17, 1763.

[5] D.M.L. MS., printed in *George Mercer Papers*, pp. 181-82.

terms only that "the OHIO COMPANY have agreed to Lay off a Number of Lots for a TOWN at Fort Cumberland . . . and that each Purchaser may have an Opportunity of attending, and choosing the Lots he may judge most convenient, they will be SOLD to the Highest BIDDERS on Friday the 15th of April next." The resolution of March 2, 1763 was more specific. Its first provision was that "about fifty Acres of the Company's Land . . . be laid of (*sic*) into Town Lotts with about two hundred and fifty Acres of the adjacent high Land for out Lotts to be annexed to the Town in such manner that one such out Lott shall forever belong to and be deemed an Appurtenance of the Town Lott. . . ." A second provision was that "Col° George Mercer be impowered to lay off [6] and dispose of the same upon the Company's Account," according to certain terms. Another provision was that "George Mason is hereby impowered and required to execute Deeds and Leases . . . or that he make a power of Attorney [7] unto Col.° George Mercer to execute and acknowledge the said Deeds and Leases in his name. . . ." A final provision was that "John Mercer Esqr. be requested to draw up a Form for the said Deeds and Leases and power of Attorney. . . ."

It was probably in accordance with this resolution of March 2, 1763, that the survey was drawn up, of which a fragment has survived. It was indubitably in accordance with the resolution that George Mason signed the power of attorney to George Mercer, March 29, 1763, which was recorded the following day. Much of the language of the resolution and of the power of attorney is identical. These two hitherto unprinted documents throw much light not only on the affairs of the Ohio Company but also on the early history of the Wills Creek area.

There seems to have been in April or May 1763, an advertise-

---

[6] See the Charlottesburg survey, *ibid.*, pp. 181-82.

[7] Frederick County Deeds, Liber H, folio 350, Maryland Hall of Records. Printed below in Appendix A, pp. 233-34.

ment [8] for a meeting of the Ohio Company on the first Monday in June. The meeting, prevented by a call for the General Assembly of Virginia, was not held. Therefore another advertisement,[9] June 16, 1763, called for a meeting the "first Monday in July next."

As earlier in February, this call for a meeting was accompanied, June 16, 1763, by another advertisement proposing the sale of town lots and the lease of the *New Store Tract*. Signed by George Mercer, it repeated, with some alterations and additions, the earlier advertisement of February and parts of the resolution of March 2, 1763.

It was at this time, and probably in connection with matters as above indicated, that George Mason secured patents for the *Cove*, 510 acres, June 24, 1763; [10] for *Hunt the Hare*, 240 acres, June 25, 1763; [11] and for *Welshman's Conquest*, 260 acres, June 25, 1763.[12] This was accomplished in the very middle of a bitter struggle for the lands, carried on against Thomas Bladen and his assignee, George Mason, by Dr. David Ross of Bladensburg. The struggle in 1763 is seen clearly in a letter of Thomas Hodgkin to David Ross, August 31, 1763,[13] and a petition of Ross, September 6, 1763.[14]

Probably these important land matters were among the "Matters of the greatest Importance to the Company to be settled at their next Meeting." In accordance with the newspaper notice, a meeting of the Ohio Company was held at Stafford Court House, Vir-

[8] Not found, but mentioned in a later advertisement, *Maryland Gazette*, June 16, 1763.

[9] *Ibid.*

[10] Liber B. C. and G. S., No. 17, folios 599-600, Maryland Land Office, Annapolis.

[11] *Ibid.*, No. 15, folio 699.

[12] *Ibid.*, folio 701.

[13] Allegany County, Maryland, Judgment Record J, folio 353, printed below, pp. 236-37.

[14] Original Surveys, Allegany County, No. 2087, Maryland Land Office, Annapolis. Copies in Maryland Court of Appeals Judgments, Liber T. H. No. 16 (1815), folios 36, 69, 148, Maryland Hall of Records.

ginia, July 4, 1763.[15] But evidently a more important matter threw land squabbles and land deals out of any recorded consideration. From the internal evidence of the actual signatures of seven members of the Committee of the Ohio Company, it appears that in anticipation of action at this meeting another memorial to the Crown had been prepared.[16] In this memorial the Committee extended felicitations to George the Third, referred to the grant of 1749 to the Ohio Company, to the early activities of the Company involving expenditures of £10,000, to the early hostility of rivals in Virginia, to the interruption of activity by the French and Indian War, to their services in that war, and made mention of George Mercer as sent to present the new petition which asked for instructions from the Crown to the government of Virginia to renew the old grant of 1749, but with modifications about surveys. As an alternative they petitioned "to be Repaid the Money advanced by our Company, with Interest. . . ." In this meeting instructions were drawn up for George Mercer,[17] who was assigned the task of representing the Company in London. It was also resolved to reimburse George Mercer and repay any money not above £2,000, spent in London in behalf of the Ohio Company.[18] And, on the basis of such understanding and in possession of a letter of credit of Colonel Tayloe for his use in London, George Mercer sailed for London, July 8, 1763.[19] But by George Mercer himself, Lieutenant-Governor Fauquier wrote letters to the Board of Trade and Plantations addressed as Lords Commissioners of

---

[15] D.M.L. MS., printed in *George Mercer Papers*, pp. 182, 196, and Part II, the *Case* . . . , pp. 30-31.

[16] P.R.O. C.O. 5: 1331/421-30.

[17] D.M.L. MS., printed in *George Mercer Papers*, pp. 182-83.

[18] *Ibid.*, and also p. 296. See the MS., Emmet Collection, N.Y.P.L., printed below, p. 236.

[19] Johnson to the Board of Trade, July 8, 1763, P.R.O. C.O. 5: 1330/511; Fauquier to the Board of Trade, July 8, 1763, P.R.O. C.O. 5: 1330/138-42. On the letter of credit, see John Mercer to George Mercer, January 28, 1768, D.M.L. MS., printed in *George Mercer Papers*, p. 205.

Trade in which he discussed the Indian troubles of the summer of 1763, blaming Indian insurrections on white settlement of Indian lands, and asserting the great difficulty of stopping such settlement by whites.[20]

In the meantime Pontiac's Conspiracy was in full swing in western Virginia, western Pennsylvania, western New York, and in what later came to be known as the Old Northwest. Indian trouble was to make utterly impossible any activity in the Ohio Valley in 1763 by the Ohio Company. In fact it was nearly two years before conditions were favorable to further settlement by the Company in this particular area.

It is possible that the unfavorable circumstances in London, at Williamsburg, and in the upper Ohio Valley may have rendered impossible the meeting of the Company appointed for the first Monday in September, advertised in August.

A fascinating manuscript item of November 8, 1763, is the bond of George Mason to Thomas Bladen for £960 .. 10s, payable June 7, 1764.[21] This double indemnity bond was obviously for lands on Wills Creek, Maryland. A codicil makes an allowance for the *Pleasant Valley* tract of 300 acres (part of the 1310 acres[22] bought) for which George Mason had no patent. On this bond is a receipt, January 11, 1792, of Daniel Dulany for £692 . . 10s current money in discharge of the bond and a notation as well of the transaction. Thus on warrants of 1743–1745, surveys of 1745–1746, assignments of June 14, 1763, and patents of June 24-25, 1763, payment was made November 8, 1763, with a double in-

[20] P.R.O. C.O. 5: 1330/138-42 and 511-14. The validity of this judgment is not questioned by those familiar with the materials on the subject.

[21] MS. George Mason Papers, L.C., printed below, pp. 237-39. An early endorsement indicates that the bond was made out by George Mason, June 2, 1763, possibly in anticipation of the assignments and patents of mid-summer, 1763.

[22] Probably for the *Cove*, 510 acres; *Welshman's Conquest*, 260 acres; *Hunt the Hare*, 240 acres; and *Pleasant Valley*, 300 acres, but exclusive of *Walnut Bottom*, 500 acres, patented March 25, 1756.

demnity bond[23] which was not amortised until 1792, a lapse of nearly fifty years. Such long drawn-out transactions two centuries ago were common.

Presumably, George Mercer on his arrival in London began the active promotion of the Ohio Company claims, though circumstances were unfavorable and he was destined to wait nearly two years before presenting memorials. He wrote a letter from London to Captain (John) Rutherford, October 28, 1763.[24] Among his serious problems was that of settlement of the Hanbury Account with the Ohio Company.[25]

In late 1763 came the famous Proclamation of October 7, 1763. Governor Fauquier wrote the Lords of Trade, February 13, 1764, "there are some difficulties relating to his Majestys Proclamation arising from the present State of this Colony in Regard to some of the Lands which are the Subject of the Proclamation." To throw light on these difficulties he traced (1) the April 1745 grant to James Patton and his allies, enclosing a list of patents to settlers and entries upon this Patton grant, all of which patents and entries seemed in accordance with existing law, three statutes of which were mentioned; (2) the grant of 500,000 acres to the Ohio Company and of 800,000 acres to the Loyal Company, commenting on these grants that owing to warfare, "I am informed not much has hitherto been done in consequence of either of them." Fauquier called for interpretations and directions in applying the Proclamation. He admitted he had entered in the Journals of the

[23] The price paid for the 1,310 acres was £460 .. 10 .. 0 current money, in pieces of eight, or about seven shillings per acre. If the price per acre was uniform, £178 .. 10 .. 0 was paid for the *Cove*, £91 .. 0 .. 0 for *Welshman's Conquest*, £84 .. 0 .. 0 for *Hunt the Hare*, and £105..0..0 for *Pleasant Valley*. It is noticeable that in 1792 part of the double indemnity was paid when the bond was paid off for £692 .. 10 .. 0. Compromise on such double indemnity bonds was not uncommon.

[24] Calendared in *Calendar of Transcripts of Virginia State Library*, ed. Kennedy.

[25] John Mercer to George Mercer, March 3, 1768, D.M.L. MS., printed in *George Mercer Papers*, p. 227.

Council as a prior claim a demand of William Byrd III for 5,000 acres on the New River, but said he had done nothing more and would do nothing more without further instructions.[26]

The three year old contest between George Mason and Doctor Ross, about lands near Wills Creek, continued in 1764. In the dispute carried on before the judges of the land office, depositions [27] were taken in April from James Prather, Jarvis Haugham, and Aaron Moore; and another deposition in October from Providence Mounts [28]—depositions covering data running back ten years or more.

George Mercer, writing, March 11, 1764,[29] one of his several letters to his brother, James Mercer, complained about communications with America and the difficulties of doing business with the "Great Ones" of the English government. He foresaw very accurately that it would be more than a year after his arrival before he could initiate proceedings on behalf of the claims of the Ohio Company.

The only other surviving document of 1764 which has been found is a letter of John Mercer to Charlton Palmer, April 17, 1764,[30] in which he touches upon the Indian atrocities of 1763, criticizes the Proclamation of 1763, and elaborates upon instructions sent to Palmer through George Mercer. In this letter are mentioned three other letters: George Mason to John Mercer, December 6, 1763, and January 11, 1764; and George Mercer to John Mercer, January 25, 1764—none of which have been found.

Nor were events much more lively in the first half of 1765. The Company lost a member in the death, March 28, 1765, of

---

[26] P.R.O. C.O. 5: 1330/589-96.

[27] Maryland Court of Appeals Judgments, Liber T. H. No. 16 (1815), folios 60-65. The originals of the deposition were not found, but copies appear in official records at Cumberland, Maryland, and in the Hall of Records at Annapolis.

[28] *Ibid.*, folio 174. There is a copy in Allegany County, Maryland, Judgment Record F, folios 334-37.

[29] In the Kentucky Collection, Western State College, Bowling Green, Kentucky, a.l.s.

[30] D.M.L. MS., printed in *George Mercer Papers*, pp. 184-85.

Arthur Dobbs, governor of North Carolina.[31] John Mercer, getting old and feeble, and probably having become despondent about the Company, presented during the year his resignation as an official of the Company.[32]

But it was in midsummer of this year, June 21, 1765, that George Mercer presented the 1763 Memorial of the Committee of the Ohio Company to the Crown [33] and followed it up in a long memorial [34] of his own to the Privy Council ten days later. In the carefully worded second memorial, probably entirely the work of George Mercer himself, the memorialist mentioned the early advisability of securing the Indian trade and the possession of the inland parts of North America for the Crown, the organization for such a purpose of the Ohio Company, the petition of 1749 to the Crown, the favorable report on the petition of the Lords Commissioners of Trade, the issuance of instructions for the grant, the early activities of the Company, the injury of the war to the Company, the postwar measures taken by the Company, and the delay in submitting the latest petition, on account of the Proclamation of 1763. The memorialist, assuming that the Proclamation was intended to be temporary only, asked for the renewal of the earlier instructions of 1749, or that "your Majesty would be graciously pleased to recommend to the Parliament of Great Britain, the making some Provision for the Reimbursement of the great Expences incurred by the Ohio Company." He suggested that in case the Proclamation of 1763 were maintained, they might be given "a Grant of Land in some other part of your Majestys American Dominions. . . ."

Late in 1765 came an episode which probably injured the Ohio Company, for it certainly discredited George Mercer, its agent in London. Parliament had passed the Stamp Act in 1765, after one

---

[31] *North Carolina Colonial Records,* VI, 1321.

[32] John Mercer to George Mercer, January 28, 1768, D.M.L. MS., printed in *George Mercer Papers,* p. 211.

[33] P.R.O. C.O. 5: 1331/421-30; Privy Council Papers, II, 244. Printed in Bailey, *Ohio Company . . . ,* pp. 310-13.

[34] P.R.O. C.O. 5: 1331/416. Printed in Bailey, *Ohio Company . . . ,* pp. 310-13, and in part, p. 220.

year's notice of such intent. The unhappy position of a distributor of the stamps in America was not adequately foreseen. It may have been that the assumption of the responsibility of distributing the stamps seemed to George Mercer a means of gaining governmental and royal favor. However that may be, George Mercer (as well as other prominent colonial Americans) was caught napping in the matter. He got the position as stamp distributor for Maryland, Virginia, and North Carolina. Sailing with the stamps on the *Leeds* he reached Virginia, October 30, 1765.[35] Ten hectic days followed. At the request of Mercer, Lieutenant-Governor Fauquier wrote to Governor Sharpe of Maryland, November 8, 1765.[36] Two days later, George Mercer wrote to Sharpe furnishing full information, saying he was leaving immediately for England.[37] In a letter of Sharpe to Calvert, November 11, 1765, he wrote that Mercer had been compelled to resign his position.[38]

It is noteworthy as well as remarkable that nowhere has been found any highly relevant material of 1766 on the Ohio Company, whether in England, Virginia, Maryland, or on the trans-Appalachian frontier. Newspaper discussion of George Mercer is the main item.[39] Probably the matter of the Ohio Company was dimmed by the Stamp Act quarrel, and the problems relating to the Great Lakes and Illinois.

Some documents of early 1767 furnish valuable information on Ohio Company matters of the previous decade.[40] George Mason left to posterity the statement, "Upon being informed that Mr. Croghan claimed some Credit on his Bond to the Ohio Company for part of the Money recovered by Captain Trent from Governor Dinwiddie, George Mason sent to Mr. John Mercer (who managed the Suit for Captain Trent) desiring a particular Account of the Matter. . . ." To this letter of Mason, reply came in the form of a general answer, along with the financial Account.

35 *Maryland Archives*, XIV, 236-37; Rowland, *op. cit.*, I, 125-26.

36 *Ibid.*

37 *Ibid.*, p. 236.

38 *Ibid.*

39 *Virginia Gazette*, No. 1607, September 26, 1766.

40 E.g., H.S.P. MS., printed below, pp. 239-41.

As reported by John Mercer, Captain Trent, an employee of the Ohio Company, presented against Dinwiddie claims of £222..18..0 for pay for himself and his men; of £68..7..9 for provisions, of £247..18..10 for going out with the first present; and of £126..11..5 for going out with the second present. The total claim against Dinwiddie for services rendered to the colonial government by the employees of the Ohio Company was £665..16..0. The full amount, according to Mercer, was recovered and credited to the Ohio Company. Since the total recovered from Dinwiddie is said to have been £800, John Mercer's fee must have been £134..4..0.

George Mason took the trouble to check the account sent by Mercer with the accounts filed with the trial and found only a small discrepancy. Any credit to Croghan on his bond was denied by the Company. Seemingly George Croghan had, 1753–55, either secured Ohio Company goods or handled some of their furs and skins on his credit. The Ohio Company held his bond, probably a double indemnity bond of £2,000, and proceeded against Croghan in the Philadelphia Court. This possibly caused further trouble in the involved finances of Croghan, already seriously injured by his losses in Indian Trade, 1753–1763. The transaction is further explained in a letter of Thomas Cresap of May 20, 1767.[41] In it he confirmed the Dinwiddie transaction of late 1758, and claimed the money recovered was due the Ohio Company for money and provisions furnished Trent in western Pennsylvania in the early months of 1754. Cresap examined the Ohio Company books kept by Trent as factor and concluded he owed the Company £540..4..3, exclusive of his joint account with Croghan in the partnership of Trent and Croghan.

A good illustration of the difficulties of the Ohio Company is seen in the fact that on June 26, 1767, the Board of Trade finally got around to the petition of 1765, in a report [42] to the Lords of the Committee of the Privy Council for Plantation Affairs. It said the

[41] Cresap to (Tilghman), a.l.s., H.S.P. MS., printed below, Appendix A, pp. 241-42. It is found in Bailey, *Thomas Cresap* . . ., pp. 211-12.

[42] P.R.O. C.O. 5: 1368/324-28.

petitioner did not appear to "prosecute his Suit," that the royal proclamation of October 1, 1763, precluded action upon the business but that George Mercer had lately renewed his application and asked some determination upon it. The report recommended merely that first of all "an exact and full Report" should be required of the Governor of Virginia and suggested that it might be advisable to discountenance further schemes. The responsibility for securing "an exact and full report on the Ohio Company" rested upon Lord Shelburne.

Since 1767 there has been among the papers of Lord Shelburne a long undated and anonymous document on the Ohio Company.[43] By both external and internal criticism it is possible to date this document as of October 8, 1767, and as having been hurriedly written and handed in to Lord Shelburne by George Mercer, the London agent and representative of the Ohio Company. Based both on papers in his possession and on matters observed in America by himself the document presents only a general picture of the years 1747 to 1767. Its adherence to facts, easily established by surviving materials, is remarkable for such hurried composition. Its authorship by George Mercer explains much of the historical factuality of the manuscript and gives the document greater significance as a step in the long process of petitions, memorials, etc., which led finally to the printed *Case* of 1770.

It was on October 8, 1767, that Lord Shelburne in accordance with this report of June 26, 1767, wrote Governor Fauquier.[44] Repeating almost the language of the report, in a final paragraph he stated, "I am therefore to signify to You His Majesty's Commands that You transmit to me for His Majesty's Information an exact Account of the Nature of the Claim which the Ohio Company have to the Lands petitioned for, what circumstances first gave Rise to the Formation of the Company; and what Sums they have expended in consequence of the first Cession of Lands made

---

[43] Shelburne Papers, L, 93-97, William L. Clements Library, Ann Arbor, Michigan. Printed in Appendix A, below, pp. 243-46.

[44] *Ibid.*, LIV, 67-69, printed below, pp. 246-47. Copy in P.R.O. C.O. 5: 1345/385-90.

to the Company by the Indians, or His Majesty's Instructions to His Lieutenant-Governor of Virginia in the year 1748 [45] directing him to grant the above mentioned 500,000 Acres." [46]

Many papers of John Mercer, once in his own possession at *Marlborough*, appear to have vanished, including both letters sent to him and copies of letters written by him, if perchance he kept letter book copies as was customary at that time. Among such letters are the following, mentioned in the long letter to his son, George, January 28, 1768: [47] letters from John Mercer to his sister Phipps in Ireland, January, 1766; to his son George in London, January 8, 1766; and letters from George Mercer to his father, March 27, 1766; May 8, 1766; September 26, 1766; December 11, 1766; to his brother, James Mercer, in 1766; to his father July 8, 1767; September 18, 1767; to George Mason, October 10, 1767; to the Governor of Virginia, October 10, 1767; and again to his father, November 5, 1767, and November 25, 1767.

The two letters of October 10, 1767 [48] may have been of great importance. They came in the form of pacquets, one of them from the Office of the British Secretary of State, along with a printed copy of the *Case* of the Ohio Company.[49] The contents of the

[45] Really March 16, 1749, our calendar.

[46] As indicated above, material relating to the "Proceedings of the Ohio Company" about settlement, etc., of the Ohio Country, as the undated George Mercer manuscript was formerly entitled, was in the possession of Lord Shelburne, and is now found in the Shelburne Papers, L, 93-95, William L. Clements Library.

[47] D.M.L. MS., printed in *George Mercer Papers*, pp. 186-220, and a fragment, p. 296.

[48] Not found.

[49] No copy of such an imprint of this date has been found. But there is some slight evidence that such printing was done and that it included the first thirty-two and one-half pages of the *Case of the Ohio Company* of 1770, reproduced in the *George Mercer Papers*, Part II. For such evidence, see the endorsement of George Mercer on John Mercer's letter of March 3, 1768, D.M.L. MS., printed in *George Mercer Papers*, p. 229. It is possible that George Mercer was mistaken, but it is not impossible that Governor Fauquier or Robert Carter or George Mason may not have delivered a copy

letter of October 10, 1767, to Governor Fauquier can only be conjectured. Probably it was short, mainly a report on the action of the Board of Trade, June 26, 1767, with emphasis on the request of Lord Shelburne, October 8, 1767.[50] But the letter to George Mason, October 10, 1767, may have had contents greatly similar to the important letter of October 10, 1767 to the Committee of the Ohio Company.[51]

Significant effort was badly needed in 1767. As late as October 2, 1775, George Mason, looking backward, wrote to Colonel William Aylett about "Garlin imported by the Ohio Comp'y several years ago," [52] and, that late, "packed up in a chest. . . ." The mercantile or trade business of the Company had obviously come to an early end.

But interesting things, some general, others highly personal, continued to happen. A petition of Augusta County inhabitants for land on the Ohio was presented to the Virginia legislature, with the complaint that sundry other claims granted in England were impeding the progress of the settlement of the backcountry.[53] And George Washington at this time of uncertainty and anxiety for the Ohio Company set actively about getting title to military lands on the Ohio using William Crawford and his brother, Valentine Crawford, as his scouts and agents in the region. In a letter to William Crawford, September 21, 1767, in regard to the lands being selected and surveyed, Washington wrote, "It may be a Matter worthy your enquiry to find out how the Maryland back line will run and what is said about laying of Neale's (I think it is

---

to John Mercer, February 24, 1768, the date of the arrival at Stafford Courthouse of the pacquet, one week only before he signed the long letter of March 3, 1768, which he probably began more than a week earlier and in which he expressed his regret that his "case" had not been printed. The imprint of 1767, if made, may have been unbound, composed of long printed sheets comparable in size to the sheets of the bound imprint of 1770.

[50] He may have mentioned his "State of the Company's Affairs" of October 8, 1767, and thus, unwittingly, have retarded, if not prevented, immediate, or possibly later, compliance with Lord Shelburne's request.

[51] L.C. Ac 2203, printed below, pp. 248-51.

[52] *Tyler's Quarterly, Historical and Genealogical Magazine*, I, 87-88.

[53] *Journal of the House of Burgesses . . .*, 1766–69, p. 37.

and Companys) Grant."[54] He added, "I will inquire particularly concerning the Ohio Company that we may know what to apprehend from them."[55] In reply, William Crawford, September 29, 1767, wrote, "As to the Ohio Company you are the best judge yourself, what will be done in it, or where it will be laid."[56] Highly interesting as well as informational is a surviving receipt of William Trent, September 25, 1767, from George Croghan for the "Sum of One Hundred & Eleven pounds ten Shillings being in full of his obligation to Francis Wafer dated the twentieth day of February 1750 given at the time to Christopher Gist by said Wafer for the use of the Ohio Company."[57]

Two highly personal items relating to those connected with the Ohio Company appear in the records. George Mercer, August 15, 1767, eloped with Mary Neville of Lincoln, England,[58] a young lady who had already written her prospective father-in-law, John

[54] *Writings of Washington,* ed. Fitzpatrick, II, 467-71. Possibly the grant mentioned was the McMachon grant of April 22, 1747. The McMachons and Neals of Frederick County, Virginia, were and long remained active land speculators.

[55] *Ibid.,* and *The Washington-Crawford Correspondence . . . Concerning Western Lands,* ed. C. W. Butterfield, p. 4. The last sentence is good evidence, long ago in print, that George Washington was not a member of the Ohio Company.

[56] *Washington-Crawford Correspondence . . . ,* p. 9.

[57] The implications of this receipt are many and varied. Christopher Gist in February, 1751 (old calendar 1750) may have sold furs and skins belonging to the Ohio Company to Francis Wafer (elsewhere Water), who in turn sold them on credit, a promissory note or bond, to George Croghan, the great dealer in furs and skins. Then Wafer (or Water) may have assigned the note or bond to Gist for the use of the Ohio Company. But it is possible that Wafer bought Ohio Company cargo goods from Curran (or Gist), with a promissory note or bond of George Croghan, and that Curran turned in to the Ohio Company, Croghan's note or bond in part payment on his own bond of September 14, 1750. Gist, Croghan, Wafer (Water), and probably Curran were among the Shawnee Indians at the mouth of the Scioto at the time. It is probable that this receipt is closely related to the suit of the Ohio Company against Croghan in the Philadelphia court, in which a judgment was attained in December, 1767.

[58] *Va. Mag.,* XIV, 234 f.

Mercer.[59] Quite evidently this marriage did not immediately disconcert him, for in October he gathered material to be sent back to Virginia,[60] and on October 10, wrote a long querulous letter to the Committee of the Ohio Company,[61] saying that in four years he had received no reply to his letters to the Company, that he had not been informed of the petition of the inhabitants of Augusta County, that the existing ministry was favorable to western enterprises, that a full report to the ministry should be secured from the Governor, that he had presented "a state of the Company's Affairs" on October 8, 1767,[62] that he had been shockingly mistreated, that "There are some Persons here Petitioning for a New Government at the mouth of the Ohio" and that copies of the Treaty of Logs Town should be sent over.

George Mercer, who was possibly driven to action by the lobbying in London of Samuel Wharton, William Trent, Benjamin Franklin, Thomas Walpole, and others, wrote again to the Ohio Company, November 21, 1767.[63] He mentioned current investigations of proposals being made for establishing new governments in the West, saying he himself had been called in by the Board of Trade and had established the superiority of the Potomac route to the West. He protested, so he said, the activities of the Mississippi Company and asserted the superior claims of the Ohio Company. He was told, so he wrote, the "Company's affairs were discharged from their consideration and that they could not resume any care or debate upon them without orders from the King." The letter says he had already prepared a memorial to the King which he thought would be immediately referred to the Board of Trade. But hurried action by the Governor of Virginia was essential,

---

[59] Mentioned, John Mercer to George Mercer, January 28, 1768, D.M.L. MS., printed in *George Mercer Papers*, p. 207.

[60] Above, pp. 134-35.

[61] L.C. MS., Ac 2203.

[62] George Mercer wrote, "I am ashamed that I have not Time to make a Copy of it to send you." This "State of the Company's Affairs," submitted by George Mercer to Lord Shelburne, is printed below in Appendix A, pp. 243-46.

[63] Printed in *W. & M. Quarterly*, I, 200-3.

thought Mercer, and he mentioned being questioned about the possibility of the Ohio Company establishing a colony in the West. He also reported the imperial cost of Indian affairs as £100,000, annually.

In a typical undated memorial [64] of this time, probably of late November, 1767, George Mercer referred back to his Memorial of 1765, and to the report of the Board of Trade of June 16, 1767, and commenting on the prospects of the Proclamation of 1763 being waived in the near future, restated the claims and activities of the Ohio Company and asked for either a renewal of the old grant or for Parliamentary provision for the reimbursement of the great expenses of the Company.

This memorial, tabled, it would seem, for nearly two years, was taken up by the Privy Council and submitted to the Board of Trade, as late as November 20, 1769.[65]

In 1767, the relations of the Ohio Company with George Croghan had become a matter of distress to Croghan and so continued for many years. The Company, with James Tilghman III, as its attorney, obtained a judgment against his Philadelphia property in December 1767.[66] Nevertheless he mortgaged it in 1768 as security to William Franklin for endorsement of a loan to Croghan by the Burlington Company of Burlington, New Jersey. A voluminous correspondence of Franklin and Croghan followed and is indirectly a part of the history of the Ohio Company.[67]

The scanty financial circumstances of some of the members of the Company are indicated by a letter of Robert Carter, of *Nomini Hall*, December 11, 1767, to George Mason, asking for a loan of

[64] P.R.O. C.O. 5: 1332/301-6. Printed in the *Case* . . . , pp. 24-35, in *George Mercer Papers*, Part II. Though compiled in November, 1767, it was not acted upon until November 20, 1769, and is commonly given the latter date.

[65] *Acts of the Privy Council*, V, 119. See the confirmation of this in the *Case* . . . , 35, *George Mercer Papers*, Part II.

[66] Several documents, printed below, Appendix A, under dates March 1, 1767, May 20, 1767, and October 26, 1772, bear upon this matter.

[67] See the calendared list, in Appendix D, below, pp. 339 and 341.

money,[68] an unsuccessful appeal, for George Mason, January 23, 1768 replied, regretting that he was unable to accede to the request because he simply did not have the money.[69] Late in December, 1767, John Mercer began to take measures for a full meeting of the Ohio Company. He wrote Robert Carter, December 21, 1767, a short letter in which he spoke of his own inactivity and enclosed a copy of parts of a letter from his son George Mercer, September 18, 1767.[70] John Mercer asked Carter to look into the matter of the report of the Governor called for by Lord Shelburne. Copies of George Mercer's letter were also sent to John Tayloe, Philip Ludwell Lee, and George Mason. Possibly in connection with this enclosure from John Mercer, the letter was written by George Mason to Robert Carter, January 23, 1768,[71] saying he had written to the Governor. Probably John Mercer wrote more fully to George Mason about the same time.[72] Richard Lee in a letter to George Mason, January 8, 1768 [73] called for a meeting of the Ohio Company for January 12, 1768. Circumstances must have caused a postponement, for the meeting was actually held at Stafford Court House, February 23, 1768.[74] A letter of George Mason to John Mercer late in January [75] enclosing the letter of Richard Lee, of January 8, 1768, may have contained an account of the circumstances. The extant letter of George Mason to Robert Carter, January 23, 1768, specifically announced a meeting of the Ohio Company on February 23, 1768, informing him that the Case of the Ohio Company had been referred by order of the King in Council to the Governor and Council of Virginia, and that he him-

[68] Mentioned, Rowland, *op. cit.*, I, 131-32.

[69] D.M.L. MS., printed in *George Mercer Papers*, pp. 185-86.

[70] MS., Emmet Collection, No. 6302, a.l.s., N.Y.P.L.

[71] Rowland, *op. cit.*, I, 131-32.

[72] Mentioned, John Mercer to George Mercer, January 28, 1768, D.M.L. MS., printed in *George Mercer Papers*, pp. 186-220.

[73] Mentioned, *ibid.*, p. 212.

[74] Rowland, *op. cit.*, I, 131. See the advertisement in *Maryland Gazette*, February 4 and 11, 1768, and in the *Virginia Gazette*, February 11, 1768.

[75] Mentioned in John Mercer to George Mercer, January 28, 1768, *loc. cit.*

self had written to the governor about the matter.[76] Also, in a long letter to George Mercer, January 28, 1768, John Mercer discussed the status of the Ohio Company affairs.[77] This rambling letter throws more light on colonial Virginia plantation life and problems than upon the Ohio Company. It involves such matters as the difficulty of correspondence, the poor health of John Mercer, his bad financial circumstances, a five thousand word account of John Mercer's brewery, the small income from his legal business, the educational situation of his small children, a brawl of James Mercer with Arthur Lee about George Mercer's stamp act episode, a discussion about relatives and property in Ireland, and the iron works of Hunter. Only at the end of nearly eighteen thousand words did John Mercer get around to comment on the Ohio Company, mentioning having sent copies of his son's letter of September 18, 1767, to Mason, Tayloe, Philip Lee, and Robert Carter, and enclosing a copy of an interesting letter from John Tayloe. Trouble about arranging for a meeting of the Company was revealed, along with troubles with Mercer tenants. The latter part of the long letter is taken up with orders for nails, agricultural instruments, clothes for slaves, and volumes of magazines and books.

There was evidently considerable stir among the shareholders in the Ohio Company in the late winter of 1767–1768, for references are found to a letter of Governor Fauquier to George Mason,[78] and of another of John Mercer to Colonel Tayloe, February 10.[79] A third letter of Robert Carter to George Mason, February 10, 1768,[80] has been found, which mentions other letters of George Mason, George Mercer, and John Mercer, comments on the necessity of a full report to Shelburne, reports rumors from

[76] D.M.L. MS., printed in *George Mercer Papers*, pp. 185-86, and in Rowland, *op. cit.*, I, 131 f.

[77] D.M.L. MS., printed in *George Mercer Papers*, pp. 211-12.

[78] Mentioned, Blair to Shelburne, March 21, 1768, P.R.O. C.O. 5: 1346/13-15.

[79] Mentioned, John Mercer to Robert Carter, February 23, 1768, printed in Appendix A, below, pp. 256-57.

[80] Dreer Collection, French Refugees, p. 44, a.l.s., H.S.P., printed in Appendix A, below, pp. 254-56.

London, and gives an analysis of the "Interrogatories" about the Ohio Company.

The meeting of the Ohio Company called for February 23, 1768, at Stafford Court House,[81] seems not to have officially assembled, but random business was nevertheless transacted. Among other things taken up, a draft of a new plan of boundaries of the lands in the proposed renewal of the Ohio Company grant, in the handwriting of John Mercer, was brought before the meeting,[82] a copy of which was sent to George Mercer by John Mercer, March 3, 1768.[83] John Mercer wrote a letter to Robert Carter on the business of the Ohio Company, February 23, 1768,[84] and a few days later, February 26, 1768, George Mason wrote to John Mercer about mistakes made in the draft of the boundaries of the Company.[85]

While concerned with the boundaries of the lands in the proposed renewal of the old Ohio grant beyond the Alleghanies, George Mason kept an eye on the Company lands on the Potomac. In a note by Thomas Bryan Martin, land agent for Lord Fairfax, to John Moffett, a surveyor,[86] is found valuable data as follows: "Whereas George Mason Esq.[r] of Fairfax County hath inform'd that there are waste Lands adjoining the Ohio Companys three Lotts [87] called the new store tract on Potomack river (Viz) N° . . 14 . . 15 . . & 16 in Hampshire County . . .

And desiring to resurvey the same in order to include the whole in one Deed being ready to pay the Composition & Office Fees these are therefore to impower you to resurvey the s.[d] Lands for the s:[d] Mason . . ."

---

[81] See John Mercer to Robert Carter, February 23, 1768, *loc. cit.*

[82] D.M.L. MS., printed in *George Mercer Papers*, pp. 229-32.

[83] *Ibid.* This made it a George Mercer Paper, as most of the Darlington Ohio Company papers seem to have been.

[84] Dreer Collection, French Refugees, p. 45, printed below in Appendix A, pp. 256-57.

[85] D.M.L. MS., printed in *George Mercer Papers*, pp. 231-32.

[86] Land Office Papers, Virginia State Library.

[87] Lots 1 and 5 in the George Mason Patents of October 25, 1754, are not included. They were personal and not for the use of the Ohio Company.

On March 3, 1768, John Mercer wrote a letter to his son, George.[88] In it he commented on the difficulty of getting together a meeting of the Company in the bad weather of late February, stated that the correspondence and packet of papers had just arrived after four months and fourteen days on passage, that a letter from Robert Carter [89] discussed the report desired from the Governor, and that the meeting lacked a quorum. Also he lamented that the Case had not been printed; [90] said he was sending over a copy of the Case and other papers, complained of Councillors of Virginia, especially Richard Corbin and William Beverley, indulging in land jobbing. An item about the Ohio Company said "There has not been a meeting of the Comp.ª or Committee since you wrote you had settled Hanbury's Acco.ᵗ but I am sure there will be still some Objections to it." Six days later he indited another,[91] in which he attacked the Penn family land and Indian policies, the role of Conrad Weiser, the somewhat similar role of George Croghan and other Pennsylvania agents. George Mercer properly endorsed this letter, "Chiefly concerning M.ʳ Penn & the People of that Province—their Behaviour in Respect to the Indians & People of Virginia." But the letter does mention Christopher Gist's first journey, the Indian deed of 1744 to Virginia, and Virginia gifts to the Indians from 1744 to 1750. Fragments of yet another letter have survived.[92]

The letter of Lord Shelburne to Governor Fauquier of October 8, 1767, must have been also delayed more than four months for it was not put before the Virginia Council until March 10, 1768.[93]

---

[88] D.M.L. MS., printed in the *George Mercer Papers*, pp. 221-29.

[89] Not found, but probably similar to, if not a copy of, the letter of Carter to Mason, February 10, 1768, printed below, pp. 254-56.

[90] But see the endorsement of George Mercer on this letter, where he says, "see the printed Case O Comp,ª Pages 33 & 34, sent in the Gov.ʳˢ Pacquet Octʳ 10.ᵗʰ" If this is not a misrepresentation, bad memory, or miserable rhetoric, the printed pages must have been secreted from the public and from posterity.

[91] D.M.L. MS., printed in *George Mercer Papers*, pp. 297-310.

[92] *Ibid.*, p. 296.

[93] Executive Journals, Council of Colonial Virginia, photostats, from P.R.O. C.O. 5: 1435, Virginia State Library.

In a letter of John Blair to Lord Shelburne, March 21, 1768,[94] announcing the death of Fauquier on March 3, instant, and his own accession to office, Blair said he found in the Book of Letters of Fauquier [95] a copy of a letter of Fauquier's to members of the Ohio Company.

The resurvey [96] of the Lots 14, 15, and 16 of the *New Store Tract* in Virginia, opposite the mouth of Wills Creek, authorized by the warrant of March 1, 1768, was made by John Moffett on the 3rd, 4th and 5th of May 1768. The resurvey included the intermediate wasteland and totaled 1,083 acres.[97] The resurvey, properly endorsed, is accompanied by a rough draft of the acreage and the surrounding territories, showing the hairpin curve of the Potomac River, Fort Cumberland, and the mouth of Wills Creek with the new store immediately opposite, on the extreme point of Virginia of that day, but now of Mineral County, West Virginia.

In the second half of May and the first half of June, 1768, the Board of Trade and Plantations had before it, one after another, a number of Virginia items [98] dealing respectively with a petition of the House of Burgesses asking royal approval of settlements made prior to the Proclamation of October 1, 1763; a comment on George Mercer's hearing by the Board, May 31, 1768; the preparation of a reply to the House of Burgesses; the transcription of the reply; and finally the signing of the representations in the report and letters to Lord Hillsborough.

A letter by John Mercer to Philip Ludwell Lee, probably in 1768, is mentioned by the latter in a letter to James Mercer, January 21, 1772.[99] In his letters to his son George in England, John Mercer wrote of his advancing age and indicated something

---

[94] P.R.O. C.O. 5: 1346/13-16.

[95] Most unfortunately, this "Book of Letters" of Governor Fauquier has not been found. It was probably shipped in a trunk, 1785, from Robert Carter to Francis Fauquier, Jr. in London. See Nellie Norkus, unpublished Ph.D. thesis on Francis Fauquier, University of Pittsburgh Library.

[96] Land Office MS. Virginia State Library.

[97] *Ibid.*

[98] All mentioned in *J.B.T.*, 1768–75, pp. 28-32.

[99] D.M.L. MS., printed in *George Mercer Papers*, p. 320.

of his many worries and burdens. He died, October 14, 1768, at the age of sixty-four.[100] His death, like that of Thomas Lee and Lawrence Washington earlier, was probably a disaster to the Ohio Company. At his death its affairs were at a low ebb. George Mason from then on assumed leadership in what proved to be an impossible cause.

Within one month after the death of John Mercer the famous Treaty of Fort Stanwix with the Iroquois Indians was negotiated, November 5, 1768. Among the agreements made there, the lands long claimed by the Ohio Company were granted by the Indians to a group including George Croghan, William Trent, and others known as the "Suffering Traders," who had suffered losses at Indian hands, 1750–1754.[101] Others like the great mercantile firms of Baynton, Wharton and Morgan of Philadelphia made similar appeals to the Indians for damages done in Pontiac's Conspiracy of 1763.[102]

After 1768, the affairs of the Ohio Company began to drag badly. Most of the activity was in London. On November 20, 1769, the Privy Council finally reported on the Memorial of 1765, presented by George Mercer.[103] But in the same month of 1769 a mixed group of old traders, land speculators, and politicians presented a petition to the King for a large tract of lands situated back of the English settlements.[104] Under the name of the Grand Ohio Company [105] they were contestants for the same lands against the representatives of the Ohio Company of Virginia, and they had powerful backing in both Pennsylvania and London.

George Mercer, however, did not immediately throw in the

[100] *Va. Mag.*, XIV, 233 f., and *W. & M. Quarterly*, XVII, 87.

[101] Etting Collection, Ohio Company Papers, H.S.P. It is printed in Wharton, *op. cit.*, pp. 86-87.

[102] *Ibid.*

[103] Mentioned in the Memorial of November 27, 1767, and in P.R.O. C.O. 5: 1332/301, and printed under date of its reception, November 20, 1769, in Bailey, *Ohio Company . . .*, pp. 314 f.

[104] Etting Collection, Ohio Company Papers, H.S.P.

[105] Bailey, *Ohio Company Papers*, p. 14, speaks of the Grand Ohio Company as organized, officially, December 27, 1769.

sponge. On November 20, 1769, the Lords of the Committee on Plantation Affairs of the Privy Council referred his Memorial on behalf of the Ohio Company to the Board of Trade,[106] and on December 18, 1769, Mercer presented yet another memorial in behalf of the Ohio Company of Virginia protesting the consideration of other petitions for a grant of the same territory and claiming among other things that the Ohio Company had first prepared a chart of the Ohio region, now petitioned for by others. He offered "to justify the Companys Pretentions." [107]

Highly valuable light on the papers of the Ohio Company and their provenance is furnished in a letter of Charlton Palmer to George Mercer, December 27, 1769,[108] in which he mentions a Petition and asserts that he had turned over, either to George Mercer or to Mr. Jackson, all Ohio Company papers sent to him and that Mr. Jackson in turn had handed them over to George Mercer.[109]

---

[106] P.R.O. C.O. 5: 1331/301-10, printed in Bailey, *Ohio Company . . .*, pp. 314-16.

[107] P.R.O. C.O. 5: 1331/307-10, printed in Bailey, *Ohio Company . . .*, p. 317.

[108] D.M.L. MS., printed in *George Mercer Papers*, p. 310.

[109] *Ibid.* This indicates the George Mercer provenance of much of the originals of the Ohio Company Papers in the Darlington Collection. Probably before George Mercer's death, most of them were sent back to his brother James Mercer. See George Mercer to (John Robinson), November 28, 1775, T 1 Bundle 445, folio 134. A few may have been sent back after George Mercer's death in April, 1784. All of the George Mercer Papers thus became the property of James Mercer and James Mercer's descendants. In a sense they are all James Mercer Papers.

X

Acceptance and Rejection of Defeat

1770–1773

MATTERS IN LONDON had reached a crisis by the end of 1769—distinctly unfavorable to the old Ohio Company.

The order of the Lords of the Committee of the Council, November 20, 1769, referring to the Board of Trade the petition of George Mercer, was considered [1] on January 3, 1770. The group variously known as the Vandalia Company, the Walpole Company, and the Grand Ohio Company, abetted by Benjamin Franklin, was so active at this time that Edward Montague, the agent of the colony of Virginia, put in before January 18, 1770, a petition [2] against the proposed grant. He called it "a Grant of certain Lands in & part of his Majestys Colony & Dominion of Virginia" involving the proposal "to sever such Lands from the said Colony & erect a new & distinct Governmt thereof." He mentioned that "no less than 1,350,000 Acres of such Land have already been granted, partly to a Society of Gentlemen called the Ohio Company." These prior grantees he credited with having made surveys and achieved progress in settlement and cultivation of lands of their grant before they were driven out by war and after the war restrained by

[1] *J.B.T.*, 1768–75, p. 89.
[2] P.R.O. C.O. 5: 1332/323.

the royal Proclamation of October 7, 1763. With considerable boldness for a petitioner and a colonial agent, he asserted, "they have not yet been restored to their just rights." He petitioned that before any imperial action should be taken the consent and approval of Virginia should be considered. His stand seems to have been influential on later policy.

The Board of Trade and Plantations had on its hands not only the petitions of the Virginia House of Burgesses, of George Mercer, of Thomas Walpole, and of Edward Montague, but also one of Arthur Lee and his relatives and friends. On January 24, 1770, the Board [3] ordered that not only Lee's memorial and petition but also copies of the original petition [4] of the Ohio Company and of the memorial presented on their behalf by Colonel Mercer on the 3rd instant [5] be "transmitted to the Secretary to the Lords of the Treasury for their information, as having reference to the application of Mr. Walpole and others, then before that Board."

Of all these petitioners the most influential and most aggressive were those associated with Walpole, Wharton, Franklin, and others in the Grand Ohio Company. In a letter both of apology and of forewarning, Thomas Walpole wrote Osgood Hanbury, February 7, 1770, admitting asking for lands on the Ohio, but saying he sought no lands that were legally claimed by another.[6] On the twenty-sixth of March, 1770, Conway Richard Dobbs [7] wrote to George Mercer in reply to a letter [8] of the latter to him, March 8, 1770,

[3] *J.B.T.*, 1768–75, p. 163.

[4] By the "original petition" is meant, probably, the Hanbury petition of January 11, 1749, rather than the earlier petition of October 24, 1747, to the Governor and Council of Virginia. No copy of the latter has yet been found. A copy may have been furnished John Hanbury in late 1748. Any copy of it, if extant, would probably be found in surviving papers of John Hanbury, or of the Privy Council, or possibly of the Treasury.

[5] Of December 18, 1769.

[6] D.M.L. MS., printed in *George Mercer Papers*, p. 311. Somewhat significantly he underlines, in this letter, the words "*legal Grants*," implying skepticism of the legality of the old Ohio Company grant of July 12, 1749.

[7] *Ibid.*, pp. 311-12. Note that it is a reply to a letter of George Mercer, March 8, 1770.

[8] Not found.

concerning the share in the Ohio Company of his father, Arthur Dobbs, who had died on March 28, 1765.[9] It may have been in connection with this correspondence that George Mercer left among his papers, later purchased by William Darlington, a statement of the account [10] of Arthur Dobbs with the Ohio Company showing levies upon his share in 1749 of £125; in 1750 of £11 .. 11s .. 11d; in 1751 of £30 and in 1753 of £50, April 7, of £32 .. 8 .. 2 and £20 November 2; a total, calculated possibly in British money, of £301 .. 17s .. 3d. Multiplied by twenty shares this total accounts for about £6,000 laid out by the Ohio Company by the end of 1753. Arthur Dobbs was credited with having paid only £200 of his assessments of more than £300. It is not impossible that the accounts of other shareholders were similarly in arrears.

George Mercer, in London in early 1770, had in his possession copies of many of the important documents of the Ohio Company, copies now located in the George Mercer Papers of the William L. Darlington Library of the University of Pittsburgh. He also had two or more long expositions of the Case of the Ohio Company, compiled or dictated by his father, John Mercer of *Marlborough.* These expositions contained copies of some material long accessible to the public in print or in depositories such as the British Public Record Office. But they contained copies of private letters not found today elsewhere. The printing of this material was long desired by the Ohio Company. An imprint, which could not be found, may have been made as early as 1767.

But in early 1770, George Mercer edited, somewhat, and had printed *The Case of the Ohio Company, Extracted from Original Papers.* The sole imprint known to have survived was found in 1950 in the New York Historical Society among the papers of the Rufus King Collection in a pamphlet volume from the library of John Pownall, one time secretary of the Board of Trade.

Permission to reprint a facsimile edition of this sole surviving imprint was graciously extended by the New York Historical Society. It contains editions of many Ohio Company documents and

[9] North Carolina *Colonial Records,* VI, 1321.

[10] D.M.L. MS., printed in *George Mercer Papers,* p. 183.

serves as a history of the company as it was known in 1770. Edited by Lois Mulkearn and used as an Appendix to the *George Mercer Papers,* it should be canvassed carefully by anyone interested. In retrospect, the imprint appears to have been the last desperate effort of the Company's London agent.

George Mercer himself, by the spring of 1770, must have abandoned hopes of realizing anything from the claims of the Ohio Company of Virginia. In a letter to George Washington March 28, 1770, he wrote not about the Ohio Company lands in the West, but about his own personal land claims under the Dinwiddie Proclamation of 1754.[11] About five weeks later, May 7, 1770, George Mercer in London, without special authority from the members of the Company, submitted to the incorporation of the Ohio Company of Virginia with or into the Grand Ohio Company.[12] This act he followed up with a Memorial the next day to the Board of Trade and Plantations, withdrawing earlier Ohio Company petitions.[13] A letter of George Mason, December 6, 1770, to a young relative, then in England, well reveals the uncertainty and inactivity of the Ohio Company at the time.[14]

It is a matter of interest that at the very time the affairs of the Ohio Company were collapsing in London, some of its old Ohio Valley pretensions were being honored in that area, in processes destined to continue for fifteen years and bring emoluments to some of the Ohio Company settlers of 1753–54. Rejections and qualifications appeared it is true, as on June 26, 1770, when William Cromwell sued Samuel Lyon and Isaac Pearis before the Pennsylvania Board of Property,[15] which gave as its opinion that "the Settle-

---

[11] *Writings of George Washington,* ed. Fitzpatrick, I, 66 f.

[12] See P.R.O. C.O. 5: 1332/365-66 and *Gist's Journals . . . ,* p. 244. Printed in *American Historical Record,* ed. B. J. Lossing, III, 205, and in Bailey, *Ohio Company . . . ,* pp. 260-62. According to Rowland, *op. cit.,* I, 157, George Mercer did not immediately inform members of the Ohio Company.

[13] P.R.O. C.O. 5: 1332/383.

[14] George Mason Papers, a.l.s., Library of Congress, Division of Manuscripts.

[15] *Pa. Arch.,* third series, I, 301.

ments made heretofore under the Ohio Company cannot have so much weight as to overthrow the rights of those regular Appliants." But Samuel Lyon, June 27, 1770, paid William Cromwell twenty pounds for a quit claim to 316 acres in dispute.[16]

It must not be overlooked that Virginians had long been interested in the southwestern Indians. It was in 1769 that Virginians began to move into the Wautauga and Holston areas and came into troublesome relations with the Indians of Tennessee. The Darlington Ohio Company manuscripts contain a letter of John Stuart, southern Indian agent, to Lord Botetourt of April 27, 1770.[17]

Among the Virginians and Marylanders who crossed the Allegheny Mountains and moved into the Monongahela Valley, 1760–63, and again 1765–70,[18] were claimants under the Ohio Company and Christopher Gist settlements of the period 1753–54. Thomas Gist and Nathaniel Gist, sons of Christopher Gist, and William Cromwell, son-in-law of Christopher Gist, put in claims for large tracts of land. In the next decade such claims by old Ohio Company settlers were to receive consideration and recognition.

In Virginia the land grant situation in 1770 remained as troublesome as it had been in the period 1745–55. On the death of Lord Botetourt, October 15, 1770, William Nelson, as president of the Council of Virginia, became acting governor. In a letter to the Board of Trade and Plantations October 18, 1770 he discussed Virginia land grants, defended the claims of the Ohio Company, and enclosed a list of Virginia land grants.[19]

Lord Hillsborough, in a letter to Nelson, January 3, 1771,

[16] Fayette County, Pennsylvania, Deed Book A, folio 85, printed below, Appendix A, pp. 258-59.

[17] It is merely one letter in an extensive correspondence between Stuart and Botetourt, most of which is in the Public Record Office in London.

[18] James, "The First English Speaking Trans-Appalachian Frontier."

[19] P.R.O. C.O. 5: 1348/321-30. On Virginia land grants, see *ibid.*, 323-53 and *Va. Mag.*, V, 175 f. and 241 f. See also Etting Collection, Ohio Company Papers, printed in Bailey, *Ohio Company Papers*, Governor Nelson's list included and supplemented the earlier list by Walthoe, under John Blair.

wrote, "I have received your Dispatch N° 2, and Duplicates of those N^{s} 5 & 6, but the Originals of them, as well as N.^{s} 3 & 4 have not been received,"[20] an illustration of difficulty then of communication. Hillsborough said he had no doubt that "Attention will be given to the equitable Claims of those *bona fide* Settlers whose Possessions are derived from the Grants made to the Ohio Company in 1754 or from such others as were passed in consequence of Instructions from his late Majesty or of Lieut. Governor Dinwiddie's Proclamation at the Commencement of the last War." In the minutes[21] of the Executive Council of Virginia, April 12, 1771, there is a restatement of the contents of the letter. In his reply[22] of April 17, 1771, William Nelson expressed his pleasure at the contents of the letter.

Numerous letters were written during this period by George Mercer from London to his brother, James Mercer, and to the Ohio Company,[23] but none of them has been found. His letter[24] to Conway Richard Dobbs, May 8, 1771, about the Dobbs share in the Ohio Company is largely personal, though it reflects a vague light on the general situation of the Company. Another letter[25] of August 8, 1771, to George Mason is of great importance. He complains of his neglect by members of the Company for eight years, having received no answers to his letters and no further orders or instructions. He claimed and complained that he had spent £1,000 of his own money. He asserted that the London credit of the Company was not worth a shilling. The letter was probably received in October and shown to Robert Carter and possibly others.

On December 5, 1771, James Mercer, who doubtless had received similar complaints from his brother in England, after a con-

[20] P.R.O. C.O. 5: 1349/1-3.

[21] *Ibid.*, 12-13.

[22] *Ibid.*, 173-176.

[23] George Mason to James Mercer, January 13, 1772, D.M.L. MS., printed in *George Mercer Papers*, pp. 315-18, 321, and George Mercer to the Ohio Company, August 1, 1771, printed in Rowland, *op. cit.*, I, 156.

[24] Arthur Dobbs Papers, a.l.s., North Carolina State Archives.

[25] V.S.L. MS. 20624.

ference in Williamsburg with three members of the Ohio Company, put in the *Virginia Gazette*, December 5, 1771, an advertisement calling for a meeting [26] of the Company at Stafford Courthouse on December 16, 1771, "on Business, though soon done, yet of the utmost importance to the Company."

A short letter [27] of Robert Carter to James Mercer from Williamsburg, December 9, 1771, mentions a proposed Ohio Company meeting at Stafford Courthouse December 28, 1771, and requests a copy of "the Resolutions that shall then be made" since he could not be present. In this letter Carter incorporated an excerpt from the letter he wrote George Mercer, October 24, 1771, in which Carter had agreed to be responsible for his share of the claims of George Mercer against the Ohio Company and had put at his disposal £200 in London, available on George Mercer's bond.[28] Writing December 31, 1771,[29] probably in reply to Carter's letter of December 9, James Mercer touched upon several important matters. He mentioned his advertisement of December 5, 1771, saying "not a single member regarded my advertisement." He reported that he had felt obligated to send a letter to each member (Col. Tayloe excepted) of the Ohio Company. He enclosed a copy of George Mercer's appointment of July 4, 1763, and indicated that he wished to secure £200 per share to remit to his brother.

John Mercer, in spite of the fact that he was a lawyer, on his death must have left his account with the Ohio Company in some disorganization, for George Mason, on January 13, 1772,[30] re-

[26] It will be recalled that George Mason in his letter, December 6, 1770, to a young relative then in England, said, after a paragraph on the unhappy history and circumstances of the Ohio Company, that there had been no meeting of the Company from 1763 to 1770.

[27] Virginia Historical Society MS., printed in Appendix A, below, pp. 261-62.

[28] See the letter of Hunt to Carter, February 29, 1772, below, pp. 264-65, and Carter to Taswell, July 24, 1773, below, p. 268.

[29] Letter formerly in the possession of W. Garnett Chisolm, whose Mercer and Garnett papers are now deposited in the Historical Society of Virginia. A few years before his death in 1955, he furnished a copy and gave his permission to print. It is in Appendix A, below, pp. 262-64.

[30] D.M.L. MS., printed in *George Mercer Papers*, pp. 315-18, 321.

quested a copy from his son, James Mercer, also a lawyer. And George Mercer in London was in financial straits. He tried to borrow £50 from Thomas Adams of 41 Fleet Street, London, in connection with marriage expenses,[31] and he seems to have decided to use his brother, James Mercer, to secure funds and compensation from members of the Ohio Company resident in America.[32] The letter of Robert Carter to George Mason, October 24, 1771, may have been related to this situation.[33] George Mason showed concern about the account rendered of Mr. Charlton Palmer,[34] and in the same month wrote Mr. Waller, asking for a copy of Mr. Hanbury's account as settled by George Mercer in London.[35] And in his letter to James Mercer, January 13, 1772, George Mason asked him to bring to a meeting of the Ohio Company the Order Book which had been in possession of John Mercer for many years before his death.

In time, James Mercer, at the instigation of his brother George, sent a circular letter to various members of the Ohio Company resident in Virginia.[36] In this circular letter he mentioned George Mercer's letter to the Ohio Company, the Grand Ohio project, his brother's expenses and dilemma, his earlier ignored call for a meeting, the proposal to enter the Grand Ohio Company scheme, and a request for £150 per share at the least to be sent to George Mercer. In some cases the circular letter was accompanied by a personal letter to the member addressed.[37] Fortunately this correspondence has survived, as it is among the Mercer papers purchased by William Darlington.[38] A striking fact about this correspondence

[31] *Va. Mag.*, XVII, 326-27.

[32] Statement based on data immediately following.

[33] Mentioned in George Mercer to Robert Carter, August 6, 1774, N.Y.P.L. MS., Emmet Collection.

[34] George Mason to James Mercer, January 13, 1772, D.M.L. MS., printed in *George Mercer Papers*, pp. 315-18, 321.

[35] *Ibid.*

[36] D.M.L. MS.. printed in *George Mercer Papers*, 312-15, 321.

[37] E.g. James Mercer to Philip Ludwell Lee, January 9, 1772, *ibid.*, p. 323.

[38] *Ibid.*, pp. 312-24. Obviously these are James Mercer Papers, never handled nor seen by George Mercer, though they are about George Mercer.

is the repudiation by most of the members of the contract made by George Mercer with the Grand Ohio Company. Very evidently, also, the members of the Ohio Company of Virginia were not prepared at that time to put any additional funds into the enterprise.

According to a letter of George Mason to James Mercer, January 13, 1772,[39] the date for a meeting of the Ohio Company was set as of March 30, 1772. But it was not held, for an advertisement[40] of May 14, 1772, in the *Virginia Gazette* said, "The expected meeting of the Ohio Company, on the 30th of March last, being prevented by the sitting of the Assembly, a Meeting of the said company, at Stafford Court house, on Monday the 25th of May next, on Business of the utmost Importance, is desired by George Mason, Treasurer." No minutes of such a meeting have been found, and as in March, no meeting may have taken place,[41] for in the *Virginia Gazette* of July 22, 1772, appeared another call by George Mason, this time for a meeting on Tuesday, August 27, at Stafford Courthouse.

Presumably at some such meeting the matter of alliance with the Grand Ohio Company was considered and repudiated. Possibly further funds for the use of George Mercer were discussed and very likely declined. Another appeal to the Virginia government must have been decided upon, for a letter was received by the Governor during the summer from Colonel Richard Lee enclosing a petition from the Ohio Company complaining of George Mercer's agreement with the Grand Ohio Company and praying that a warrant be issued to survey their old grant of 1749. This petition of the Ohio Company of Virginia was ordered to be entered in the

---

[39] *Ibid.* See the advertisement in the *Virginia Gazette*, March 5, 1772.

[40] It was published in the *Maryland Gazette*, April 23, 1772.

[41] Since John Mercer was dead and could no longer make journalistic notations nor write letters to his son George at London, and since George Mercer was being neglected and, in 1772, in disfavor, one may well believe that some meetings were held of which no minutes have survived, because of the loss by fire of the Ohio Company papers in the possession of George Mason and his descendants. There is, indeed, some indirect evidence that one or more meetings were held in 1772.

journal of the Council of Virginia, July 27, 1772,[42] the day the Governor laid it before the Board. A letter of the Clerk of the Council of Virginia, July 27, 1772, indirectly evaded renewal of the Grant of the Ohio Company whose grant of 1751 had expired, in law if not in right, in 1771, by saying the Company already "had such an Order in their favor" and there was no precedent for such a re-warrant.[43]

In the meantime the relations of George Mercer in London with the Grand Ohio Company were being more closely knitted. On August 5, 1772, George Mercer drew a draft for £250 on Samuel Wharton, a leading agent for the Grand Ohio Company.[44]

The Grant to that Company, commonly called the Walpole or the Vandalia Scheme,[45] was conditionally confirmed by the Privy Council, August 4, 1772. Samuel Wharton in a letter to George Mercer, August 20, 1772,[46] informed the latter of this fact and that according to the agreement,[47] a government should be established thereon. He asked if it were Mercer's desire for Walpole and Wharton to continue to push the project. Actually as the biographies of Trent and Croghan reveal, the affairs and finances of the Walpole group were also in bad shape.

The next twelve months, August, 1772 to August, 1773, seem to have been taken up in a quarrel in both the New World and in the Old World, between the Grand Ohio Company and the Ohio Company of Virginia. The former put out its own Case with re-

---

[42] P.R.O. C.O. 5: 1440/42-46. Minutes of the Virginia Council, photostat in Virginia State Library, printed in Appendix A, below, pp. 265-66. It is mentioned in the Memorial of November 20, 1778, V.S.L. MS., printed in Bailey, *Ohio Company* . . . , p. 324. The petition of 1772 was not found.

[43] Note its misinterpretation in the Memorial of 1778. As extant material reveals, some members of the Ohio Company optimistically gave this evasive statement of the Council a positive rather than a negative or even a neutral interpretation.

[44] D.M.L. MS., printed in *George Mercer Papers*, p. 324.

[45] Bailey, *Thomas Cresap* . . . , pp. 126-27; P.R.O. C.O. 5: 27/34; and sundry items in the Etting Collection, Ohio Company Papers, H.S.P.

[46] D.M.L. MS., printed in *George Mercer Papers*, pp. 324-25.

[47] Printed pamphlet, N.Y.P.L.

spect to Virginia and claimed priority over Virginia patentees in lands on the Ohio. In turn George Mason, as spokesman not only of the Ohio Company of Virginia, but of Virginia's government's rights, drew up a sharp condemnation of the Walpole Company grant.[48] Probably this document was brought up in a meeting of the Ohio Company of Virginia, which was advertised to meet August 27, 1773.[49] Seemingly at this meeting it was decided to take up lands in Kentucky, possibly to avoid trouble with Pennsylvania and with the Indians north of the Ohio, but probably as a result of the great contemporary Kentucky craze. In accordance with Virginia Statutary regulations, a commission from the President and Masters of William and Mary College was secured for William Crawford as surveyor for the Ohio Company.[50] Shortly after, a similar commission was obtained for Hancock Lee.[51] As will be commented upon below, extensive surveys followed within two years.

An anonymous and undated document,[52] probably of October 26, 1772 and almost certainly drawn up by Joseph Galloway, is highly relevant. A short paragraph covers a matter stretching from 1754 to 1772 and beyond. Excerpted, this paragraph reads, "1767, Dec[r] A *Judgement* on a Bond to a certain Geo. Mason—(Agent for the Ohio Company) was obtained against Geo- Croghan and Fi-Fa Issued—Penalty Two Thousand Pounds—which as Ja.[s] Tilghman

---

[48] Printed in Rowland, *op. cit.*, I, 393-414, from the MS. in the Bancroft Collection, N.Y.P.L., pp. 125-37.

[49] *Virginia Gazette*, July 22, July 29, August 5, and August 19, 1773. Mentioned in Thomas Glasscock to George Washington, August 21, 1773, MS. in Washington Papers, in L.C., printed in *Letters to Washington*, IV, 251.

[50] Memorial of 1778, V.S.L. MS., printed in Bailey, *Ohio Company . . .*, pp. 320-27.

[51] *Ibid.*, and see the letter of George Rogers Clark, April 1, 1774, Draper MS., I L 16, a.l.s., in Wisconsin Historical Society, printed in *Collections* of the Illinois State Historical Library, VIII, 9.

[52] MS. in Free Library of Philadelphia, Ridgeway Branch, printed below, p. 267. Unfortunately, actual research has failed to locate either the bond or the court record of the trial in Philadelphia, or, indeed, of any final settlement of the claim.

the Attorney on Record says, is not satisfied. i.e. on the 26th Octo.r 1772." This note, not in the handwriting, but from the office of Joseph Galloway, gives some idea of the business done by George Croghan, as commissioner of military supplies and fur trader, with the Ohio Company, 1750–54. The bond was doubtless a double indemnity penal bond and therefore the account was probably of one thousand pounds, or less, for expenses or costs were sometimes included in such claims of damages.

A long drawn out correspondence [53] between William Franklin and Croghan, 1772–73, makes frequent mention of this Ohio Company business and the Judgment obtained against Croghan in 1767.

George Croghan, in answer to a letter of William Franklin of November 21, 1772, about his financial obligations wrote, December 26, 1772, ". . . the Balance I owe the Ohio Company is very trifling when Capt. Trent settles his part of those Accounts which I have nothing to do with; I have given M.r Gratz directions as soon as Cap.t Trent settles the Ohio Company's affairs to sell the House and Lotts, and to pay you the Money." [54] It is obvious that this financial statement refers to the 1753–54 operations of Trent and Croghan with the earlier Ohio Company of Virginia rather that with the more recent Grand Ohio Company of Pennsylvania.

In the midst of all the above troubles of George Mason, both with the Ohio Company of Virginia and its Pennsylvania rival, came the deed [55] of Thomas Lord Fairfax to 1,083 acres of land on the *New Store Tract*, surveyed, May 5, 1768, by John Moffett.

The year 1773 marked the end of an era in the matter of imperial land grants. In this year the Privy Council reversed itself and decided against the consummation of the Walpole grant. Samuel Wharton put in one last forlorn petition which was virtu-

---

[53] Some of it is calendared in Appendix D, below, pp. 339-41. Much of it is in the Society Collection, H.S.P.

[54] In Miscellaneous Collection, H.S.P. A statement of the financial relations of Croghan and Trent accompanied the letter. The statement is now in the Ridgway Branch of the Free Library of Philadelphia.

[55] Northern Neck Grants B, 1771–75, Land Office, Archives Division, Virginia State Library.

ally ignored. Benjamin Franklin nominally dropped out of the group, at the sacrifice probably of his earlier advances of time and money. The colonial hostility to the Tea Act of May, 1773 put an end to the prospect of imperial land grants to restive and revolutionary colonials across the Atlantic. All such projects whether old like that of the Ohio Company or new like that of the Grand Ohio Company were doomed. The only possible recourse which remained to those concerned was appeal to various governments in the colonies, notably to Virginia, which claimed title to all lands west of the Chesapeake Bay, Maryland, and Pennsylvania as far as the Mississippi River. And in Virginia first claim to such lands seems to have been considered as belonging to military claimants, under the Dinwiddie proclamation of February 19, 1754, and the Royal Proclamation of 1763.

The letter, above mentioned, of Glasscock to George Washington in which he refers, August 22, 1773, to a forthcoming meeting of the Ohio Company is indicative of a situation seen very clearly in the correspondence of Washington during this period, when military claims produced numerous warrants, entries, surveys, and patents in much disregard of earlier land company grants.

Already, since the arrival, June 1, 1773, of a royal proclamation of April 4, 1773, forbidding further Western land grants save to soldiers in the late war, the Virginia Executive Council was narrowly restricted in all such matters.

A side glance at George Mercer in London at this time reveals him in an unfriendly correspondence with George William Fairfax whom he accused of retarding matters by his opposition to the Vandalia Scheme.[56] To Mercer's accusation Fairfax replied in a letter [57] of December 14, 1773, vindicating himself from any such charges.

---

[56] Letter of December 2, 1773, mentioned in Edward Duffield Neill, *The Fairfaxes of England and America in the Seventeenth and Eighteenth Centuries*, p. 140; Rowland, *op. cit.*, I, 157; and Bailey, *Ohio Company* . . . , p. 261.

[57] MS., in N.Y. Hist. Soc.

XI

The Kentucky Episode

1773–1779

As already indicated, the Ohio Company by 1773 had become vitally interested in finding in Kentucky its long sought grants of from 200,000 to 500,000 acres of land.[1] The ambiguous report of the Council of Virginia July 27, 1772, that they already "had . . . an Order in their favor" [2] may also have influenced them.

At that time all of present day Kentucky was organized as Fincastle County, Virginia, with William Preston as the official county surveyor. By recent Virginia legislation all surveys to become valid in law had to be made by the official county surveyor through assistants deputized directly or indirectly by him. That the Ohio Company recognized this is seen in a letter of John Tayloe of *Mount Airy* to William Preston, January 28, 1775,[3] announcing the appointment of Hancock Lee as the Ohio Company surveyor in Kentucky and seeking as a personal favor his "deputation" by William Preston.

As early as 1773 Hancock Taylor, a deputy surveyor of Fin-

[1] Above, p. 156.

[2] Above, p. 155.

[3] Draper MS. 4 QQ 5, printed in Appendix A, below, p. 268.

castle County, was in Kentucky making surveys.[4] These earliest official Kentucky surveys were usually made near the Ohio River at places such as Limestone (Maysville of later days) or the Falls (Louisville of later times) or on the navigable reaches of large rivers such as the Kentucky, the Salt, the Green, and the Licking. Taylor in 1773 had as an assistant Willis Lee, brother of Hancock Lee and a relative of the Lees of Stratford. For Willis Lee, Hancock Taylor in 1773 "mark'd out" 20,000 acres "on the N.E. side of Kentucky and on Elkhorn Creek & other Branches. . . ."[5]

A later deputy surveyor of William Preston, John Floyd, appointed such March 2, 1774,[6] surveyed in 1774 and early 1775 several hundred thousand acres on the Kentucky River and its tributaries. On Elkhorn Creek alone about fifty surveys totaling 89,000 acres were made for about forty individuals, of whom one was Patrick Henry, who secured for himself 7,000 acres in four surveys in the region.[7]

These surveys made by John Floyd in 1774 and early 1775 are commonly designated as military surveys. On Elkhorn Creek the general direction of these military surveys was at first up stream southeast, but on the headwaters the northern line of the military surveys ran in the general direction S 45 E.

Hancock Lee probably reached Kentucky late in 1774. His assistants, among whom was George Rogers Clark, all arrived in early summer of 1775.[8] The Ohio Company survey was begun late in May or early in June. Setting out from the Kentucky River and probably establishing headquarters near Stamping Ground,

[4] Draper MS. 4 QQ 5, printed in Appendix A, below, p. 268.

[5] Entry Book (Fincastle County), on file in the office of the Clerk of the Court, Montgomery County, Christiansburg, Virginia.

[6] Typescript minutes of Fincastle County, 1773–75, Virginia State Library. These minutes show that William Russell, another surveyor of Kentucky lands, 1774–75, was appointed deputy surveyor of Fincastle County, August 2, 1774.

[7] Record of Plotts A (Fincastle County) *passim*. The volume is in the office of the Clerk of the Court, Montgomery County, Christiansburg, Virginia.

[8] *The Journal of Nicholas Cresswell, 1774–77*, pp. 67-77.

Scott County, of the present day, a small group under Benjamin Ashby began the Ohio Company southeasterly survey line on McConnells Run and ran the line S 70 E along the East fork of McConnells Run. By the middle of July they reached a point due north of Georgetown of the present day and arrived at an old John Floyd military survey corner, north of the Elkhorn near the center of present day Scott County. From there the lines were run into Fayette County of the present day. Other groups, of whom no record has yet been found, must have completed the survey. Seemingly this survey was never filed in Fincastle County or in later Kentucky County, nor in the land office of colonial Virginia at Williamsburg. And no copy of the survey is known to have survived. It is impossible to be exact about its size and location. But legal and historical research by Kentuckians in the first half of this century has revealed abundant evidence of the actuality of the survey and of its location in the very heart of the famous blue grass region. Surviving documents [9] show that from the old Floyd corner north of the Elkhorn, on the western ridge of Lanes Run, Benjamin Ashby seems to have run the line, mainly S 70 E, south of Newton, Scott County, to a point in Fayette County about seven miles south of Centerville. From this point the line appears to have been run to the neighborhoods of Jimtown, Fayette County; Muir, Fayette County; Avon, Fayette County; Winchester, Clark County; Grass Lick, Montgomery County; Sharpsburg, Bath County; Moorefield, Nicholas County; Myers, Nicholas County; Headquarters, Nicholas County; Lair, Harrison County; Lees Lick, Harrison County; Rogers Gap, Scott County; and probably seven miles west of Rogers Gap and then South 20 W. to join, on the waters of McConnell Run, the beginning of the Benjamin Ashby line. A continuous line connecting the above points shows that the survey enclosed virtually

[9] Notably, the later depositions of Hancock Lee and of Benjamin Ashby. The former is in the "Land Trials" book of the Fayette County, Kentucky, Circuit Court, pp. 121-22 and the latter, enclosing a John Floyd letter of July 17, 1775 is found, *loc. cit.*, in the Complete Records Book B, pp. 339-40. Both can be found in print.

all of Bourbon County, about one half of Nicholas County, and one fourth of Clark County, but only small strips of Scott, Fayette, Montgomery, Bath, and Harrison counties. A recent local historical marker wrongly claims the survey included 800,000 acres; it is very certain that it included only about 400,000 acres. No eighteenth century evidence indicates any intent on the part of the Ohio Company to survey 800,000 acres. It is possible that the Ohio Company remembered its old petition for 500,000 acres. It was also customary at that time to extend surveys unduly and there is the possibility that the Ohio Company anticipated the necessity of recognizing within their survey the claims of several adventurers who had established, in 1774 and 1775, rights to later preemption claims.

Seemingly the aim of the Ohio Company surveyors, apart from that of avoidance of earlier surveys for others, was to take in entirely the fertile upper valley of the South Fork of Licking River and its tributaries. This could have been done, and probably was done greatly short of 800,000 acres, particularly if some of the infertile upper valley of Hinkstons Creek were omitted. The Virginia surveyors were excellent judges of land. They knew limestone lands. They knew trees and weeds. The height of a regional weed served as a guide. The surveyors may be said to have limited the lines to the rich limestone blue grass region of central Kentucky and changed directions whenever they reached its end and the beginning of poorer land. In general the lines followed the ridge of the drainage basin of the South Fork of Licking River. Only in avoiding the military surveys of 1774 and early 1775 by John Floyd on the Elkhorn and the large Gist surveys on Hinkstons Creek, was there serious departure from lines along the marginal limestone.

As indicated above, much scattered evidence reveals that the Ohio Company was not without competition for this rich, officially unentered, wilderness Eden. Earlier, or contemporaneously, a few bold individuals, commonly designated as adventurers, established holdings along the branches of the South Fork of Licking River, branches which are named for such individuals as George Michael

Approximate shape and location of a survey for the Ohio Company of Virginia, made in the year 1775 and containing about 400,000 acres, as laid down from deed and survey references by W. T. Smith, of the Lexington, Kentucky, Bar, June 15, 1951.

Stoner, Joseph Houston, John Hinkston, John Townsend, and John Cooper. Some of these later secured title by improvement or preemption rights.

Before Hancock Lee and his assistants had completed the survey for the Ohio Company, the American Revolutionary War and Indian hostility had begun to cast dark shadows upon Kentucky. But the ominous situation did not deter Hancock Lee and his assistants from locating, entering upon, and surveying in 1775, for themselves and their relatives, thousands of acres each in Kentucky, many of the surveys along or abutting the earlier Ohio Company survey lines. Duly entered upon the entry and survey books of Fincastle County, these surveys later became valid and descended in many cases to the claimant's heirs.

That from this extensive and expensive Kentucky project, nothing of profit accrued to the Ohio Company, can be explained. Their effort was circumvented by politics and law. Viewed from the standpoint of ethics and justice it should have been otherwise. No other Virginians were more entitled to a share in the frontier in Kentucky than the gentlemen of the Ohio Company.

A letter of George Mason to Robert Carter, March 12, 1776, is very specific in regard to the activities of the Company surveyors in early Kentucky.[10] This very important letter stated, "Capt. Hancock Lee and one Leet are returned, from surveying the Ohio Companys 200,000 acres of land . . . They have got it all in one tract, upon a large creek called Licking Creek, which falls into the Ohio river on the southeast side, about 150 miles below the Scioto river. . . ."[11] The letter refers to a notable Ohio Company operation. Its definitiveness is marred only by the lack of a more specific location of the land surveyed. The history of the operation is damaged by the lack of a copy of the survey, the failure to get a patent, and the quick elimination of the claim.

Almost contemporary with the employment of William Craw-

[10] The first permanent settlements in Kentucky were made at Harrodsburg in 1774, not at Boonesboro, which dates from 1775.

[11] Rowland, *op. cit.*, I, 214-15.

ford and Hancock Lee as surveyors for the Ohio Company in Kentucky, George Mason presented a memorial to the Virginia government stating that he had purchased "a considerable Number of Importation Rights founded on the Charter granted by King Charles the second, whereby he conceived himself to be entitled to fifty Acres of Land for each Right. . . ." [12]

Documentary evidences of any other than Kentucky activities, 1774–1775, by the Company are few and far between. One important document of the year 1774 is a letter of George Mercer to Robert Carter, August 6, 1774,[13] in which he defended not only his own actions, but the claim of the Grand Ohio Company as found in their printed *Case,* agreeing with the claim therein, that the earlier Ohio Company lands were ceded by Indian and imperial sanction to others at Fort Stanwix in 1768, included in the Walpole Grant, and accepted by the royal Treasury in 1770.

The minutes of a meeting of several grantees of lands from the Six Nations to the Suffering Traders as reported by William Trent, September 22, 1775, containing extracts of the meeting of the Grand Ohio Company of September 27, 1769,[14] is a document of only indirect connection with the Ohio Company of Virginia, though the two groups had conflicting claims. Equally indirect in relation is an account, January 19, 1776, by Thomas Richardson

---

[12] Executive Journal, Council of Colonial Virginia, photostat from P.R.O. C.O. 5: 1440, in Virginia State Library. There is a record of these purchases in the official records of Fairfax County, Virginia, at the Fairfax County Courthouse. From 1780 until his death in 1792, George Mason was deeply engaged in this private transaction which involved locations, entries, surveys, caveats, and patents relating to more than 60,000 acres in Kentucky. His oldest son, heir to the Kentucky claims, was similarly involved during his later years. Voluminous materials are found in the Virginia State Library, Department of Archives, and in Kentucky, particularly in the Land Office at Frankfurt. The records of a dozen or more county courthouses should be consulted.

[13] MS., N.Y.P.L. Printed in part in Bailey, *Ohio Company . . .* , pp. 262-63.

[14] Etting Collection, Ohio Company Papers, H.S.P., printed in Bailey, *Ohio Company Papers,* pp. 288-301.

of bales of goods remaining among the possessions of the Vandalia Company.[15]

Much more direct was a bill from Thomas Walpole, February 6, 1776, to George Mercer for the assessment on him of £22 . . 19 . . 6 for his proportion of the expense incurred in connection with the Vandalia purchase.[16] At the same time, on March 12, 1776, George Mason was presenting a bill to Robert Carter for his share of the £600 expense of the Ohio Company of Virginia in its Kentucky surveys of 200,000 acres and offering to buy the shares of Carter if he wished to sell, an indication that Mason had not abandoned all hopes of eventual profit, even at that late date.[17] That there were debts due the Ohio Company at this date is indicated by a letter of William Franklin to William Trent, March 14, 1776,[18] in which the writer complained that he could not realize on the Philadelphia property of George Croghan, because of a Judgment against it in favor of the Ohio Company. "If what he (Croghan) writes is true, that Judgment is for a Debt you owe to the Ohio Company, and which he has nothing to do with."

The sole greatly important document of the Ohio Company of 1777 is an account of the Grand Ohio Company with George Mercer in favor of S. Wharton and the Grand Ohio Company, 1776-July 17, 1777 for £74 . . 11 . . 3, mainly a matter of expenses for improvements on the Ohio tract.[19] There exists a petition to the House of Delegates of Virginia to take into consideration the grants of land to the Ohio Company, Walker's Company, etc., and warrants granted to soldiers.[20]

Throughout his last years, George Mason maintained his interest and activity in the Ohio Company of Virginia. In 1778 and

---

15 *Ibid.*, p. 285.

16 D.M.L. MS., printed in *George Mercer Papers*, p. 325. This action, almost a year after the outbreak of the War of the Revolution, was primarily a matter of financial honor, but somewhat in the nature of salvage.

17 See Rowland, *op. cit.*, I, 215, and Bailey, *Ohio Company . . .* , pp. 275-77.

18 MS., a.l.s. American Philosophical Society.

19 D.M.L. MS., printed in *George Mercer Papers*, p. 326.

20 Miscellaneous Petitions, Folder 140, p. 541, Virginia State Library.

1799, along with his historically famous campaign for the assertion and maintenance of Virginia's rights, whether against alien land companies or against Congressional assumptions, he carried on in the House of Burgesses a great effort to secure what he considered the just rights of the Ohio Company. On January 8, 1778, he presented a bill "for establishing a land office and for ascertaining the terms and manner of granting waste and unappropriated lands" [21] which was deferred January 17, 1778.[22] On January 14, 1778 he presented a bill "for adjusting and settling titles of claimers to unpatented lands, under the former government" [23] which was deferred January 21, 1778.[24] In the autumn session the land bill was again entered [25] and deferred until the following year. The matter came up again in May 1799 and the bills much modified were enacted into law in late June 1799.[26]

In connection with such activity Mason wrote a short letter to James Mercer, February 6, 1778,[27] in which he mentioned a bill on land measures which he had introduced in the Virginia Assembly and which he expected to be passed, remarking "it is encumbent upon the members of the Ohio Company to take preparatory steps for making good their title and obtaining a patent for the 200,000 acres actually surveyed, in Kentucky, which is all I have any hope of. . . ." A meeting of the Company was also suggested. In the *Virginia Gazette*, April 24 and May 1, 1778, he advertised a meeting of the Ohio Company for Monday, May 18, 1778. While no minutes of this meeting have been found, it presumably dealt with at least three matters, the status of George Mercer in London and his act of affiliation with the Grand Ohio Company; the Kentucky surveys and prospects; and, a new memorial to be presented

[21] *Journal of the House of Delegates of Virginia*, p. 105.

[22] *Ibid.*, p. 119.

[23] *Ibid.*, p. 115.

[24] *Ibid.*, p. 124.

[25] *Ibid.*, p. 11.

[26] *Ibid.*, pp. 34, 37, and Hening, *op. cit.*, X, 35-50, 50-65.

[27] Printed in full, Rowland, *op. cit.*, I, 291-92, and in part, Bailey, *Ohio Company* . . . , p. 273. In the Harvard University Library is a fragment of a letter of George Mason to George Mercer, October 2, 1778, in which the data are similar to that in the earlier letter.

to the General Assembly of Virginia. In connection with the first of the three matters mentioned, Mason wrote George Mercer, October 2, 1778.[28] In connection with the second matter Mason wrote Mercer, "We have had 200,000 acres of land laid off, marked and bounded in one survey for the Ohio Company." [29] In connection with the third matter there was drawn up and presented to the General Assembly of Virginia by George Mason, November 20, 1778, a comprehensive and weighty memorial of the Ohio Company.[30] According to Bailey,[31] this memorial was never acted upon by the Assembly of Virginia. But its historical value is indubitable. Probably drawn up, written, and submitted by George Mason, it is an excellent condensed history of the Ohio Company. In chronological perspective it touches upon the formation of the Ohio Company "in or about the year 1748"; the purposes of its founders; the petition to the Crown; the royal instructions of March 16, 1748/9; and the terms of the grant. The mistakes in the personnel listed in the first petition are indicated, and reference made to the entry of the grant in the Virginia Council Books, July 12, 1749. The activities of the Company in building storehouse and ordering cargoes of goods are correctly stated. The first and second explorations of Christopher Gist are mentioned. Reference is made to the Articles of Agreement of 1751, and to the construction of a road "over the Alleghany mountains" and the construction of a warehouse near the mouth of Red Stone Creek within two years. Here in this memorial is found a flat statement that Christopher Gist was duly commissioned a surveyor for the Company and

[28] Printed in Niles, *Principles and Acts of the Revolution*, from an incomplete copy, then in the Mason family. Another copy is in the Lee Papers, Harvard University Library. It is also in Rowland, *op. cit.*, I, 297-301, and in the *Virginia Historical Register*, II, 28.

[29] *Ibid.*

[30] Miscellaneous Petitions, Folder 266 A, Virginia State Library. Printed in Bailey, *Ohio Company . . .*, pp. 320-27. On its presentation, see *Journal of the House of Delegates . . .*, 1778, p. 74. George Mason was personally aware of the facts, but in 1778, he was probably in possession of all of the books and business papers of the Company. It is regretted that it has seemed unwise to reprint, with a score of annotations, this long document.

[31] Bailey, *Ohio Company . . .*, p. 273.

made surveys in 1753 around Red Stone Creek and at the Forks of the Ohio. The work on the fort at the latter place and its capture by the French, with the loss of property involved is stated. The claim is made that colonial troops did great damage to Ohio Company buildings and property along Wills Creek without compensation or redress to the Company. One sentence, that "the Nature of the Trade your Memorialists were engaged in was such that they were obliged to give large Credits to the Indian.—Traders, most of whom were killed, captivated, or ruined in the Course of the war, and the Debts due to your Memorialists thereby lost" is most interesting but greatly inadequate as to detail.

The ruinous effect of the war of 1754–1763 and of the Proclamation of 1763 upon the activities and expectations of the Company is pointed out; as also the loss of the territory above Mason and Dixon's Line to Pennsylvania and of lands lower down the Ohio to veterans under the Dinwiddie Proclamation of February 19, 1754. Reference is then made to the petition of 1772 to the Governor and Council, and to the action of George Mercer in merging with the Walpole group.

The Memorial asserts (without validity) the recognition of the old rights of the Ohio Company by the Virginia Council, July 27, 1772. It mentions a commission to William Crawford as surveyor in 1773 and another to Hancock Lee in 1774. Finally the memorial reaches the survey in 1775 of 200,000 acres in Kentucky, and the interruption of the project by renewed warfare.

Most valuably, the Memorial sets forth the holders of Ohio Company shares in 1778 and asks that the Virginia and Maryland members may receive individual grants of proportionate shares of the Kentucky lands surveyed for them. An exact plot of the lands indicated was said to be ready.

The approval of the petition is endorsed by Richard Lee,[32]

---

[32] Richard Lee's endorsement, dated April 25, 1778, indicates that the petition was, in accordance with the idea of George Mason in his letter of February 6, 1778, to James Mercer, drawn up at an informal meeting at Gunston Hall, April 25, 1778. It was probably presented, ratified, and signed at or before the formal meeting of the Ohio Company, May 18, 1778.

James Mercer, Pearson Chapman, Richard Henry Lee (administrator of the estate of Philip Ludwell Lee), and James Scott. Seven of the fourteen Virginia and Maryland shares are not represented in these approvals, but there is little doubt that all of them agreed and would have accepted such individual grants. The failure of the Virginia Assembly to recognize the essential justice of the petition and make the grants, apart from the dreadful exigencies of war, was somewhat deplorable.

A letter of George Mason to Richard Henry Lee, June 19, 1779, is full of general historical significance. Seven lines say, "The Indiana Company's title after two or three days debate and every effort within and without doors, to support it, is rejected; and an act [33] passed in the most explicit terms, firmly asserting the Commonwealth's exclusive right of pre-emption from the Indians, within our own territory, declaring that all deeds or cessions heretofore made to the Crown shall inure to the use and benefit of the Commonwealth, and that all deeds which have been or shall be made by Indians, for the separate use or benefit of any person or persons whatever, are void and of no effect." This provision was a deadly blow not only to George Croghan, William Trent, and others with expectations from the Indian cession of Fort Stanwix of 1768, but also to Richard Henderson and others in Kentucky. Mason's land office bill was not, he said, yet acted upon by the Senate.

According to Mason, the shareholders of the Ohio Company were not permitted a special investigation of their claim and were obliged to submit to the description in a "general bill," though efforts were made by its enemies to exclude them by "particular words." He thought, "the only chance now left is to get their claim referred to the Court of Appeals," in which he still had "hopes of succeeding." [34]

The Memorial of 1778 and the letter of George Mason to Richard Henry Lee of June 19, 1779, throw light on some Ken-

---

[33] Hening, *op. cit.*, X, 35-71, under May, 1779.

[34] MS., a.l.s., in Lee Papers, a.l.s., in University of Virginia Library; George Mason Papers, L.C. Printed in Rowland, *op. cit.*, I, 333-50.

tucky transactions of the following decade. In the former, mention was made of a demand for proportional individual grants in Kentucky for the Virginia and Maryland shareholders in the old Ohio Company. One fortieth of 200,000 acres would have provided 10,000 acres for each holder of a two-fortieths share. The possibility of 10,000 acres in Kentucky was highly intriguing in 1778–1779. But in the letter of June 19, 1779, George Mason, in addition to his reference to the old Ohio Company claim, mentions his "charter rights." This may be held to refer to his Importation Rights, mentioned above, which he had presented in 1774. His statement, "My charter rights I believe will be established, and my location preserved to me, upon resurveying the same lands," if it applies to Kentucky lands, is an implication that Hancock Lee and others may have surveyed in 1775 not only 200,000 acres for the Ohio Company but additional lands for George Mason. On the other hand the caveat [35] of George Mason against John May, entered April 17, 1787, states that the particular lands in litigation were located or entered upon in 1780 though not surveyed until 1783.

On June 22, 1779, George Mason tried to secure the passage of a Virginia act of the Assembly to validate the Ohio Company surveys,[36] but the result was negligible, for only county surveyors were sanctioned by law, and the Ohio Company surveyors lacked this sanction. Unpatented for four years, the Ohio Company survey of 400,000 acres in Kentucky could not be patented under the Virginia legislation of 1779. As unpatented land these rich acres were open to entries, warrants, and patents by others. Within five years they fell into the possession of others.

The Ohio Company lost one of its important members in this year on the death of John Tayloe of *Mount Airy*, whose will was filed, July 5, 1779.[37] A petition of William Trent to Congress, September 11, 1779 [38] in behalf of himself and his associates in

---

[35] Caveat Book, II, 23, Virginia State Library.

[36] Bailey, *Ohio Company* . . . , p. 279; Hening, *op. cit.*, X, 35-50, 50-65. See also the *Journal of the House of Delegates*. . . .

[37] Filed at the Richmond County Courthouse, Warsaw, Virginia.

[38] MS. H.S.P.

the Vandalia Company is of value here only as an illustration of the general difficulties of land speculators during the American Revolutionary War. Unfortunately, no records are known of a meeting of the Ohio Company late in 1779, which was advertised in the *Maryland Gazette*, November 11, 1779.[39]

Of Ohio Company activities east of the Blue Ridge mountains, extended research revealed no highly relevant documents of 1780, the year when tidewater Virginia was overrun by British invasion under Arnold and Phillips.

During this trying period, however, old Ohio Company activities along the Youghiogheny, 1752–1754, received retro-active attention. Virginia Commissioners, sent out to issue certificates to settlers believed to have valid claims to lands in Monongalia, Yohogania, and Ohio counties, were active in such works in 1780. They certified, February 4, 1780, that Thomas Gist was "entitled to four hundred Acres of Land in Yohogania County on Gist Run to include his Improvement made thereon in the Year of our Lord, 1773. Also a Right in Preemption to one thousand Acres Adjoining thereto." [40] As a result of later validation of such claims by Pennsylvania, the Ohio Company settlers at Gist's Place, 1752–1754, eventually secured several thousand acres in the Youghiogheny Valley.

In this same winter of 1779–1780, similar Virginia Commissioners, sent out to Kentucky, validated claims of many individuals to lands in Kentucky, some of them within the Ohio Company Survey of 1775. The Virginia land law of June 1779 and the adjudications of these land commissioners on the Monongahela and in Kentucky marked the end of further land expectations for the Ohio Company.

The old troubles of George Mason and the Ohio Company

---

[39] Bailey, *Ohio Company* . . . , p. 279. This advertisement could not be found. The paper was supposed to appear in an issue, November 12, 1779.

[40] The Land Office, Department of Internal Affairs, Harrisburg, Pennsylvania. By an earlier agreement, the Virginia certificate was accepted by Pennsylvania and the 400 acre tract resurveyed, October 19, 1785. See document printed in Appendix A, below, pp. 270-72.

about their landed tracts in Maryland, in the neighborhood of Wills Creek, became acute again in the summer of 1780. Dr. David Ross who had begun activities in 1761 left, at his death in 1778, a badly involved estate. His heirs and their assignees and lessees took action on July 25, 1780 against the tenants of lands long held by George Mason and the Ohio Company. The usual writ of ejectment [41] was sued out against James Guest (Gist) in occupation of *Pleasant Valley*, occupied earlier successively by John Fraser and Samuel Plumb. In accordance with the writ, which was served September 1, 1780, litigation began in the General Court of the Western Shore,[42] in the October term, 1780. Litigation, thus begun, carried over into the next decade. The docket books of the court, 1780–1797, contain not less than twenty-nine items, of which the second was in the May term and the third in the October term of 1781.

There are several documents of 1781 relating to the Ohio Company. In a letter, Robert Carter to a friend, April 14, 1781, he discusses the attitude of the Assembly toward the Ohio Company claims, which the House of Delegates had rejected on the ground that their surveys were not made by legally appointed surveyors.[43] But since the Assembly had approved some military claims, similarly surveyed, he hoped the claims of the Ohio Company would be revived and proposed to join the partners in a petition. Yet another letter, Robert Carter to George Mason, May 11, 1781,[44] dealt with Ohio Company affairs, and contained the same idea and suggestions. It is evident that eighteen years after his purchase of two shares and ten years after the nominal expiration of the Articles of Agreement, Robert Carter had not abandoned hope.

---

[41] Original Papers, Box R, 1793, Western Shore General Court, Maryland Hall of Records.

[42] Docket Book, Western Shore General Court, October Term, 1780, folio 45, printed in Appendix A, below, p. 272.

[43] Robert Carter Letter Books, IV, 55-61, No. 82, Duke University Library, printed in Rowland, *op. cit.*, II, 5. The letter was to John Sutton, a clergyman friend.

[44] Robert Carter Letter Books, IV, 75, printed in Appendix A, below, pp. 272-73. Mentioned in Rowland, *op. cit.*, II, 6.

This attitude of Robert Carter and George Mason in 1781 is one year later seen in the Last Will and Testament of James Scott where as an item he leaves his friend Colonel George Mason his agent to manage his "share of the Ohio Company to Pay the money of my part to be added to my personal estate," and twice uses the phrase "my Share of the money Goods or Debts in the Ohio Company"—but in a codicil distinguished this item from his "Share of the land as a member of that Company" and devised the latter to his three sons and to two grandsons as tenants in common, share and share alike.[45] It is highly interesting that long after potential reality of expected land grants had closed, the reverend gentleman had not abandoned his claims, now of thirty-three years antiquity.

The old expectations of the Ohio Company, in regard to a 200,000 acre grant, did not expire abruptly and easily. In a letter of October 19, 1782, George Mason thanked Edmund Randolph and the other gentlemen of a congressional committee "for stating the title of Virginia to her western territory" and, possibly at the request of the committee, added a long exposition of Virginia's claim to the western territory. In this matter he touched upon early Virginia council entries of grants in the west, the royal instructions of 1749, the proclamation of Dinwiddie of February 19, 1754, and the patents granted thereunder, and settlements beyond the mountains. He made particular mention of the district of West Augusta and the Virginia counties of Ohio, Monongalia, and Yohogania on the upper waters of the Ohio, and of the county of Kentucky and its later subdivisions. The Virginia capture of Kaskaskia and Vincennes was not overlooked. He mentioned the Indian deed to Virginia of 1744, the instructions of Gooch of 1749. He derided the purchase at Fort Stanwix of lands already sold earlier, and the claims of the Indiana Company. One important sentence states, "The English and American maps have uniformly laid down Virginia across the continent, to the westward, until the Treaty of Paris in 1762, and since to the river Missis-

[45] Prince William County, Virginia, Will Book G, folios 180-83, printed in Appendix A, below, p. 273.

sippi." According to Mason, the Virginia Constitution of June 1776 "plainly described and declared the extent of our western territory," and this claim was guaranteed by the Articles of Confederation, any violation of which "dissolves the federal compact." Congressional claim on the territory claimed by Virginia was denounced in the name of state rights. Even a charter to Virginia by Charles the Second in 1667 was used as an argument by Mason, who on the strength of it declared the Proclamation of 1763 "was absolutely illegal and void."

XII

The End: Land Disposal and Land Litigation

FOR A DECADE after 1782, the relevant materials about the Ohio Company revolve around the official actions of George Mason as treasurer of the Company, engaged as such mainly in winding up its accounts and affairs. His activities were much concerned with land titles and litigation about the Ohio Company lands along the Potomac, and with his own personal holdings in central Kentucky.

Since there is much indefiniteness and uncertainty about the Kentucky lands of the Ohio Company and of George Mason as a private citizen, attention may well be given to matters in Kentucky before it is turned to the well-documented matters of the Ohio Company lands on the Potomac. That the Ohio Company survey in Kentucky was considered invalid, probably by reason of the surveyors not being county surveyors, and that the lands of the survey were looked upon as unpatented and open to new entries upon warrants, is borne out by the fact that entries, surveys, warrants, and patents to part or parts of the territory surveyed by the Ohio Company in 1775, began about 1780 and continued for a decade or more. No evidence has yet been located that the Company contested in litigation or in political activity this steady evaporation of their extraordinarily valuable surveyed territory in Kentucky. George Mason, Richard Lee, Robert Carter, and others seemed to have properly interpreted the situation, though they may not have fully realized that they were losing, in the heart of the blue grass region of Kentucky, 200,000 acres of the fairest region of the earth, later to be worth many millions of dollars.

Private individuals stepped in the Ohio Company tracks and secured vast estates, which enriched their descendants for many generations.[1] The fate of the Ohio Company Kentucky lands was disastrous, but George Mason himself, using in part importation rights, obtained 65,000 acres of land in widely scattered large holdings in Kentucky,[2] in the last decade of his life. His oldest son, George Mason of Lexington, not only inherited these lands but added to them before his death.

In matters concerning lands along the Potomac, George Mason was heavily engaged in Ohio Company affairs and was obtaining substantial results. In May 1781, he leased a part of the resurvey of *Walnut Bottom* for ten years, and in 1782 was involved in a law suit about it in the Washington County, Maryland, Court.[3] Thomas Cresap, living at Old Town near the Ohio Company's Maryland tracts probably knew of George Mason's activities and expectations. He doubtless knew much about the dispute about *Pleasant Valley* and about the unpatented acres in the old resur-

---

[1] Particularly valuable in this matter are the records of the Virginia Commissioners of 1779–80, who validated settlement and preemption claims to many thousands of acres of land, some of it within the old Ohio Company survey of 1775. These records are printed in the Kentucky State Historical Society *Register*, XXI.

[2] As suggested in an earlier footnote, there is a vast amount of material on all this in central governmental archives at Richmond, Virginia and at Frankfort, Kentucky.

[3] *Ibid.*, Judgment Records, No. I, folios 34-41. Entered, March 15, 1783, in the General Court of the Western Shore of Maryland; the suit was there struck off, according to the Docket Book, May Term, 1783, folio 69, printed in Appendix A, below, p. 273. Here the Ohio Company lost a claim based on the unpatented resurvey of *Walnut Bottom*.

vey of *Walnut Bottom.* He may have known of the writ of November 11, 1782, for the resurvey of *White Oak Level* and *Pleasant Valley*. Whatever his information, or lack of it, on April 19, 1783, he made out a notable deed to his share or claim in all Ohio Company lands, assets, etc. to his son Daniel and grandsons, children of Michael Cresap.[4]

It was in connection with the resurvey of April 28, 1783, that depositions of Thomas Cresap, Jarvis Haugham, Daniel Cresap, James Prather, James Gist, and Elizabeth Guest were taken in April 1783.[5] The Ross suit came before the court term, May 1783.

Doubtless with a view to later resale, George Mason, May 2, 1783, for £50 Maryland money, secured from Daniel Cresap and his wife Ruth an indenture or deed [6] to *Limestone Rock*, 63 acres of land, along the Potomac. This tract had been patented to Daniel Cresap August 10, 1753. Six months later, October 24, 1783, Mason made a lease [7] to Thomas Beall of Washington County, Maryland, on consideration of five shillings, for, first, a tract of land called *Walnut Bottom* of 500 acres, patented in 1745 and surveyed for Mason, March 25, 1756; and, second, to *Limestone Rock*, the tract of 63 acres obtained May 2, 1783 from Daniel Cresap and his wife. On the following day he deeded [8] the land included in the above lease to Thomas Beall for £1,407 .. 10s, Maryland money "in Specie." [9] Two years after the first sale, George Mason, in consideration of five shillings hand money, made, July 13, 1785, a lease Indenture [10] to James Maccubbin

[4] Washington County, Maryland, Land Record, Liber C, folios 5-6, printed in Appendix A, below, pp. 275-78.

[5] Original Papers, Box R, 1793, a.l.s., Evan Gwynne Sheriff Western Shore General Court, Maryland Hall of Records. Copies are found in the Maryland Court of Appeals Judgments Liber T. H. No. 16 (1815), folios 153-56, 156-57, 157-58. These depositions are sources of valuable information about the Ohio Company as well as about the region near Wills Creek.

[6] Washington County Deeds, Book C, folios 480-82.

[7] *Ibid.*, folios 513-16.

[8] *Ibid.*, folios 516-21, calendared below, p. 344.

[9] This may be the language of the deed, but George Mason accepted two double indemnity bonds, which later were the subject of extended litigation.

[10] Washington County, Maryland, Deeds, Book D, folios 353-56.

Lingan of Montgomery County, Maryland, for a tract of land on the Potomac of 240 acres, called *Hunt the Hare,* which had been patented to Mason, June 25, 1763; and for a similar consideration a lease indenture for the *New Store* tract. On the following day, in consideration of the payment to him in specie of £480 Maryland money [11] he deeded *Hunt the Hare* to James Maccubbin Lingan, and on the same day, July 14, 1785, deeded [12] to Lingan on payment in specie of £2,166 Maryland money, the famous *New Store Tract,* opposite the mouth of Wills Creek, containing 1,083 acres. In contrast with the above data, no record of the disposal of *Welshman's Conquest* by George Mason was found, though it was resurveyed for Samuel Ridout, December 5, 1798. Ridout, on friendly terms with both the Ross family and the Mason family, may have bought from the latter who had valid title to it.

Meanwhile the litigation about *Pleasant Valley* continued. Four depositions [13] of February 28, 1786 respectively, of Daniel Cresap, John Nicholas, Elizabeth Gist, and James Gist, are certainly related to the suit and probably to another resurvey or amendment of earlier surveys. The information in such depositions gives facts not found elsewhere. Both in May and in October 1786, the suit was docketed. And the dockets of the suit for May and October 1787 constitute the only relevant Ohio Company documentation of the year.

On May 1, 1788, Mason wrote to John Francis Mercer about Ross's suit against him for Ohio Company lands.[14] He was also

---

[11] Washington County, Maryland, Deeds, Book D, folios 356-58. No evidence of bonds and of failure to pay the amount indicated was found anywhere.

[12] D.M.L. MS., Ohio Company Papers. No evidence of failure to pay this in specie has been found anywhere.

[13] Original Papers, Box R, 1793, Western Shore General Court, Maryland Hall of Records.

[14] Rowland, *op. cit.,* II, 212. "Ross's suit" was the old suit of David Ross, and others later, against George Mason, 1781, which ran on until 1797. The items are found mainly in the Docket Books of the General Court of the Western Shore. They are calendared in Appendix D, below, pp. 342-48. A few samples are printed below in Appendix A, pp. 272 and 290-93.

at this time concerned about "the Ohio Company's title to a tract of land adjoining Fort Cumberland, called the *Treasury of Walnut Bottom* fraudulently granted by Governor Eden to one French, a creature of his." If the letter is accurately published, Mason confused the *Resurvey of Walnut Bottom* with *Treasury of Walnut Bottom* and since the resurvey was never patented, wrongly accused Governor Eden and Thomas French, the latter of whom in 1773–1774 merely secured good title to unpatented lands. However unethical, their acts were not legally fraudulent.

The Ross suit, which so troubled Mason in his last years, came before the court in both May and October terms of 1788, 1789, and 1790. The litigation resulted in 1790 in another warrant [15] for another resurvey of the land in dispute; and, in 1791, in four depositions,[16] and a resurvey.[17] The lawyers of the litigants endeavoured in May 1791 to reach some agreement in a statement of the case.[18] But the suit dragged on from the May term to the October term of the court.

In 1791, the very last twelve months of the life of George Mason, the Board of Property of Pennsylvania, in dismissing a caveat, upheld old titles of Richard Gist, Thomas Gist, and Nathaniel Gist to 2,800 acres of land, formerly part of the Ohio Company's settlement at or near Gist's Place of 1753.[19] On November 5, 1792, a month after Mason's death, these titles were again validated.[20]

Contrary to long established opinion, the interests of the Ohio Company did not cease with the death of George Mason, October 4, 1792. He may have desired to wind up its affairs before his death but did not do so. They ran on indeed for another thirty years, coming to an end no earlier than October 1821. The two

---

[15] Original Papers, Box R, 1793, Western Shore General Court, Maryland Hall of Records.

[16] *Ibid.*, printed in Appendix A, below, p. 279.

[17] Resurvey Plot No. 2, Maryland Hall of Records.

[18] Original Papers, Box R, 1793, Western Shore General Court, Maryland Hall of Records.

[19] *Pa. Arch.*, third series, I, 757-58.

[20] *Ibid.*, II, 51.

double indemnity bonds of October 27, 1783 were not paid off in accordance with their terms. On both bonds it was necessary to sue not only Thomas Beall but his three co-signers William Deakins Junior, James Maccubbin Lingan, and Brooke Beall. Two warrants against each of them, eight in all, were issued in the General Court of the Western Shore of Maryland, June 4, 1791.[21] Eight separate declarations, each with a copy of the bond at issue, were made June 15, 1791.[22] One of the bonds for £1408 had fallen due November 1, 1784. The bond is endorsed with an item payment of £91 . . 18 . . 8, June 20, 1789, in payment of interest. The other bond for £1407, which became due May 1, 1786, contains no such indorsement. In the October Term of 1791, eight suits were docketed [23] severally against Thomas Beall and his three co-signers to the two bonds. These suits, and also the old Ross suit of 1780, came up again in the May Term of 1792.[24] Probably owing to the death of George Mason, the bond suits were not brought up on the October Term of 1792. But the Ross suit against George Mason came up both in the October Term of 1792 and in the May Court of 1793, where it was discontinued and so recorded.[25] And the executors of George Mason of *Gunston Hall* continued in 1793 action in the eight suits against the signers of the two bonds.[26] Eight Sci Fa writs were issued, January 7, 1793,

[21] Original Papers, Box R, 1793, Western Shore General Court, Maryland Hall of Records. One warrant is printed in Appendix A, below, p. 280, and the others are calendared in Appendix D, below, pp. 345-49.

[22] *Ibid.* One warrant is printed in Appendix A, below, pp. 280-82, and the others calendared in Appendix D, below, pp. 345-49.

[23] Docket Books, October Term, 1791, folios 212-13, Western Shore General Court, Maryland Hall of Records.

[24] The Docket Book, October Term, 1791, folio 46, shows that in the Ross suit judgment was secured for "Possession and Costs," but with a continuation nevertheless.

[25] See the Docket Book, May Term, 1793, folio 59 #1, and, also, Judgment Record, J. G. No. 21, folio 217.

[26] Original Papers, Box C, May Term, 1793, Western Shore General Court, Maryland Hall of Records. No. 74 is printed in Appendix A, below, pp. 283-85, and the others calendared in Appendix D, below, pp. 346-47.

and the eight suits came before the May Court, 1793. The suits were renewed to May 1794.

Brought up again in October Term, 1794, they were renewed to May Term, 1795, at which, brought up again, they were renewed to October 1795, at which time, brought forward again, they were renewed to October 1797.

In the meantime, the old Ross suit, which had resulted in a resurvey in 1791, was, seemingly, renewed in a new narrative in ejectment, March 10, 1795, prosecuted in May, 1795, October 1795, May 1796, October 1796, and, after yet another resurvey [27] in April 1797, finally abated in May 1797.

The eight bond suits, begun in October 1791, and buttressed September 7, 1797, by another set of eight Sci Fa writs,[28] came before the Court in the October Term, 1797, and were again continued. To the writs of Sci Fa, the attorneys of Thomas Beall, James Maccubbin Lingan, and William Deakins Junior entered disclaimers [29] alleging no recordation in the case of Deakins and previous satisfaction of the bonds in the cases of Beall and Lingan. But by the October Term 1798, the two suits against Thomas Beall and Brooke Beall on each of the two bonds were not docketed and only the four suits against William Deakins Junior and James Maccubbin Lingan were prosecuted. But in the May Term of 1799, the four suits were now against Thomas Beall and James M. Lingan, but they were continued to the October Term 1799, where they appeared again in the docket books, but with no notice of renewment, and probably with judgment and costs against the defendants.[30]

The old Ross case against George Mason and the Ohio Company received a new turn on August 14, 1799, with the deed of the Ross estate to William Stewart for the purpose of paying the

[27] Original Papers, Box R, 1797, Western Shore General Court, Maryland Hall of Records.

[28] *Ibid.* One sample document is printed in Appendix A, below, p. 283, and the others calendared in Appendix D, below, p. 347.

[29] *Ibid.*, Box C, October, 1798 and Box C, May, 1779.

[30] Some of the highly relevant docket items are printed below, pp. 278-86, and the others are calendared in Appendix D, pp. 347-49.

old debts of the family.[31] Eight months later a new ejectment writ [32] was issued to get the tenant off the *Pleasant Valley* tract occupied for a whole generation by the Ohio Company. The suit was prosecuted in the May and October Terms, 1800–1805. Transferred to the Allegany County Court,[33] it came up in October, 1805, April 1806, and October 1806, when a judgment was rendered in favor of the defendant, but exceptions were made in court and transference to the Court of Appeals resulted.

Meantime, by the order of the Chancery Court of Maryland, on June 28, 1803, the heirs of George Mason of *Lexington,* eldest son and heir of George Mason of *Gunston Hall,* in keeping with Last Will and Testaments of both testators, received £471 . . 5 . . 11 for the *Cove,*[34] the old Ohio Company tract patented June 25, 1763. This transaction has the appearance at least of a belated Ohio Company share inheritance.

Somewhat similarly, heirs of George Mason, who were continuously involved in litigation with William Stewart and his heirs from 1800 to 1815, managed, nevertheless, to secure, September 3, 1805, a patent [35] to *Pleasant Valley,* possession of which had been in dispute for more than forty years. Referred to the Court of Appeals, the suit, at the end of ten years, was returned in 1815 to the Allegany County Court, where this tract remained in dispute from 1815 to 1821. It ran on in Allegany County Court, October 1815-October 1816. But a verdict in favor of Ross was followed by an ejectment writ on the part of William Mason. At last, after an Allegany County Court order of October 9, 1820, the Mason heirs agreed to sell the tract for $951.00, to William

---

[31] Deed Book, Liber J. R. M. No. 7, folios 264-66, Prince Georges County, Maryland.

[32] Copy in Maryland Court of Appeals Judgments, Liber T. H. No. 16 (1815), folios 39-40.

[33] April, 1805. See the Allegany County, Maryland, Docket Book under that date, and also the original papers of the court, October Term, 1816.

[34] Deed Book C, folio 668, Allegany County, Maryland. It is printed in Appendix A, below, pp. 287-89.

[35] Patents, J. C. No. 2, folios 248-49, Maryland Land Office, Hall of Records, Annapolis.

Lamar, possessor of a rival Ross title, and gave a deed to the property according to the court order. This deed of April 14, 1821, appears to have been the last act of hereditary disposal of lands held under Ohio Company title and therefore to mark a terminus in the affairs of the famous company.

It was early claimed by members of the Ohio Company, and often asserted afterwards, that the Company expended £10,000 in its activities and enterprises, with the implication that this sum, and more still in connection with the Kentucky survey of 1775, was lost by the shareholders. That there was no such dead loss of about £11,000, is amply proved by surviving documents, some of them herein published. If surviving records are taken at their face value, the Ohio Company invested £6,000 in three cargoes of goods imported from Great Britain. As indicated above, the first two cargoes were sold at a price above original cost, of one and a half times. Theoretically the sales of the first two cargoes brought in a profit of £6,000, not deducting expenses of purchase, importation, of handling sales. The goods of the third cargo were not all sold, but part of them were taken over by military authority, 1753–1755, and later paid for. Naturally, some of the credit accounts were risky even where promissory notes and bonds were taken. But payment of accounts of the Company by debtors such as Aaron Price, Barney Curran, William Trent, Robert Dinwiddie, George Croghan, Thomas Caton, James Martin, Richard Pearis, and others cannot be overlooked. It is doubtful therefore that the Ohio Company lost any considerable sum of money in its trading activities. They may have bought and paid with good money 1747–1754, and received depreciated currency in payment in later years, but that is another matter, affecting the whole society of the time.

Of the approximately £11,000 invested, only about £5,000 could have been spent on lawyers' fees, surveys, explorations, roads, storehouses, personal services, lands, etc. Any analysis of the land transactions of George Mason for the Ohio Company reveals a favorable financial situation greatly similar to that of trade transactions. For the *New Store Tract* in Virginia, £2,166 was received. For *Walnut Bottom* (500 acres) and *Limestone Rock* (63 acres),

£1407 .. 10 .. 0 was taken in. For *Hunt the Hare* (240 acres) Mason secured £480. For the *Cove* (510 acres) the descendants of George Mason secured £471 .. 5 .. 11. For *Pleasant Valley* (300 acres) these descendants got $951, possibly the equivalent of about £200. The total of these sales thus amounted to £4,724 .. 16 .. 11. But the account is incomplete by reason of the lack of records of the disposal of *Welshman's Conquest* (260 acres) which, if sold at a price comparable to that of *Walnut Bottom* and *Limestone Rock*, must have produced more than £275 and thus resulted in total of £5,000 or more received from land sales. If fluctuations in the value of currencies and sundry unrecorded expenses are left out of consideration, the gentlemen of the Ohio Company, not necessarily as individuals but as a group, suffered no actual financial losses from their land investments. The distribution of the funds received from trade sales and land disposals is another matter, not revealed by documents which have survived. George Mason in 1792 had not only a small cash balance but bonds as security for the sale of 1783 to Thomas Beall and titles to *Welshman's Conquest, the Cove* and *Pleasant Valley*. Since he had probably largely paid for the Kentucky survey of 1775, and his estate probably paid off the Bladen bond, these claims when added to his share may have justified him and his heirs in their receipt of all surviving assets.

Thus with the data now available, one can no longer accept the old idea of the great financial losses of the Ohio Company. The losses were in fact not real but losses of possible speculative profit, losses of expectations not fulfilled though not beyond the bounds of reason.

In several senses the Ohio Company was not a failure. In one respect it was a notable success. Its place in history is beyond cavil. Its story is important in the history of Virginia, Maryland, Pennsylvania, and of what is now West Virginia, Kentucky, and Ohio. It is an essential part of the larger history of Anglo-French rivalry and struggle in North America. It fits into the picture and pageantry set forth by Francis Parkman. The Ohio Company was highly important politically, not only at Williamsburg, Annapolis, and

Philadelphia, but also at Quebec in New France, as well as at London and Paris in the Old World.

The gentlemen of the Ohio Company in the devotion of time and money to exploration, trade, and settlement, won an imperishable place in American and modern world history.

Appendix A

SELECTED DOCUMENTS FROM THE A. P. JAMES COLLECTION

Collated Transcripts of Manuscripts Relating to the Ohio Company of Virginia

More than one thousand documents, faithful collated transcripts of original manuscripts, are gathered into slipcases in the Darlington Memorial Library. Only a selection of them is printed here.

TABLE OF TYPES OF DOCUMENTS

Accounts, Expense
Accounts, Mercantile
Advertisement of Meetings of the Ohio Company
Advertisement of Proposed Land Sales
Articles of Agreement
Bills of Sale
Bonds, Commercial
Bonds for Land Purchases
Certificates of Land Surveys
Certificates of Survey Warrants
Commission of Court
Contemporary Comment
Declaration of Law Suits
Deeds of Real Estate
Deed of Shares in the Ohio Company
Depositions
Docket Books, Maryland
Docket Papers
Gift or Bequest of Shares in the Ohio Company
Journals
Judgment Records, Maryland
Jury Lists
Land Grants
Land Lease Indentures
Land Patents
Land Surveys
Laws
List of Mercantile Goods
Letters
Maps and Map Notations
Memoranda
Memorials
Minutes of the Board of Trade and Plantations and of the Privy Council including Reports
Minutes of the Ohio Company
Newspaper Items
Notations or Attestations of Lawyers
Order Books, Virginia
Petitions of the Ohio Company and Others for Land, etc.
Petitions for Warrants, Commercial
Power of Attorney
Proclamations
Promissory Notes
Purchase and Sale of Shares in the Ohio Company
Resolutions of the Ohio Company or of the Committee of the Ohio Company
Resolutions of Governmental Authorities
Resurveys of Lands
Suits, Mercantile and Land
Statement of Cases
Surveys of Land

Treaties, Indian
Warrants, Commercial
Warrants for Surveys and Resurveys and Renewals thereof
Wills and Testaments, Last
Writs of Attachment
Writs of Ejectment
Writs of Scire Facias

Warrant to Thomas Bladen for 3,000 Acres of Land

(Maryland Land Office, Warrants, Liber L. G. No. d, folio 397.)*

[April 16, 1745]

Lay out for his Excellency Thomas Bladen Esq.r three thousand acres of land.[1] in any part of this Province, not formerly surveyed for nor cultivated by any person, or lands leased or reserved for his Lordship's use, and return Your certificate of the survey thereof unto his Lordships Land office, with all convenient speed, with the name of the place, and of what manor to be held; and for your so doing this shall be your warrant. Given under his Lordships lesser seal at arms this sixteenth of April Anno Domini 1745. To Capt.n Thomas Cresap, Surveyor of Prince Georges county.

* Copies, folios 32, 105, 140, 144, 209. Printed in *Report of Cases. . .*, III, 519.

1. Three tracts of land, *Walnut Bottom,* 500 acres, *Hunt the Hare,* 240 acres, and *Pleasant Valley,* 300 acres, surveyed on this warrant, were assigned to and patented by George Mason for the Ohio Company.

Survey Calendar

(Maryland Land Office, Book RR No. 34, folio 152.)

[June 1, 1745]

500 / 1..0..0 / Walnut Bottom [1] Surveyed for Thomas Bladen Esq.r the 1st June 1745 beginning at 2 bound White Oaks Pat.d 25 March 1756[2] to George Mason Poss.s 500. 1. 0. 0. George Mason.

1. This document is published here because *Walnut Bottom* was later assigned to George Mason and became an important part of the lands of the Ohio Company on Wills Creek, Maryland. It was the site of later Cumberland, Maryland.
2. Printed, below, under that date.

Walnut Bottom Survey. Identification Notations.

(Maryland Land Office, Original Surveys, Prince Georges County, No. 2241.)

......2.2.4.1......
PRINCE GEORGE'S COUNTY.

.........Walnutt . Bottom.........
....
Acres...500.........................

SURVEYED FOR
.........Thomas..Bladen.........
.........1st...June.1745.........
Returned ....
Ex'd and Passed.12th..Aug.1746.....
Comp. $...Pd.17th..March.1756...
PATENTED TO
.........George..Mason.........
......25th...March.1756.........
Rec. of Cert.BC&GS.No5.folio.170..
Rec. of Patent....................
....

Original Survey of Walnut Bottom Tract

(Maryland Land Office, Original Surveys, Prince Georges County, No. 2241.)

Prince Geo County Ss [3]

[June 1, 1745]

By Virtue of a Warrant [4] Granted out of his Lordships Land Office of this Province unto his Excell Thomas Bladen Esq for Three Thousand Ac of Land, bearing date the 16. day of April Anno Domini 1745
I therefore Certifye as Deputy Survey of Prince Georges County, under his said Excell I have carefully laid out for & in the Name of him the said Thomas Bladen Esqr all that Tract of Land lying in the said County called the Walnutt Bottom beginning at Two bounded White Oak Trees standing on a Clift of Rocks at the Lower End of a bottom near half a Mile below the Mouth of Wills Creek near the River Side & running thence South Thirty Deg East Seventy Four Per,[5] then North Fifty Seven Deg East Twenty Eight Per, then North Twenty Seven Deg East Twenty Per, *then North Forty Deg East Eighty Per* then South Eighty Four Deg East Twenty Per, then North Forty Nine Deg East Twenty Six Per, then North Fifteen Deg East Sixteen Per then North Seven Deg West Fifty Four Per, then North Thirty Five Deg East Twenty Per, then North Twenty Eight Per, then North Fifty Four Deg West Thirty Six Per, then North Eight Deg West Fourteen Per, then North Sixty Two Deg West Twenty Eight Per then North Twenty Seven Deg East Thirty Per, then North Eight Deg West Twenty Per, then North Thirty Eight Deg West Forty Per, then West Fifty Two Per, then North Eighty Five Deg West Forty Five Per, then North Sixteen Deg West Twenty Six Per, then North Three Deg West Sixteen Per, then North Fourteen Deg West Sixteen Per, then North Forty Seven Deg West Twenty Per, then North Seventy Three Deg West One Hundred & Thirty Four Per, then South Thirty Seven Deg West Twenty Per then South Fifty One Deg East Ninety Six Per, then South Thirty Six Deg West Thirty Six Per, then South Seventy Eight Deg West Forty Per, then South Thirty Deg West Forty Four Per, then

South Sixteen Deg West Fifty Four Per, then South Forty One Deg East Fourteen Per, then South Sixty Five Deg East Twenty Two Per, then South Six Deg East Seventy Eight Per, then South Eighty Three Deg East Forty Two Per, then North Eighty Two Deg East Twenty Per, then North Sixty Nine Deg East Twenty Per, then North Fifty Deg East Sixty Eight Per, then South Sixty Four Deg East Forty Per, then by a strait line to ye beginning Trees,[6] Containing & now laid out for Five Hundred Ac of Land to be held of Culverton or Conegocheeg Mannor, Surveyed this 1st day of June Anno Domini 1745

p Me Thos Cresap Dty Surv^{r}
of prince georges County

N	C	D	P	N	C	D	P	N	C	D	P	N	C	D	P
1	S	30 E	74	10	N	..	28	19	N	16 W	26	28	S	30 W	44
2	N	57 E	28	11	N	54 W	36	20	N	3 W	16	29	S	16 W	54
3	N	27 E	20	12	N	8 W	14	21	N	14 W	16	30	S	41 E	14
4	N	40 E	80 S	13	N	62 W	28	22	N	47 W	20	31	S	65 E	22
5	S	84 E	20	14	N	27 E	30	23	N	73 W	134	32	S	6 E	78
6	N	49 E	26	15	N	58 W	20	24	S	37 W	20	33	S	83 E	42
7	N	15 E	16	16	N	38 W	40	25	S	51 E	96	34	N	82 E	20
8	N	7 W	54	17	..	.. W	52	26	S	36 W	36	35	N	69 E	20
9	N	35 E	20	18	N	85 W	45	27	S	78 W	40	36	N	50 E	68
												37	S	64 E	40

then by a strait line to ye big Trees
by a Scale of 100 Equal parts in an inch

P G Cty ss Ent.^{d}
The Platt & Certificate of the
Walnutt Bottom 500 Ac
Thos Bladens Esqr: Land

[*Endorsed:*]
for the Office mem.^{o} to charge
fees to Bayne
Smallwood [7] of Charles
County ——————

Novr 1, 1745
The Platt & Certificate
disagree in the Direction of
the 4th Course Disallowed
Ex^{d} B Young [8] Exam.^{r}
Corrected ye 4th Course
12th August 1746 3.^{sds} & Ass.^{t}
Examined and passed
J. Ross [9] Exam^{r}

Pat. 25 March 1756 to George Mason Rent ℘ anno
£ 1: 0: 0 Sterling ————
Ch.d to the Rent Roll

Recorded in Lib BC & GS N° 5 folio 170 [10] .... I hereby assign [11] & make over to George Mason [& the Ohio Company] * all Mr Bladens right & Title to the within mentioned Land & Premises for the consideration of Twenty Pounds as Witness my Hand & Seal this 11 September 1753

Benj Tasker Jun [12]

Wittness John Campbell [13] Attorney in fact for Tho: Bladen,

I have received the sum of Ten pounds fifteen shillings for ten years & three Quarters of a Years Rent to Lady Day next Patent may therefore issue with his Excellencys Approbation

Edw Lloyd [14]

17 March 1756

Hor..° Sharpe [15]

* [These words were crossed out in the document.]

3. The common abbreviation for scilicet.
4. Printed, above, p. 188.
5. An abbreviation for "perches."
6. This survey will be recognized as typical, by those familiar with surveys in the eastern states of the Union.
7. A delegate for Charles County in the Maryland Assembly, 1738 following. His son, William Smallwood was a Major General in the Revolutionary Army and Governor of Maryland, 1785–1788.
8. Benjamin Young, Examiner General 1738, Judge of Admiralty Court, 1742, Surveyor General of Eastern Shore of Maryland, 1745.
9. John Ross, Examiner General and Deputy Receiver of Quit Rents, 1743–1760. See the deposition of Joseph Tomlinson, August 13, 1761, calendared below.
10. The reproduction of this extant record copy would be superfluous.
11. This assignment is the particular justification for publishing the entire materials relevant to the transaction.
12. Born 1720, died 1760. Of a distinguished family. His father, of the same name, outlived him. His signature on this and other assignments is autograph as may be the assignment, though in dissimilar penmanship.
13. Probably John Campbell, who lived near Annapolis. The name, appearing in six counties, was a common one.
14. Seemingly an official in the land office, without other personal distinction, though of a family of importance for several generations.
15. *D. A. B.*

Title Page of Survey of Pleasant Valley [1]

(Maryland Land Office, Original Surveys, Allegany County, No. 2087.)

2087
ALLEGANY COUNTY.
"Pleasant Valley"
Acres 300
SURVEYED FOR
Thomas Bladen
1st June 1745
Returned 1st June 1861 [2]
Ex'd and Passed 14th June 1863
Comp. $ ______ Pd. ______
PATENTED TO
William Thompson et al [3]
3rd Sept 1805
Rec.[4] of Cert. I.C. No 2 folio 1805
Rec. of Patent don't find

* Two copies are located in the Allegany County, Maryland, Judgments, F and J-K; and another two in the Maryland Court of Appeals Judgments, Liber T H., No. 16 (1815).

1. This tract was claimed by George Mason and the Ohio Company and was involved in dispute and litigation from 1761 to 1821. As many as six later copies, no two of them *literatim* alike, can be found at Annapolis and Cumberland.
2. This failure to return the certificate for sixteen years was one cause of trouble.
3. The patent of September 3, 1805, below, p. 289, shows that it was made out to William Mason, Thompson Mason, and John Mason, surviving executors of George Mason of Lexington.
4. The record of the certificate, though available, is omitted herein.

Survey of Pleasant Valley

(Maryland Land Office, Original Surveys, Allegany County, No. 2087.)

[June 1, 1745]

Prince Georges County ss

By Virtue of a Warrant Granted out of his Lordships Land Office of this Province unto his Excellency Thomas Bladen Esqr for Three Thousand Acres of Land, bearing Date the 16th day of April, Anno Domini 1745.[5] I therefore Certifye as Deputy Surveyor of Prince Georges County under his said Excellency, I have carefully laid out for and in the Name of him the said Thomas Bladen Esq, all that Tract of Land lying in the said County, called the Pleasant Valley, beginning at Two bounded White Oak Trees standing near the River Bank about a Mile below the Mouth of Everts Creek, a Branch of Potowmac & running thence North Nine Deg West Seventy Two

Per, then North Twenty Six Deg West Thirty Four Per, then North Twenty Four Deg West Sixty Six Per, then North Fory Nine Deg West Twenty Per, then North Sixty Deg West Eighty Per, then North Five Deg West Forty Two Per, then North Fifty Eight Deg East Twelve Per, then North Twenty Six Deg East Seventy Per, then North Twelve Deg East Twenty Two Per, then North Eight Deg West Forty Six Per, then North One Deg East Fourteen Per, then North Twenty Six Deg East Forty Two Per, then North Six Deg East Forty Per, then North Thirty Deg East Fifty Per, then North Thirty Two Per, then North Twenty Four Deg East Sixteen Per, then North One Deg West Eighteen Per, then North Fifty Deg East Twenty Four Per, then North Thirty Nine Deg East Twenty Six Per, then North Fifty Eight Deg East Fifty Eight Per, then South Forty Nine Deg East Twenty Four Per, then South Seventy Nine Deg East Twenty Two Per, then North Seventy Seven Deg East Thirty Two Per, then South Nineteen Deg East Twenty Two Per, then South Seventy Five Deg West Thirty Eight Per, then South Forty Five Deg West Eighteen Per, then South Seventy Three Deg West Twenty Eight Per, then South Four Deg East Twenty Four Per, then South Forty One Deg West Sixty Four Per, then South Five Deg East Twenty Two Per, then South Thirteen Deg West Thirty Four Per, then South One Deg East Twelve Per, then South Twenty Eight Deg West Twenty Six Per, then South Forty Eight Deg West Forty Per, then South Five Deg East Thirty Four Per, then South Fifty Seven Deg East Twenty Four Per, then South Six Deg East Thirty Per, then South Twenty One Deg West Forty Two Per, then South Ten Deg East Fifty Two Per, then South Forty Four Per, then South Sixteen Deg East One Hundred Per, then South Forty Six Deg East Thirty Two Per, then South Twenty Five Deg East Sixty Per, then South Seven Deg West Forty Per, then by a strait line to the beginning Trees, Containing and now laid out for Three Hundred Acres of Land, to be held of Culverton or Conegocheeg Mannor, Surveyd this First Day of June Anno Domini 1745

p[r] me Tho:[s] Cresap Dty Surv[r]
of prince georges County

N	C	D		P	N	C	D		P	N	C	D		P	N	C	D		P
1	N	9	W	72	12	N	26	E	42	23	N	77	E	32	34	S	48	W	40
2	N	26	W	34	13	N	6	E	40	24	S	19	E	22	35	S	5	E	34
3	N	24	W	66	14	N	30	E	50	25	S	75	W	38	36	S	57	E	24
4	N	49	W	20	15	N	..	..	32	26	S	45	W	18	37	S	6	E	30
5	N	60	W	80	16	N	24	E	16	27	S	73	W	28	38	S	21	W	42
6	N	5	W	42	17	N	1	W	18	28	S	4	E	24	39	S	10	E	52
7	N	58	E	12	18	N	50	E	24	29	S	41	W	64	40	S	..	..	44
8	N	26	E	70	19	N	39	E	26	30	S	5	E	22	41	S	16	E	100
9	N	12	E	22	20	N	58	E	58	31	S	13	W	34	42	S	47	E	32
10	N	8	W	46	21	S	29	E	24	32	S	1	E	12	43	S	25	E	60
11	N	1	E	14	22	S	79	E	22	33	S	28	W	26	44	S	7	W	40

then by a strait line to the beg Trees
by a Scale of 100 Equal Parts in an Inch

[*Endorsed:*] Prince Geo County ss
The Platt & Certificate of
the Pleasant Valley
300 Acres

— — — — — —

for the Office
May 18.th 1761
The Certificate & Plat disagree in the Direction of the
20.th Course—Disallowed
U Scott Exr [6]
Corrected June 1st, 1761
June 14.th 1763
Examined & Passed
U Scott Exr
Caveated ℘ Doctr [Da]vid Ross 6 Sept 1763

I have recd [7] ten pounds sixteen shillings for Eighteen years Rent of the within Land to Midsum. 1763
14 June 1763 Edw Lloyd

I Hereby Assign [8] over all my right Title Interest Property Claim and demand Whatsoever of in and unto the within mentioned Certificate and the Land and Premisses therein contained unto a Certain Col.o George Mason of the Colony of Virginia and Desire patent may issue in his name for the same as Witness my hand this 14 June 1763

Benj:n Tasker
att.y in Fact for
Tho:s Bladen

Caveated [9] July 24. 1780 by David Ross son & Heir
at Law of D.t David Ross Deced.—
5¼ sd.s/

5. Above p. 188.
6. Upton Scott. Examiner of surveys, patents, etc. connected with the land office. He had succeeded John Ross in 1760 and was later Clerk of the Council.
7. Presumably from George Mason or his attorney, in behalf of the Ohio Company.
8. This assignment justifies the publication of the material.
9. Original caveat not found, but see the Writ of Ejectment of July 25, 1780, Maryland Hall of Records, W.S.G.C., Original Papers, Box R, 1793. Copies of the caveat are found in the Maryland Court of Appeals Judgments, Liber T.H. No. 16 (1815).

Thomas Lee to Conrad Weiser [1]

(H.S.P. Peters Papers, II, 89, a.l.s.)

Stratford [2] Feb^{ry} 13, 1747/48

Sir

I am very much obliged to you for your last letter in which you give me soe particular account of the Six Nations, whose conduct seems to me to be wise and honest, we have noe [allies] y^{t} will serve us on such easy terms. and without we will help our Selves it seems [un]reasonable to expect more from them. If the Warr continues, the govern^{t} at home will probably [pursue] their first design and it seems possible to drive the French out of North America, if the good disposition of the Indians be layd hold of in time.

I know you have lately conducted a treaty [3] at Philadelphia, if it is printed [4] I hope my fr^{ds} Messrs Strettels [5] will send it me. Our Gover^{t} [6] is extending our frontiers by large grants of land as far as Ohio, and I am concerned in one,[7] which when we begin to Settle I shall hope for your help to make it agreeable to the Indians the vine you were soe kind to send me I have sav^{d} ab^{t} 10 of the plants, which I will cultivate as fast as I can, and you shall be sure of an invitation to the first Vintage. I am glad you have not forgot the Indian Songs, which I long to see. I hope you have success in your good natured application for Poor Shikallemy. his son [Jack?] was kill ab.^{t} 2 years agoe, by a Catawba boy, who Observing Jack to lye behind a log, when he lifted his head to fire into the Cabbin, shot him dead with his pistole. I wish you health and prosperity with all my heart, being very truly,

Your affectionate & humble Servant
Thomas Lee [8]

I am glad
to hear y^{t}
Conosotogoe is well

1. Conrad Weiser, famous Indian interpreter. *D.A.B.* See Wallace, *Weiser,* p. 262.
2. Name of the famous Lee residence in Westmoreland County, Virginia.
3. *Pa. Col. Recs.,* V, 145-53.
4. Printed in 1748 in *Indian Treaties Printed by Benjamin Franklin,* pp. 101-7.
5. Amos and Robert, prominent merchants, the latter, councillor of the city of Philadelphia.
6. The government of Virginia.
7. The Ohio Company.
8. The eleventh of a series of letters by Lee to Weiser, all in H.S.P. Peters Papers, II, 19-89.

The Committee of the Ohio Company to Thomas Lee and Other Members of the Ohio Company

(N. Y. P. L. Emmet MSS. 14853, d. s.[1])

Cameron[2] Feb.ry 23d 1748/9

Sir

We the Committee of the Ohio Company met here have order'd the Hundred Pounds Sterling from each Member as A Stock for goods from London to be paid at or before the 15th of April next,[3] We therefore desire you'l send that Sum to M.r Nathl Chapman or order at or before that time who's to give Receipts for the Same to order of—Sir

Yr humble Servts

P:S: We have Appointed the 18th day of May Next for a General Meeting at Cameron where Business of Importance Relating the Comp:y will be Transacted & We desire Your Attendance Without fail[4]

Law.e Washington
James Scott
Nathl Chapman
John Carlyle

1. Handwriting of John Carlyle.
2. Residence, near the Potomac, of Nathaniel Chapman.
3. The order was delayed until June and the goods were not for sale until May 24, 1750.
4. See minutes of the meeting of June 21, 1749. D.M.L. MS., printed in *George Mercer Papers*, pp. 141-42, 168-70.

Thomas Lee to Members of the Ohio Company

(N. Y. P. L. Emmet MSS., 6214, a. l. s.)

[Williamsburg] Thursday June 1. 1749

Gent.m

as I am advised[1] by Mr Hanbury yt our Grant for 500,000 Acres is ready for the Kings Sign & will be sent in his next, I think it will be in our mutual intrest to put of [*sic*] our meetg untill the [third] Tues day, and [then to be at the Cou]rt, [where I] shall be too much [occupied for anything] further The Man of Warr & other ships are dayly expected & I hope to have the Grant before I return & settle what will be necessary to settle with the Gover.t here.

I am
Gent
Yr most hble Servt
Thomas Lee

1. Documentation of this advice was not found. The Hanbury letter was probably sent March 17, 1749.

Last Will and Testament[1] *of Thomas Lee. Disposal of Two Shares in the Ohio Company*

(Westmoreland County, Virginia, Deeds and Wills, II, folios 311-15. Excerpt from folio 314.)

[February 22, 1749/50]

. . . Item I give my share in the stock in trade and of the profit of the land to be granted by virtue of the Kings warrant to my second son,[2] he paying on every Division made by the Company an equal third part of the profitts of his share to my third son[3] and fourth son,[4] to each an equal part with himself, or this Gift to him to be void and he only to come in for one third to be paid him by the Comp. and an third to each of his two brothers aforesaid. Item whereas I have given to my eldest son[5] one share in the said Company both Trade and Land, which I paid for him in the stock in Trade, I hereby confirm my said Gift absolutely. . . .

Test

George Lee, Clerk

1. Probated July 30, 1751. Recorded August 2, 1751. This item throws light both on the expectations of the Ohio Company, 1750–51, and on the distribution of the two shares of Thomas Lee. It also indicates how his sons became members.
2. Thomas Ludwell Lee, 1730–1778.
3. Richard Henry Lee, 1732–1794. *D.A.B.*
4. Francis Lightfoot Lee, 1734–1797. *D.A.B.*
5. Philip Ludwell Lee, 1726–1775. The gift antedated June 21, 1749.

Account[1] *of James Ross*[2] *with George Mason and the Ohio Company*

(D. M. L. George Mason Papers.)

May 24, 1750-March 23, 1750/1

D.^R THE ESTATE OF MR JAMES ROSS TO GEORGE MASON AND THE OHIO COMPANY

1750			
May 24	To Sundrys sold himself Viz^t		
	1 half barrell of Gunpowder.......	£ 5.. 0.. 0	
	100 lb of Lead	2.. 6.. 0	£ 7.. 6.. 0
July 21	To Sundrys Viz^t		
	1 Gro mixt col.^d Garters	£ 1..10.. 0	
	2 Ps of Garlix	5..13.. 0	
	1 doz Buck hand knives	0..12.. 6	
	1 doz brass Penknives	0.. 9.. 8	
	1 doz Scissors	0.. 5.. 6	
	50 Ells of Oznabrigg...a 20.^d Ell..	4.. 3.. 4	£12..14.. 0

26 To Sundrys sold himself Viz[t]

1 Pce of Chintz	£ 2..10.. 0	
2 lb of Pepper ....a 3/3 lb..	0.. 6.. 6	
1 Match Coat	0..12.. 6	
1 Gunlock	0.. 5.. 6	
1/2 Pce of Garlix .....a 4/6pce..	1.. 3.. 0	
3 Looking Glasses ...... a 1/3..	0.. 3.. 9	
3 1/2 oz of thread	0.. 5.. 3	
1 Pce of white half thicks	4..10.. 0	£ 9..16.. 6

Mar 23 To Sundrys sold himself Viz[t]

1 Quire of paper	£ 0.. 1.. 4	
1/2 Pce of Callimancoe..a 75/pce..	1..17.. 6	
1 Pce of 7/8 Garlix	2..12.. 6	
1 Pce of Irish Linnen...........	3.. 2.. 4	£ 7..13.. 8
To Cash given him to buy Oats..........		£ 0.. 7.. 6
		£37..17.. 8

C.[R]

1750		
Mar 23	By Entertaining Mark Foy[3]	£ 0.. 2.. 0
	By 8 bushells of Oats	0..16.. 0
		£ 0..18.. 0
	Ball.[a] due to the Ohio Company..	£36..19.. 8
	Errors Excepted	£37..17.. 8

[*Endorsed:*]

James Ross's Acco[t]

Ball.[a] due £ 36..19..8

Maryland Fred. Cty ss

This day came Jarvis Haugham [4] before me one of his Lordships Justices of the Peace for the said County, who made Oath on the Holy Evangelists of Almighty God, that the within written Accompt is a true and just Copy taken from M.[r] Hugh Parkers Books [5] for the use of the Ohio Company, sworn this 8th day of July 1751 before me

Tho:[s] Cresap

We of the Jury [6] finde for the plentiv £-28:8:3: Damage Sam:[l] Boyd [7]

1. One of the two earliest trade transactions of which any record has been found. Handwriting probably that of a clerk, not identified, but possibly of S. S. Welder. The account is not merely a family account. If not a regional store owner, Ross must have been an Indian trader.
2. James Ross died in 1751.
3. Not further identified.
4. Copyist and Clerk of Thomas Cresap.

5. Not found. Probably burned in the fire which destroyed or damaged the George Mason papers. This "copy," attested July 8, 1751, postdates the death of Ross and of Hugh Parker.
6. Notation of February 7, 1759. See Ross item calendared below, p. 330.
7. Not further identified. He signed, probably, as a foreman.

Account[1] *of John Hammer*[2] *Against the Ohio Company*

(D. M. L. George Mason Papers.)

[July, 1750]

		£	S	D
July 1750	Dr Ohio Company by Hugh Parker	£	S	D
	To hauling two cannoe loads[3]	0.	5.	0
	To Hauling goods from [—?][4] to the Store[5]	0.	5.	0
	To making 20 Indian Shirts	[0	16.	0]*
	To making 3 Shirts & one pear trousers for the traders	0	3	0
	To hauling goods to unload the boat	0	5	0
	To helping a cart[6] load of goods with me and my horses one day towards Carolina[7]		5	0
	To work done in the store house making a dore cutting out a joice and making a post and a latter and sundre other things	0	10	0
	To haking up one treading horse	[0	5	0]*
	To four days a helping with [a boat]* the boat		12	0
	To two bushels of Corn	0	4	0
		3	14	8
Per John Hammer[8]		paper money		
		2	9	0
		2	17	9z
	V.m.° 6.ˢ 6¾[9]	m m e8		9z

[*Collector's mark*]
N A 980 B
[*Endorsed:*]
Ohio Comp
to } acct
Hammer

* [These figures and words were crossed out in the document.]
1. In the handwriting of Hammer, whose name is sometimes, but rarely, spelled as Hamer.
2. Not mentioned in Swem's *Index*. He may have been a Marylander, for he had lands in Maryland. But the documents are of Virginia provenance.
3. Probably at Wills Creek on the Potomac. See Minutes of February 6, 1753, printed in *George Mercer Papers*, pp. 144-47, 176.
4. Probably from the landing place.
5. Seemingly the New Store, opposite Wills Creek, and thus evidence that the first cargo reached Wills Creek in July, 1750.

6. Early use of a cart on the frontier.
7. Possibly *Carolina,* a tract of land in Frederick County, Maryland. But the trip may have been southward, up Pattersons Creek where settlement was already made.
8. He was also a purchaser of Ohio Company goods. See the petition and warrant of March 18, 1753, calendared below, pp. 316-17.
9. See the acceptance of the above account and the verdict of this account by the Court April 4, 1753, calendared below, p. 318. "V. m.°" means Virginia money.

Promissory Note[1] *of William Richey*[2] *to the Ohio Company*

(D. M. L. George Mason Papers.)

July 24, 1750

I PROMISE to pay to the Ohio Company or order the sum of Four pounds fifteen shillings Current Lawful Money of Maryland[3] on or Before the Twentieth Day of Novem.r next Ensuing as Witness my hand p.r Value Receved this Twenty Fourth Day of July in the year of our Lord 1750—

WITNESS

his
William Richey
mark

Tho:s Caton[4]
[*Collector's mark*]
NA 105 D
[*Endorsed on back:*]
WILLIAM RICHEYS NOTE
for £ 4..15..0
OHIO
Wm Richeys'
Note £ 4:00:0

1. Handwriting of Thomas Caton.
2. Bail for Caton in 1752. Probably moved later to the Monongahela Valley.
3. Most of these early accounts are in Maryland money, a matter partially explained by the fact that both Thomas Cresap and Hugh Parker were Marylanders.
4. Influential early settler in Frederick County, Virginia. His transactions with the Ohio Company and its litigation with him are indicated in many documents printed or calendared below.

Bond[1] *of Aaron Price*[2] *and Barney Curran to the Ohio Company*

(Frederick County, Maryland, Judgment Record H, folios 575-76.)

[September 14, 1750]

Exd ℘r Com

At the request of the Ohio Company the following Bond was Recorded October the fifteenth day in the Year of Our Lord Seventeen hundred and Fifty Four To wit Know all men by these presents that we Aaron Price &

Barny Currun both of Frederick County in the Province of Maryland Traders are held and firmly Bound unto the Ohio Company in the sum of Fifteen hundred and Eighty five Pounds Six Shillings Current Lawfull money of Maryland to be paid to the said Ohio Company their Certain Attorney Executors Administrators or Assigns to which payment well and Truly to be made and done We bind ourselves our Heirs Executors and Administrators and each of us our Heirs Executors and Administrators & each & every of them Jointly & severally firmly by these presents sealed with our seals Dated this Fourteenth Day of September in the year of our Lord one thousand seven hundred & fifty 1750 The Condition of this Obligation is such that if the Above Bounden Aaron Price & Barny Currun their Heirs Executors or Administrators or either of them their Heirs Executors or Administrators shall and do well & truly pay or cause to be paid unto ye above named Ohio Company their Certain Attorney Executors Administrators or Assigns the just & full sum of Seven hundred and Ninety Two Pounds Thirteen Shillings & two pence 1/2 Current Lawfull money afs^d on or before the first Day of May Next ensuing the date hereof without fraud covin or other delay then this Obligation to be Void or else to stand & remain in full Force & Virtue

Seal'd & deliver'd in the presents of — Aaron Price (seal)
James Dickson[3] John Trohock[4] — Barny Currun (seal)

on the back of which Bond was thus Indorsed Towit Received this 20.th August 1752 One Hundred Thirty three Pounds twelve Shillings and Eleven pence being the Ballance of their Accounts[5] then Settled.

1. The significance of this document is obvious. It, fortunately, happens to have been recorded and thus preserved. There may have been similar transactions, neither involved in litigation nor recorded. Add such transactions to those indicated by litigation and published or calendared herein, and one has definite data that the Ohio Company successfully disposed of its imported cargoes. The possibility that this was a surety bond for Hugh Parker is weakened if not invalidated both by the irregular sum and by the endorsement. This bond shows that the Ohio Company was active in Indian trade in 1750.
2. He signed as a witness of the Indian Deed of June 13, 1752. In his bill of sale, of March 1, 1751, he describes himself properly as "Trader." See below, p. 204.
3. Not identified.
4. Nephew and a devisee of Hugh Parker. His signature may indicate some connection of Hugh Parker with this transaction.
5. The complete lack in Frederick County, Maryland, of court files relating to the Ohio Company, similar to those found in Frederick County, Virginia, is a great historical loss. The use of the plural suggests mercantile actions. According to Gist's first *Journal* for December 26, 1750, Barney Curran was with him on Ohio Company trading business, on the Big Beaver and on the Muskingum. He probably exchanged the goods for furs and skins. He may have sold the skins to other traders. Certainly this circumstantial evidence indicates that some of the first cargo of the Ohio Company was taken to the Indian country.

Account[1] *of Abraham Johnson*[2] *with the Ohio Company*

(From photostat in Abraham Johnson Scrapbook, West Virginia University Collection. Original MS. in the possession of Mrs. J. H. A. Brown, Keyser, West Virginia.)

[October 5, November 27, 1750]

	Dr Abraham Johnson to the Ohio Company		Cr
1750			
Octr 5	To Sundrys sent P. Wm Johnson[3] Viz^t 1 Blankett £0.. 16.. 0 ½ yd of red Stroud a 12/6 yd 0..6..3	£ 1—2—3	Nov 6 by cash £0-5-8
Novr 6	To 1½ yd of half thicks a 3/6 yd	£ 0..5..3	Ball^a due to the Ohio Company
27	To 1 Match Coat	£ 0..12—6	
		£ 2..0..0	£1..14..4
			Errors Excepted
			£2..0..0

1. An ordinary family mercantile account. His descendants claim that Abraham, who settled on Pattersons Creek before 1742, was the proprietor of the New Store. This account disproves that. He may have worked at the store after the death of Hugh Parker in 1751. The scrapbook contains much random biographical data.
2. Prominent settler on Pattersons Creek. Later J. P. of Hampshire County.
3. Probably the son of Abraham Johnson, whose other son was named Okey.

Excerpts[1] *from the First Journal of Christopher Gist*

(*George Mercer Papers*, pp. 10, 13, 100, 103. *Case*..., Appendix, p. 3.)

[November 26, 1750] . . . to great Beaver Creek where I met one Barny Curran a Trader for the Ohio Company, and We continued together as far as Muskingum . . .

[December 4, 1750] Set out late S 45^d W about 4 m—here I killed three fine fat Deer so that tho' we were eleven in Company We had great plenty of Provisions.

[December 26, 1750) . . . then Barny Curran desired Leave to bury Her, which He, and his Men, and some of the Indians did just at Dark.

1. These items showing Christopher Gist traveling a month with Barney Curran, and with these two agents of the Ohio Company and their aides making a party of eleven, are significant as showing the Ohio Company trading in the Ohio Valley in late 1750. The bond of Aaron Price and Barney Curran of September 14, 1750, above, p. 200, and the Wafer bond of February, 1751, paid off September 25, 1767, below, p. 242, are obviously related to this trip.

Bill of Sale to Hugh Parker in behalf of the Ohio Company

(Frederick County, Maryland, Deeds B, folios 347-48.)*

[February 9, 1750/1]

Ex[d] ℘ Comm.[r]

At The Request of Hugh Parker the following Bill of Sale was recorded March the Nineteenth day Anno Dom seventeen hundred and fifty (Viz) Know all men by these presents that I Neal Ogullion [1] of Frederick County in the Province of Maryland Farmer for and in Consideration of the sum of One hundred & Eighty pounds Current money of the province aforesaid, to me in hand paid by Hugh Parker of the said County and province, Merch:[t] for and in the behalf of the Ohio Company the Receipt whereof I do hereby Acknowledge and myself therewith fully Satisfied Have Bargained, Sold & delivered and by these presents do bargain, Sell, and Deliver unto the said Hugh Parker for and in the behalf of the Company afores.[d] Three Red Cows, and one brown Cow, and two Brindled coloured Steers branded on the off horn H P also two Horses and three Mares branded under their Tails H P also Six Ewe Sheep with their Lambs, mark with an half Crop in the under side of the near Ear also thirty four swine Marked as the sheep before mentioned also four hundred Weight of Bacon as also all my right Title and Interest of in and to a Bond given under me by Col. Thomas Cresap in behalf of Daniel Dulany Esq.[r] [2] for the making over a certain Tract of Land unto me the said Neal Ogullion whereon I the said Neal now dwell, called sugar Bottom,[3] which said Bond is now in the Care and Custody of Doctor Charles Carroll [4] of the City of Annapolis as also Eleven Acres of Wheat and Rye sowed on the said Plantation, also a stock of Rye that stands in the sugar Bottom Field, one other Horse a Roan Branded on the near shoulder I on the near Buttock H and under the Tail H P To have and to hold the said Bargained Premises unto the said Hugh Parker in the behalf of the said Ohio Company his or their heirs, Executors, Administrators and Assigns, and to his & their proper use and Behoof for Ever, And I the said Neal Ogullion do promise the aforesaid Premises against me the said Neal Ogullion, my heirs, Executors and Administrators And against all and all manner of person or persons whatsoever to him the said Hugh Parker in Behalf of the Company aforesaid, his & their heirs Executors Administrators and Assigns to Warrant and forever defend by these presents. In Witness whereof I have hereunto set my hand and Seal this ninth day of February in the year of our Lord One thousand seven hundred and fifty, fifty one. 1750/51

Signed Sealed and Delivered
In the presence of
Jarvis Hougham [5]
Elizabeth Lamy [6]

the mark of
Neal Ogullion (Seal)

On the foot of which Bill of Sale was thus Indorsed

Frederick County ss. This day Neal Ogullion came before me and Acknowledged the above to be his hand and seal and the goods & stocks and Plantation [7] above mentioned to be the property of Hugh Parker for use above mentioned Exam.[d] /____________/ Thomas Prather [8]

* This and similar documents found by the author indicate the value of county records.

1. An illiterate small farmer whose name appears often in the records of Frederick County, Maryland. The markings of his livestock indicate that he was an associate if not, indeed, a dependent of Hugh Parker.
2. The Maryland lawyer of the Ohio Company. See *D.A.B.*
3. Probably *Sugar Bottom,* a tract of land based on Bladen surveys. Nine tracts so named are known in the Maryland Land Office.
4. See *D.A.B.*
5. Probably in his handwriting. Haugham, born in 1707, came to Maryland in 1744, settling at Old Town. He was living in 1783.
6. Not listed in Swem's *Index*. She was well known to Hugh Parker and Thomas Cresap.
7. No evidence was found that the purchase of the bond resulted in the transfer of the ownership of the plantation. The *Sugar Bottom Tract* in Allegany County, Maryland, was patented to Dr. David Ross in 1765.
8. Colonel Thomas Prather, of a well known local family and probably a justice of peace of Frederick County, Maryland. He lived near the Conococheague.

Bill of Sale to Hugh Parker in behalf of the Ohio Company

(Frederick County, Maryland, Deeds B, folio 343-44.)

[March 1, 1751.]

At The Request of Hugh Parker the following Bill of Sale was Recorded March the Nineteenth day Anno Dom seventeen hundred and fifty (VIZ) Know all men by these presents that I Aaron Price [1] of Frederick County in the Province of Maryland Trader for & in Consideration of the sum of Sixty pounds Curr.[t] mony of Maryland to me in hand paid by Hugh Parker for and in Behalf of the Ohio Company the receipt whereof I do hereby Acknowledge have Bargained and Sold and made over and by these presents do bargain sell and make over unto the said Hugh Parker for the use of the said Ohio Company their Heirs and Assigns Eighteen Months service of a servant Woman called Mary Maugride Four feather Beds and their furniture Twelve Chairs and a Table one large Iron pott one Middle sized pott one small Ditto one Large Brass Kittle one Tea Kittle a Coffee Mill one Box Iron & Heater one Dozen plates three Dishes three Basons Six Porringers one pewter pint one pewter Tankard two Wooden Bowls Six Trenchers three pails two Tubs three Barrels, onę spinning Wheel one Box one old Trunk one Churm one frying pan, One Brown Cow wth a Star Called Starry one red Cow with a White face Called Black Eyes, one small red Cow w:[th] a Star Called Conrod one small red & White Cow one Bull Stagg and three Calves Two plough Horses bright Bays with Stars a Plough and Tackling for two Horses one young rhoan Mare branded IC part of the Estate of my father in

Law James Couborn [2] Deceased, Twenty Hoggs Young and old all my Share of the Grain now in the Ground and what grain and flax & hay is in the Barn or elsewere belonging to me To Have and Hold the said Bargained Premises unto the said the said [*sic*] Hugh Parker his heirs & Assigns for the use and Behoof of the said Ohio Company their Heirs and Assigns and I the s[d] Aaron Price the said Bargained Premises to the said Hugh Parker his heirs & Assigns for the use and behoof of the said Ohio Company their Heirs and Assigns shall and will Warrant and forever defend Witness my hand & Seal this 1.st March 1750/1

Sealed and Delivered Aaron Price (Seal)
In presence of
James Dickson [3]
John Trohock [4] On the foot of which Bill of Sale was thus Written (Viz) Fred:[k] County ss../ Then Came Aaron Price before me one of his Lordships Justices for Fred: County & Acknowledged the written Bill of Sale [5] to be his Act and Deed March 16th 1750/1
Exam[d] ______________________/ Thomas Prather

1. A small trader of Frederick County, Maryland, who in 1752 secured a license to operate at the mouth of the Conococheague. See his bond September 14, 1750, above, p. 200.
2. Not identified. Possibly the resident of Talbot County, Maryland, whose estate was inventoried in 1748. But more probably James Coburn of Augusta County, who was living in 1747 and whose son Jonathan was a debtor of the Ohio Company.
3. Not identified. Probably a later resident of Virginia, a soldier in the Revolutionary War.
4. One of the three nephews, heirs, assignees, and devisees of Hugh Parker.
5. Since Price sold for £60 virtually as much as Ogullion, February 9, 1751, sold for £180, the conclusion must be that the earlier transaction involved either the bond and plantation of Ogullion or possibly overpayment and collusion.

Articles of Agreement and Copartnership for the Ohio Company for the Space of Twenty Years

(Typescript, transcribed, and collated from photostat in Darlington Library taken from photostat in the Virginia Historical Society at Richmond, Virginia.)*

[May 23, 1751]

THIS INDENTURE made the twenty third Day of May in the year of our Lord One thousand Seven hundred and fifty, one BETWEEN John Hanbury Esq:[r] of the City of London in the Kingdom of Great Brittain Merchant of the first Part, Arthur Dobbs of the Kingdom of Ireland Esquire of the second Part, Robert Dinwiddie of the said City of London Esquire of the third Part, Capel Hanbury of the said City of London Merchant of the fourth Part, Samuel Smith of the said City of London Merchant of the fifth Part, Richard Corbin of the County of Middlesex in the Colony and Dominion of Virginia Esq.[r] Gawin Corbin Philip Ludwell Lee and Thomas Ludwell Lee all of the County of Westmoreland Gent. Executors of the last Will and Testament of Thomas Lee late of the said County of Westmoreland Esquire deceased in trust for the said Thomas Ludwell Lee of the sixth Part, the said Philip Ludwell Lee of the seventh Part, John Tayloe of the County of Richmond in the said Colony Esquire of the eighth Part, Presley Thornton of the County of Northumberland in the said Colony Esquire of the ninth Part, the aforesaid Gawin Corbin of the tenth Part, Richard Lee of the County of Westmoreland aforesaid in the said Colony Esquire of the eleventh Part, Augustine Washington of the said County of Westmoreland in the said Colony Gent. of the twelfth Part, Lawrence Washington of the County of Fairfax in the said Colony Esquire of the thirteenth Part, Nathaniel Chapman of the said County of Fairfax in the said Colony Merchant of the fourteenth Part, James Scott of the County of Prince William in the said Colony Clerk of the fifteenth Part, George Mason of the aforesaid County of Fairfax in the said Colony Gent of the sixteenth Part, John Mercer of Marlborough in the County of Stafford in the said Colony Gent. of the seventeenth Part, James Wardrop of Prince George County in the Province of Maryland Merchant of the eighteenth Part, Jacob Giles of [the aforesaid] County in the said Province Gent. of the nineteenth Part, and Thomas Cresap of Frederick County in the said Province of the twentieth Part. WHEREAS the said several Parties to these Presents now are & for sometime past the greatest number of them have been concerned together in Company and Copartnership by the name of, THE OHIO COMPANY,[1] for the taking up and settling a Tract or Territory of Land of about Five Hundred Thousand Acres on the Branches of the Ohio and other Branches of the River MISSISSIPPI within the Colony and Dominion of Virginia aforesaid [2] and for the carrying on a Trade [3] with the INDIANS in those Parts with a joint and common Stock [4] for the joint and mutual Benefit and Advantage of the said several & respective Partners and their respective Heirs Executors Administrators and Assigns, And the said several Partners have respectively advanced and paid several Sums of money as and for their respective Parts and Shares of the said common and general Stock for the Purpose aforesaid and divers Goods Wares & Merchandizes have been purchased imported and Sold, and divers Sums of money have been expended and laid out for the Account of the said Company.[5] AND WHEREAS by the Death of the above named Thomas Lee [6] and of Hugh Parker [7] late of the aforesaid County of Frederick in the Province of Maryland aforesaid Merchant deceased (who was one of the said Company) and for divers other Reasons, it is necessary that the Accounts of the said Company should be made up settled and adjusted with all convenient Speed, more especially as the said Hugh Parker hath had the Custody & disposal of most of the said Goods Wares & Merchandizes imported on the said Company's Account [8] and that some certain Rules and methods should be agreed upon and established in the carrying on the said Company's Affairs for the time coming as the said Partners live so remote one from the other. NOW THIS INDENTURE WITNESSETH [9] that each and every of the said

Partners, Parties to these Presents, HATH, and by these Presents every of them DOTH for himself his Heirs Executors Administrators and Assigns covenant promise and agree to and with all and every other of the said Partners and in and with their & every of their respective Heirs Executors Administrators and Assigns, That each and every of them the said Partners His Heirs Executors Administrators and Assigns shall and will from time to time and at all times hereafter during the Continuance of the said Copartnership well and truly observe perform fulfill and keep all and singular the Covenants Articles Agreements Rules and Directions herein after mentioned and expressed, that is to say: IMPRIMIS That all and every the said Parties to these Presents shall & will be and continue Copartners and jointly concerned as a Company by the name of THE OHIO COMPANY for the taking up and settling the said Tract or Territory of Land and carrying on an Indian Trade for and during the term of TWENTY YEARS [10] from henceforth next ensuing and fully to be compleat and ended. And in Case of the death of any of the said Partners during the said Term the Heirs Executors Administrators or Assigns of such Partner or Partners so dying shall become a Partner or Partners in the said Company in the room and stead of such Partner or Partners so dying for the residue of the said Term. ITEM That the said Companies lands and common or general Stock shall be divided into forty equal Parts or Shares and every of the said Partners Parties to these Presents, his Heirs Executors Administrators and Assigns shall have and be entitled to TWO such Parts or Shares thereof, and every of the said Partners his Heirs Executors Administrators and Assigns shall from time to time contribute advance and pay to the Treasurer or Receiver of the said Company for the time being such and so many Sum & Sums of money as shall from time to time be found necessary for carrying on the said Company's Affairs: So as the whole Sum to be advanced & paid by each & every of the said Partners shall not exceed in the whole the Sum of Three Hundred Pounds Sterling (including what hath been already advanced) for every two Shares as aforesaid.[11] ITEM That all & every of the said Partners shall and will be just true & faithful to each other in all their Buyings Sellings Accounts Reckonings Disbursements & Dealings concerning the said Copartnership & shall every of them endeavour respectively by all just Care & Diligence to advance & promote the said joint Trade & Stock without Fraud or Deceit & give their Attendance upon the said Companies Affairs as often as shall be necessary or they shall be required so to do in such Parts & Places as the said Partners respectively live and reside. ITEM That every of the said Partners & his several & respective Heirs Executors Administrators and Assigns shall from henceforth have a several & separate Right & Interest in the Lands & Stock aforesaid and the Encrease, Rents and Profits thereof in just & equal Parts & Proportions to their several & respective Shares & Parts in the said Lands & common or general Stock. And that all Losses Adventures Costs Charges and Damages to happen or arise in or by the said Copartnership shall be from time to time allowed, reckoned sustained and born[e] out of the whole Stock and Encrease. ITEM That the major Part of the said Partners living and residing in the Colony & Dominion of Virginia & Province of Maryland shall yearly [12] on the first Monday in September meet at the Town of Alexandria in the County of Fairfax then & there to view inspect & examine the Accounts of the preceding year and finally to settle allow & sign the same: After which Allowance & signing the same by the majority of the said Partners then & there present the same shall be conclusive & binding upon the said Company; But any Partner or Partners keeping such Accounts so to be examined allowed [and signed] shall not be admitted to Vote concerning any Article of such Accounts which may be then & there [accepted] ITEM That the said major Part of the said Partners at every such party meeting shall have full Power & Authority to nominate & appoint agree with [such of the said Partners as they shall think proper to be Committee [13] which shall have power to act for the] said Company & to order & transact all matters & things which they shall judge proper & necessary for the carrying on the said Company's Affairs to their best Profit Benefit & Advantage for the year then next ensuing: Subject nevertheless to such Rules Orders & Directions as the said major Part of the said Company shall at such their yearly meetings agree upon & cause to be entered in a Book [14] to be kept from time to time for that purpose: which Rules Orders & Directions so agreed upon & entred shall be binding & conclusive on the said Company: Subject nevertheless to be altered or revoked by an subsequent Rules Orders & Directions to be made by the major Part of the said Partners living & residing in Virginia & Maryland as aforesaid at any of their general meetings. ITEM That the said major Part of the said Partners as aforesaid at every such yearly meeting shall also have full Power & Authority to nominate appoint & agree with such of the said Partners as they shall think proper to be Treasurer or Receiver of the said Company who is hereby authorized impowered & required to receive & pay away all such Sum & Sums of money tobacco or other Effects belonging to the said Company as the major Part of the said Company at their meetings or the Committee to be [by them] from time to time appointed shall order & direct: For all which Payments he shall be obliged to produce proper Receipts & Vouchers upon the passing his Accounts. And all Bonds Bills promissory notes Bills of Exchange & other Securities for the Payment of any money or other Effects belonging to the said Company shall be taken by such Treasurer or Receiver for the time being in his own name; FOR THE USE OF THE OHIO COMPANY and shall immediately upon his receiving the same be by him endorsed in blank,[15] that in Case of his Death they may be delivered over to such other Treasurer or Receiver as shall be appointed by the major Part of the said Partners as aforesaid, who shall also immediately upon receiving the same endorse the same in blank, that they may from time to time continue & remain to be the Property of the said Company & subject to their Direction and Orders. ITEM That the said major Part of the said Partners at [every such] yearly meeting shall also have full Power & Authority to nominate appoint and agree with such & so many Person or Persons as they shall judge proper for the keeping the said Companies Books selling or disposing of their Effects, livings warehouses or other stores, surveying or settling the said Company's Lands or buying or taking up any Lands, buying Horses Waggons & all other Necessaries directing any & other Sum or Sums of money to be advanced & paid by the several Partners into the joint & common Stock [16] and finally to agree upon any matter or thing whatsoever which they shall judge to be for the Benefit and Advantage of the said Company & especially the drawing up the Orders & Instructions for the Committee for the ensuing year. PROVIDED always that all Bonds Bills promissory notes Bills of Exchange other Securities for the Payment of any money or other Effects belonging to the said Company to be taken by any Factor or Factors or other Person or Persons to be employed by the said Company shall be taken in the name of the Treasurer or Receiver of the said Company for the time being; FOR THE USE OF THE OHIO COMPANY & be by the Person or Persons taking the same delivered as soon as conveniently may be to the said Treasurer or Receiver to be by him endorsed in blank as aforesaid.[17] ITEM That the several matters to be agreed upon by the said major Part of the said Partners at their yearly general meetings as aforesaid shall be determined by the majority of Votes and that any of the said Partners so meeting shall have and be entitled to one Vote for every fortieth Part or Share in the Lands and common Stock such Partner is entitled to but for no less part or Share than one fortieth Part. And where any Heirs Executors, Administrators or Assigns are or shall be entitled to any Share or Shares of the said Company's Lands & common Stock, they shall not have or be allowed any more than one Vote among them for every fortieth Part or Share thereof which they shall be entitled to: And if they shall differ in their Vote the Share shall be disallowed where the number is equal but if the major Part of such Heirs Executors Administrators or Assigns entitled to one or more fortieth Part or Parts of the said Company's Lands & common Stock do agree in their Vote or Votes the same shall be allowed according to the number of their fortieth Parts as aforesaid.[18] PROVIDED always that no Partner or Partners present at any such meeting shall be admitted to vote in any matter or thing which shall be disputed at any of the said meetings wherein the particular Interest of such a Partner or Partners is concerned, but in such Case the majority of the Votes of the other Partners present shall be conclusive and binding [except such as the] Partner or Partners so interested choose to refer the same to some subsequent meeting. ITEM In Case it should happen that the major Part of the said Partners living in Virginia & Maryland should not meet at the time & place appointed for such yearly meeting as aforesaid: It shall & may be lawful to and for such of the said Partners as shall then & there meet to proceed in the same manner as if such majority had met: PROVIDED no order or Agreement shall in such Case be made or enterd or have any force or Effect whatsoever except the same shall be made and agreed to by at least five of the said Partners who shall be entitled to ten fortieth Parts or Shares of the said Companys Lands & general Stock at the least: And if the said Partners so met cannot proceed or agree for want of a sufficient number present it shall & may be lawful for them to adjourn to such other time & place as aften as shall be requisite & until such major Part shall meet or at least five of the said Partners entitled as aforesaid can agree: And in the mean time the Committee then in being shall have full Power & Authority to act as they shall think proper & most for the Benefit & Advantage of the said Company. ITEM That the several Committees to be from time to time appointed in pursuance of these Presents or any three of them shall have full Power & Authority to meet at such times & places as they shall appoint them there to [consider] & agree upon such matters & things as they shall judge to be for the Benefit & Advantage of the said Company and to make such Orders & Agreements as they shall judge most conducive to that End. And shall cause all their Proceedings & Orders to be fairly enter'd in a proper Book or Books [19] to be kept for that purpose & to be signed by them: PROVIDED no other Agreement or other Proceeding of the said Committee shall be valid or binding except the same shall be made & agreed to by at least three [members. Item that the Committee] of the said Company for the time being upon any extraordinary Emergency which they shall judge requires the same the said Committee may & shall cause or Advertise as aforesaid in the Virginia Gazette requiring the Attendance of the several Partners living & residing in Virginia & Maryland at such time & place as they shall appoint in order to nominate & choose a new Treasurer or Receiver for the said Company or to provide against such Emergencies as shall require it: At which meetings so to be appointed the majority of the said Partners shall have the same Power & Authority and shall proceed in the same manner as is herein before mentioned & directed at their yearly general meetings. ITEM That it shall & may be lawful to & for the Treasurer or Receiver of the said Company for the time being when he shall think it necessary upon any particular Occasion to appoint a meeting either of the Committee or the majority of the said Partners in Virginia & Maryland at such time & place as he shall appoint for that purpose: [20] At all & every of which meetings the said Committee & majority of the said Partners shall have the like Power & Authority as at any other meeting appointed in pursuance of these Presents. ITEM That the several Committees from time to time shall have full Power & Authority to order & direct that each & every of the said Partners shall advance & pay unto the Treasurer or Receiver for the said Company for the time being any Sum or Sums not exceeding in the whole thirty pounds Sterling for every two fortieth Parts or Shares of the said Companies Lands & common Stock if to the said Committee it shall seem necessary for defraying any extraordinary Expence that may accrue before the general annual meeting of the majority of the said Partners before mentioned.[21] And if any of the said Partners his Heirs Executors Administrators or Assigns shall refuse or fail to pay within one month after notice unto the said Treasurer or Receiver for the time being such Sum or Sums of money as shall from time to time be directed to be advanced & paid into the said Companys common or general Stock which the Committee for the time being or the majority of the Partners at any of their general meetings as aforesaid according to the true Interest & meaning of these Presents: It shall & may be lawful for the said Treasurer or Receiver for the time being to borrow or advance upon Interest so much money as the Parts or Shares of such Partner or Partners his or their Heirs Executors Administrators or Assigns so refusing or failing to pay shall amount unto. And if such Partner or Partners his or their Heirs Executors Administrators or Assigns so refusing or failing to pay the same shall not at the next general meeting of the said Partners pay down their special & respective Parts & Shares of the money so advanced together with the lawful Interest thereof then & in such Case it shall & may be lawful to & for the said Partners at the said next or any other general meeting to assign & transfer the Part or Parts Share or Shares of such Partner or Partners his or their Heirs Executors Administrators or Assigns of & in the said Company's Lands and common Stock to any other of the said Partners who will advance & pay unto the said Treasurer or Receiver the Part & Proportion of such Partner or his Heirs Executors Administrators or Assigns so refusing or failing to pay the same together with the lawful interest thereof & will also agree to & pay unto such Partner his Heirs Executors Administrators or Assigns so refusing or failing so much more money as together with the Principal & Interest so paid to the said Treasurer or Receiver as aforesaid shall amount to the value of the said Companys Lands & common Stock belonging to such Partner his Executors Administrators or Assigns so refusing or failing as aforesaid, to be paid or secured to be paid within three Calendar months the next ensuing: And if none of the Partners belonging to the said Company will accept & take the Part or Parts Share or Shares of such of the said Partner or Partners his or their Heirs Executors Administrators or Assigns who shall so refuse or fail to pay their respective Parts of Shares of the said Company's common or general Stock as aforesaid upon the Terms herein before mentioned that then & in such Case it shall & may be lawful for the said major Part of the said Partners at their general meeting as aforesaid to take in any other Person or Persons who shall be willing to become a Partner or Partners of & in the said Company in the room & stead of such Partner or Partners his or their Heirs Executors Administrators or Assigns refusing or failing to pay his or their Share or Shares of the common stock as aforesaid, such new Partner or Partners first paying or securing to be paid UNTO the said Treasurer or Receiver of the said Company so much money with the lawful Interest thereof as the Partner or Partners his or their Heirs Executors Administrators or Assigns so refusing or failing to pay ought to have paid for his or their Part or Parts of the general or common Stock as as [*sic*] aforesaid & also paying or securing to be paid within three months then next ensuing unto such Partner or Partners his or their Heirs Executors Administrators or Assigns so much as the value of his or their Part or Parts Share or Shares of & in the said Company's Lands & general stock shall amount unto after discounting the [account] so much as shall have been paid to the Treasurer or Receiver of the said Company for Principal & Interest as aforesaid, which value of every Partners Share or Part of the said Company's Lands & common Stock shall in all such Cases be accounted rated & ascertained by the said Companies Books according to what such Partner shall be respectively charged therein for the same & no otherwise or in any other manner whatsoever: And every such new Partner shall at the time of his Admission as aforesaid, enter into bond of the penalty of one thousand pounds Sterling conditioned that he his Heirs Executors Administrators & Assigns shall & will on his & their several Parts & behalf well & truly observe perform fulfill & keep all & every the Articles Covenants Agreements Rules & Orders there in being & subsisting between the several Partners of the said Company of which shall at any time thereafter be made in pursuance of & according to the tenor & true meaning of these Presents. And thereupon it shall and may be lawful to & for the said Partners at su[c]h general meeting to make & enter an Order in the said Company's Books that such Partner or Partners, Person or Persons so [complying] with & performing the several Conditions & making such Payments as are herein before mentioned be admitted & received as a Partner or Partners of the said Company in the room & stead of such of the said Partner or Partners his or their Heirs Executors Administrators or Assigns who shall be excluded for the nonpayment of his or their Part or Parts as aforesaid, as a such Partner or Partners so to be admitted & received shall immediately upon such Admission be entitled to the Part or Parts Share or Shares of & in the said Company's Lands & common or general Stock to which such Partner or Partners his or their Heirs Executors Administrators or Assigns was or were entituled at the time of his or their Exclusion as fully to all Intents and purposes whatsoever as if such excluded Partner or Partners his or their Heirs Executors Administrators or Assigns had in due Course of Law transferred and assigned the same: And such Order & Determination of the major Part of the said Company at any of their said general meetings touching or concerning the admitting or excluding any of the Partners of the said Company for nonpayment of any of their Parts or Shares of the common or general Stock as aforesaid shall and is hereby agreed to be conclusive and [b]inding on all & every the said Partners Parties to these Presents their & every of their respective Heirs Executors Administrators and Assigns: And each & every of the said Parties & their respective Heirs Executors Administrators and Assigns shall & may be compelled to perform the same by a Rule of the General Court of the Colony & Dominion of Virginia pursuant to the Statute in the like Cases [22] made & provided to be moved for & obtained at the proper Costs & Charges of such Partner or

Partners so to be admitted & received in the room & stead of any other Partner or Partners his or their Heirs Executors Administrators or Assigns so to be excluded as aforesaid. ITEM That the several Committees to be from time to time appointed as aforesaid shall have full Power & Authority to take state & settle the Books and Accounts of the said Hugh Parker deceased & of all & every Factor & other Person or Persons that is or shall be chargeable or accountable to the said Company for any matter or thing whatsoever touching or concerning the said Copartnership, and to report the same to the next succeeding general meeting of the major Part of the said Partners as aforesaid in order to have the same finally adjusted & settled. ITEM That all & every the Part & Parts Share & Shares of & in the said Company's Lands & common Stock belonging to all & every of the said Partners his & their respective Heirs Executors Administrators & Assigns shall principally & in the first Place be chargeable & liable to satisfy & pay all & every the Demands whatsoever which the said Company may or shall have against any of the said Partners respectively or his Heirs Executors Administrators or Assigns for any matter or thing whatsoever touching or in anywise concerning the said Copartnership: And if any of the said Partners his Heirs Executors Administrators or Assigns being found indebted to the said Company for or on Account of the said Copartnership shall refuse or fail to pay unto the Treasurer or Receiver of the said Company for the time being for the Use of the said Company what shall be justly due & owing from such Partner his Heirs Executors Administrators or Assigns within Six Calendar months after the same shall become due: It shall and may be lawful to & for the major Part of the said Partners at their next or any other general meeting [ensuing] to sell & dispose of one or more fortieth Part or Parts Share or Shares of the said Companies Lands & common Stock belonging to such Partner his Heirs Executors Administrators or Assigns sufficient to satisfy and pay what shall be due to the said Company [——?——] such Partner his Heirs Executors Administrators or Assigns [——?——] the said major Part of the [said Partners proceeding in the sale] & disposal thereof in the same manner as is herein before directed for the Sale & Disposal of any of the said Partner's Parts or Shares in Case of their nonpayment of the several Proportions of the money to be from time to time advanced & paid for carrying on the said Copartnership. ITEM In Case it shall at any time hereafter happen that any Attachment or other legal Process shall be sued out or prosecuted for the making the Part or Parts Share or Share of any of the said Partners his Heirs Executors Administrators or Assigns of & in the said Companies lands & common Stock liable to the Payment of the Debts of such Partner his Heirs Executors Administrators or Assigns that then & in such Case if such Partner his Heirs Executors Administrators or Assigns shall not within Six months after service & due notice thereof satisfy and pay such Debt or Debts or other Demands and cause or procure such Attachment or other Process to be dismissed or otherwise in due form of Law discharged so that the several & respective Partners of the said

Company and their respective Heirs Executors Administrators & Assigns may be idemnified therefrom without being put or held to answer the same, or being put to any trouble charge or Expence for or by reason thereof. It shall & may be lawful to & for the said major Part of the said Partners as aforesaid at their then next or any other, general meeting to sell or dispose of one or more fortieth Part or Parts Share or Shares of the said Company's Lands & common Stock belonging to such Partner his Heirs Executors Administrators or Assigns to such Partner or Partners of the said Company or such other Person or Persons as the said major Part of the said Partners shall approve of who shall be willing to buy and purchase any such fortieth Part or Parts Share or Shares at such a price & value as each & every such fortieth Part shall appear by the said Companies Books to have cost such Partner his Heirs Executors Administrators or Assigns, out of which Purchase money shall be in the first place satisfied and paid all & every such Debts & Demands which shall be due & owing to the said Company by & from such Partner his Heirs Executors Administrators or Assigns for any matter or thing whatsoever touching or concerning the said Copartnership, and the residue of the said Purchase money or the whole thereof in Case nothing shall be due to the said Company to be lodged in the Hands of the Treasurer & Receiver of the said Company for the time being in order to satisfy & pay thereout in the first place all such Costs Charges & Expenses as the said Company or any of them shall be at or be obliged & be paid for or by reason of the said Attachment or other process, & in the next place to pay & satisfy such Judgment or Judgments Decree or Decrees as shall or may be obtained against such Partner his Heirs Executors Administrators or Assigns upon such Attachment or other Process, if the same shall be sufficient for that purpose or as far as the same will thereunto extend paying & rendering unto such Partner his Heirs Executors Administrators or Assigns the Overplus of such Purchase money, if any there be, the major Part of the said Partners proceeding in the Sale or disposal thereof in all things in the same manner as is herein before directed for the Sale & Disposal of any of the said Partners Part or Shares in Case of their nonpayment of several Proportions of the money to be from time to time advanced and for carrying on the said Copartnership. All & every which Sales or Sales Disposal or Disposals of any such Part or Parts Share or Shares of & in the said Companies Lands & common Stock belonging to any of the said Partners his Heirs Executors Administrators or Assigns in all & every the Cases herein before mentioned & provided for shall be and are hereby declared & agreed upon to be valid conclusive & binding upon all & every the said Partners Parties to these Presents, respectively & their respective & several Heirs Executors Administrators and Assigns. PROVIDED always and it is hereby declared & agreed upon to be the true Intent & meaning of these Presents & of the Parties thereto, that for the better carrying on & managing the said Company's Affairs & preventing & avoiding as for as may be too great a number of Partners dividing the said Companies Lands and common Stock into too many considerable Parts or Shares, no sale Disposal Assignment Devise or other Disposition of any less Part or Share than one fortieth Part or Share of the said Company's Lands & common Stock shall in any Case whatsoever be made allowed or admitted of. And that in every Sale & Disposal of every such fortieth Part or Share by the major Part of the said Partners at any of their general meetings in all or any of the Cases herein before mentioned & provided for any of the Partners of the said Company willing to purchase any such fortieth Part or Share so to be sold or disposed of shall be preferred & admitted to make such Purchase preferably to & before any other Person or Persons whatsoever: And the Price or Purchase money of every such fortieth Part or Share shall in every such Case be settled & ascertained by the Books of the said Company & no otherwise: Except the value of the said Companies Lands & common Stock should fall so low that none of the said Partners or any other Person or Persons will purchase such fortieth Part or Share at the Price or Value thereof appearing in & by the said Books: In all & every which Case or Cases [23] every such fortieth part or Share may & shall be exposed to publick Sale at the time & place of the general meeting of the major Part of the said Partners & the same shall & may be sold for the most than can be got for the same at such publick Sale. Anything contained in these Presents to contrary or seeming to be contrary thereof in any wise notwithstanding: And the money thereby accruing shall be applied & paid in such manner & to & for such Uses and Purposes as are herein before mentioned and expressed & not in any other manner whatsoever. ITEM That all Orders Agreements Resolutions & Proceedings of the several Committees from time to time shall be carried & determined by a majority of Votes according to the number of Persons constituting such Committee: So as such majority shall consist of three Votes at the least: And that it shall & may be lawful to & for any of the Partners of the said Company who shall be present at any meeting of the said Committees [although not appointed a Member thereof] to [cast] his Vote in any of the Resolutions Debates or Proceedings of the said Committee at such meeting: But if by this admitting any such Partner's Vote (not being one of the said Committee) [the manner of the dispos]al the matter or thing in dispute shall be adjudged to be carried & determined on that Side on which the majority of the Members (who are of the said Committee) shall have Voted, So as such Equality shall consist of three Votes at the least. ITEM That as often as any of the Partners of the said Company living & residing in Great Brittain or Ireland shall signify [under his or] any of their hands any matter or thing which they desire to be provided for or concerning the said Copartnership or the Benefit or Advantage of the said Company the same shall be proposed to the Committee or general meeting of the said Company [———— ? ————] and such shall be [———— ———— ? ————] Great Britain & Ireland shall be reckoned & accounted according as they shall have signified under their hands as aforesaid & according to their respective Parts or Shares in the said Company's Lands & common Stock. ITEM That once every year as soon as conveniently may be after the general meeting of the said Partners as aforesaid a true Copy of all the Proceedings of the said Company & their Committees for the year preceding shall be transmitted by the Clerk of the said Company for the time being to the aforesaid John Hanbury Esquire or to any other Person the said Partners residing in Great Brittain and Ireland shall nominate & appoint for that purpose.[24] ITEM That the Accounts of & concerning the said Company's Lands and common Stock and also all the Buying's Selling's Dealings Gains Debts & Credits which shall grow arise happen or be made of or by means of the said Copartnership and joint Trade or anything incident or belonging thereto shall from time to time during all the said Term of the said Copartnership be truly enter'd & fairly written in some convenient or fitting Book or Books to be kept for that Purpose by such Person or Persons as the majority of the said Partners shall from time to time employ and appoint: Of which said Books the several Partners, Parties to these Presents their respective Heirs Executors Administrators & Assigns or any of them shall freely at all times have the Sight & Perusal when & as often as it shall be desired & shall have Liberty to transcribe & copy out all or any Part thereof without any Let Hindrance or Denial.[25] ITEM It is expressly agreed & concluded by & between the said Parties to these Presents & the true Intent & meaning of the said Parties is hereby declared to be: That if any of the Parties to these Presents shall happen to dye during the Continuance of the said Copartnership, yet nevertheless no benefit or Advantage of Survivorship shall accumulate or be had or taken by the Survivors of them in any wise whatsoever: Any Law Usage or Custom or anything herein contained to the contrary or seeming to the contrary thereof in any wise notwithstanding, but the Part or Parts Share or Shares of such Partner or Partners so dying shall descend & come to the several & respective Heirs Executors Administrators or Assigns of such Partner or Partners so dying in the same manner as if such Partner or Partners so dying had been severally and respectively seised & possessed thereof in his & their own Right severally & not joyntly: Subject nevertheless to all & singular the Covenants Articles Restrictions Limitations & Agreements mentioned contained & expressed in this Present Indenture or to be hereafter made entered into or agreed upon by the majority of the said Partners at any of their general meetings in pursuance of the Power & Authority lodged & reposed in them by virtue of these Presents. ITEM That it shall & may be lawful to & for any of the said Partners at any time hereafter by Deed duly executed in his lifetime or by his last Will & Testament in writing to bargain sell dispose of give alien or devise his Part or Parts Share or Shares of & in the said Company's Lands & common Stock to any other Person or Persons whatsoever: Subject nevertheless to all & singular the Covenants Articles Restrictions Limitations & Agreements mentioned contained & expressed in this present Indenture or to be hereafter made enter'd into or agreed upon by the majority of the said Partners at any of their general meetings in pursuance of the Power & Authority lodged & reposed in them by virtue of these Presents. ITEM In Case at the end & Expiration of the said Copartnership the money & stock belonging to the said Company shall not be sufficient to clear & discharge all the Debts owing upon Account of the said Copartnership that then & in such Case each & every of the said Partners his Heirs Executors Administrators or Assigns shall advance & pay such Part & Proportion the said Debts as the Part or Parts Share or Shares of the said Company's Lands & common Stock belonging to such Partner shall amount unto or in default thereof or otherwise well & sufficiently saving harmless & keeping indemnified the rest of the Company therefrom the Part or Parts Share or Shares of such Partner his Heirs Executors Administrators or Assigns or as much, thereof as shall be sufficient for that Purpose shall be immediately sold to the highest bidder & the money arising by such Sale applied to pay & discharge the proportion of the said Debts which ought to have been paid by such Partner or his Heirs Executors Administrators or Assigns. ITEM That at the End & Expiration of the said Copartnership all the Lands belonging to the said Company shall at the joint Charge & Expence of the then Partners & Proprietors to be defrayed & born[e] in proportion to their several & respective Shares & Interests therein be surveyed laid off & divided into forty several Shares or Lots as equal in value as the same can be done having respect to the quantity & quality, Which Surveys of the said several Shares or Lots shall be marked & numbered from One to Forty, inclusive. And each of the said Partners or Proprietors entitled to one or more Share or Shares thereof, having first drawn Lots to determine who shall be first entitled to draw & so second & successively to the last, shall then draw in that Order & Succession the several Surveys & lots of Land so surveyed, & every Person & Proprietor so drawing shall have hold & enjoy to him & his Heirs & Assigns forever thereafter in Severalty the several & respective Lot or Lots of Land which he shall so draw. And after such drawing all & every the said Partners and Proprietors shall join in & duly execute one or more proper Deed or Deeds of Partition for the confirming & establishing such Division and Partition: And if any of the said Partners or Proprietors shall not be present at such Partition or Division by drawing Lots as aforesaid: It shall & may be lawful to & for the major Part of the said Partners & Proprietors present at the same to nominate & appoint one or more Person or Persons to draw the [lots] for such absent Partners or Proprietors in Case the said absent Persons who are Partners & Proprietors shall not have nominated & appointed some Person or Persons to be present & draw such Lots for them: And such drawing Lots & the Division & Partition to be thereby made is by these Presents declared & Agreed to be binding & conclusive upon all & every the Parties to these Presents & their several & respective Heirs Executors Administrators & Assigns. PROVIDED always that public Notice of the Time & Place of such final Partition & Division shall be advertised in the Virginia Gazette [at least] two months before such Petition [& Division announced to be] advertised in the said Gazette for the [space] of the [—?]. ITEM That the general or common Stock of and belonging to the said Company shall at the same time & place be divided by & between the several Partners & Proprietors of the said Stock in proportion to their several & respective Rights & [Interests]. ITEM That it shall & may be lawful to & for the said major Part of the said Partners as aforesaid at any of their general meetings if they shall judge it to be for the Benefit & Advantage of the said Company to order & direct any such Part of the said Company's Lands, as they shall think proper to be sold or disposed of to such Person or Persons & upon such Considerations & Terms as they shall order & direct: Anything in these Presents contained to the contrary or seeming to the contrary notwithstanding [in] which Case it shall & may be lawful to & for the Treasurer or Receiver of the said Company for the time being in his own name and as Attorney of & for the said Company to sign seal and execute & deliver proper Deeds of Conveyance which are hereby declared and agreed to be good valid & binding on any & every of the said Partners & Heirs & Assigns as fully to all Intents & Purposes as if all & every of the said Partners had signed sealed executed & delivered the same. ITEM That all & every Deed & Deeds Articles & Writings whatsoever heretofore made signed or sealed by all or any of the said Partners touching or concerning the said Copartnership before or immediately after signing & executing this present Indenture void null & of no effect so far as the same relate to or concern any matter or thing agreed upon or provided for by these Presents. ITEM If any Doubt Question or Controversy shall arise between the said Partners to these Presents or any of them their or any of their Heirs Executors Administrators or Assigns for or about or concerning this present Indenture or any Clause Provision or Agreement herein comprized or any defect or want of Explanation on any matter or thing relating to this Copartnership then as often as such Doubt Question Controversy or Difference shall arise or happen the same shall be referred to the Determination of any three indifferent Persons or any two of them to be nominated by the major Part of the same: [—?] the said Partners aforesaid at their next general meeting after such Controversy shall arise or happen & each & every of the said Parties to these Presents their several & respective Heirs Executors Administrators & Assigns shall stand to abide perform & keep such Order & Determination therein as if the said three Persons or any two of them shall make & give up: So as such Order Judgment & Determination of the said three Persons or any two of them of or concerning the Premises be from time to time made & set down in writing under their hands & Seals within two months next after they shall have been so nominated and appointed as aforesaid. Which said Determination is hereby agreed to be conclusive to the said Parties to these Presents & every of them there & every of their Heirs Executors Administrators & Assigns and every of them shall be compelled to perform the same by Rule of the General Court aforesaid pursuant to the form of the Statutes &

in like Cases made & provided. LASTLY It is hereby agreed & concluded upon that the major Part of the Partners Parties to these Presents may & shall have full Power & Authority at any of their general meetings during the Continuance of the said Copartnership, if they shall see fit & judge it to be for the Benefit & Advantage of the said Company to alter revoke & change [26] all or any of the Articles Covenants & Agreements in this present Indenture mentioned & contained, & to conclude & agree upon any other Covenants Articles or Agreements in their place & Stead: Provided always that in such Case the said major Part shall consist of so many of the said Partners as shall be entitled to one full equal moiety or half Part of all the said Companies Lands & common or general Stock, at the least. IN WITNESS whereof the said Parties to these Presents have hereunto interchangeably set their hands & Seals [27] the day & year first before written.

[*Signed:*]

Rob.t Dinwiddie	Phil: Lud: Lee	Presly Thornton	Richard Lee
	John Tayloe	Gawen Corbin	Aug.st Washington
Lawrence Washington	James Scott.	J. Mercer	Jacob Giles
Nath.a Chapman	George Mason		Thomas Cresap

[*Endorsed: top, left*]

Sealed and delivered by the within named Presley Thornton, Richard Lee, Augustine Washington, Lawrence Washington, Nathaniel Chapman, James Scott, George Mason, John Mercer, Jacob Giles, Thomas Cresap in the presence of us:

[James Polick]
[John Trohock]
Henry Haskin
John Trohock

[*Endorsed: right side*]

Sealed and delivered by the Hon.ble Robert Dinwiddie Esq & Philip Ludwell Lee in the presence of us

Henry White
Francis Southall

Sealed and delivered by Thomas Ludwell Lee Esq. July 25, 1753, being then of full Age in the presence of us

Richard Henry Lee
George Mercer
Francis Lightfoot Lee

Sealed & delivered by John Tayloe [28] Esq. Sept. 3rd 1753 in presence of us

Thomas Cumming
Adam Stephen
William Garrard

[*Endorsed: bottom right*]

The Articles entered into by the Ohio Company

May 23rd 1751

* The photostat is of the John Tayloe family original later in the possession of Alvin F. Embery, Esq., of Fredericksburg, Virginia. The work of establishing the text consumed many hours of the author.

1. As noted above, in the History, one has here the legal nature of the Company and its official name. Hitherto it has often been called the "Ohio Company of Virginia," but the last two words when so used are merely a convenience and not a part of the official designation. Capitalization is retained as found in the original.
2. The Ohio Company by the terms of its Indenture had no rights to any land property falling within the terms of the Pennsylvania Charter of 1681.
3. The full story of Virginia trade with the Ohio Valley Indians has never been revealed.
4. Note the similarity with the Virginia Charter of 1606.
5. A comprehensive footnote on this sentence, with reference to the documents herein printed or calendared, is not needed.
6. Died 1750.
7. Died April-May, 1751.
8. See, herein published or calendared, many references to amounts of goods and sums involved.
9. It is fairly obvious that the language following is that of contracts of that day.
10. As indicated in the History, above, the Ohio Company, thus organized, came to the end of its legal organization as such in 1771.
11. A possible total of £6,000, the equivalent today, in purchasing power, of about $200,000—not a small sum of money.
12. Annual meetings are hereby prescribed, but they may not have been held, owing to unforeseen circumstances; and certainly they were not held regularly at Alexandria, Virginia, as is indicated in the History, above, and shown in the various documents herein printed or calendared.
13. It will be noticed from the History and the documents herein printed that much of the real work of the Ohio Company was done through such committees.
14. There are printed many references to this "Book." A number of the documents are copies of material from this "Book." Its fate is unknown, further than that it was, in sequence, in the possession of Thomas Lee, John Mercer, and George Mason.
15. Note, herein printed or calendared, many documents of George Mason, published now for the first time.
16. The documents printed or calendared herein contain many references to the exercise of such authority by those so empowered. Cf. *George Mercer Papers, passim.*
17. Cf. footnote 16 above.
18. No comment on the law or on the ethics of this is in order, but its relation to democracy is significant.
19. An implication at least that there may have been two or more "Books," possibly not the Ohio Company "Books" referred to above but a "Book" or "Books" of the Committee of the Ohio Company. No such books have been found.
20. The documents herein listed indicate many such appointments of a meeting by the Treasurer. Cf. pp. 300-42.
21. This provision was followed more than once. Cf. History, above, p. 15.
22. This is a legal formula. Consult Hening, *Statutes* . . . , I-V, as indexed under "Partnership."
23. This is probably the usual legal provision of a partnership agreement, and not therefore a foreboding of things to come.
24. It may be that some of these copies will eventually be located in Great Britain. Some of them are in the George Mercer Papers.

25. An item which may explain finding, by research, duplicate materials.
26. There is no extant record of any such change in this indenture.
27. Note that the Indenture is not signed by John Hanbury, first part; Arthur Dobbs, second part; Capel Hanbury, fourth part; Samuel Smith, fifth part; Thomas Lee's Executors, sixth part; James Wardrop, eighteenth part.
28. It will also be noted that the signatures of Dinwiddie, Philip Ludwell Lee, Thomas Ludwell Lee, and John Tayloe postdated May 23, 1751.

George Mason and Company against Daniel Ashcraft[1]

(Frederick County, Maryland, Dockets[2] 1751, p. 154)

[August, 1751]

D D	19th	George Mason & Com^y^		Casa[3]
120	sbre.[4]	vs	po	
		Daniel Ashcraft		NE[5]

1. Not identified.
2. The old dockets of Frederick County are in the Hall of Records at Annapolis, and not in Frederick.
3. This is the earliest commercial litigation item found. No additional items in this case are recorded.
4. September 19, 1750, probably the date of a petition and warrant and probably relating to a sale of May-June, 1750.
5. Abbreviation for *Non Est Inventus,* meaning he was not found by the sheriff.

Warrant[1] *of George Mason for the Arrest of John Tucker*

(Frederick County, Virginia, Court Docket Papers.)

[February 23, 1752]

George the second by the grace of God of great Britain France & Ireland K[ing] Defender of the Faith &c To the sheriff of Frederick County greeting we command you that you take[2] John Tucker and him in your safe Custody keep so that you have his body before the Justices of our s^d^ County Court at the Court house of the s^d^ County on the second Tuseday in May next to answer George Mason of a Plea of Debt[3] for Eleven pounds Six shillings and Ten pence Pens^a^ money of the Value of Eleven pounds Six Shillings 6 Ten pence Cur^t^ money damage Twenty Shillings and have then there this writ witness James Wood Clk of the s^d^ Court at the s^d^ Court house the 23 day of Februa^y^ in the 25 year of our Reign

J Wood

[*Endorsed:*]
Mason
v } Caps
Tucker
Executed
℔ T Wood D.S.
filed June 1752

Com ord a deft and Shff
Att ordered to Issue on
behalf of shff ag.[t]
the Estate of Deft.[4]

7.10
15
4.6
7
8.10.1

1. The earliest item found of the Virginia litigation of the Ohio Company. No petition, declaration, mercantile statement, promissory note, or bond was found in the files. Such items may not have been filed, but they may have been filed and later lost or pilfered.
2. Common legal terminology for the first warrant of arrest.
3. A common plea, seemingly not always based on a declaration, or complaint of debt. Where a warrant mentions a petition or a declaration the files usually contained it.
4. See the item of June 5, 1752, calendared below, p. 310.

Petition[1] *of George Mason against William Castleman*

(Frederick County, Virginia, Court Docket Papers.)

[February 24, 1752]

To the worshipful Court of Frederick County George Mason Gent Humbly sheweth that Will[m] Castleman stands indebted to him the sum of three pounds seven shillings & two pence Maryland Money

due by note[2] and refuseth payment Wherefore you Petitioner prays Judgment for the same [with] Costs and shall pray

[*Endorsed:*]

Mason
v } Pet[n]
Castleman

1. Almost invariably the petition and warrants of George Mason and Company in these old documents are in the handwriting of James Wood. In a few cases a printed form is used, as elsewhere in the docket papers. The undated petition is here given a conjectured date, based on the dated warrants.
2. Of October 28, 1751, calendared below, p. 308.

Bond of James Martin[1] *to George Mason for the Use of the Ohio Company*

(D.M.L. George Mason Papers.)

[March 31, 1752]

KNOW all Men by these presents, That I James Martin of the County of Frederik in the Province of Maryland, Trader am held and firmly bound unto George Mason of the County of Fairfax in the Colony of Virginia Gen.[t] for the use of the Ohio Company in the Sum of One hyndred and Sixty two Pounds Eleven shillings and three pence[2] Current Lawfull Money of the Province of Maryland————— To be paid to the said George Mason or his Assigns for the use aforesaid: To the which Payment well and truly to be made, I bind myself My + Heirs, Executors & Administrators + + + + + firmly by these presents, Sealed with my Seal, Dated the thirty first day of March Anno Domini 1752

THE CONDITION of the above Obligation is such, that if the above bound James Martin—his + + + + + + + + + + + Heirs, Executors or Administrators, do and shall well and truly pay or cause to be paid unto the said George Mason or his Assigns for the use of the said Ohio Company the sum of Eighty one Pounds five shillings and seven pence half penny of like Lawfull money of Maryland + on or before the thirtieth—day of June[3]—next ensuing the date of these Presents, then the above Obligation to be void, other wise to remain in full Force and Virtue

SEALED & DELIVERED
in the presence of
Thomas Cresap Jun:[r] James Martin
S. S. Welder (Seal)

[*Collector's mark:*]
N A 978 o(2)

[*On the back of this bond:*]
James Martin's
Bond to Geo.
Mason & Com:[y]
for L 81:5:7½
pay:[ble] 30th June 1752

1. A common name. Obviously an important Indian trader, but not listed in the General Index to Deeds, Frederick County, Virginia. Presumably he exchanged the goods for furs and skins, but he had to be sued for payment of the bond. The goods may have been from the third cargo, which possibly reached Virginia in November, 1751.
2. A typical double indemnity penal bond. It is in the handwriting of S. S. Welder.
3. The traditional ninety days.

Declaration[1] of George Mason against Abraham Teagarden

(Frederick County, Virgina, Court Docket Papers.)

[June 1, 1752]

Fred[k] County ss

George Mason of Fairfax County in the Colony of Virginia Complains of Abraham Teagarden otherwise lately called I .... in Custody &c of a plea that he render to him Eight pounds & three shillings Pennsylvania money of the value of Eight pounds three shillings Virginia money which to him he owes & from him he unjustly detains &c For that Whereas the s.^d Defendant the seventeenth day of July MDCCLI at the County afores^d by his certain penal note in writing [2] seald with the seal of the Defendant and to the Court now here shown whose date is the same day and year aforesaid did promise & Oblidge himself to pay unto the s.^d Plaintif the sum of four pounds one shilling & six pence to the use of the Ohio Company on or before the first day of October next ensuing the date of the s^d Penal note

To which payment well and truly to be made to the s^d Plaintif He the s.^d Defendant did Bind himself in the penal sum of Eight pounds three shillings of the money afores.^d of the Value afores^d and the s^d Plaintif in fact sayeth that the s^d Defendant did not on or before the Last day of October aforesaid pay the above mentioned sum of Four Pounds one shilling & three pence of the money of the value aforesaid By which action accrued to the S^d Plaintif to have & demand of the s^d Defendant the first mentioned sum of Eight pounds three shillings of the money afores^d of the Value afs^d Yet the s^d Defend^t (altho often required) the s^d last mentioned sum of money or any part thereof to the Plaintif hath not paid but ye same to pay hath refused and still doth refuse to the Plaintifs damage Twenty shillings .... and thereof He Brings suit &C

Jones for Ptf Pled^s &c { [J.] Doe / R. Roe }

[*Endorsed:*]
Mason
v } Decl
Tegarden
filed June 1752
Com Ord
1753
Sep Judg w Inq [3]
June. 1755.
Jury Sworn Verd^t Ptf
Judg^t [4]
55
15
71
23
80
244 &c 15^s

We of the Jury find for Plt
£6. 2. 3 damages
John Brisco form^n

1. In accordance with custom, declarations are made out by Attorneys. The Virginia declarations herein are in the handwriting of Gabriel Jones.
2. Of July 17, 1751, calendared below, p. 308.
3. See Calendar, below, p. 322, under September 5, 1753.
4. See Calendar, below, p. 328, under June 5, 1755.

Warrant for the Attachment of the Goods, etc., of John Tucker

(Frederick County, Virginia, Court Docket Papers.)

[June 16, 1752]

George the Second by the Grace of God of Great Britain France and Ireland King Defender of the Faith &c To one of our Coroners of Frederick County Greeting We Command You that You attach [1] so much of the Goods and Chattles of the within named John Tucker as will be of Sufficient Value to satisfy and pay the within mentioned Sum and Costs and so to secure the Same in Your hands or otherways provide that it may be liable for payment thereof as our Justices of our said County Court at the Court house of Our said County on the First Tuesday [in] July next shall in that part Consider And have then there this writ [2] [Wit]ness James Wood Clk of our said Court at the said Court house the 16 day of June In the 26 Year of Our reign

J Wood

[*Endorsed:*]
Mason & Hite [3]
v } Attachm^t
Tucker
Executed on a
Sorrell Mare
℘ T Wood D S

1. See the court item of June 5, 1752, calendared below, p. 310.
2. Note the court report of June 5, 1752, also found here on the reverse of this warrant.
3. On a writ of attachment, a county official, commonly the sheriff, was a participant.

Debt of Frederick Ice to George Mason and the Ohio Company

(D.M.L. George Mason Papers.)

[August 18, 1752]

Fred.^k Ice . D:^r

To a Note [1] you Assigned me of Benjamin Roger's for 6£ Pens money, due from one Joseph Gough, who proved Insolvent) £ 4. 10 [2]
)

George Mason for
Self & Co. [3]

[*Collector's mark*]
N A 979 C 2
[*Endorsed:*]

		Joseph Gough's
¼	1645	Note assign'd by
	411¼	Frederick Ice
	1233¾	for £6.
		sue Frederick Ice

1. See note of May 27, 1751, calendared below. All the Frederick Ice items are related to this note.
2. Note that Pennsylvania currency in 1752 was at a discount of 25 per cent of Virginia currency.
3. The entire manuscript is in the handwriting of George Mason.

George Mason versus Evan Shelby [1]

(Frederick County, Maryland, Judgment Record G, 1752–1753, pp. 713-15.)

[November Court 1752]
[November 21, 1752]

DD GEORGE MASON
vs } Judgment Confessed
PP EVAN SHELBY

COMMAND was Given to the Sheriff of Frederick County that he should take Evan Shelby late of Frederick County farmer if he should be found in his Bailiwick and him should Safe keep so that he might have his Body Before his Lordships Justices of his Lordships then next County Court to be held at Frederick Town in said County on the third Tuesday in November then next to Answer unto George Mason of a plea of Trespass upon the Case and that thereof he the said Sheriff should not fail at his Peril and that he Should have then and there that Writ c.[t]

And the said George Mason Declared against the said Evan Shelby in the plea aforesaid as followes

[*Approximately 40 lines left blank for the unrecorded declaration*]

A Copy of the aforegoing declaration was made out and Sent with the Writ which issued in the plea aforesaid —

At which said Third Tuesday of November to wit the twenty first day of the Same Month Anno Domini Seventeen Hundred and fifty two being the day of the Return of the aforegoing Writ Comes the said George Mason by his Attorney aforesaid and the Sheriff of Frederick County to whom the Same Writ was Directed also Comes and makes Return thereof to the Court here Thus Indorsed To wit Cepi Copy in time GEO GORDON Sher[f]

AND the said Evan Shelby In his Proper Person says that he Cannot Gainsay the Action aforesaid of him the said George Mason nor but that he did Assume upon himself in Manner and form as the said George Mason above Thereof in his Declaration against him does Complain and as to the Damages of the said George Mason by Occasion of the Premises in this part Sustained the said Evan Shelby says and Acknowledges that the said George Mason has Sustained damages by Occasion aforesaid besides his Costs and Charges to three pounds Current Money and no more and because the said George Mason does not Gainsay but the Allegation afs[d] is True he Prays Judgment and the

Damages above Acknowledged together with his Costs and Charges to him to be Adjudged c[t]
NOVEMBER THE 24th 1752 [2] THEREFORE of the Assent of the Parties aforesaid It is Considered by the Court here that the said George Mason Recover against the said Evan Shelby his Damages by Occasion of the Nonperformance of the Promise and Assumption in the Declaration above Mentioned to Three Pounds Current Money in form aforesaid Acknowledged as also One hundred and Ninety Nine pounds and One Quarter of a pound of Tobacco to the said George Mason by Discretion of the Justices here of his Assent Adjudged for his Costs and Charges by him about his Suit in that part Laid out and Expended by the Court here Adjudged and the said Evan Shelby IN MERCY &c.[a] [3]

1. The Shelbys lived near Hagerstown. Evan Shelby, Senior, died in 1752. His son, Evan Shelby, Junior, was farmer, fur trader, and military figure. *See D.A.B.* His son, Isaac Shelby (born in 1750), became a famous Kentucky settler.
2. Consult the Docket Book, November Court, 1752, calendared below, p. 314.
3. This seems to be a clerical error for November 21, 1752. Probably it was the date of recordation.

Gawin Corbin's Statement Assigning his Shares of the Ohio Company to Robert Carter

(Chicago Historical Society. Gunther MSS.)

[December 5, 1752]

I do hereby assign all Right and title to my Shair [1] of the Ohio unto Robert Carter Esq[r] of Westmoreland County given Under my hand this fifth day of December 1752.[2]

Gawin Corbin

1. One-twentieth of the forty shares in the Ohio Company. See the Articles of Agreement of May 23, 1751, above, p. 207.
2. Note the purchase by R. Carter of another twentieth part, the share of Augustine Washington, June 2, 1753, immediately below.

Receipt of Augustine Washington to Robert Carter. Sale of Share in the Ohio Company

(Chicago Historical Society, Washington Collection MS., a.d.s.)

[June 2, 1753]

June the second seventeen hunder [*sic*] and fifty three received of R. Carter three hundred and sixty Pounds [1] Current Money for My Part of the Ohio company [2]

Aug.[st] Washington

George Lee [3]
Tho:[s] Bentley [4]
Will Booth [5]

1. Probably the equivalent of the exact outlay of each member of the Ohio Company before the above date, of which possibly three hundred Pounds were for cargoes of goods and the remainder for exploration, roads, handling of goods, construction of storehouses, etc. The total before June 2, 1753, thus was £7,200.
2. Note the acquisition by R. Carter of the share of Gawin Corbin, December 5, 1752, above, p. 227.
3. Probably of Westmoreland County, Virginia. A George Lee was one of the two executors of William Fairfax, 1755.
4. Not definitely identified, but probably a militia official and possibly later active in the old Northwest.
5. A common name in Virginia, but probably the brother-in-law of Augustine Washington.

Expense Account of Thomas and Richard Penn *

(H.S.P. Penn MSS., Large Folio, II, 15.)

[April 3-July 8, 1754]

Thomas Penn & Richd Penn Esq.^{rs}
About the Ohio Company

1754		£	S	D
Apr 3.	Att.^{d} at Co.^{11} office & saw Pet.^{n} from the Ohio Company	—	10	—
	Note thereof, to Mr Penn & p.^{d} Mess.^{r} therewith	—	2	6
5.	Att.^{d} Mr Penn at Westm.^{d} & he orders me to get out Copy of the Ohio Company's New Pet.^{n} & the Refer-rences	—	6	8
	Att.^{d} at Co.^{11} Office to bespeak the same	—	6	8
	Coach & Expences	—	2	—
	Letters to Mrs Dickinson [1] & to the Clerk of the Council,[2] for the same, & p.^{d} Mess.^{r} therewith	—	2	6
6.	Att.^{d} at Co.^{11} Office, & got out Copy of the Ohio's Comp.^{a} Pet.^{n} & Ref.^{nce} to the Com.^{tee} & Ref.^{nce} to the Board of Trade	—	13	4
	P.^{d} Mr Wm Sharpe [3] for the same	2	—	—
	P.^{d} Porter	—	—	6
	Copy of the s.^{d} 3 Papers for Mr Penn	—	18	—
	P.^{d} Mess.^{r} with the same	—	—	6
May 1.	Att.^{d} Mr Penn, consulting abo.^{t} the Ohio Comp.^{as} Pet.^{n}	—	6	8
June 29.	Att.^{d} Mr Penn, on News arrived from Ohio	—	6	8
	Letter	—	—	2
July 1.	Att.^{d} Mr Penn on this & sundry other Affairs	—	6	8
3.	Att.^{d} Mr Penn taking Instrus for an Agreem.^{t} from the Managers here, from the Ohio Company	—	6	8
	Draw.^{g} s.^{d} Agreem.^{t} [4]	—	10	—
	Fair Copy sent Mr Penn	—	5	—
	Letter of Advice to him therewith	—	2	
	P.^{d} Porter	—	—	6

		£	S	D
4.	Att.[d] M.[r] Penn, settling the Dra.[t]	—	6	8
	Engross.[g] 3 Parts thereof & paid Stamps	—	19	6
6.	Two Clerks attend at M.[r] Hanburys & at two other Gentlem.[ns] Houses in the City, & saw all the 4 Gent.[n] execute the Instrum.[ts],[5] but M.[r] Hanbury keeps them all, on Pretence that some *other* Terms were agreed upon	—	13	4
	Letter to M.[r] Spring [6] thereon	—	2	—
	P.[d] Clerks Expences	—	2	—
8.	P.[d] Letter from M.[r] Penn	—	—	3
		£ 9	10	9

* The author is indebted to Mrs. Lois Mulkearn and to Mr. Nicholas B. Wainwright for the location of this item.

1. Not identified.
2. William Sharpe, secretary to the Privy Council.
3. William Sharpe, clerk of the Privy Council.
4. Not found. It is mentioned in the Petition of April 2, 1754.
5. Not found.
6. Not identified.

George Mason and Company against Christopher Gist

(Maryland Hall of Records, Frederick County, Dockets, March, 1755, folio 31.)

[March 20, 1755]

D D	[6th Jan	George Mason & Company		Case
72	1755]	vs	N E	En[d] in Liber H, folio 800.
	id		p[o]	
		Christopher Gist		

Writ of Attachment in behalf of George Mason and the Ohio Company against Richard Pearis

(D.M.L. George Mason Papers.)

[September 7, 1756]

Frederick County ss

Where as Complaint is this day made to me John Funk Gent.[1] one of his Majesties Justice of the peace for the County afores.[d] by George Mason Esq.[r] that Richard pearis [2] is indebted to him & the Ohio Company in the Sum of four hundred pounds and do Abscond as the ordinary Process Law cannot be found upon him.

These are therefore in his Majestie's name to will & require you to Attach the Estate of Mes.[r] Richard Pearis sufficient [pay] * to Answer the s.[d] Debt and Costs and the same in y.[r] hands to Secure that y.[e] same maybe liable to further proceedings here in to be had at the next Court to be held for the s.[d] County-here in fail not as you'l answer the same at y.[r] peril. Given under my hand this 7th. day of Sep[t]. 1756—

To the Sherif of Fredrick John Funk

Attach in the hands of Sam.[l] Welder[3] Christopher Gist & Sam.[l] Gist.[4]

[*Collector's mark*]

N A 961 H

Know all Men by these presents that we George Mason of the County of Fairfax & George Mercer of the County of Frederick are held & firmly bound unto Richard Pearis late of Frederick County in the Sum of Eight hundred pounds[5]—lawful Money of Virginia: To which payment to be made to the said Richard Pearis, or his Heirs Executors Administrators or Assigns, We bind ourselves & each of us our & each of our Heirs, Executors, & Administrators jointly and severally by these presents. Witness our Hands & Seals this 7th Day of September in the Year 1756—

The Condition of the above obligation is, That whereas the above bound George Mason hath this present Day—before John Funk ——— Gent one of his Majesty's Justices of the peace for the County of Frederick prayed an Attachment on behalf of himself & Company against the Estate of the said Richard Pearis for the Sum of four hundred pounds Current Money & hath obtain'd the same returnable to the next Court to be held for the said County of Frederick If therefore the said George Mason & Company shall pay to the said Richard Pearis all Damages which shall be to him awarded, in Case the said George Mason & Company shall be cast in their said Suit; Then this obligation to be void; or else to remain in full force—

Sealed & delivered
in presence of
W.[m] Eilbeck[6] G Mason (Seal)
Thomson Mason[7] G.[o] Mercer[8] (Seal)

[*Endorsed:*]

I

Mason
vs } Att
Paris

Attachd in the
hands of Sam'l
Welder and
Summoned him
as a Garnishe
℘ L Stephens[9]
Sheriff

Feb 1757
discont.[d]. by ptf[10]

* [This word was crossed out in the document.]
1. John Funk. On the Shenandoah River in 1749; voter in Frederick County, Virginia, 1758; captain of militia, 1779.
2. Important Indian trader. Traded with the Cherokees, 1750–1755. Used in negotiations with the Cherokees, 1754–1755. Commandant at Fort Frederick, Maryland in 1756. He lived on the Holston River in 1756. His signature is found in Augusta County record of 1769. Mentioned by the *Virginia Gazette,* March 24, 1774. This debt may have been for Ohio Company goods taken to the Cherokees or consumed at Fort Frederick.
3. Samuel S. Welder, a clerk of George Mason and the Ohio Company.
4. Probably one of the many collateral relatives of Christopher Gist. A resident of Virginia.
5. Double indemnity. The sum is too large for other than goods for Indians, for troops, or for trade with Indians of the South.
6. Father-in-law of George Mason?
7. George Mason's younger brother.
8. Incidental item of Ohio Company activity on his part. George Mercer, however, in 1755, inspected the Ohio Company goods at Rock Creek.
9. Voter in 1758. Member of important local family.
10. See the item of February 2, 1757, immediately below.

George Mason against Richard Pearis

(Frederick County, Virginia, Order Book No. 7, 1755–1758, p. 181.)

[February 2, 1757.]

	George Mason......Esq. Ptf	On attachment
discont[d]	ag.[t]	
	Richard Pearis..........Dft	

On the Ptfs motion this Suit is discontinued [1]

1. See endorsement on Declaration of September 7, 1756, above, p. 230. Settlement of the large account may be presumed, for Richard Pearis continued land transactions (fourteen in all) in Frederick County, Virginia, from December 2, 1761 to November 6, 1770.

List [1] of Papers sent by William Trent to M.r Mercer

(H.S.P. Society Collection.)

Philadelphia April 11th 1759

My Commission from Governor Dinwiddie dated 26.th January 1754—
My Instructions from the Governor of Virginia
Governor of Virginia Instructions to M.[r] Gist wherein he acknowledges the sending of Goods to the Ohio Indians
Coll: William Fairfax's Letter dated Winchester 26.th May 1753
Coll: Washingtons Letter to Coll: Cresap dated the 18.th April 1754
Coll: Washingtons Letter to myself
Governor of Virginias Letter to me dated Williamsburg May 31.st 1753

Coll Wm Fairfax's Letter to me dated Belvoir June the 9.th 1753
Coll Wm Fairfax's Letter to me dated Winchester September 1.st 1753
M.r Walthoe Clerk to the Council's Letter to me dated at Williamsburg September 26.th 1753—about the Carriage of Amunition &c to Ohio
My Accounts

[*Holograph notation of Trent:*]

April 11.th at Night wrote Cap.t Robert Stewart a letter[2] desiring him, to deliver my Letter[3] to M.r Mercer which had all my papers inclosed in it Agreeable to the Acct.s on the other side, & sent Them to him by Cap.t Ward & requested of him in my letter if M.r Mercer should not be at Wmsburg to deliver them to any of the Ohio Company that might happen to be there.

W. Trent

[*Endorsed:*][4]

List of Papers &c sent to M.r Mercer by Cap.t Stuart
April 11.th 1759
Amt of my Acct 449.18.1½ besides the payment due to myself & Men who I have chiefly pd

[*H.S.P. Notation:*]

W.m Trent
Soc. Coll.

1. The list is in unidentified handwriting. It was probably submitted in connection with the suit against Dinwiddie which was initiated in 1757, and still before the court in 1760.
2. Not found.
3. Not found.
4. Seemingly in the handwriting of Trent.

George Mercer to William Trent

(H.S.P. Etting Collection, Ohio Company Papers, a.l.s.)*

Nov. 8, 1760

Dear Sir

I am just returned from Wms Burg, where I had the Pleasure to be present at your Trial[1] with Govr Dinwiddie, where I may assure You that all his malicious Attempts & Aspersions agt. your Character & Credit, were sufficiently cleared up both to the Court[2] & Jury; the former were sensible of the ill Treatment your Character had suffered, & the latter so well satisfied of the Injury done you in both Respects, that they have brought you in a Verdict for £800 besides your Costs—I give you Joy of this Piece of real Justice & am

D.r Sr Your Friend & hble Servant
G:o MERCER

I expect to have the Pleasure of seeing you in Philadelphia, I shall be there next month & the rest of the Winter.

* Printed in Bailey, *Ohio Company Papers*, p. 347.
1. See the items of Mason, Mercer, and Cresap, of 1767, below, pp. 239 f. This case began

in late 1757. Such length of time of a trial was common. The decision of 1757 was probably appealed and continued until 1760.
2. The General Court of Virginia.

Power of Attorney from George Mason to George Mercer

(Maryland Hall of Records, Frederick County Deeds, Liber H, folio 350.)

[March 29, 1763]

Fre.^{d} Cy
ss

At the Request of George Mason the Following Power of Attorney was recorded March the 30.th [1] one thousand seven hundred and sixty Three To Wit To all whome these presents shall or may concern I George Mason of the [Coun]ty of Fairfax in the Colony and Dominion of Virginia send Greeting—
[W]hereas the committee of the Ohio company by their resolve of the second day of this Instant March [2] did agree and direct that about Fifty Acres of the said companies Land at Wills Creek adjoining to Fort Cumberland [shou]ld be laid off into Town Lotts with about Two hundred and fifty Acres of [t]he Adjacent high Land for out Lotts to be Annexed to the Town / which is to be Called Charlottesburg / in such manner that one such out Lot shall forever belong to, and be deemed an appurtenance of the Town Lott to which it was at first annexed and on no Account separated from it & [t]hat Col^{o} George Mercer be Impowered to lay off and dispose of the same upon the Companies Account either by Leases for Three lives with privilege of renewing the said Leases for two lives more upon paying a fine of twenty Shillings sterling for each life so renewed or for the term of fifty years at an Annual Ground rent of Ten shillings Sterling or if the purchasers insist upon having a fee simple estate in their Lotts that the said lotts be sold to the highest bidder receiving in the Deeds an Annual Ground rent of Five shillings Sterling Money That the persons who take lotts either by Leases or Deeds be obliged to Build on each Town Lott within Three Years from their Respective Titles one House at least Twenty feet long and sixteen feet wide with a Brick or Stone Chimney which is always to be kept in repair under penalty of forfeiting their Lotts and that no houses or Buildings whatsoever shall be erected on the out Lotts except stables or Cow Houses and that the usual covenants for distress and reentry upon the nonpayment of the recorded Rent be inserted in the said Deeds and Leases And as the land upon which the said Lotts are to be laid off or pattented in the name of me the said George Mason in Trust for the said [Ohio Company...] [*Whole line missing, from the badly preserved original.*]
As above mentioned to the persons purchasing and leasing the said Lotts or that I should make a power of Attorney to the said George Mercer to execute and acknowledge the said Deeds and Leases in my Name Know ye therefore that I the said George Mason in pursuance of the said resolve have made

Ordained constitued and appointed and by these presents Do make ordain Constitue and appoint the said George Mercer my true and Lawfull Attorney for me and in my name but on trust for the said Ohio Company to make seal and deliver as my Deeds all and every such Deeds and Leases as may be Necessary to grant and Demise unto all and every person or persons willing to Lease and purchase the same all or any of the Lotts in the said Town of Charlottesburg and the out lotts appurtenant to the same at and under the several Rents purchases Conditions and Agreements mentioned in the above recited resolve of the said Committee of the Ohio company and also for me and in my Name to Acknowledge all and every such Deeds and Leases by him so made Sealed and Delivered pursuant to the Laws and practice of the Province of Maryland, so as to render the same Valid and Effectual to all intents and purposes to the several purchases and Lessees and to receive from the several purchasers the purchase Money for such Lotts and the Counterparts of their several Deeds and Leases to be signed Sealed Executed and Acknowledged by the several purchasers and Leases and generally for me and in my Name to do perform and execute all & every such Act and Acts thing and things as shall or may be requisite and Necessary on or about the premisses in as full and ample manner to all intents Constructions and purposes as I myelf might or could if I was personally present Ratifying confirming and holding for good and Valid whatsoever my said Attorney shall lawfully do or cause to be done in or about the premisses by Virtue of these presents In Witness whereof I have hereunto set my hand and Affixed my Seal this Twenty ninth day of March in the Year of our Lord one thousand Seven hundred and sixty Three

Sealed and Delivered in Presence of G Mason (Seal)

mark

George Horyford Robert R Haskins

On the Back of which Power of Attorney was the Following Indorsment to Wit March the 30:th 1763 Came before me the Subscriber one of his LShips Justices of the Provincial Court of Maryland Geor Horyford and Robert Haskins Subscribing Witnesses to the within power of Attorney and made oath on the holy Evang.^{s} of Almighty God that they saw the within Named Geo Mason sign and execute the within power of Attorney and that they Subscribed their Names as Witsesses thereto

John Darnall

1. Unless George Mason was in Frederick, Maryland, March 29, 1763, considerable speed was made in getting this document recorded.
2. See the resolution as found in the D.M.L. MS., printed in the *George Mercer Papers*, pp. 181-82.

George Mason and the Ohio Company against Thomas Caton

(Frederick County, Virginia, Order Book, No. 11, 1763–1764, p. 92.)

[May 4, 1763.]

Mason & Co vs Caton	Judg.t	George Mason & the Ohioh Company—Ptfs Agt Thomas Caton— Defts	In Case

This day came the Parties by their Attorneys and thereupon Came also a Jury to wit George Rice[1] John Hogdale[2] John Howard[3] John Lindsey[4] William Lochry[5] Henry Earnest[6] Richard Stephenson[7] Lawrence Snapp[8] James Lindsey[9] Morgan Morgan Enoch Enoch[10] and James Fowler[11] who being Elected tryed and sworn the truth to speak upon the Issue Joined upon their oaths do say that the defendant did Assume upon himself in manner and form as the Plaintifs against him hath Declared, and they do Assess the Plaintifs damages by Occasion of the nonperformance of that Assumption to One hundred & thirty Two Pounds Twelve Shillings and Nine Pence Three farthings, Whereupon It is Considered by the Court that that [*sic*] the Plaintifs Recover against the said Defendant his Damages aforesaid In form Aforesaid Assessed and their Costs by them about their Suit in this behalf Expended & the Said Defendant in Mercy &C.[12]

1. Not further identified.
2. On the accompanying jury list, spelled "Stogden."
3. Common name. Not further identified.
4. Last will and testament probated 1795.
5. Not further identified.
6. Private in George Mercer's Company in 1754.
7. Voted in 1758. His last will and testament was dated 1765.
8. Mentioned in the *Virginia Gazette*, May 19, 1774.
9. His last will and testament was dated 1795.
10. Not further identified than as earlier debtor to the Ohio Company.
11. Not further identified. A common name. Name mentioned in the *Virginia Gazette*, May 23, 1771. In the Frederick County, Virginia, General Index to Deeds are two items, 1765, 1767, under James Fowler.
12. Printed here as, among other significances, the last item found recorded in Virginia mercantile litigation by the Ohio Company.

Resolution of a Meeting of the Ohio Company

(N.Y.P.L. Emmet MSS., 13417, d.s.)

[July 4, 1763]

At a Meeting of the Ohio Company at Stafford Court House on Monday July 4.th 1763

The Members present approve of the Terms recomended by their Comittee at their last Meeting[1] proposed by Col.^{o} George Mercer to sollicit their Grant in England; and agree that their Treasurer do give Credit to Messrs Hanbury's Account with the Company, for the Amount of Mr Samuel Smith's Share of the Company's Lands & Stock & close Mr Smiths Account in the Company's Books by Credit for the same

Committee { Phil: Lud: Lee
J Mercer
Thos Lud: Lee }
John Tayloe
Lunsford Lomax
Presly Thornton
Richard Lee

1. Probably the meeting of March 2, 1763. In the handwriting of George Mercer. It should be observed that this item is not in the George Mercer MSS. in D. M. L. It furnishes additional data.

Thomas Hodgkin to David Ross, the Elder

(Allegany County, Maryland, Judgment Record F, folios 353-54.) *

[August 31, 1763]

Sir,

I have received the five Warrants inclosed; You send me a tithing for 500 acres, and direct the location to be in two distinct places; as I do not remember to have Known different Locations in the Same Warrant, (except by renewment) I must beg you.^{ll} to excuse me for delaying the matter untill I have the Judges direction thereon Nothing further has been done with Mr Bladens Certificates that I Know of except those mentioned herein the locations of which I insert[1] at your request

David Ross's Patent (by the name White oak Level) for "300 acres Pleasant valley[2] beginning at two bounded white oak trees Standing near the River Bank about a mile below the mouth of Evits Creek,"

Mr Bladens, "510 Acres, The Cove, Beginning at the bounded white oak Standing at the upper end of a Bottom called the cove on the north side of the North Branch of Potomack about Six or Seven miles above the Upper Old Town."

Mr Bladens, "240 acres Hunt the Hare, Beginning at a Spanish or red oak

Standing on the Bank of Potomack River about three miles from the mouth of Wills Creek"

M.r Bladens, "260 acres The Welchmans Conquest Beginning at two bounded White Oaks Standing on the brow of a hill, between a Small road and a mountain to the Eastward of the trees."

These four Tracts have been assigned to Col George Mason and the patents made out in his name [3] tho not yet Signed by the Governor, Doctor Steuart is out of Town when he returns will immediately apply for his order in respect to the Special Warrant, and if possible Send it by your post tomorrow in the mean time Shall note your application on this day so as the Warrant may be in force from the 1st March last. I have deld your patents to the Bearer, I am

Sir your most humble Servt
T Hodgkin
Annapolis 31.st August 1763

* The original could not be found. Other copies in Maryland Hall of Records, Court of Appeals, Judgments Liber T. H. No. 16 (1815), folios 102-3, 206-7. Printed in part, *Report of Cases in Court of Appeals, Maryland,* III, 525-26.

1. Inside information, bordering on, if not, collusion.
2. This nomenclature, 1763, is significant.
3. The patents, duly found, are calendared below.

Double Indemnity Bond [1] of George Mason to Thomas Bladen

(L.C. George Mason Papers.)

[Nov-8-1763] [*sic*]

Maryland

Duty Paid
John Bruce [Cl]

KNOW all Men by these Presents, That I George Mason of Virginia Gent. am held and firmly bound unto Thomas Bladen Esq.r in the full and just Sum of Nine hundred & Sixty pounds Ten Shil.s Cur.t Money to be paid unto the said Thomas Bladen his certain Attorney, Executors, Administrators, or Assigns: To the which Payment well and truly to be made and done, [I] bind my self My Heirs, Executors, and Administrators, & every of them firmly by these Presents. Sealed with My Seal, and Dated this 8 — — — Day of November Anno Domini, One thousand seven hundred and sixty & three

THE CONDITION of the above Obligaion [*sic*] is such, That if the above bound George Mason do, and shall well and truly pay, or cause to be paid unto the said Thomas Bladen his certain Attorney, Executors, Administrators, or Assigns, the just and full Sum of Four hundred Sixty four pounds Ten Shil.s Cur.t Money in p:s of Eight at Seven Shil.s & Six pence each—at or upon the first Day of June 7 next ensuing the Date hereof, w.th Legale

Interest for the same then the above Obligation to be void, else to remain in full Force and Virtue in Law.

Sealed and Delivered in Maryland
in the Presence of

Tho:^{s} Cresap George Mason (Seal)
James Tootell

[*Endorsed:*] 2 June Virginia
1763

[*Endorsed on back of document:*]

Whereas their is a Tract of Land called Pleasant Vally[2] containing 300 Acres par.^{t} of 1310 Acres[3] purchased of Mr Bladen for the Consideration of the w..th in Bond wch said Tract is not Pattented to Col.^{o} Mason Now its hereby agreed before Signing & Sealing this Bond that unless Patent is made out for It that Col.^{o} Mason is to be allowed in proportion of it's Value & also that He is to be allowed his reasonable Costs in Serving out or Obtaining a Patent for the same Witness my hand this 8 Novr 1763

Benjn Tasker

Virginia

2 June
1763

Col^{o} Geo: Mason
Bond £ 464:10: p.^{s} 8
at ye 6

Reced the
11th Jany 1792[4]
six hundred &
ninety two pounds
ten Shillings
Current money
in discharge of
the within Bond
Danl Dulany
Adm.^{r} of the
within Obligee
discharged; and a Receipt indorsed,
from Daniel Dulany Esq..^{r} Adm..^{r}
to Thos Bladen Esqr the Obligee.—
dated January 11..th 1792—

1. This is a highly complex manuscript. It covers the purchase, from Thomas Bladen by George Mason for the Ohio Company, of 1,310 acres of land in Maryland along the Potomac near Wills Creek. The first two paragraphs are a printed form filled in by the handwriting of Benjamin Tasker. An early endorsement indicates that it was first drawn up in Virginia, June 2, 1763. The signature of George Mason, save for the

capital *G* is well crossed out. The seal has been pulled off though its former presence and location are clearly evident. The transaction was consummated in Maryland on November 8, 1763. It is attested by the signatures as witnesses of Thomas Cresap and James Tootell and the payment of the customary duty is attested by the signature of John Bruce, Clerk. An endorsement on the document of the same day November 8, 1763 is in the nature of a qualifying clause and is in the handwriting of Tasker. A fourth endorsement of satisfaction or discharge of the bond, January 11, 1792, is in the handwriting of Daniel Dulany and accompanied by his autograph signature. The fifth and last endorsement records the satisfaction of the bond. It is in the handwriting, possibly, of George Mason or of some executor of his estate. Since this bond is contemporary with the patents to three tracts its genesis is obvious.

2. On this tract see particularly, George Mason to John Francis Mercer, May 12, 1792, calendared below, p. 346.
3. The exact acreage of the *Cove* (500), *Hunt the Hare* (400), *Welshman's Conquest* (260), and *Pleasant Valley* (300). To this acreage must be added *Walnut Bottom* (500) obtained early, and the purchase from Daniel Cresap of *Limestone Rock* (63) in 1783.
4. The lapse of time, twenty-nine years, is noteworthy. If no adjustment of the debt is involved, payments on the bond or of interest must be assumed.

George Mason to Colonel James Tilghman. Statement of William Trent's Account with Virginia, while Factor of the Ohio Company, enclosing Letter of John Mercer

(H.S.P. John Cadwallader Papers.)

[March 1, 1767]

Upon being informed that M.r Croghan claimed some Credit on his Bond [1] to the Ohio Company for part of the Money recovered by Captain Trent from Governor Dinwiddie, George Mason sent to M.r John Mercer (who managed the Suit for Capt.n Trent desiring a particular Acco.t of the matter, and received from Mr Mercer the following Answer and Account.

(copy)

"D.r Sir [March 1, 1767]

Your memorandum [2] by my son gave me a good deal of trouble to search for Captain Trents papers, tho I was almost certain that they would not turn to M.r Croghans advantage any further than by returning an Account of his which our Assembly refused to allow" [3]

	£
"Captain Trents claim for his own £35..4..2 and his Men's pay in the whole	222..18..0
for provisions for himself and Men	68.. 7..9
for going out with the first present, himself £100 Horses £90..16..0 Wampum £16..4..—provisions £11..14..9—Owen £6..11..4 bringing in Skins £6..9..0—Interpreter £5..16..0—an Express £5—French Deserters Express 40/1 Halfthicks 38/9 A ruffled shirt 15/—one p.s rib on 9/1 a Skin for Belts 5/.	247..18..10

For going out with the second present, himself £50.—Horses £37..2..—presents £9..15..0 Wampum £8..9..6 Match Coats £7..10..0 Expresses £6..12..—Skins for Belts £4/0 Halfthicks £2..12..11............	126..11..5
	£ 665..16..0[4]

"Of that sum £324..11..2 was due to himself and £344..4 to his [Men. He] offered me any part of what I could recover of it, and I realy believe it would have been lost, if I had not by a good ffee procured M.r Dinwiddie to be arrested at York. Even afterwards the Court [5] put me upon such proof of the Account as they were almost certain I could not procure but meeting Colo. Washington and Col.o Mercer, who recommended me to some other witnesses then luckily in Town [6] and having a good Jury who resented the Treatment Trent met with; they not only allowed the whole Acco.t but gave such Damages as satisfied me, and therefore I according to Capt. Trents order gave the Ohio Company Credit [7] for the whole £665..16..0 I hope this will be satisfactory, & am

Dr Sir

your most Obedient Servant
John Mercer
March 1.st 1767."

George Mason was also at the Expence and trouble of procuring from the Secretarys office [8] Authentic Copys [9] of all Capt. Trents Acco.ts &.c in the Suit with M.r Dinwiddie and found them to agree exactly with the above state of Mr Mercer's except the Article for provissions of £68..7..9 which in the Office Copy is £70..9..9—but whence this difference of £2..2—arises, is not apparent This it is presumed will be sufficient to satisfie both Capt: Trent & M.r Croghan, that M.r Croghan is not entitled to any Credit from the Ohio Company on this Acco..t and if by any private agreement between Mr Trent and M.r Croghan the latter has a right to any part of it (which does not appear to be the case from the papers in the Suit) Capt.n Trent ought to pay M.r Croghan himself, as Mr Mercer has given Capt. Trent Credit for the whole [sum to] the Ohio Company.

M.r Croghans Acco.t Certificates,[10] for which the Virginia Assembly refused to make him any Allowance are inclosed herewith, Col.o Tilghman [11] will be pleased to return them [12] to [me] And oblige his most Hble Serv.t

G: Mason

1. Not found. Probably a double indemnity bond covering the indebtedness indicated in the Account of June 2, 1753-September, 1755, calendared below, p. 319. A judgment was secured on this bond, December, 1767.
2. Not found and, unfortunately, not dated by John Mercer. Presumably the son was James Mercer, the lawyer.
3. Not found. Not mentioned in *Journal of the House of Burgesses of Virginia.*
4. It seems impossible to harmonize the varied statistics of Trent's accounts.

5. The General Court of Virginia. See *Journal of the House of Burgesses of Virginia, 1758–1761*, p. 255. But the trial may have begun at a local court in York County.
6. Probably Williamsburg.
7. Since Trent was the Factor and on the pay roll of the Ohio Company and had probably used Ohio Company money to pay his men, the money recovered belonged at least indirectly to the Ohio Company. The amount recovered has to be added to the other credits of the Ohio Company. It seems to have remained in John Mercer's hands as late as 1767. See Cresap to Tilghman, May 20, 1767, below, p. 335.
8. The Secretary of Virginia, 1767.
9. Some of them have survived. See the Account of April 8, 1754, calendared below, p. 325.
10. Not found.
11. James Tilghman III, the Philadelphia attorney of the Ohio Company in the suit against Croghan, December, 1767. The proposed suit was doubtless responsible for this inquiry of George Mason. This material ties in with the William Franklin-George Croghan correspondence, some of which is calendared below, pp. 339; 341.
12. They were probably returned to Virginia and there lost by fire, either in 1781 or in 1865.

Thomas Cresap to [James Tilghman III]

(H.S.P. Society Collection, a.l.s.)

[May 20, 1767]

Sir: In regard to Cap.t Trent; Mr Mercer[1] did Receive from Gov.r Dinwiddie a Sum of Money but what sum I know not, whatever the Sum was I am apt to believe it was for Goods[2] Belonging to the Ohio Company Except what was due him[3]—as Cap.t of a Company four or five Months as he was directed by Dinwooddie to Build a Fort at the Mouth of Monongahalia and not being furnished with money by the Gov.r he was Obliged to make use of the Company's money as well as Goods Such as Blankets, Guns, Powder, Lead &c to pay the Workman And furnish them with Provisions for that Purpose as appears in the Company's Books Charged to the Government of Virginia,[4] and Fort S.t George So called in the Company's Books, to the Amo.t of £269—13..5¾ Exclusive of Several Articles the Amo.t of which is Left Blank.

There is also in the Company's Books which were Left by Cap.t Trent an Open Acc.t wherein he Charges himself with Sundries to the Amo.t of £926..14..6¾ Exclusive of Some Blank Articles. and in the Same he gives himself Credits to the Amo.t of £366. 10. 3 So that there appears to be a Ballance due the Company of £560.. 4.. 3¾ Exclusive of his Joint Acco.t with Croghan[5]—

This is the best State of the Affair that I can furnish you with at this time. I should be Heartily glad that Cap.t Trent wou'd Call on me at my own House wheare Several Matters might be Settled by us greatly to his—Advantage, which woud inable him the better to Settle. with the Company who are very disireous to have their Affairs Settled. and without him it cannot be done—if I am not Mistaken Col.º Mason told me that the money Recovered from Dinwooddie is Still in M.r Mercer's hands.

The above is an Exact State[6] of the Books Kept by Cap.t W.m Trent. Examined by—

Tho.s Cresap

20th May 1767

[*Endorsed:*][7]

Colº Cresaps Let concerning the Ohio Company's demand upon Trent & Croghan

1. John Mercer.
2. Used by Trent in 1753–1754. See Ward's deposition of June 30, 1756, calendared below, p. 329.
3. Captain Trent's military pay. Since he was on the Ohio Company pay roll and probably paid himself with Ohio Company funds, debiting the government of Virginia, the sum of his pay recoverable was due the Ohio Company.
4. See the Account of April 7, 1754, calendared below, p. 329, and John Mercer's letter of March 1, 1767, above, p. 239.
5. Croghan seems to have been indebted, in 1767, to the Ohio Company for supplies of the Ohio Company used by him as commissary for military forces in 1754 and for furs and skins sold him by the Ohio Company on credit supported by his bond. The Ohio Company furs and skins were probably largely secured in exchange for other goods, thus accounting in part for the disposal of its imported cargoes.
6. On being consulted, teachers of accounting and of statistics have found it virtually impossible to harmonize the six different relevant items herein calendared. Unfortunately, the "Books Kept by Cap.t W.m Trent" were not found.
7. In the handwriting of James Tilghman III.

Receipt for Money Received by William Trent

(H.S.P. Cadwallader Collections, d.s.)

[September 25, 1767]

Received[1] at Philadelphia this 25 September 1767 of George Croghan Esq r the Sum of One Hundred & Eleven pounds ten Shillings being in full of his obligation to Francis Wafer[2] dated the twentieth day of February 1750 (1751) given at the same time to Christopher Gist by said Wafer for the use of the Ohio Company[3]

℘ William Trent
Factor[4] for the Ohio Company

59
85–
64–10
20–10

[*Endorsed:*]

Wafer Bond[5]

1. This receipt is probably related to the Trent, Croghan, Mason, Mercer, Cresap letters of the early months of 1767, and to the suit, against Croghan, of 1767.

2. Unidentified. Possibly a fur trader, elsewhere named Francis Water. He may have secured supplies on credit from the Ohio Company in 1750, and sold his furs to George Croghan, on the latter's bond, with which he paid his Ohio Company account. On the other hand, he may have bought the furs from Gist or from the Ohio Company on credit, sold them to Croghan, and turned in Croghan's bond in payment of the original purchase. It is a relatively large transaction. The sum of money should be added to the gross receipts of the Ohio Company. In February, 1751, Gist was at Pickawillany, as was Croghan and probably Francis Wafer (or Water).
3. Was this money turned in to George Mason by Trent? No record was found.
4. This status must have been nominal in 1767.
5. Not found. Possibly returned to Wafer and thus lost. This Wafer bond may have been an item in the Ohio Company suit against Christopher Gist, March 20, 1755, above, p. 239.

*George Mercer's Report * to Lord Shelburne on the State of the Company's Affairs*

(W.L.C.L. Shelburne Papers, L, 93-97. See P.R.O. C.O. 5: 1532/33.)

[October 8, 1767]

Proceedings of the Ohio Company, about the settlement of the Ohio.

About the Year 1748 or 49 several Gentlemen in Virginia and Maryland formed a Scheme of settling the Ohio, and opening a Trade with the Indians of that Country and those of the Great Lakes; and to forward this Design wrote to some Gentlemen in England pointing out the Advantages that must accrue from it to Government & Themselves, recommending it to Them to become Members of a Company which they proposed to form, as the most probable Method of accomplishing their Undertaking, not only because it would require a large Sum of Money, but it would also be necessary to have some established Regulations to conduct so Extensive a Concern. These Gentlemen if they approved the Scheme were desired to petition the King for a Grant of Lands, and Privileges which they thought the Govr of Virg.^a^, could not give Them; and because too they thought there were just Grounds to apprehend the French would not allow such Settlements to remain undisturbed, therefore no Step should be taken but with the Knowledge & Approbation [1] of his Majesty's Ministers.

The Company prayed from his late Majesty a Grant or Grants of 500,000 Acres of Land between Romanettoe's & Buffaloe's Creeks on the S.^o^ Side, and between the two Creeks and Yellow Creek on the N.^o^ Side of the Ohio; and that 200,000 Acres Part thereof might be immediately granted, upon Condition of their settling at their proper Expence 200 Families in 7 Years, erecting a Fort, & maintaining a Garrison &c. and that the remaining 300,000 Acres should be granted so soon as they should comply with the Terms of the first Grant on Condition they should settle 300 Families more in 7 Years; and the Lords Com.^rs^ of Trade having reported upon a Reference of the

Petition to their Lordships That it was their Opinion it would be for his Majesty's Service to grant the Prayer of the Company, as such a Settlement would be a proper Step towards checking the Incroachments of the French, by interrupting their Communication from their Forts on the Lakes to the Mississippi, by Means of which the British Settlement were much exposed to their Incursions, and those of the Indians in their Interest; and that beside many Benefits would arise from the Execution of the Company's Proposal.[2]

His late Majesty having been pleased on this Report to order Sir Wm Gooch then Lt Govr of Virg.^{a} to make a Grant or Grants to the Company on the Terms they prayed—they on the first Notice thereof from their Association in London, who agreeable to the Plan that had been formed immediately shipped Them a large Quantity of Goods suitable for the Indian Trade, not only applied to the Govr for the Grants ordered, but at their own Expence employed proper Persons to Uncover the Lands on the Ohio, and to make a Survey and Map of the country the only one ever made of it, till after the Conclusion of the last War, and cultivate a Friendship with the Indians there; to effect this and to begin and carry on a Trade with Them, they were obliged immediately to advance several thousand Pounds, beside taking every other Step to comply with the Conditions of their promised Grant until the French Encroachments on those Parts brought on a War.

The Company during this Time met with several Obstacles from the Govr & Council in Virg.^{a} notwithstanding his Majesty's Instructions, chiefly as they believe on Account of very large Grants of Lands being made to private Persons on the very first Report of the Instruction in Behalf of the Comp.^{a} being sent to the Govr and before it appeared, as the Members of the Company in Virg.^{a} were informed of it many Months before the Govr acknowledged the Receipt of it, tho they were assured by the Members here,[3] it was sent out at the same Time [4]—and no less than 1,350,000 Acres of Land were granted by the Govr & Council to borrowed Names and private Land-Mongers who were incapable of making effectual Settlements, & whose Grants could only therefore serve to frustrate the Ends of those to which the Comp.^{a} were entitled under the Kings Instructions and while the Company were thus engaged in removing these Difficulties, & in conciliating the Affections of the Indians residing on the Ohio at a very considerable Expence, having at the Treaty at Logg's Town in 1752 obtained the Indian's Leave to settle those Lands, of which the Indians at the same Time signed a Deed of Conveyance of them to the King, to the Purchase of which in his Majesty's Name the Company contributed largely [5] and having engaged and settled several Families on the Waters of the Ohio within the Limits of their intended Grant and having also begun a Fort at the Place now called Pittsburg, and raised a Garrison for that Service, the whole Force of the French in Canada was employed by the Govr of that Country to disappoint their Measures; and those Forces too powerful for a private Company of only 20 Members to resist effected their Design, by the Destruction of that Fort they had begun at Pittsburg, and another Fort or Blockhouse which they had actually completed at the Mouth of Red Stone Creek on the River Monongahela, together with some Store Houses they had built on the Comunication to Red Stone Creek, at a Place called in the Maps *Gists* on the West Side of the Mountains, and by plundering their Effects, which ruined most of the Traders they had employed, and the rest being chiefly killed, or the Indians whom they had traded with, being mostly engaged against Them the Company lost all [6] the Money they had advanced for the Trade

The Government of Virg.[a] pitched upon the Spot [7] now called Pittsburg where the Comp.[a] had begun a Fort, as a proper Post to fortify, and finding it necessary to raise [forces] for the Defence of that Country, gave by Proclamation 200,000 Acres of Land 100,000 Acres to be contiguous to the Fort, to the officers and Soldiers employed on that Expedition free from any Rights or the Payment of any Quit Rents for 15 Years—a Step the Company immediately acquiesced in, though the Proclamation had been made without any Application to one of their Members, and judging it for the Good of the Service, they immediately publickly gave up all their Pretensions to any Lands the Governm.[t] might allot the Military, as everyone in that Country knew their Claim to the very Lands which had been promised without their Consent to the officers and Soldiers—

The Company were obliged to remain without attempting any Thing during the War, but on the Proclamation of the Peace immediately resumed their Plan of settling the Country that had been promised Them, and which from former Possession they claimed a Right to, and thinking an Establishment on the East Side of the Mountains the first Step that ought to be taken proposed to lay out a Town,[8] and dispose of the Lots to Persons, particularly Mechanicks who were willing to settle there and pitched upon the Spot at Wills's Creek for that Purpose as the most proper Place, being the first Spot where Goods could be embarked in Boats on the Potomac and immediately on the Communication to the Country to the Westward The Ohio Company informed of the Convenience of this Spot had bought it of private Proprietors at a large Price,[9] and built Store Houses there before the War—called in the Maps the New Store—and had at their own Expence opend a Road from thence over the Mountains (which Route General Braddock took with his Army in 1755) to the Mouth of Red Stone Creek on the Monongahela, where Goods might again be embarked in flat bottomed Boats, & sent down to the Ohio. A Fort was built, at this Place, by his Majesty's Troops, called *Fort Cumberland* & the Company's Store Houses which cost Them a large Sum, not only constantly used while necessary for the Troops, but when they abandoned Them and returned to the Fort, were pulled down to build Barracks, and the Timber for above a Mile round cut down and destroyed to the Amount of some hundred Pounds, yet the Company never complained, or asked a Recompense for the Damages, but purposed to pursue their original Plan, and build new Store Houses which they were permitted to compleat, but were absolutely refused Leave by the Commander in Chief [10] to whom personal Application was made by one [11] of the Company in Behalf of the rest, to lay off or build the Town [12] they proposed—as it was thought probable from the Convenience of the Situation a Royal Magazine might be established there, and the Company were obliged to give up their Design.

The Company have actually expended above £10,000 in Support of their Undertaking, and have never been able notwithstanding their frequent Applications first to the Gov.r & Council in Virginia,[13] and afterwards to his Majesty [14] to obtain a Renewal of their Grant, which of Course prevents Them from every other Proceeding which they originally proposed.[15]

* The handwriting, not that of Fauquier nor of Blair, has not been fully identified. It seems to be that of George Mercer. This impression of the author was confirmed by the William L. Clements Library.

1. This is the language of the George Mercer Memorial of June 21, 1765.
2. This paragraph parallels the above memorial.
3. The word "here" implies that the document was written in London. Seemingly it was written by George Mercer.
4. Probably March 17, 1749, arriving in May.
5. Inside information, not found elsewhere.
6. An erroneous conclusion, as seen in documents herein published.
7. This language is used elsewhere.
8. See items of 1763, calendared below, pp. 333-34.
9. See land documents, printed above, pp. 188 f., and others calendared below in Appendix D.
10. Amherst, 1763.
11. George Mercer. The information here fits George Mercer as author.
12. Reference, as in footnote 8.
13. Not found.
14. See the Memorials of 1763, 1765, 1767, printed or reproduced in the *George Mercer Papers*. George Mercer knew best these memorials.
15. The excellence of this "State of the Company's Affairs," may be due in part to an imprint of the *Case* of the Ohio Company, which George Mercer claims to have sent to Virginia, October, 1767.

Lord Shelburne to Governor Fauquier

(W.L.C.L. Shelburne Papers, LIV, 67-69. Copy.) *

Whitehall 8:th Octob:r67 1767.

Sir,

The Lords Commiss:rs of Trade and Plantations have had under their Consideration a Petition [1] presented to His Majesty in the Year 1765 by Coll:o George Mercer, on Behalf of the Ohio Company, setting forth, amongst other Things "That on the 16:th of March 1748 His late Majesty was pleased to give an Instruction to the Lieut:t Governour of Virginia to grant the said Company, under certain Conditions, 500,000 Acres of Land between Romanettoes & Buffaloes Creeks, on the South Side of the Ohio, & between the Streame called the Two Creeks and Yellow Creeks on the North Side of the said River, and humbly praying for the Reasons therein contained that His Majesty will be pleased either to renew the said Instruction to the Lieu:^{t} Gover:^{r} of Virginia, for the Time being; or recommend to Parliament the making some Provision for reimbursing the great Expences incurred by the Ohio Company, or that the said Company may receive by a Grant of Land in some other Part of His Majesty's American Dominions, or otherwise, such Compensation, as His Majesty in His Bounty shall be graciously pleased to bestow upon them"; which Petition was referred to the Lords of Trade by an Order of His Majesty in Council of 21:st June 1765, with Directions to Report what might be adviseable to be done thereupon, but the Petitioner not appearing to prosecute his Suit, and that Part of the Country where the Lands petitioned for by the Ohio Company lie, having been thought precluded from Settlement by His Majesty's Proclamation of the 7:th Octob:^{r} 1763 they did not think it necessary at that Time to proceed any further upon this Business; but some late Proceedings of the House of Burgesses of Virginia having given Cause to suspect that some Measures may be taken there to encourage and support Persons in making Settlements beyond the Mountains, Col:^{o} Mercer has thought fit to renew his Application, and to solicit some Determination of his Petition.[2]

I am therefore to signify to You His Majesty's Commands that You transmit to me for His Majesty's Information an exact Account [3] of the Nature of the Claim which the Ohio Company have to the Lands petitioned for, what Circumstances first gave Rise to the Formation of the Company; and what Sums they have expended in consequence of the first Cession of Lands made to the Company by the *Indians*, or His Majesty's Instructions to His Lieu:^{t} of Virginia in the Year 1748 directing him to grant them the above mentioned 500,000 Acres.

I am
Sir &c.[a]

[*Endorsed:*]

Lieut:^{t} Gov:^{r} Fauquier
on the claim of the Ohio Company to certain lands.

* P.R.O. C.O. 5: 1345/385-90. Copy.

1. See the History, above, pp. 132-33, for the report of June 26, 1767, P.R.O. C.O. 5: 1368/324-28.
2. See petition of June 21, 1765, printed in *George Mercer Papers*, Part II, the *Case. . .*, pp. 30-31. See also the report of the Lords of Trade, June 26, 1767, *loc. cit.*
3. No such "Account" was found in the correspondence of Fauquier, John Blair, William Nelson, or Botetourt.

George Mercer to the Committee of the Ohio Company

(L.C., Ac. 2203. Copy.)

London October the 10· 1767

Gent[n]

I know not which of the Ohio Company to blame for their strange neglect of me here, or I may rather say for Neglect of their own Business in July 1763 the Comp[a] employed me as their agent and ordered me to proceed immediately to England to attend their further orders. I came over & hope I have done my Duty, as I will venture to say of myself, that I have been always attentive to the Company's Interest, have constantly employed myself in their service when an occasion presented, and never failed regularly to advise them of my Proceedings How loudly then ought I to complain when I recollect it is more than four years since I have attended their further orders without having received a single Instruction from them or even an Answer to any one of the Letters I have wrote, and my Astonishment at their Neglect has been greatly increased by a late occurrence, I presume the Company cannot be ignorant as some of their Members have the Honour to set both Houses of Assembly, of the Petition preferred by the Inhabitants of Augusta [1] &c demanding Leave to take away the Companys Lands, and laying the fault of that Country being so long unsetled, to their and other Grants, and yet I have a right to think if they knew of it and the steps taken by the Assembly on that Petition they should have informed me or some one else have of a proceeding which they [will]* certainly will allow most materially affected their Interest, nevertheless I imagine no one of them will say any such Information was sent there by him. I found it out by accident, & the Comp.[a] will know what steps I took, by the inclosed reports [2] of the L.[ds] of Trade a Copy of which I sent to the Committee about a month ago, and which is now also sent to the Gov[r] of Virginia by the Secretary of State. I have been so often disapointed, and so long neglected without being able to guess at any other Cause than the Possibilitie of my Let.[rs] miscarrying that I have taken care to obtain a sure Passage for this, as it will go from the Secretary of States office [3] to the Gover.[r] and I hope the Comp[a] will not remain unactive when they are told their interest is so much concerned, If it will be any Inducement to Them to employ some of their Time on this occasion I can venture to assure them they can never have a more favourable opportunity to obtain Justice The present M—try I know wish that Country to be settled & will give the Comp[a] every Indulgence such an Undertaking can merit, it is the opinion of many that you have been hardly treated, and suffered many unnecessary Delays & oppositions. I hope these reflections will induce the Comp.[a] to enter wth Spirit and Dispatch on the Business & that they will endeaver to procure a full & explicit Report from [4] the Gov.[r] after which I am sure they will meet with no Difficulty in gett.[g] their Grant renewed, for the Gov[r] must report in Your Favour.

I am well convinced this Business once settled, & y.r Petn allowed, I mean y.r Lands granted, that the whole Number of Settlers might be got in one Summer from hence, Ireland France the Protestant Provinces, & Germany as I have seen in these Countries more than 5000 Families starving for want of Employment and of Course for the Common Necessarys of Life, or draging the Chains of their Despotic Princes who treat them much worse than the meanest Black ever was by the most inhuman Oversear in Virginia The Comp.a though will no Dout recollect before they give ord.rs for the Ex.n of such a Plan, that it will absolutely necessary to tell whoever they employ, where they Lodge money to defray the Charges of it, and give him an ord.r to recieve it as no one will go from hence to Germany to Virg.a for their Expences, nor travel thro those Dominions to recieve several Months after his Expences with the addition of 5 per C.t Com.n for his Trouble tho on a former Occasion, this was thought by one of the Comp.y a most extravagant allowance

I have lately two Days since had the Honour to present a very full State [5] of the Company's affairs which was much attended to; I am ashamed, that I have not Time to make a Copy of it to send you, tho I am sure the Comp.a in their future Representation of their Case will not contradict any Thing I have said which would be all that would necessary to avoid I have stated only real Facts from my own Knowledge which the Comp.a if they will ever again only venture to think they were once called the Ohio Comp.a and that it has cost them £10,000 as I do not remember they have any other advantage to boast to Themselves—cannot fail to recollect tho indeed it is so long since I have attended their further orders, that I begin to imagine they forget their own Records

I hope I shall not be thought impertinent in my Hints or Charges ag.st the Comp.a but I cannot possibly prevail upon myself to believe they have not most shamefully neglected their own Business, the Certain Consequence of their Neglecting me, or not appointing another if they did not think me a proper Person & treating me as an Agent not fit to Manage any Thing except a Whip Top or a T to turn surely no Comp.a before ever employed an Agent & made him Undertake a Journey of 3,000 Miles without intending he should do something for Them, and they generally when that was the Case, told him what it was they expected he should do or removed him immediately that he might not do any thing & the Comp.a most undoubtly have had sufficient Time to deliberate what orders were proper for one as they have had above four years to consider of Them.

There are some Persons [6] here Petitioning for a New Government at the Mouth of the Ohio, & offer to undertake the Expences for maintaining it I do not know what success this Proposal may meet with tho I am inclined to believe it will be well received & the Petition granted—this is mere surmise in me tho I dare not say a word as certain I have seen the whole Plan, and it has been referred to the Board of Trade who have yet come to no Determination Would not a Separate Government within the Limits of your Grant be more easily settled and maintained and of course more advantagious to you,[7] than a settlement lower down can be to any other Company? I should imagine in a [few]* very few Years defray the Expences of a civil Establishment, but of this you must judge better than I can, and whether too it may not be very Material for you to begin the first settlement in that Country [8]

I must take Leave [to beg]* again to beg you will immediately take this affair into consideration and endeavor to obtain with all possible Dispatch, the Governors Report I am certain afterwards every thing will be easy, and whoever you please to give the execution of your orders to, shall meet with every Help and Information I can give, & I am convinced no one who knows the State of the Comp.ª can possibly be so well Acquainted with the Country as myself

It may perhaps be Necessary to tell you why your Case at present is referred to the Gov.ʳ so many Complaints have been made of Persons from America obtaining Lands, or what else they had no right to, that it is become at most an invariable Rule in the public offices to admit no Claim from the Plantations unless Authenticated by the Gov.ʳˢ You will see the Necessity there is to make the Gov.ʳ thoroughly acquainted with your affairs, or to get him to attest every Testimony you send over

I think it will be Necessary to send over the Treaty of Logs Town made in 1753 and the several Speeches the Indians made at seperate times in the Comp.ᵃˢ Favor together with the Deed of Sale [9] they made at Logs Town of the Lands on the Ohio to the King, and it will be certainly necessary to mention the Buildings the Comp.ª had erected at every Place, and if they would ascertain the Number of Families they had settled on those Lands, it would have great weight.

I dare not presume to tire you longer with my Remarks or advice If what I have said is taken as I mean it only, no one can blame me I am sure I have ever been ready to Obey your Commands & convince you that I esteem myself Gentlemen

Your much Obliged & Most Obedient
humble Servant
Gᵉᵒ Mercer

[*Addressed:*]
To the Committee of The Ohio Company
[*Endorsed:*]

Copy, of a letʳ fᵐ Col Geo Mercer to the Committee of the Ohio Cº 1767.

* [These words were crossed out in the document.]
1. *Journal of the House of Burgesses of Virginia,* 1766–1769, p. 37.
2. Probably including that of June 26, 1767, P.R.O. C.O. 5: 1368/324-28.
3. This letter obviously was in the pacquet sent on October 10, 1767. The pacquet probably contained the letter of October 8, 1767, of Lord Shelburne, the secretary of state.
4. Not found.

5. Of October 8, 1767, above, pp. 243-46.
6. The Vandalia and Grand Ohio Company group including Trent, Croghan, Samuel Wharton, Thomas Walpole, Benjamin Franklin, etc. But this may well be a reference to the Mississippi Company.
7. This suggestion foreshadows the Kentucky enterprise of the years following 1773.
8. Indirect reference to Kentucky lands.
9. Printed in *George Mercer Papers,* Part II, the *Case. . .* , pp. 21-22.

George Mercer to the Committee of the Ohio Company

(*William and Mary Quarterly*, I, 200-3.)

London, November 21st, 1767.

Gentlemen:

The circumstance of establishing new governments in America, which I mentioned in my last letter, is now no longer secret. Thursday last and the two preceding days, the Board of Trade were entirely employed in examinations on that subject. Among others I was called upon and interrogated very particularly, as to the practicability, necessity, use, advantage to Great Britain, expense, etc., etc., etc., of such establishments. I found my answers to these questions were very agreeable to the adventurers, and I hope to their lordships. I took an opportunity in the course of my examination, to mention the disappointments of the Ohio Company, to show the use and necessity of their scheme of settlement, and made the petitioners for the new governments acknowledge, they were convinced it was the best, if not the only, communication they could have for transporting any goods from Great Britain to the countries they proposed to settle. An officer,[1] who was in the Illinois country twelve months and who went up the Mississippi with the troops, declared that, under the most favorable circumstances, he believed it impossible to go from Orleans to Fort Chartres, where he was and where the settlement is proposed, up the Mississippi, under three months; that he had been himself four in accomplishing it, and had at times, more than half the soldiers complaining, and really worn out with fatigue. He told their lordships at the same time, that expresses, etc., had arrived there twice or thrice in eight and ten days from Fort Pitt. This declaration was much in favor of the Company, as I understand the Illinois will be settled and formed as separate governments at all events, as they find it the only method to procure the Indian trade on that quarter. I took the liberty to remark to their lordships, that from the first report of settlements being intended on that quarter, and from the beginning of my application, I had not only as my private conversation and opinion, but in every memorial I had the honor to present, pointed out that communication as absolutely necessary to be used, being the most practical and cheapest, and that it must be the door to all the new acquired countries of Indians and those in amity formerly with us, and at the same time I thought it hard treatment to the Ohio Company, that a set of gentlemen just informed of the fertility of that world, should be allowed to settle it, and have all the advantages which the first execution of a settlement there must first enjoy over a later one, while the Ohio Company were restrained from what they esteemed a right, and for which they had paid very heavily, while these adventurers acknowledge themselves, not only indebted to the discoveries made at the expense of the Company for part of their information, but for the passage they had, at a great expense too, opened for them through the mountains, as they should always use the Company's road to convey everything and their settlers to their government. Indeed, I complained as much as I thought I dared to do, of the delays the Company had met with, and especially in the last reference [2] of their claim to the Governor of Virginia. I told them I was prepared with every proof he can possibly send a copy of,[3] and could tell them more of my own knowledge than the Governor could write them, but, even without considering our former claim, I could hope we might be put on a footing with other new petitioners, and, as they acknowledge they must use the communication the Company had made for them, I should scarce imagine they would injure the Company's interest so far as not to allow them to begin their settlements at the same time with the new Adventurers. I was told the Company's affairs were discharged from their consideration,[4] and that they could not resume any care or debate upon them without orders from the King. I immediately determined to put in a memorial to the King setting forth the facts I have here stated, and have accordingly prepared one [5] which I shall present on Thursday next when I am told there will be a Council, and I have not the least doubt in my mind but it will be immediately referred to the Lords of Trade, and I think it is as clear to me the Company's claim will be allowed without waiting for the Governor's report, though I would not permit myself to think the Company will be less assiduous in endeavoring to procure that as soon as possible, for it is mere opinion I speak upon, and no one's judgement is infallible. The Governor's report I am sure cannot hurt, if the business should be done before it arrives, but if they determine to wait for it, I believe you will agree no time should be lost in sending it over. I am willing to save all I can for the Company, and have really been so hurried about their business lately that I have not had time to copy my memorial to send you.

A question has been put to me, which, as [I] was neither authorized or prepared to answer fully, I did evasively. I was asked if the Company would establish a government on the Ohio at their own expense. I replied that they only asked what they had a very long claim to, which I hoped they would obtain, and, afterwards I believed I might venture to say on proper encouragement, the Company would do everything in their power for the public good, and certainly were as capable of an extensive undertaking as any of the new petitioners.

I am told, I think from authority, that the government will give up the expense and management of the Indians and the trade to several Provinces. I was examined on this subject by the Lords of Trade, and could scarcely believe the information that had their of the annual expense; indeed I should not have credited it had been less authenticated, for the annual expense I am told, is near as not about £100,000 to the crown. God knows whether the poor savages get it.

I shall write you again as soon as I know the success of my memorial.[6] Permit me to assure you I am with great regard and esteem, Gentlemen,

Your obliged and obedient humble servant,

Ge.[o] Mercer

1. Major Farmer.
2. See above report of June 26, 1767, and letter of Shelburne of October 8, 1767, above, pp. 132-33 and pp. 246-47.
3. Not an idle boast. The George Mercer Papers, in so far as they have survived, are these proofs.
4. See the unfavorable report of June 26, 1767, above, pp. 132-33.
5. Probably the memorial of November 27, 1767.
6. This remark and comment by John Mercer in his letter to Robert Carter, February 23, 1768 (below, pp. 256-57), would seem to indicate that this letter of November 21, 1767 was not completed and dispatched before November 25, 1767.

John Mercer to Robert Carter

(N.Y.P.L. Emmet MSS., 6302.)

[December 21, 1767]

Dear Sir

As you are one of the greatest Proprietors in the Ohio Company, I have to save the Expences of Postage sent you on the other side a Copy of so much of a Letter reced last week from my Son—George dated London Sept. 18 last [1] as relates to that Comp.[a] It is now above two years since I gave notice to the other members of Committee that my ill State of health & private Affairs would not permit me to attend the Company's business [2] any longer & recommended Col.[o] Tho.[s] Lee as a very proper person to be appointed in my stead, but I apprehend my Son still looks upon me as an acting member & doubt he has not wrote to any other of the Comp.[a] I should therefore have thought myself inexcusable if I had not given the Comp.[a] the earliest notice I could of a matter that so nearly concerns them & in which no time is to be lost. I should if I had time contrived a Copy to each member as it is I have besides this sent Copies [3] to Col.[o] Tayloe Col.[o] Phil Lee & Col.[o] Mason. The Report [4] my Son mentions never came to my hands nor did I before hear of the Governor's having any directions to report what Steps the Comp.[a] had taken. If he had reced such I should have imagined that he would have called upon the Comp.[a] that he might have reced proper information in that matter & as I am persuaded he is not an Enemy to the Comp.[a] (whose interest is strongly connected with that of the Colony) his Report [5] must have been to their Advantage but of this you have the best Opportunity of any of the Comp.[a] to be truly informed.

Wishing you, your Lady, & family the Compliments of the approaching Season I am with great regard

Dear Sir

Your most obed.^{t} Servt

J. Mercer

Dec. 21, 1767

1. Not found.
2. This vague phraseology implies that John Mercer was secretarial executive from 1751 to 1765.
3. Not found.
4. Probably the report of the Board of Trade, June 26, 1767. P.R.O. C.O. 5: 1368/324-28.
5. Fauquier died before making such a report. No such report seems to have been sent back to London by his successors.

Robert Carter to George Mason

(H.S.P. Dreer Collection, French Refugees, Colonial and Indian Affairs, p. 44, a.l.s.)

To Col: Geo: Mason

W$^{m's}$burg

10th Febry 1768

Sir

Your friendly Letter [1] inclosing one for his honor the Governor, also a notification (which will be published to-morrow in both gazettes [2]) was put into my hands this day. His honor doth not open Letters after candles are alighted, therefor the Consideration of yours & a large packet are postponed, till Sol's rays shall re-illuminate our atmosphere

I have before me a transcript of part of Col: Geo: Mercer's letter dated the 18th day of last Sep^{r},[3] which is addressed to his Father: It is annexed to a letter,[4] written by mr Mercer of Malbrough; [*sic*] who saies thou hast a Copy [5] of the same. The Copy of the Report [6] of the Lords recom̃ended to his Majesty, & the Order [7] in consequence thereof, I fear are lost: For neither the former, nor the latter have been received: and our only expectation, is on the Duplicates. The Company will have a firm Basis to build on when the Report & order shall arrive; and not otherwise: I apprehend every Resolution, every Request without them, will be premature. I beg leave to remark that the expected order issued on account of our own memorial: [8] Can we consistently echo it, or recogitate anew, without considering the royal Order?—I think we cannot: But what ever shall be determined by the Gentlemen, who shall attend, I shall submit to, believing they will deliberately attend to the Papers & Information, that will be layed before them.

I would cheerfully have obeyed the sum̃ons if my state of health would have allowed me, so Sir, be pleased to present my Compliments to those Gentlemen who shall attend

Mr Mercer begs leave to resign his Place, & recomends Col: Thos Lee, as a very proper Person to act in that office;[9] if the Col will Do the business, he hath my vote freely.

12th day—

The Packet mentioned above,[10] inclosed a Copy of an order of his Majesty[11] relative to the Ohio Company. I asked for a Copy of said transcript, but it was thought uncivil to give one before it was communicated to a full Council. His honor comprises in the inclosed letter[12] the general purport of the whole Order in two words, Viz: Proceedings, & Circumstances. See his Letter.

The Governor is also directed[13] to run a line from the lead-mine (comonly called Chiswell's) to the Place the late comissioners ended at [*sic*]; who were employed by the Lord Baltimore & Messrs Penn.

It is said that two, or three new Governments will be created to the West & north-west of the presen[t] ones; & if neither of them shall include the ter- [*sic*] territory situate betwixt this Government, and Ohio-river, then the Restrictions in his Majesty's Proclamation published in the year 1763, will be taken off.

Intelligence from London. It is said the following Interrogatories[14] will shortly transpire

Who were the first Advisers, & Establishers of the Ohio-Company?

Have the Company ever given any Consideration, to the Indians for the Land they are claiming? And was the Cession made to Govern^t, or to the Company

What sum of money have they imbursed?

Do the Company say his late Majesty directed either of his Governors to grant 500,000 acres of Land to them, in the year 1748? And if that shall be insisted on, they must produce the Warrant

I design, that this article of news shall be imparted to a few Gentlemen only, & not made public I read it only once, & write f^m memory, therefor make a proper allowance. Pray furnish me with Answers to these Questons

I am, Sir,
Your most obed^{nt}
& very hum Ser^t
Robt Carter

P.S.

I shall answer the last Paragraph of your Letter, when I have more Leisure. R.C. Will not the Gov$^{r's}$ Report necessarily require y^e Company to meet?

1. Of January 23, 1768, calendared below, p. 336.
2. Of February 11, 1768.
3. Found on the reverse of the letter of John Mercer to Robert Carter, December 21, 1767, but greatly illegible.

4. Of December 21, 1767, above, p. 253.
5. *Ibid.*
6. Of June 26, 1767.
7. Of October 8, 1767, above, p. 246. Adequate proof that Fauquier made no reply before his death, March 3, 1768.
8. Probably that of June 21, 1765.
9. See the letter of December 21, 1767, above, p. 253.
10. Of October 8, 1767, above, pp. 243-47.
11. Possibly a reference to the contents of Shelburne's letter of October 8, 1767.
12. Not found.
13. The source of this information is not indicated. It may have been in another letter to Fauquier.
14. These questions are found in the above mentioned Report and Order.

John Mercer to Robert Carter

(H.S.P. Dreer Collection, French Refugees, p. 45, a.l.s.)

[February 23, 1768]

Dear Sir

Tho I sent Col.[o] Mason a copy of my Son's Letter [1] at the same time I forwarded that [2] to you I was greatly surprized that I never heard till last week that a meeting was appointed, tho Col.[o] Tayloe on the 8.th Instant wrote to him on that head & promised to attend if he had timely notice. I went about ten days ago to Fredericksburg where I catched a violent cold & was detained longer than I expected by the bad weather, so that I did not get home till Friday night & it has been raining more or less every day since. I should notwithstanding have gone today to Stafford court, tho it rained, if M.[r] Rob.[t] Brent [3] had not come in just as I was setting off & assured me that Col.[o] Mason was at his brother's & would not be at the courthouse. As I was therefore unwilling to encrease my cold, I sent my man to see if any of the Comp.[a] met & sent by him a Letter [4] from my Son of Nov.[r] 15. directed to the Committee: I desired if any of the Gent met to desire them to wait Col.[o] Mason's coming down tomorrow, when I should be sure to attend. He returned with a Letter [5] from Col.[o] Rich[d] Lee in which he informs me that he was the only person there that he opend you Packet in consequence of your orders endorsed on it, which he forwarded to me with the Pamphlets, for which I return you thanks, he added that Col[o] Tayloe intended up & that he himself would wait. I therefore hope at least five of us will be there tomorrow. Col[o] Philip Lee wrote home by him excusing his attendance on account of Westmorland court, & for some other reasons that astonished me he says a meeting would be to no end before my Son arrived, that he would have left London before he received our Letter or if not the ministry would look at nothing of that kind before all the Elections were over, which would not be before the middle of Summer. Had he come up, I coud have satisfied him by a Letter [6] from my Son dated Nov 25 & reced but Sunday last that he would not leave Lond.o till May, & that in consequence of the Report of the Lords of Trade & their Advice he had prepared a memorial [7] to his Majesty which he intended to present the Thursday following when a Council was to be held. Your Packet conveyed me a Letter from him w.th another to the Committee dated [8] October 10.th with a Copy of the Report [9] of the Lords of Trade which occasioned the direction to the Gov.r so that Col.o Lee would have found enough to have deliberated upon, but I think that my Son very justly charges the Comp.a & Committee with a most shameful neglect of their Interest. And it happens that Cap.t Anderson who lies at Leedstown has fixed the first of March for his sailing to London. The Hanbury's Claim ought also to be consider'd. I think what has been said will answer the greatest part of yours, & as you will see the order [10] & report [11] before this will reach you, there would be no occasion if I had him to send you a copy. Your Queries have been already answered in a State of the Company's Case [12] which I drew, comprehending copies of the original Papers, among them the Copy of an additional Instruction [of]* to S.r W.m Gooch dated March 16, 1748/9 to grant the Comp.a the Land petitiond for the original was sent to M.r W.m Nelson & by him delivered to S.r Wm [13] & I suppose may be found among the Council papers.[14] I am

Dear Sir

Your very humble Servt
J Mercer
Feb. 23, 1768

* [This word was crossed out in the document.]

1. Not identified, and (if not one of the two letters of October 10, 1767 and of November 21, 1767), not found. Probably the letter of September 18, 1767.
2. Not found. The date was probably December 21, 1768.
3. Relative of Mason. Brother of George Brent.
4. Not found under the date November 25, 1767; but by internal criticism really the letter of November 21, 1767, printed above, pp. 251-53. It may have been completed and mailed November 25, 1767.
5. Not found.
6. Not found. But see letter of November 21, 1767, above, pp. 251-53.
7. Of November 26, 1767.
8. Above, pp. 248-50.
9. June 26, 1767, P.R.O. C.O. 5:1332/301-6.
10. Shelburne to Fauquier, October 8, 1767, above, pp. 246-47.
11. Probably that of June 26, 1767.
12. Here, in early 1768, is indicated the origin of the printed *Case* of 1770, which is reproduced in facsimile in the *George Mercer Papers.*
13. Sir William Gooch. The fact mentioned explains the delay in June and July, 1749, in making the Ohio Company grant.
14. Not found. Probably burned in 1781 or 1865.

Memorandum of George Croghan for Mr. Gratz

(H.S.P. Etting Collection, Ohio Company Papers, I, 83, a.d.) *

[January, 1770]

Memorandum for Mr. Gratz

....

Please to Examine the Clarks offise for ye Judgt.[1] Tighlman
Entred against Trent & Croghan & See ye. amount.[2]

* Printed in Bailey, *Ohio Company Papers*, p. 485. It is not certain for which of the brothers, Barnard or Michael, the memorandum was made. The bracketed date is an editorial conjecture.

1. The record of this judgment could not be found. The reference is to a suit by the Ohio Company. It should be noted that the suit is against Trent and Croghan, and not against Croghan only.

2. See the Notes on Financial and Legal Transactions of George Croghan, October 26, 1772, below, p. 267, and W. Franklin to Croghan, November 21, 1772, calendared below, p. 339.

Indenture [1] between William Cromwell and Samuel Lyon

(Fayette County, Pennsylvania, Deed Book A, p. 85.)

[June 27, 1770]

THIS INDENTURE, made this twenty seventh Day of June in the Year of Our Lord Seventeen hundred and Seventy Between William Cromwell of Baltimore County in the Province of Maryland of the one part and Samuel Lyon of Cumberland County in the Province of Pennsylvania of the other part Whereas the said William Cromwell made a Settlement in or about the Year of Our Lord Seventeen hundred and fifty three under a Grant from the Ohio Company on a Tract of Land lying on the waters of the Yochiogeni near Bradocks Road adjoining Isaac Pearse and Thomas Gist computed to be three hundred and eighteen Acres now in the Possession of the said Samuel NOW this Indenture Witnesseth that the said William Cromwell for and in Consideration of the Sum of Twenty Pounds to him in Hand paid by the said Samuel Lyon the Receipt whereof he doth hereby acknowledge and thereof and from every part and Parcell thereof doth hereby exonerate acquit and discharge the said Samuel Lyon his heirs Executors & Administrators hath granted bargained sold aliened released and confirmed and by these Presents doth grant bargain sell alien release and confirm unto the said Samuel Lyon all the said three hundred and eighteen acres of Land and Premises with the Appurtenances to have and to hold unto the same Samuel Lyon his Heirs and Assigns forever to the only proper Use and Behoof of the said Samuel Lyon his Heirs and Assigns forever and the said William Cromwell for himself his Heirs Executors Administrators and Assigns doth Covenant to and with the said Samuel Lyon his Heirs and Assigns that He said William Cromwell and

his Heirs the same Lands and Premises unto him Samuel Lyon *and his Heirs* against all Manner of Persons whatsoever claiming or to claim by from or under him then or any of them shall and will Warrant and forever defend In Witness whereof the parties to these presents have hereunto set their Hands and Seals the Day and Year first above mentioned.
Sealed and Delivered in Presence of Us. Thos. Gist.[2] Isaac Peairs.

Wm Cromwell (Seal)

Pensylvania Fayette County. On the 22^d^ of September in the year of our Lord one thousand seven hundred and Eighty five Before me one of the Justices of the Peace and Pleas in and fors^d^ County came the within named Isaac Pearce and made Oath that he was present and an Evidence to the within Bill of Sale and that he and Mr Thomas Gist set their Names to it as such. Sworn and Subscribed the day of the above Date.
James Finley Isaac Peairs

1. The relevancy is slight yet adequate. It is a quit claim. It may be recorded in Cumberland County whose early records are inaccessible.
2. Son of Christopher Gist; householder at Gist's place, 1753; soldier, 1758; captive; pensioner of Virginia, 1763; returned to Monongahela country; made entry of Kentucky lands, 1774. Died at Mount Braddock, 1786. George Washington dined with him in 1770 and again in 1784.

George Mercer to George Mason

(V.S.L., 20624. Copy.)

Holles Street London August the 8:^th^ 1771

Col Mason

My dear Sir

I have so often troubled you on the Subject of the Ohio Company's Affairs that I am Afraid even you will think I give myself and you unnecessary Employment—but as there are at least half of the Members who compose that *extraordinary Company* whom I really do not esteem half as much as I do you, I mean as Gentlemen if they can be so called and Abstracted from the Affinity you used formerly to Claim with me, I have made the matter extremely plain to them in the enclosed Letter,[1] which though short I assure you fully contains my Resolutions as to their Concern: And I should hope if there is a Power of thinking left in the Majority of the Members, I know many of them always think right, they will not, I am sure Judgment however would be given against them in a court of equity and good Conscience, Condemn me for demanding *one* clear Answer to all the Letters I have wrote for eight years past to my Friends, my Relatives, my Acquaintances, the Committee of the Company, and the Company at large, concerning the Agentcy the Company appointed me to, on the 3.^d^ of July 1763, giving me full Power and Authority to Act for them as Seemed best to me, and I would appeal to Themselves and the world for the uprightness of my conduct towards Them; And I may at the same time venture to say that I can prove I might have gained as good terms for myself as I have for the Ohio Company at large, as their Grant seemed rather an object of contempt in their opponents, than a matter which merited Serious Attention, and the only time I could ever prevail on the English Members to go one yard to assist me, because they found my American Constitutents treated me with so little respect, it was publicly declared by the opposite party in their presence, that they did not value the claim of the Ohio Company at Six Pence, tho' they would all wish to Serve me, And as I before hinted to you in my general letter, I could have procured the Same terms for myself, And should have been moreover amply rewarded for my Assistance, and discoveries of what I knew of the Country and I can Assure you that no step has been taken without my Privity Since the Agreement [2] I entered into on Behalf of the Company. I have frequently represented to the Members of the Company in America, the trouble and fatigue and Expence and opposition I have encountered—and have notwithstanding never been honored with a Line of their Orders—they entered into a Resolution the 3.[d] July 1763, that they would repay me any Expence not exceeding £2000 I should subject myself to in Consequence of that appointment—I have wrote them several Times, that Resolution would not procure *me* here 2000 Farthings on their Credit—and I am obliged again to repeat that—I have wrote them too, that I had expended for Them near £1000 raised on my own private Credit, and I had wrote them that I had strained my Credit for them as far as it would stretch—but not one word of answer to all this—no money, no Credit, no approbation of my past Conduct, or orders for my future—Is this Sir treatment for an Agent, for one whom the Company reposed such a Confidence in? You give in Virginia your Negro Agents whom you call Gang Leaders Approbation, and sometimes an additional allowance of Meat or cloath at Christmas, and yet the Ohio Company, out of their great Generosity and politeness, have never said to me well done good and faithful Slave, nor have they ever troubled themselves about repaying me the money I have put out of my pocket for Them, I believe if I recollect, Some of the Company know that if Money does lie in the Streets to be picked up here, that they have not been able to find out the man who would or could do it for Them, And I fancy the Company *in general* know that their Partner H[anbur]y is not very Alert in giving them Credit and I can assure Them he is as Costive of his Cash to me as any man in England is, and that he has assured me a thousand times, he never will again trust them for a Shilling—how then do the Company guess I am to raise £2000 they are to repay me on the *very first* notice, after I have given them Notice at least twenty times [3] that I was half that sum in advance, and have never been able to get 12.[s] in Return, or even an Answer to one of my Letters? The curse of dancing attendance on the ministers and public Boards I have frequently mentioned though with less than a thousandth part of the humiliating Circumstances that are forced upon the poor wretch who is obliged to cringe and ask a Favor of them—Let the Company too, if ever they will trouble themselves to think of the Agreeable State they have put, and endeavour, nay appear, to resolve to keep me in, remember they will see an Article in my account [4] if they ever mean to peruse it of £125 charged as So much paid for House Rent, Expences for Clerks, Coach Hire pr year, and two Guineas pr Day for Extra Charges allowed by the English Members to their Agent here who has besides an allowance of £1000 pr Annum from them for his Trouble—and the Members in America Allow the same person £2000 per Annum more,[5] in which we are not concerned.

[*Endorsed:*] 1771 Private.

Copy of a letter to Col Mason Treasurer to the Ohio Company dated Aug.st the 8.th 1771 complaining of want of Instructions and Remittances

[*Endorsed on back:*]

London Aug. 8. 1771
Col George Mercer
to
Col George Mason, Treas.r Ohio Co.
Letter Complaining of want of
Instructions and Remittances—

1. Not found.
2. Probably the agreement of May 7, 1770, P.R.O. C.O. 5:1332/365-66.
3. Probably not mere exaggeration, though but a few of the letters have survived.
4. Not found.
5. Reference, probably, to the Grand Ohio Company and to Samuel Wharton, though William Trent represented also the "suffering traders." But it may be a reference to Charlton Palmer. The statistics seem incredible.

Robert Carter to James Mercer

(V.H.S. MS., a.l.s.)

Williamsburg 9th Decembr 1772 [1771] [1]

Sir, . . .

If a sufficient number of, members of the Ohio Co shall attend on the 16th of this Instant at Stafford Court-house to do business,[2] pray obtain a Copy of the Resolutions that shall then be made & transmit the same to me; also any Remarks hereon that may occur to you—I ask this favor being unable to attend the meeting, which is desired—

I wrote a Letter the 24th day of last Octobr [3] to your Brother Coll. G, M— part thereof is in these Words—"I was not present when your agentcy co͠menced, nor have I seen either the original Entry relative thereto, or a Copy of the same, nor did I hear of your Letter of the 10th of October 1767 [4] & the four other Letters written last year,[5] till now—My-self Colll T. Lud: Lee & Tayloe are the only members of the Ohio Co now in Town We think that any Resolution or opinion of ours on your Letter now before me, tho' notified, would not be obligatory on the [other members] of the Ohio Co We also thought, that the said Members residing in this Province & Maryland should convene speedily, or as many of them as can be gotten together, & that they should transmit to you their Sentiments touching your Conduct &c In the Interim, I say, in Confidence, if thou art properly authorized to act for the Ohio C^o^ I will patronize you, tho the measures have not succeded, wch you adopted—because I do not suspect your Integrity—You say that the money Lenders in Great Britain will not advance upon the Credit of the Ohio C^o^ only, & you declare that you will not make any overture to borrow money for their use—I have a little money deposited with Messrs Thos & Rowland Hunt, merchants of London,[6] who will deliver to you 200 £ Sterling, on your Bond [7] payable to me—I told Lee & Tayloe that I should order a house in London to put into your hands 200£, if you should call on them and then advised Lee & Tayloe to give you further Credit"—I am,

Sir, Your most hu st
Robt Carter

N.B. I intend that N,[8] H,[9] shall be sued in the County Court & not in the General Court ——————

To James Mercer Esq
Attorney at Law
Fredericksburg

[*Addressed:*]
To James Mercer Esq:r
Attorney at Law at
Fredericksburg

1. The contents indicate that this letter should be dated 1771.
2. No further documentation of such meeting found.
3. Not found. "Last October" seems to mean, October, 1771. See Hunt to Carter, February 29, 1772, below, pp. 364-65.
4. Printed above, pp. 248-50.
5. No letters of 1770 have been found. The phrase may mean "last twelve months." See letter of August 8, 1771, above, pp. 259-61. Other three not found.
6. Not identified. But see the letter of Hunt to Carter, February 29, 1772.
7. Not found. But see mention of the bond in Hunt to Carter, February 29, 1772, below, pp. 264-65, and Carter to Taswell, July 24, 1773, below, p. 268.
8. Not identified. Possibly Nathaniel Harrison, if merely the first of two initials.
9. Not identified, if not the second initial of Harrison.

James Mercer to Robert Carter

(Formerly in the possession of W. Garnett Chisolm, Leesburg, Virginia. Now on deposit with the Historical Society of Virginia, a.l.s.)

[December 31, 1771]

Honble Sir

Your favours [1] covering Mr. Carter's Bond to you & protested Bill passed to Mrs. Tasker, Mr. Grymes's Bond & Bill to the late Colo. Tasker, came to Hand today; your Instructions regarding them shall be immediately observed, having—thank God—now & not till a few Days past resumed Business being confined to my Room with slow Fevers ever since I had the pleasure of seeing you, except when I ventured to Mr. Selden's expecting to meet the Ohio Company at Stafford Court House agreeably to my advertisement, by which I was not a Little worsted in my Health.

Not a single member regarded my advertisement, so that I have in compliance with my Inclination to oblige & obey my Brother, been obliged to write [2] each member (Colo. Tayloe excepted for he agreed at Wmsbg.) by express requiring their immediate & explicit answers as to the requisitions made by my Brother in his last Let. to the Compy, which you saw during the last Genl Court & to which I beg leave to refer you.

As you seemed a total Stranger to my Brother's appointment, and thought it necessary for your Government, I have inclosed you a Copy [3] to which I ought to add their impowering of him to take up & apply to the amount of 2,000 £ on the Company's Acct. promising to reimburse him immediately on notice. This with the Letr allready referred to will give your Honour all the Knowledge I have of this affair & convince you how justly my Brother calls on all the Members of the Company for their proportions of his advance, which If I mistake not, at his last writing amounted to 1300 & odd pounds Sterl., exclusive of what everybody must think he ought to ask in part of his very great expense & trouble incurred in the prosecution of their Business, and what must necessarily occur at the completion of the Grand Company's Grant, (which was expected to be on the 25th of October last) with whose Fate he had involved that of the Ohio Company, as the best he thought cou'd be done for that Company; in confirmation of which procedure, (waving the opinion I hope you & all his acquaintances, have of my Brother's Integrity) I beg leave to observe he is more interested in the Ohio Company than any member of it (your Honour excepted) holding one share and a half in his own Right.[4]

I am now to request, as desired of the other Members, that your Honour will favour me with your immediate answer,[5] in writing, saying with precision will you, aye or no, engage to abide by my Brother's agreement for the Ohio Company in the Union with the Grand Company? and will you, remit him your proportions of his advances? I hope you will determine in the affirmative! if you do, I shall be much obliged to you for your Bills For 400 £ Sterl by next post, that I may forward them to his Relief (want them he certainly must) before he quits London. I ask 400 £ of you, understanding you hold two shares, if I am mistaken half that Sum will do. I wish you happy new year and all felicity and have the Honour to be

Yr Honour's most obedient & very
humble Servant
Js Mercer

St. James's Dec. 31st 1771

P.S. I beg your answer by next Post, I doubt not, you will not delay it, when you reflect you will not be at full Liberty to make your Election, shou'd the advices of the 25th of Oct. relative to the Grand Company's Grant arrive here, before you declare your Sentiments as to the present Propositions.

Fredg [*not clear numerals*]

To The Honble Robert Carter Esquire
Williamsburg [*Armorial red wax seal*]

[*Across the end in another handwriting*]
James Mercer 1771

1. Not found.
2. See the correspondence of January, 1772, D.M.L. MS., printed in the *George Mercer Papers*, pp. 312-24.
3. This copy not found, but see the copy D.M.L. MS., printed in the *George Mercer Papers*, pp. 182-83 and 296.
4. Note the discrepancy with George Mercer's claim of ownership of two shares, May 28, 1771, calendared below, p. 337.
5. Not found.

Richard Lee to James Mercer

(N.Y.P.L. MS., Misc. Papers, Richard Lee folder, a.l.s.) *

Lee Hall Jan.y 21.st 1772

Sir/

The relation in which I stand to the Ohio Company forbids me by every kind of principle from doing any thing by which the Gentlemen concerned may be affected without their previous knowledge and approbation. You will find me Sir in March next very readily disposed to comply with whatever shall be the result of the United councils of the Company. The late Advertisement for the meeting of the Company I never saw untill the time appointed for the meeting was expired.

I am Sir Your
Humble Serv.t
Richard Lee

[*Addressed:*] To
M.r James Mercer
at
Fredericksburg
By his Express

[*Endorsed:*]
Richard Lee
1772

* Copy in D.M.L. MS., printed in *George Mercer Papers*, p. 323.

Thomas and Rowland Hunt[1] *to Robert Carter*

(Maryland Historical Society, Tench Tilghman Papers, 1770-1772.)

London 29th Feb.y. 1772

Sir

Since ours of 31.st. Dec.r.[2] ℘ Captn Dunsley we have reced yours dated 24th Oct.r. 1771,[3] covering a Remittance for £150 . . . . which is accepted

& shall be passed to y^r credit when due. Agreable to your desire Col^o George Mercer called for £200 . . . . which we let him have on his signing 2 Bonds[4] (both of the same tenor & date) one of which we now enclose you—

We have sold 4 more hhd^s of y^r Tob.^o. at 10½^d ℔ lb.

At the time we procured the Glass Bowls from Mr. Dobbs[5] we mentioned to him the sound of the Delph Bowls to which he gave no credit & he was so short with us that it was a doubt whether the Glass Bowls could be obtained from him.

We have placed Master B. . Benson[6] at an Academy where he is improving himself in such Accomplishments as are necessary, for the Military Life which he has chose—or as a Gentleman & will wait y^r Determination concerning him.

We hope by the middle of next Month to send out Captn Clark in a Ship to load in York River as usual & shall be much obliged by any kind assistance you give him in his Loading

We are Sir
Your very hble Serv^ts
Thos. & Rowl^d Hun[t]

[*Addressed on side:*]

Robert Carter Esqr.

[*Not endorsed.*]

1. London merchants, prominent in colonial trade and finance. See Robert Carter to James Mercer, December 9, 1771, above, pp. 361-62.
2. Not found.
3. Not found, but see the letter of the same date of Carter to George Mercer imbedded in Carter to James Mercer, December 9, 1771, above, pp. 361-62, and non-payment of the bonds, in Carter to Taswell, July 24, 1773, below, p. 268.
4. Not found.
5. Not identified.
6. Not fully identified. Probably Benjamin Benson, scion of a Maryland family. He was left a legacy by Benjamin Tasker, Senior. Robert Carter was one of the executors of this legacy. See *Va. Mag.*, XVIII (1910), pp. 83-84.

Minute of the Virginia Council

(P.R.O. C.O. 5: 1440/43-46. V.S.L., photostat, p. 45.)

At a Council held July 27. 1772.
Present
His Excellency
William Nelson William Byrd
Thomas Nelson Robert Burwell
John Page Esquires.

His Excellency laid before the Board a Letter[1] from Col Richard Lee, inclosing a Petition from the Ohio Company,[2] wherein they complain of their Agent Col George Mercer's having undertaken without their Consent or

Authority to make an Agreement of Copartnership to subsist between the said Company and Thomas Walpole Esq.[r] and others his Associates in Great Britain with respect to the said Company's Grant of Lands on the Western Frontier of this Colony, and praying that they may have a Warrant to survey the said Grant.

WHEREUPON it was ordered by Advice of the Board, that the substance of the above Representation be entered on the Council Journals,[3] and that the Clerk inform [4] Col. Lee that as there is no Precedent of any other Warrant to Survey Lands, than the order by which they are granted, and the Company having already such an Order in their Favour,[5] it does not appear necessary for the Board to do any Thing farther. . . .

1. Not found.
2. Not found. Probably of July 7, 1772. See the petition of 1778, printed in Bailey, *Ohio Company of Virginia,* pp. 320-27. The decision to present such a petition may have been reached at a meeting, May 25, 1772.
3. Not found.
4. Not found.
5. It is hard to classify this remark. Is it a confirmation, a rejection, or merely an evasion? But it may have served as a justification for the later Kentucky Survey of the Ohio Company. Note that the Board came from southern Virginia.

Advertisement for Sale of George Croghan's Philadelphia Property

(*Pennsylvania Gazette*) *

[August 19, 1772]

To be SOLD by PUBLIC VENDUE, on the 23d of September next, at 6 o'clock in the evening, at the London Coffee-house, Philadelphia.[1]

A CERTAIN tract of good LAND, containing 18 acres and 23 perches, with a good two story brick house, two small brick outhouses or offices, a good barn, stable and coach-house, a good large garden and orchard; the place is generally called Monckton Hall, situated in Poplar Lane, in the Northern Liberties, within two miles of this city, finely situated for a gentleman's country seat; a plan to be seen at said Coffee-house, at the Indian King, and Queen. Any person [2] inclinable to purchase the same by private sale, may know the terms, by applying to MICHAEL GRATZ, on Fourth-street, Philadelphia.

* Repeated September 9, and September 23, 1772.
Reprint in William Vincent Byars, *B. and M. Gratz . . . Papers* (Jefferson City, Mo., 1916), p. 200, from the supplement to issue of August 26, 1772, omitted in the microfilm.

1. The advertisement is relevant to the judgment of the Ohio Company, December 1767, against this property, thus described.
2. A Mr. Jones seems to have made an offer of £1,100. See William Franklin to George Croghan, November 21, 1772, calendared below, p. 339, and to William Trent, March 14, 1776, calendared below, p. 341.

*Notes * on Financial and Legal Transactions of George Croghan*

(Free Library of Philadelphia, Ridgway Branch, McAllister Collection MS.)

[October 26, 1772]

A State of the Case respecting the Mortgage on Croghan's House & Lotts in the Northern Liberties

1766

May 2[d] G. Croghan mortgaged to Thomas Wharton [1] his three Brick Messuages or Tenements & about *four* Acres of Land in the Northern Liberties for £500 Pensylv.[a] Money

May 17. The said Mortgage was recorded [2]

1767

Dec[r] A *Judgement* [3] on a Bond to a certain Geo. Mason (Agent for the Ohio Company) was obtained against Geo- Croghun and Fi-Fa- issued- Penalty Two Thousand Pounds—which as Ja.[s] Tilghman the Attorney on Record says, is not satisfied. i. e. on the 26th Octo.[r] 1772

1768 Dec.[r] 12th Satisfaction was entered upon Record [4] for the Mortgage to Tho.[s] Wharton

Dec.[r] 13. Geo- Croghan purchased of H. Roberts & others [5] two Lotts containing *Fourteen* Acres & 54 Perches of Land adjoining to his place before mentioned in the Northern Liberties—The same day (Viz. Dec.[r] 13) Geo- Croghan mortgaged [6] to William Franklin the three Brick Messuages & 4 Acres of Land, and also the 14 Acres & 54 Perches adjoining.

Quere, Whether the *Judgment* above mentioned (supposing it to be regularly obtained and recorded) can affect a bona fide Purchaser of both or either of the said Tracts?—[7]

* Seemingly by Joseph Galloway, but not in his usual handwriting.

1. Thomas Wharton (1735–1778), prominent Philadelphia merchant. *D.A.B.*
2. Recorded in the Recorders Office of Philadelphia County, Pennsylvania, in X-10, p. 338.
3. The official records of this suit have not been found, though carefully sought. The judgment, and possibly the bond, should have been recorded. The penalty of £2,000 indicates an account of approximately £1,000.
4. See footnote 2. In the light of the Judgment of December, 1767, this transaction suggests that Croghan made some effort to clear his property before mortgaging it to William Franklin on December 13, 1768.
5. Recorded in Office of Recorder of Deeds, Philadelphia, Book D-68, p. 653.
6. That this mortgage was recorded in Philadelphia is not indicated by the context, but it is in X-13, p. 335, Office of the Recorder of Deeds, Philadelphia.
7. This is a lawyer's question, probably notations of Joseph Galloway, though seemingly not in his handwriting. In his letter to Croghan of November 21, 1772, calendared below, p. 339, William Franklin mentions Galloway's "State of the Case."

Robert Carter to John Taswell at Williamsburg

(Duke University Library, Carter Papers.)

Nomony Hall
July 24,th 1773

Sir,

Coll Geo Mercer, now beyond Sea, owes me 200£ Sterling on his bond,[1] only, Penalty thereof 400£. Has G. M. Effects in this Colony and if he has can part thereof be taken to satisfy my Demand Against him [2]

1. See Carter to James Mercer, December 9, 1771, above p. 261; and Hunt to Carter, February 29, 1772, above pp. 264-65.
2. No reply by John Taswell is found among the Robert Carter MSS. in the Duke University Library. George Mercer did have extensive landholdings in Virginia in 1773, but they were heavily mortgaged. The well-documented matter of their sale in November, 1774, is only indirectly an Ohio Company matter. No participation in the proceedings by Robert Carter was revealed in the records.

John Tayloe to William Preston [1]

(W.H.S. Draper MSS., 4QQ5, a.l.s.)

[January 28, 1775]

Sir

As Cap.t Hancock Lee [2] is appointed by the Ohio Company to survey their Land (of which Company I am a member) thinks he may possibly be able to do some other work. Wishes to have a deputation [3] from you, I take leave to ask the favor of you to grant his desire which please consider as an Obligation done to

S.r

Your Obed.t hble Serv.t
John Tayloe

Mount Airy
Jany. 28th 1775

1. Born 1729. Son of John Preston, the associate of James Patton. Surveyor of Fincastle County, January 5, 1773, of Montgomery County, September 2, 1774, and probably official surveyor of Kentucky County. He moved to Kentucky, where he died in 1783. In addition to the voluminous Preston Papers in the Draper MSS., there are many in the Library of Congress.
2. Son of Hancock Lee of "Ditchley" and brother of Willis Lee; in charge of the Ohio Company surveyors in 1775; afterward lived in Kentucky, dying there about 1820. Nicholas Cresswell (*Journal*, Dial Press, 1924), on Sunday June 11, 1775, "Found Captn Hancock Lee camped at Elkhorn, surveying land."
3. Somewhat obviously this letter represents an indirect and inside effort of the Ohio Company to have its surveyor made a deputy surveyor of Fincastle County and thus meet the legal requirement of possession of such status. The favor seems not to have been granted. Preston represented frontier rather than tidewater interests.

Survey for Francis Ash[1]

(Fayette County, Kentucky, Fayette Surveys D, p. 385.)

[Reference to the Ohio Company's Survey of 1775.]

January 4th 1783.

. . . upon the East side of Stoner's fork of Licking,[2] in the county of Fayette, and bounded as follows (To-wit): Beginning at an old marked Locust and a Young Elm, in the line of survey made for the Ohio Company, thence So. 70 E. at 162 poles crossed a branch, at 368 poles crossed a Run, the Course continued, in all 382 poles, to a Red Oak and Linn, a corner to Anne Churchill,[3] thence along her line No. 34 E 260 poles to a Cherry tree and Ash, in the line of James Ware,[4] then along his line No. 70 W. 382 poles to an old marked Buckeye and Walnut in the Ohio Company's line, thence along that line So. 34 W. 260 poles to the Beginning . . .

1. Probably of Fauquier County, a second lieutenant in 1779. By a Virginia grant and a survey of December 14, 1784, he got 1,400 acres of land on Cabbin Creek, Fayette County, Kentucky.
2. Here the Ohio Company survey line is found in the northeast corner of Clark County of the present day, or possibly in Montgomery County.
3. Her grant of 207 acres on Stoner's Forks was also dated January 4, 1783. Her name is not prominent in Kentucky annals.
4. A soldier in the Second Virginia State Regiment.

Kentucky Land Entry of Daniel Leet[1]

(Fincastle County, Kentucky, Entry Book A, p. 32.) *

[December 7, 1775]

Daniel Leet produced his memorandums and demanded to have noted in this Book as Above (to wit) 400 Acres of Land upon the north fork of Elkhorn Creek 7 or 8 Miles Above the forks Including an Improvem^{t} & Cabbin. Also 400 acres joining the above at a Cabin & Improvem.^{t} Also 400 Joining the Ohio Co.^{ys} Survey, Beginning at a Hicory & Sug.^{r} Tree the 3^{d} Corner[2] in the Survey . . .

* Printed in Wilson, *Ohio Company*, pp. 56-57.

1. Born in New Jersey, 1748, surveyor under William Crawford, West Augusta County, Virginia, Revolutionary soldier. Died in 1830 in Leetsdale, Pennsylvania, so named in his honor.
2. Probably in Scott County of today. Very likely the first two surveys were made in June, 1775 and the third in midsummer, 1775. Daniel Leet was awarded 1,000 acres on the north fork, in 178c. *Register,* XXI, 160.

Marker on the west side of Russell Cave Pike, six miles south of Centerville, Kentucky, Marker No. 20

COMMONWEALTH
of
Kentucky
OHIO COMPANY
OF
VIRGINIA
SOUTHERLY[1] LINE OF SURVEY OF 800,000[2]
ACRES (NOMINALLY 200,000)
MADE BY CAPT HANCOCK LEE
IN 1775 FOR COMPANY FORMED
IN 1748 TO ACQUIRE LANDS
IN OHIO VALLEY—A CORNER
IS S 70° E ABOUT 1 MILE
HISTORICAL MARKERS SOCIETY.

1. "Southerly Line," here probably means not only the direction but also the south side of the polygon of the survey. The farthest south point of the survey seems to have been another corner about two miles southeast of Winchester, Kentucky.
2. Incorrect. It was not more than 400,000 acres.

Land Claims of Thomas Gist

(Pennsylvania Department of Internal Affairs, Land Office Bureau, Harrisburg, Pennsylvania.) *

[February 4, 1780]

Thomas Gist in Right of Christopher Gist
by Certificate for 400[a]

Situated on Gist's Run on both Sides of Braddock's Road in Union and Franklin Townships Fayette County and Surveyed the 19th Day of October 1785. In Consequence of a Certificate Issued by the Commissioners for adjusting and Settling Claims to unpatented Lands &c of which the following is a true Copy

We the Commissioners for adjusting Claim's to unpatented Lands in the County's of Monongalia Yohogania & Ohio Co herby Certifie that Thomas Gist Ass[e] of Nath.[l] Gist is intitled to four hundred Acres of Land in Yohogania County on Gist Run to include his Improvement made thereon in the year of our Lord, 1773. Also a Right in Preemption to one thousand Acres Adjoining thereto. Given under our hands at Cox fort the 4 day of Feb[y] 1780. & in the fourth year of the Commonwealth

Test Saml Irwin,[1] Clk Pro.r Temp.e — Francis Peyton[2]
Feby 4th Entd Book No 1 fol.o 13 Entry N.o 96. — Phil Pendleton[3]
Mar 18t 1785. Copy Teste W: Crawford S.Y.C. — Joseph Holmes[4]

B Johnston[5]

Note, the Northern part of this Survey includes an Improvement or Small Messuage and Plantation Claimed by Thomas Rogers who in Cosequence thereof Caveats the acceptance of this Survey

P.r Alexander Mclean[6] Depty

To John Lukens[7] Esqr
Surveyor General

[*Endorsed:*]
1785,
Fayette County
Thomas Gist in Right of
Nathaniel Gist
B. 4. 58 458.a & all
192.a66
Red &c 11 June 1864 on
Wt to Accept to
Jacob Murphy[8]
266a 54
Retd &c 4th Nov. 1864

Pat. Nov. 4—1864
Mary Meason[9]
H 58—137

* The Virginia certificate and surveys of 1780 and the later Pennsylvania confirmations and acceptances are well preserved in the Land Office at Harrisburg. Their specific location and shape are, for Gist items, seen in the maps of Union, Franklin, and Dunbar townships, Fayette County, Pennsylvania in the *Horn Papers*, III. Based on improvement and preemption claims of Christopher, Nathaniel, Richard, and Thomas Gist, they involve nine surveys, totaling about 2,680 acres.

1. Probably a Pennsylvanian who had gone to the upper Potomac and from there to the Monongahela area where he became an important figure.
2. Of Loudoun County, Virginia, burgess, 1768–1769–1771–1774.
3. Colonel in the Berkeley County, Virginia, militia, 1777.
4. Colonel in the Frederick County, Virginia, militia.
5. Deputy surveyor from Fredericksburg, Virginia, where he was innkeeper and townclerk. Came to Ohio Valley in 1776–1777. Accumulated great landed estate. His descendants scattered over the West. Many of the family papers are in the possession of Stanton C. Crawford of the University of Pittsburgh.
6. Of Westmoreland County, Pennsylvania. Deputy surveyor under John Lukens.
7. Famous surveyor of Pennsylvania.

8. Not identified.
9. Member of the famous Isaac Meason heirs, who long owned the old lands of the Gist family.

Suit [1] of David Ross and Others against James Guest, Tenant of George Mason and the Ohio Company

(Maryland Hall of Records, Docket Books [2] of the General Court of the Western Shore of Maryland, 1780, October Term, p. 45.)

Oct 1780 Jgs	appls for	David Ross, Horatio Ross & Archibald Ross their Lesse		Eject. Service 1st Septem.r 1780
3.	Geo. Mason [3]	a	Wash.	Leave
T S J H.[4]	Land Lord July 21	James Guest Tent.		

1. The case in suit was mainly concerned with the dispute about a tract of 300 acres, called *Pleasant Valley* by the defendant but *White Oak Level* by the plaintiffs.
2. The many items from the docket books are accompanied by many warrants, surveys, plats, depositions, and judgment records. Similar data is embedded in the records of Allegany County, Maryland, and of the Maryland Court of Appeals. In addition there are three items from a similar suit in Washington County, Maryland, 1783.
3. Hereby George Mason became the defendant as seen in later items of the case. Eventually his executors and heirs were involved.
4. The initials in such dockets are those of the lawyers connected with the case. Here the initials are those of Thomas Stone (1743–1787) and John Hall.

Robert Carter to George Mason

(Duke University Library, Robert Carter Letter Books, IV, 75, a.l.s.)

Nomony Hall May the 11.th 1781

Sir—It is Said that the Legislature of this State have Established Some officer Claims founded on works returned by Surveyors [1] acting under the like authority of M.r H. Lee, who was appointed to Survey, by Some members of the late [2] Company Styled the Ohio Company—if this Report should be well found—I apprehend that the Claims of Such of the Members who choose to appear in a petition addresed to the house of delegates, may be revived im̄ediately [3] relying therein on the Establishment mentioned above as a president [*sic*], to bottom their Claims—If this Idea Should be approved on & a petition [4] Shall be prepared & presented, pray have my name inserted therein for two [5] fortieth parts, I having purchased two Shares of the late M.r Aug.t Washington and M.r Gawin Corbin, members of the Ohio Company

I am Sir

Your very Hum.e Ser.t
Robt Carter

Col.o George Mason

1. *Journal of the House of Burgesses of Virginia*, 1779–1781, *passim*.
2. Indication that the Ohio Company was considered to have expired before 1781.
3. A vain expectation. But compensation elsewhere in Kentucky, as in the case of Richard Henderson, would have been reasonable.
4. Not found.
5. It seems this should be four-fortieths or possibly "two Shares each," for each share was two-fortieths.

Last Will and Codicil of James Scott

(Prince William County, Virginia. Will Book G, folio 180 f.)[1]

August 2, 1782

Folio 181. "Item I leave my friend Col.° George Mason my [*sic*] agent to manage my share of the Ohio Company & to pay the money of my part to be added to my personal estate." ————————————————.

f. 182. "Item I do Declare it to be my meaning & Intention that the money goods and Debts only of my share in the Ohio Company are to be Considered as personal Estate included in the Bequest to my wife & Daughters, but that my Share of the lands as a member of that Company Shall be equally divided Share & Share alike to take as tenants in Common and not as jointenants between my said Grandson Alexander Scott Son of James my three Sons John Gustavus and William and my Grandson Alexander Scott Son of my late Son Robert Scott deceased and their Heirs forever, but if my Grandson Alexander the son of Robert Scott Should Die without issue before he arrives at the age of twenty years then his share of my Lands in the Ohio Company is to be equally Divided between my said Grandson Alexander the son of James Scott and my said sons John Gustavus and William and their heirs for Ever as tenants in common.

f. 183. Mention again of "my Share of the money Goods or Debts in the Ohio Company."

1. As stated earlier above, this item is evidence that the Ohio Company was a matter of importance and concern for decades after its supposed legal end in May, 1771.

Suit[1] *of George Mason's Lessee against Charles Clinton*

(Maryland Hall of Records, Docket Books of the General Court of the Western Shore of Maryland, 1783, May Term, folio 69.)

J. g. s.	Ent[d]	George Masons Les	Eject. Wash.
V 7	March 15	a	Service March 1783.
	Cha	Charles Clinton	Stk off.[2]

1. See the record of this suit in Washington County, Maryland, November Court, 1782, Judgment Records, No. 1, folios 34-41.
2. George Mason and the Ohio Company lost the suit and, thereby, the unpatented lands of the Walnut Bottom Resurvey, and the case was dropped. But George Mason in his last years had not abandoned the claim. See his letter to John Francis Mercer, May 1, 1788, calendared below, p. 344.

Bonds Accepted as Specie

October 27, 1783

[Bonds[1] of Thomas Beall of Saml., Brooke Beall, William Deakins Junr and Js McCubbin Lingan to George Mason for, respectively, £1408 and £1407.]

1. The originals were not found. They were probably burned along with many other George Mason papers. But legal copies are embedded in items of June 15, 1791, found in Maryland Hall of Records, Western Shore General Court Original Judgments, 1792, one of which is printed below, pp. 280-81.

Deposition of Robert Johnson[1] (1806) on Ohio Company Survey Lines

(Fayette County, Kentucky, Circuit Court, Clerk's Office, Complete Record Book "B"—1805-1810, Lexington District Court, September 26 1806, p. 280.) *

[Reference to early 1783]

Deposition of Robert Johnson, taken in Fayette County, 27 May 1806; deposes—That he first became acquainted with John Floyd in 1780 when he moved his family to said Floyd's station on Bear Grass creek in Jefferson county. Said Floyd informed this deponent he had made a survey on waters of North Fork of Elkhorn for one Boyd, and as this deponent moved his family to Bryant's station, near the beginning of the year of 1781, desired this deponent to find the corner of said Boyd's survey of 1,000 acres and to run out the course and distance from the South west corner of said survey N. 20 E 400 poles and then to make a corner agreeable—to the description given by the certificate of survey. This deponent accordingly examined and found what he thought was the South west corner and—made a corner but found an old line[2] on that corner—and he thinks early in the year 1783 he had traced an old line from Boyd's S.W. corner—to a corner he supposed was intended for William Ingles—and some distance further to a corner in three sugar trees—"Ohio C", cut on a tree—he thinks one or other corners would be claimed by said Ingles.—Nor does deponent recollect to have seen any old line running from the survey supposed to be Christian,[3] Meredith,[4] Dandridge[5] or Russel[6] lines—some of the—boundaries of the surveys supposed to be Christian's, Meredith's, Dandridges or Russell's were open lines and not marked. The Line—from Boyd's S. W. corner was marked all the way.[7]

* Printed in the Kentucky State Historical *Register*.

1. Father of Richard M. Johnson. His reputation was then and has remained high.
2. In the opinion of the author, this "old line" was that of the Ohio Company of July, 1775.
3. William Christian (c. 1743–1786), prominent frontiersman and soldier of Virginia. Moved to Kentucky in 1785. *D.A.B.*
4. Samuel Meredith, burgess from Hanover County, Virginia, 1766. Captain in 1768 and Colonel of Virginia troops, 1776.

5. Bartholomew Dandridge, burgess of New Kent County, Virginia, 1771 and 1774; judge of Virginia court of 1779; council member, 1777.
6. William Russell, of Fincastle County.
7. The author believes this south line of Boyd's tract was the old main line of John Floyd's surveys of 1774.

Deed of Share of the Ohio Company by Thomas Cresap

(Washington County, Maryland, Land Record, Liber C, folios 5-6.)

[April 19, 1783]

Examined &
[d]elivered
John Jacobs.

At the reques [*sic*] of John Jacobs & Daniel Cresap James Cresap & Michael Cresap was the following Deed Recorded May 10th 1783—to wit, This Indenture made the nineteenth day of April– in the year of our Lord one Thousand seven hundred Eighty Three Between Col.^{o} Thomas Cresap of the neighbourhood of Skipton in Washington County Maryland on the one part and Daniel Cresap son to the aforesaid Thomas Cresap and James Cresap & Michael Creasap [*sic*] Infants Grandsons to the aforesaid Thos Cresap sons of Michael Cresap late of Skipton deceased all of Washington County Maryland on the other part, Witnesseth, that the said Thos Cresap as well for and in consideration of the Natural love and affection which the said Thomas Cresap hath and beareth unto them the said Daniel Cresap James Cresap and Michael Cresap, as Also for the better Mentanance [*sic*] livelyhood and preferment of them the said Daniel Cresap, James Cresap & Michael Cresap hath given granted, alien'd enfeoffed and confirmed and by these presents doth give grant alien enfeoff and confirm unto them the said Daniel Cresap, James Cresap and Michael Cresap their Heirs and assigns, all that Valuable and undivided tract of Land, Called the Ohio Compan[y] Grant,[2] (that is to say) all the claim of him the aforesaid Thomas Cresap said Grantor any part thereof in right and by Virtue of his being a member of said Company which Aforesaid grant was Originally prayed for and claimed as five hundred thousand Acres to be surveyed and laid of on the Waters of the river Ohio, one Twentieth part whereof ought and is the proper right and property of him the said Thomas Cresap as Member Aforesaid but be the same more or less either at this time or hereafter, it is the Intent and Meaning of him the said Thomas Cresap that every part, parcell Interest or Claim with which he is now possessed or ought of right to possess, or may hereaftere [*sic*] become his right and property by Virtue and in right of his being a Member of the Aforesaid company, [together, or may hereafter become his right and property by Virtue and in right of his being a member of the aforesaid company,] * together with all profits benefits commodit[ies] priviledges, liberties, advantages and appurtenances to the same belonging, or that ought or Should in any wise pertain or belong, And also all and singular the right of him the said Thomas Cresap to all Lands and Tenement which was either taken up or purchased in the name of the company or in the name of Col.° George Mason Agent, for the company or any other name or description whatsoever within the State of Maryland and Virginia for use of said company, or that was intended for the use and advantage of the said Ohio company together with all and Singular the improvements, buildings, Edificies profits rents, and Arrears of Rents, Leases) damages for forfeituers of Leases, Nonpayments of Rents or otherwise Also all advantages to the same belonging or in any wise appertaining to them the said Daniel Cresap James Cresap & Michael Cresap their Heirs and assigns, Likewise the said Thomas Cresap hath given and granted and by these presents doth give and grant to them the said Daniel Cresap, Jam[es] Cresap and Michael Cresap their Heirs and assigns all the right of him the said Thomas Cresa[p] to all goods, Moneys Debts, Morgages [*sic*] Interests and [and] * advantages of every Kind nature and denomination whatsoever with which he is now possessed, or ought of right to possess in Virtu[e] of his being a member of the company aforesaid In manner following to wit one Moiety or full half of all Lands tenements, goods Chattles, Interests and properties recited Above [said, in manner] * the said Thomas Cresap hath by these presents doth give and grant to the aforesaid Daniel Cresap his Heirs and assigns forever, the residue and remainder being one full half he the said Tho.[s] Cresap hath by these presents doth give and grant to them the said James Cresap and Michael Cresap in equal portions to be devided [*sic*] between them for the only proper use & behoof of them there [*sic*] heirs and Assigns forever—and the said Thomas Cresap for himself his Heirs Executors & Administrators doth covenant and grant to and with, to and with [*sic*] them the said Daniel Cresap James Cresap & Michael Cresap there [*sic*] heirs and Assigns by these presents that they the said Daniel Cresap James Cresap and Michael Cresap may from henceforth forever hereafter peaceably have hold use occupy and possess the said Lands Tenements, Goods Chattles and Monies hereby granted and conveyed or intended to be granted & conveyed with their and every of their appurtenances, In Witness whereof the said Thomas Cresap hath set his hand and Seal the day and year above

Signed Sealed and Delivered }
In Presents of —— } Thomas C hresap [*sic*] (Seal)

Cha.[s] Prather [3]
And[w] Bruce.[4]

On the Back of the same Deed was the following Indorsements to wit— Washington County ss,[t]—The day and year within written came the within named Thomas Cresap before us two of the Justices for the said County and Acknowledged the within instrument of Writing to be his act and Deed and the land and premises within mentioned to be the right and estate of the within named Daniel Cresap James Cresap & Michael Cresap there [*sic*] heirs and Assigns for ever According to the true inte[nt] and meaning thereof and the Act of Assembly in Such cases made and provided

Chas Prather
And.^{w}. Bruce

at the same time came Margaret Cresap wife to the said Thos Cresap who being privately examine[d] out of the hearing of her husband Acknowledged her right of Dower of the within lands to be the right and estate of the within named Daniel Cresap James Cresap and Michael Cresap their Heirs and Assigns and that she made such Acknowledgment freely and Voluntarily and of her own Accord with[out] being induced thereto through fear or threats of Ill usage from her husband or fear of his displeasure

Charles Prather
Andrew Bruce

* [These words were crossed out in the document.]

1. The significance of this deed is obvious. It is the only deed of this type which was found recorded. It shows definitely that Thomas Cresap in 1783 did not consider the Company extinct and his claim from his share as valueless. The eventful fate of the share as granted was not determined.
2. Probably merely the flamboyant idea of Thomas Cresap, but possibly the traditional concept.
3. Charles Prather, James Prather, and Thomas Prather were each prominent political figures in early western Maryland.
4. He lived near Fort Cumberland and on the establishment of Allegany County, became, in 1791, its first justice of the peace.

Depositions of Daniel Cresap, John Nicholls, Elizabeth Gist, and James Gist

(Maryland Hall of Records, Western Shore General Court, Original Papers, Box R, 1793.)

[February 28, 1786]

The deposition of Daniel Cresap aged about fifty Eight Years taken in a writ of Ejectment brought by the Executors of Doct David Ross dec.^{d} plaintiff against George Mason defendant being first sworn on the Holy Evangels of Almighty God deposeth and sayeth that two Bounded White Oak Trees standing on the bank of Potomack River—[are]* he Bounded by directions of Thomas Prather the then Dep^{y} Surveyor for the Beginning Trees of a tract of Land Called Pleasant Valley then to be surveyed for Tho. Bladen that he carried the Chain round the said Tract, that some [short]* time after making said Survey, John Frazer,[1] Erected a log Cabbin near the banks of the River within the lines they had run round, and that he understood sd Frazer had purchased the Land from Mr Tasker agent for Mr Bladen ab.^{t} the year 1754
Feby 28. 1786. Sworn before Ad^{m} Ott Shff

The deposition of John Nicholls aged ab.^{t} 77. years taken in a Writ of Ejectment brought by the Executors of David Ross deceased plaintiff against

George Mason defendant who being first sworn On the Holy Evangels of Almighty God deposeth and saith that a parcel of old Logs near the Bank of Potomack is the place where John Frazer Erected a Log House and that he understood he understood [*sic*] he settled there as a purchaser of a tract of Land Called Pleasant Valley from Mr Bladen or his agent about the year 1755 [or] 1756

Feby 28. 1786. Sworn before Ad^{m} Ott S hff

The deposition of Elizabeth Gist aged about Sixty Six Years taken on a Writ of Ejectment brought by the Executors of David Ross deceased plaintiff against George Mason defendant who being first sworn on the Holy Evangels of Almighty God deposeth and sayeth, that on or about the year 1759. Col^{o} George Mercer agent for the Ohio Company give [*sic*] her former Husband Samuel Plumb Possessn [2] of a tract of Land for which her said Husband was to pay Annually One Ear of Indian Corn, whereon her Husband Erected the House where she now lives, and has lived ever since, as a Tenant to the Ohio Comp^{y} (or Col^{o} George Mason

Sworn Before Adam Ott Shff

The deposition of James Gest aged ab.^{t} 51 years taken on a Writ of Ejectment brought by the Executors of Doct David Ross deceased plaintiff against George Mason defendant who being first sworn on the Holy Evangels of Almighty God deposeth and Sayeth that About twelve years ago he moved to the place where he now resides where he has lived ever since as a tenant to the Ohio Company,[3] that about seven years ago Mr Ross told him he should take possession of the Land where on he lived if he (this deponent) nor the Ohio Company Entered Suit—

Feby 28. 1786.— Sworn Before Ad^{m} Ott Sh ff

[*Endorsed:*]

Depositions taken on Resurvey Ross @ Mason—	Depositions of Danl Cresap, John Nicholls Eliz.^{b} Gist & James Gist Feb. 28. 1786.	167
Ross vs Mason		Ross's Les @ Mason

* [This word was crossed out in the document.]

1. The famous gunsmith of Venango, who fled to Turtle Creek in 1753, to Monongahela in 1754, to Cumberland in 1754, and settled on Wills Creek in 1755. He moved, finally, in 1759, to Bedford, Pennsylvania. See Howard Clark's thesis on John Fraser in the University of Pittsburgh Library, printed in *W. Pa. Hist. Mag.*, XXXVIII, 83-93, and XXXIX, 165-75.
2. Evidently John Fraser was a lessee rather than an owner.
3. The Articles of Agreement and some statements of George Mercer imply that the Ohio Company was an affair of twenty years. But this claim was more legal than historical for its affairs ran on for another fifty years after May 23, 1771.

Depositions of Daniel Cresap, Sr., James Prather, Christian Burkett, and James Gist

(Maryland Hall of Records, Western Shore General Court Original Papers, Box R. 1793.)

David Ross Lese }
a }
George Mason } [March 14, 1791]

Daniel Cresap Sen[r] being duly Sommoned and Sworn deposeth & Saith the Two White Oak Trees he now is at he Saw Bounded for the Begining Trees of a Tract of Land Called Pleasent Valley Surveyed for Thomas Bladen

Same day James Prather being duly Sommoned and Sworn deposeth & Saith the Two Bounded White Oak Trees he is now at is the Begining Trees of a Tract of Land Called White oak Levill Surveyed for David Ross——

Same day Christian Burkett being duly Sommoned and Sworn deposeth & Saith that about the Year one Thousand Seven hundred and eighty Nine in the Month of November he purchaced from a Certain James Gist the right of Possession of the House he now lives in and the Land Called Pleasent Valley and to hold the Same as a Tennent Under George Mason

Same day James Gist being duly Sommoned & Sworn deposeth and Saith that about the Year one Thousand Seven Hundred and Seventy five he Rented from Col.[l] Thomas Cresap [1] a Tract of Land Called Pleasant Valley & that he had Lived on the Same land under the Ohio Company until about the year 1789 when he Sold his right of Possession To a Certain Christian Burkett——

Sworn Before John Beatty Shff
Allegany County

March 14th 1791

[*Endorsed:*]

Depositions
Daniel Cresap
James Prather
Christian Burkett
James Gist
March 1791.

[*Additional longitudinal endorsement:*]

Depositions [2]
filed 10 May 1791

1. Thomas Cresap as a member of the Ohio Company acted on several occasions as the agent of the Company, but no record was found of any power of attorney.
2. The depositions and other data show that *Pleasant Valley* was occupied by John Fraser, 1755–1759, by Samuel Plumb, 1760–1775, by James Gist, 1775–1789, by Christian Perkey, 1789–1799, and by Jacob Perkey, 1800—.

Warrant of George Mason for the Arrest of Thomas Beall

(Maryland Hall of Records, Western Shore General Court, Original Judgments, 1792.)

[June 4, 1791]

THE State of Maryland, sc. To the Sheriff of *Allegany* county, Greeting. We command you that you take *Thomas Beall late of Allegany County Geneleman otherwise Called Thomas Beall son of Samuel Beall of the County of Washington in the state of Maryland* if *he* shall be found in your bailiwick, and *him* safe keep, so that you have *his* body before the judges of our general court, to be held at the city of Annapolis on the second Tuesday of *October* next, *to answer unto George Mason of Fairfax County in the Commonwealth of Virginia of a plea that he render unto him the sum of fourteen hundred and seven pounds Current Money of Maryland in Specie* [1] *which to him he owes and from him unjustly detains and so forth*—Hereof fail not at your peril, and have you then and there this writ. Witness [Robert Hanson Harrison],* *Thomas Johnson* Esquire, chief judge of our said court, the 4.th day of June. anno domini 1791 Issued the *15.th* day of *June 1791.*

J. T. Mason *John Gwinn Clk*

[*Endorsed:*] N° 13.

George Mason
a } Cap
Thomas Beall of Saml
Debt £1407.0.0 Cur.t
All.y
Cepi and
Declaration Left 15.
Aug.t

John C Beatty Shff

* [These words were crossed out in the document.]

1. This, one of a series of eight related documents, obviously is connected with the land transactions of October 25, 1783. The "Specie" mentioned in the deed of that date seems to have been merely bonds. There were two double indemnity bonds, one for £1408 and another for £1407. The two bonds have each the same four co-signers. Eight suits resulted. On the basis of the data found it seems that the entire compensation of the deed of October 25, 1783, was covered by two separate bonds.

George Mason against Thomas Beall

(Maryland Hall of Records, Western Shore General Court, Original Judgments, 1792, No. 74.)

[June 15, 1791]

Western Shore State of Maryland Allegany, County to wit,

Thomas Beall late of Allegany County Gentleman otherwise called Thomas Beall (son of Samuel Beall) of the County of Washington in the State of

Maryland was summoned to answer unto George Mason of Fairfax County in the Commonwealth of Virginia of a Plea that he render unto him the Sum of fourteen hundred and eight pounds current money of Maryland in Specie which to him he owes and from him unjustly detains & so forth. And whereupon the said George by John Thomson Mason his Attorney says that whereas the said Thomas on the twenty seventh day of October in the year of our Lord one thousand seven hundred and eighty three at the County of [Allegany] * Montgomery in the State of Maryland by his certain Writing Obligatory acknowledged himself to be bound to the said George in the said fourteen hundred and eight pounds current money of Maryland in Specie to be paid to the said George whenever he the said Thomas should be thereunto required Nevertheless the said Thomas although often required & so forth hath not paid the said fourteen hundred and eight pounds current money in Specie to the said George but hath hitherto altogether refused & still doth refuse to him the same to the Damage of the said George of fourteen hundred pounds & thereupon he brings Suit and so forth; and the said George Mason brings here in to Court the writing Obligatory aforesaid Sealed with the Seal of the said Thomas Beall which testifies the Debt aforesaid in form aforesaid the date whereof is upon the same day & year aforesaid J.T. Mason pro Que

Pledges to prosecute } John Doe & Rich. Roe

And the said Thomas Beall by his Attorney comes and defends the force & injury when & where & so forth and prays an hearing of the said Writing Obligatory & of the Condition thereof and they are read to him in the words following to wit,

[October 27, 1783]

Know all men by these presents that we Thomas Beall (Son of Samuel Beall) of the County of Washington in the State of Maryland Brooke Beall of George Town in the County of Montgomery and State of Maryland William Deakins Junior and James M. Lingan of the same Town County and State are held and firmly bound unto George Mason of Fairfax County in the Commonwealth of Virginia in the just & full Sum of fourteen hundred and eight pounds current money of Maryland in Specie, to be paid to the said George Mason his Executors Administrators or Assigns or to his or their certain Attorneys. To the which payment well and truly to be made we bind ourselves and each of us our and each of our Heirs Executors & Administrators jointly & severally firmly by these presents. Signed & sealed with our Seals, in the County of Montgomery in the State of Maryland this twenty seventh day of October in the year of our Lord one thousand seven hundred and eighty three

The Condition of the above Obligation is [such] * that if the above bound Thomas Beall his Heirs Executors or Administrators shall pay or cause to be paid to the above named George Mason his Executors Administrators or Assigns or to his or their certain Attorney on or before the first day of November which shall be in the year of our Lord one thousand seven hundred and and [*sic*] eighty four,[1] the Sum of seven hundred & four pounds current money of the State of Maryland in Specie, that is to say, in [Dollars] * Spanish silver Dollars at the rate of seven Shillings & six pence each or in other silver and gold Coin at a proportionable rate & value together with Interest thereon, at the rate of six per Centum per annum to be computed from the first day of May last past; then the above Obligation to be void; otherwise to remain in full force and power.

Signed & sealed in the presence of us the word (above) being first interlined	Signed	
Anthony Reintzel [2]	Thomas Beall of Saml	(Seal)
Tho. Beall of Geo.[3]	Brooke Beall	(Seal)
Walter Smith [4]	William Deakins Junr	(Seal)
Tho Richardson [5]	J.^s McCubbin Lingan	(Seal)
Zach.^h Warfield [6]		

Upon the back of this Bond there is an indorsement in the words & figures following, to wit,

1789 June 20th Received of the within named Thomas Beall (per the hands of his Son) the Sum of ninety nine pounds eighteen Shillings and eight pence current money of Maryland in part of the Interest due on the within Bond [7]

Signed
per
G Mason

[*Endorsed:*]

Geo. Mason v Thos Beall of Saml — Nar & Oyer nar 3¼ oyer 4½

Filed 15.th day of June 1791 and
Copy sent with the writ to
October next
Cost 699 Tob.^o
Sci fa issued in the name of
plfts Exors to May 1793 N.º 74.

* [These words were crossed out in the document.]

1. A limit of twelve months for payment is set on this £1408 bond.
2. Early inhabitant of Cumberland, Maryland.
3. Not further identified than of an influential family.
4. Not identified.
5. Not identified.
6. Early member of a well-known Maryland family.
7. This endorsement is found only on the four copies of the £1408 bond. No endorsement of the kind is found on the four copies of the £1407 bond.

Suits of George Mason against Signers of Bonds in Land Transactions

(Maryland Hall of Records, Docket Books of the General Court of the Western Shore of Maryland, 1791, October Term, pp. 212-13.)

JTM.	Same			Debt £1407. C^t my nar & oy Copy
id				
13	6	Ch^d	Ally.	sent same.
	Thomas Beall of Sam.[1]			Cepi Copy left 15 Aug
				Same am.^t
JTM.	Same			Debt. £1408 C^t my nar & oy Copy
id				
16.	9	Ch^d	Ally.	sent same.
	Thomas Beall of Saml			Cepi Copy left 15 Augs.
				Same am.^t

Suit of David Ross and others Lessees against George Mason

(Maryland Hall of Records, Docket Books of the General Court of the Western Shore of Maryland, 1791, October Term, p. 32, No. 1.)

Oct.° 80	July	David Ross & als Lessee	Eject plats Dep^s &
Jgs	21st	Copy case stated and part of	Will filed [1]
PBK1	1780	will for PBK	Judg for Possession
1 JTM		for pltf 6½ 8d	and Costs subject to
LM		Ch	the Case stated
		George Mason	
			cont.

1. The files for 1791–1799 were examined and no additional dispositions found. Probably older material was involved.

Sci Fa Writ of Martin Cockburn and George Mason, Executors of George Mason, versus Thomas Beall

(Maryland Hall of Records, Western Shore General Court, Original Papers, Box C, May, 1793, No. 74, a. d. s., J. T. Mason.)

[January 7, 1793]

The State of Maryland, sct. To the Sheriff of Allegany County greeting Whereas George Mason lately in our General Court at the City of Annapolis on the second Tuesday of May Anno Domini seventeen hundred and ninety two and by Judgment of the same Court recovered against Thomas Beall late of Allegany County Gentleman otherwise called Thomas Beall (Son of Samuel Beall) of the County of Washington in the State of Maryland the sum of Fourteen hundred and eight pounds current Money of Maryland a certain Debt and Six hundred and ninety nine pounds of Tobacco for his damages which he had sustained as well by reason of the detention of that debt as for his Costs and charges by him about his suit in that behalf expended whereof he the said Thomas Beall is convicted as it appears to us on Record And afterwards the said George Mason made his last Will and Testament, in writing, and of the same Will constituted and ordained Martin Cockburn and George Mason Executors thereof, and afterwards died; and now on the behalf of the same Martin Cockburn and George Mason the Executors aforesaid we have in Court before us understood, that although Judgment thereof is given, execution Nevertheless of the Debt and Damages aforesaid yet remains to be made; Wherefore the same Martin Cockburn and George Mason the Executors aforesaid have besought us to grant them a proper remedy in this behalf And we being willing that what is just in this behalf should be done Command you that by good and lawfull Men of your Bailiwick you give notice to the same Thomas Beall that he be and appear before the Judges of our General Court to be held at the city of Annapolis on the second Tuesday of May next to shew if he hath or can say any thing for himself why the said Martin Cockburn and George Mason the Executors aforesaid ought not to have their Execution against him for the Debt and Damages aforesaid according to the force form and effect of the recovery aforesaid, if he shall think fit and farther to do and receive what our said Court shall then and there consider concerning him in this behalf; and have there then the names of those by whom you shall give him notice and this Writ Witness the Honorable Samuel Chase Esquire Chief Judge of our said court the nineteenth day of November Anno Domini 1792—

Issued the 7.th day of January 1793. John Gwinn Clk

J T Mason.

[*Endorsed:*] No 74.

Martin Cockburn &
George Mason Exors
of George Mason
vs
Thomas Beall of Saml } Sci fa

Allegany

Debt —— £1408 Currt M.o

Costs — 699 lb Tob.o

Casa iss.d to May 1794

To be released on paym.t of £704 Current Money with Interest thereon from the 1.st May 1783 and costs—

paid 20th June 1789,

£99-18-9 currt My part of Int.

Made Known Before Jn.o. B Beall [1] & Josiah Beall [2]

March 26th 1793

John C Beatty Shff

Cost 539 Tobo

1. Not identified.
2. Prominent name and figure in Prince Georges County, 1746–1747, in Frederick County, 1748–1792, and later in Allegany County. A last will and testament of a Josiah Beall is dated February 12, 1805.

Statement of Attorney at Suit for Thomas Beall of Samuel, Defendant in Suit of Martin Cockburn, Surviving Executor of George Mason

(Maryland Hall of Records, Western Shore General Court, Original Papers, Box C, May, 1799, a.d.s., John M. Gantt.)

Thomas Beall of Sam.[1]
at Suit
Martin Cockburn Surv.[g]
Ex.[r] of George Mason—

[January 26, 1798]

And the aforesaid Thomas by John M Gantt his attorney comes and defends the force and injury when and so forth and saith that the aforesaid Martin Cockburn Surviving Executor as aforesaid his execution against him the said [Thomas Beall of] Samuel of fourteen hundred and seven pounds current money debt, the quantity of six hundred and ninety nine pounds of Tobacco damages and [Costs] * charges and also the quantity of five hundred and thirty nine pounds of Tobacco Costs and charges to have ought not because he saith that after the recovery of the Judgments aforesaid in the Writ of Scirefacias aforesaid above mentioned and before the [sai] * impetration of the said Writ of Scirefacias to wit on the day of in the year seventeen hundred and be paid to the said Martin Cockburn and George Mason Executors as aforesaid in the lifetime of the said George Mason the sum of fourteen hundred and seven pounds Current money, the quantity of six hundred and ninety nine pounds of Tobacco, and also the quantity of five hundred and thirty nine pounds of Tobacco in discharge and satisfaction of the Judgments aforesaid to wit at aleghany County aforesaid which said sums of fourteen hundred and seven pounds [of Tobacco] * current money, the quantity of six hundred and ninety nine pounds of Tobacco, and also the quantity of five hundred and thirty nine pounds of Tobacco the aforesaid Martin Cockburn and George Mason then and there received and accepted in full discharge and satisfaction [1] of the Judgments aforesaid and this he is ready to verify, wherefore he prays Judgment if the said martin Cockburn Surviving Executor as aforesaid his execution against him the said Thomas Beall of Samuel of the aforesaid sum of fourteen hundred and seven pounds Current money, the quantity of Six hundred and ninety nine pounds of Tobacco and also the quantity of five hundred and thirty nine pounds of Tobacco to have ought and so forth

John M Gantt for Defend.[t]

[*Endorsed:*]

3½
Thomas Beall of Saml
at Suit
Martin Cockburn Surv.^{g}
Ex.^{e} of George Mason.
pay.^{t} [2]
Filed 26.th of January 98

* [These words were crossed out in the document.]

1. No record of such payment and receipt was found. If this statement can be accepted as valid, George Mason and the Ohio Company must be credited with the sum herein mentioned. To this must be added a similar sum in the following statement.
2. This endorsement is indefinite, but payment is at least claimed for Thomas Beall, and, in other documents, for James M. Lingan. But no such endorsement is found for payment by Deakins, nor is any payment by B. Beall anywhere indicated.

Suits of Martin Cockburn, Surviving Executor of George Mason, against Signers of Bonds in Land Transactions

(Maryland Hall of Records, Docket Books of the General Court of the Western Shore of Maryland, 1799, October Term, p. 475.) [1]

JTM	id	Martin Cockburn surv		Casa: D.^{t} £ 1408. C^{t} m.^{o}
32.	id	Exor George Mason.		Costs ——— 699 Tob^{o}
		Ch^{d}	Ally.	Costs on 1. Scifa——539.
		Thomas Beall of Saml		Costs on 2^{d} Scifa: —686.
				ad.^{l} costs ————180.
JTM	id	Same		Casa: D.^{t} same.
33	id	Ch^{d}	Mont.	Costs ———699. Tob.^{o}
		James M. Lingan		Costs on 1. Scifa -539.
				Costs on 2.^{d} Scifa: -763.
				ad.^{l} Costs ———180.
JTM	id	Same		Casa: D.^{t} £1407. C^{t} m.^{o}
34	id	Ch^{d}	Ally.	Costs same as N.º 32.
		Thomas Beall of Saml		
JTM.	id	Same		Casa: D.^{t} same
35.	id	Ch^{d}	Mont.	Costs same as N.º 33.
		James M. Lingan		

1. No further renewal being indicated and no later items found in the docket books, it must be assumed that this October Term of 1799 saw the end of this particular matter of litigation. Probably the bonds were paid off and only costs here involved. Both Thomas Beall and James M. Lingan were wealthy.

Deed to the Cove from George Mason's Heirs

(Allegany County, Maryland, Deed Book C, folio 668.)

[June 28, 1803]

At the request of Joseph Magruder [1] John Magruder [2] Greenburg Magruder [3] & Robert White Magruder [4] this Deed was Recorded 28th day of June 1803. This Indenture made this twenty eighth day of June in the year of our Lord one thousand Eight hundred and three Between John M Gantt of Prince George's County in the State of Maryland of the one part and Joseph Magruder John Magruder Greenburg Magruder and Robert White Magruder of Montgomery County and state aforesaid of the other part. Whereas the Chancellor of Maryland by his decree [5] bearing date the ninth day of July one thousand eight hundred and one did among other things appoint the said John M Gantt trustee to convey unto Joseph Magruder John Magruder Greenburg Magruder and Robert White Magruder the Land hereafter mentioned and all the right Estate and Interest of George Mason,[6] William Mason [7] Richard Barnes Mason [8] Elizabeth Barnes Hoe Mason [9] Ann Eilbeck Mason [10] and Sally Barnes Hoe Mason [11] heirs of George Mason Son and devisee of George Mason of in and to the Same upon the payment unto the chancery office of four hundred and Seventy one pounds five Shillings and Eleven pence Current Money with Interest thereon from the date of Said decree till the time of payment and as the said sum with Interest amounting to four hundred and Eighty nine pounds Sixteen Shillings and one penny was paid [12] into the Chancery Office on the Sixteenth day of December one Thousand eight hundred and two according to the said decree as will more fully appear by reference to the proceedings of the Chancery Court

Now this Indenture Witnesseth that in consideration of the above recited premises and in Execution of the trust aforesaid The said John M Gantt hath bargained sold released aliened enfeoffed and confirmed and by these presents doth grant bargain sell release alien enfeoff and confirm unto the said Joseph Magruder John Magruder Greenburg Magruder and Robert White Magruder their heirs and assigns forever all that part of a Tract or parcel of Land called the Cove being in Allegany County which is contained within the courses and distances following that is to say Beginning at a white oak stump standing at the upper end of a bottom and on the Bank on the north side of the north Branch of Potomack River and running Thence north forty two degrees East thirty six poles then north Eighteen degrees east one hundred and six poles then north sixty Eight degrees east two hundred & fifty Seven poles north forty Eight degrees east one hundred and Eighty four poles then north Seventy five degrees east fourteen poles then South Eleven degrees east Sixty two poles then South Twenty poles then South fifteen degrees west Twenty Six poles then South Twenty degrees west fifty four poles then South Twenty Seven degrees West Eighteen poles then south thirty five degrees west fifty poles then south Sixty six degrees west twenty four poles then South

Sixty Seven degrees west thirty poles then south thirty nine degrees west twenty four poles then south Twenty two degrees west forty four poles then south two degrees west thirty Eight poles then south twenty one degrees west Seventy nine poles then South Twenty nine degrees west thirty four poles then West thirteen poles then North Seventy four degrees west fifty four poles then north Seventy nine and a half degrees west Sixty poles then south Eighty nine degrees west fifteen poles then to the Beginning containing by estimation four hundred and thirty five acres [13] To have and to hold the Said part of a Tract of Land above described and premises with every of the appurtenances unto the said Joseph Magruder John Magruder Greenburg Magruder and Robert White Magruder their Heirs and assigns forever as tenants in common and not as Joint tenants to their only use and behoof and to and for no other use intent or purpurpose [*sic*] whatsoever In Testimony whereof the said John M. Gantt hath hereunto set his hand and affixed his seal the day and year first aforesaid

Jn M Gantt Trustee (seal)

Signed Sealed and delivered
in the presence of
Jeremiah Townly Chase On which Deed was thus endorsed to Wit Western Shore of Maryland to Wit Be it remembered that on the Twenty eighth day of June in the year of our Lord one thousand Eight hundred & three Jn° M Gantt the grantor & trustee within named appeared before me the subscriber one of the Judges of the General court of the State of Maryland and acknowledged the within instrument of writing to be his act and deed according to the act of assembly in such cases made and provided

Jeremiah Townley Ch[ase] [14]

Taken before and certified to me.

1. The name Magruder was widespread in Western Maryland, though not politically prominent as early as 1803. A Josiah Magruder was married in Montgomery County in 1778.
2. Probably a brother of Josiah. He served on a jury in Montgomery County in 1777 and was married there in 1799.
3. Not further identified but probably a brother of Josiah and John.
4. Not further identified but also probably a brother of Josiah and John.
5. Not found.
6. George Mason, son of George Mason of Lexington. He might be designated George Mason the Sixth.
7. Born, February 3, 1786. Probably named for his uncle.
8. Born, January 16, 1797. Died, July 25, 1850. Governor of California. *D.A.B.*
9. Born, March 9, 1785. Married Alexander Seymour Hooe.
10. Born, April 1, 1791. Married George Nicholas Grymes.
11. Married, John Stith, January 5, 1815.
12. Presumably the money went to the six heirs of George Mason of Lexington. It was a payment for old Ohio Company lands.
13. It is noticeable here that the acreage and the lines do not correspond with the original

survey of June 16, 1746, and the patent of June 24, 1763. Additional records are implied.

14. Distinguished regional lawyer and judge.

Patent of Pleasant Valley to Descendants of George Mason

(Maryland Land Office Patents, Liber J.C.N. 2, folios 248-49.) *

[September 3, 1805]

William Mason, Thompson Mason and John Mason, Exors. of George Mason Their patent 300.[a] Pleasant Valley } The State of Maryland &c.[a] Know Ye that Whereas Thomas Bladen Esq.[r] had surveyed and laid out for him, a tract or parcel of land Called Pleasant Valley lying then in Prince Georges, but now Allegany County, and Containing three hundred acres, by virtue of so much part of a warrant for three thousand acres obtained by him out of the Proprietary's land office (according to the Conditions of Plantations then in force) the sixteenth day of April seventeen hundred and forty five, as appears. that the said Thomas Bladen paid to the Agent for the Proprietary, the sum of ten pounds sixteen shillings for rent to midsummer, Seventeen hundred and sixty three, and by his Assignment bearing date the fourteenth day of June seventeen hundred and sixty three, transferred and made over the Said Land to Col.[o] George Mason of the Colony of Virginia and desired that patent might issue to him for the same—And Whereas upon Petition, it was ordered by the Chancellor, that Patent should issue to William Mason, Thompson Mason, and John Mason, surviving Executors of George Mason late of Lexington and their heirs, in trust for, and to the uses mentioned in the Last will of the said George Mason,—The State of Maryland doth therefore hereby grant unto them the said William Mason, Thompson Mason and John Mason, the said tract or parcel of Land, Called Pleasant Valley, lying in Allegany County, aforesaid—Beginning at two bounded white oak trees standing near the river bank about a mile below the mouth of Evits Creek, a branch of Potomac and running thence. . . .[1] Containing and laid out for three hundred acres of land, according to the Certificate of Survey thereof taken and returned into the Land office, bearing date the first day of June seventeen hundred and forty five, and there remaining, together with all rights, profits, benefits, and Privileges thereunto belonging, To Have and To Hold the Same unto them the Said William Mason, Thompson Mason and John Mason, surviving Executors of George Mason late of Lexington, and their heirs, in trust for and to the uses mentioned in the Last will of the Said George Mason—Given under the great Seal of The State of Maryland this third day of September eighteen hundred and five—

Witness the Honorable Alexander Contee Hanson Esquire Chancellor

Rob.[t] Bowie (the great seal) A. C. Hanson Chan.[r]

* Copies of this survey are found in the Court of Appeals Judgments, Liber T. H. No. 16 (1815), folios 39-40, 151-52, and in Allegany County, Maryland, Judgment Record J, October Court, 1816, folios 397-98.

1. The survey description, also found in the original survey of June 1, 1745, is herein omitted by the author.

Richard Smith, Lessee of William Stewart and Others, against William Mason

(Allegany County, Maryland, Judgment Record F, folios 304-57, October, 1806.) [1]

[October 13, 1806]

John Johnson	Richard Smith Lessee of
Roger Perry	William Stewart
Philip B. Key	David Ross
Will[m] Pinkney	Horatio Ross and
Sam[l] Hughes.	Archibald Ross
	against
Luther Martin	William Mason
John T. Mason	

1. This fifty-three folio page judgment is really an Ohio Company archive. But it repeats items found in originals elsewhere. Appealed to the Maryland Court of Appeals, the suit ran on there until 1815 when, by procedendo, it was returned to the Allegany County Court.

William Stewart and Others against William Mason

(Maryland Hall of Records, Court of Appeals Judgments, May Court, 1815, Liber T. H., No. 16 [1815], folios 1-224.) [1]

[May 29, 1815]

1. This long document is an Ohio Company archive. Embedded in it are many items of which the originals have been located elsewhere. It contains duplicate but variant copies of the fifty-three folio page Allegany County judgment of October, 1806. In condensed form it is reported in print in the *Report of Cases in the Court of Appeals,* Harris and Johnson, III, 507-34. In approximate total this suit, 1800–1817, fills about 400 folio pages in Maryland judicial records.

William Stewart and Others against William Mason

(Allegany County, Maryland, Dockets. Trials to October Court, 1816.)

R.P.	William Stewart & others	Ejectment procedendo from the
B.H.	Lessees	Court of appeals & record—
[JTM] *	Haberi Facies possessionem	12 pp[d] Trial & Verdict for
4	Fi far for Costs	Plaintiff 18th Pd Jury
J A T.K.	vs fr April Court 1817.	fee paid by B. Howard Esq
[PLB] *	No 162	Judgment Recorded in Record H.B
	William Mason	No J from folio 358 to and end
		and in Judgment Record H. B. No K

from folio 1 to folio 59. 18th Trial & Verdict for Plaintiff for all the Lands Located on the plotts. in this Cause as the Claim & pretensions of the Defendant which are included within the lines of the Tract of Land Called white oak Levil as Shown upon the plotts in this Cause [*sic*] Beginning for the tract Called white oak Levil at the Green Letter A upon the said plotts and running thence with the Black dotted Lines numbered with Green Figures from 1 to 52 thence to the beginning at said Green A & one Cent damages

Plffs Costs on the General Courts	80.53
Surveyors fees	60.4
Shffs fees	8.
Witnesses & Survey & chain Carrier	4.66⅔
attorney	3.33½
Clk fees in County Court	84.16½
Cry in fees	.7
Jury fee	1.60
paid for copies of papers	17.16⅔
	260.33⅔

* [These letters were crossed out in the document.]

William Stewart, David Ross, and Others against William Mason

(Allegany County, Maryland, Judgment Record J, October Court, 1816, folios 358-402, and Judgment Record K, folios 1-59.) [1]

R P William Stewart 15
B H. David Ross
J A T.K. Horatio Ross and
Archibald Ross's Lessee
against
William Mason

1. This record of 103 folio pages is an Ohio Company archive. Embedded in it are copies of many items of which the originals have been located elsewhere and are published or calendared herein.

Deed of Pleasant Valley to William Lamar

(Allegany County, Maryland, Deed Book L, folios 144-45.)

[April 14, 1821]

This Indenture made and entered into the 14.th. day of April in the year of our Lord 1821 between John Stith and Sally B Stith his wife, Alexander L Hooe and E B Hooe his wife & George N Grymes & Ann E Grymes his wife all of the County of King George in the Commonwealth of Virginia of the one part and William Lamar of Allegany County in the State of Maryland of the other part, Witnesseth that whereas the said Sally B Stith, E. B Hooe & Ann E Grymes are the Daughters and devises of George Mason of Lexington in the County of Fairfax & Commonwealth of Virginia and as such they Claim right & Title to a certain tract of Land lying near to the Town of Cumberland in the County of Allegany in the State of Maryland Called Pleasant valley which said tract of Land was many years ago Conveyed to George Mason the elder by two Several Patents [1] Executed to him by the proper authority in the State of Maryland and whereas the title of the said George Mason the Elder of those Claiming under him, in and to the said tract of Land Called Pleasant valley or to a very large proportion thereof has for many years been Contested at Law by the said William Lamar in virtue, & on the faith of a better Title set up and claimed by him under a patent issued to a certain [Doctor David] Ross conveying to him the said Ross a very large proportion of the said tract of land. Now this Indenture therefore Witnessith that the said John Stith & Sally B Stith his wife Alex^r L Hooe & E B Hooe his wife and George N Grymes and Anne E his wife, for and in consideration of the sum of nine hundred and fifty one dollars to him in hand paid by the said William Lamar before the ensealing and delivery of these presents, the receipt whereof is hereby acknowledged, have hereby granted bargained & sold & by these presents they do give, grant, sell, alien, convey & confirm to the said Wm Lamar his heirs, and assigns forever, all that tract of land called pleasant Valley & to every part thereof to which they claim title as aforesaid, together with all & singular its rights & appurtenances. To Have and to Hold the same to him the said William Lamar his heirs & assigns forever free from the claim or demand of the said John Stith & Sally B, his wife, Alex^r L Hooe & E B his wife and George N Grimes and Ann E his wife or either of them of their heirs or assigns or of any other person or persons claiming under them, or of claiming in virtue of the patents aforesaid issued to George Mason the elder for the said Tract of Land called pleasant Valley. In testimony whereof the parties aforesaid have hereto set their hands & seals the day and year first above written

Signed Sealed & delivered	J Stith	(seal)
In presence of	Sally B [M]* Stith	(seal)
John P. Stewart	Alex.^r. L Hooe	(seal)
W.^m. F Grymes	Eliza.^th. B Hooe	(seal)
	George N Grymes	(seal)
	Anne E Grymes	(seal)

Commonweath of Virginia King George County s s

Be it remembered, that on this 14.th. day of April personally appear...... Taken and Certified this 14.th. day of April one thousand eight hundred and Twenty-one.

John E Stuart
W^m F Grymes

* [This letter crossed out in document.]

1. Not found. Probably duly made out but caveated and not recorded. See the survey of June 1, 1745, above, pp. 192-94; the endorsement, therein, of June 14, 1763; the endorsement on George Mason's bond of November 8, 1763; and George Mason to John Francis Mercer, May 12, 1792.

William Mason and Others against William Lamar

(Allegany County Court Docket Trials, April Court, 1821.)

J A T K	William Mason	Eject. Nar & Notice Nar
F A.	Thompson Mason &	& Notice D.^{d} Ten.^{t} in
1 1	John Masons Lessee	Poss.^{n} Augt 26; 1817
B H	2	Def.^{t} App. & Confesses
R P	Ch 17	lease entry & ouster
	William Lamar	Plea
		Cont.^{d} by Consent.

(Allegany County Court Docket Trials, October Court, 1821.)

J.A.T.K.	William Mason	Eject Nar & Notice
F A	Thompson Mason &	Copy of Nar & Notice
2	John Masons Lessee 9	D.^{d} Ten^{t} in possession
B.H	a [10]*	Augt 26. 1817. Def^{t}
R.P.	William Lamar	Appears & Confesses
		lease entry & ouster
		Plea
		Settled [1]

[*Partly erased:*]

Jury Sworn and Pltff called &
Not Answering Non pross Jury fee
paid by Deft

* [This figure crossed out in the document.]

1. This word seems to be properly the end of all highly relevant Ohio Company historical items.

Appendix B

TABLE OF COMMERCIAL TRANSACTIONS

Sale of Goods by the Ohio Company

Name	*Obligation*	*Amount*	*Probable Recovery*
Ashcraft, Daniel	No Data		
Baker, Isaac	Account	£ 11..11.. 6	£ 11..11.. 6
Castleman, William	Promissory note	3.. 7.. 2	3.. 7.. 2
Caton, Thomas	Account	160.. 7.. 1	119.. 3..½
Chapman, Richard	Double indemnity	5.. 6..11	10..13..10
Coburn, Jonathan	Promissory note	6.. 0.. 6	4..10.. 4
Craig, David	Account	3.. 1..10½	
Croghan, George	Double indemnity bond	1000.. 0.. 0	2000.. 0.. 0
Cunningham, John	Promissory note	2.. 9.. 6	
Enochs, Enoch	Account	6.. 1.. 5½	6.. 1.. 5½
Erwin, Robert	Promissory note bond	80.. 5.. 6	
Erwin, William	Promissory note	9..10.. 7	10.. 1.. 2
Findley, James	Account	2..19.. 0½	2.. 4.. 3½
Fowler, James and MacFaddin, John	Account	27..12.. 0	27..12.. 0
Gist, Christopher	No data		
Hammer, John		2..17.. 9	2..17.. 9
Harrell, William		10.. 5.. 5	
Hood, Jacob	Promissory note	3.. 8.. 7	
Houghland, Jacobus	Promissory note	10..16.. 0	
Ice, Frederick	Promissory Note	6.. 0.. 0	
Jack, Jeremiah	Account	12.. 5.. 4	
Johnson, Abraham	Account	2.. 0.. 0	
Johnson, John	Account embedded	7.. 3.. 0	7.. 3.. 0
Jones, John		11.. 1.. 4	11.. 1.. 4
Leans, Richard	Merchandise	10.. 9.. 3	
Leman, Robert	Bond	75.. 8..10	150..17.. 8
Long, John Adam	Bond	8..11.. 0	
Martin, James	Bond	81.. 5.. 7	69..19.. 2½ and interest
McDonogh, Mark	Account	7..19.. 3½	3..12..11
MacFaddin, John and Fowler, James	Listed under Fowler		
McGuire, Philip	No data		

Mounts, Joseph		9.. 7..11½	9.. 7..11½
Mounts, Providence	Account	7.. 3.. 7½	
Nicholas, John	Promissory note	5.. 3.. 4	5.. 3.. 4
Park, George	Promissory note	2.. 9.. 3	2.. 9.. 3
Parker, George		4..17.. 5	4..17.. 5
Patterson, William	Promissory note	7.. 0.. 0	7.. 0.. 0
Pearis, John and Isaac P.	Bond	17..16.. 3	26..14.. 4
Pearis, Richard		200.. 0.. 0	200.. 0.. 0
Price, Aaron and Curran, Barney	Bond	792..13.. 2½	792..13.. 2½
Richey, William	Promissory note	4..15.. 0	4..15.. 0
Ross, James	Account	37..17.. 8	
Ruth, Zacheus	Account	37.. 8.. 9½	
Rutherford, Thomas	Account	14.. 8.. 9	
Shelby, Evan, Sr.		3.. 0.. 0	4..15.. 0
Sutton, Jasper	Promissory note	5..13.. 9	5..13.. 9
Swearingen, Thomas	Promissory note	3.. 0.. 0	3.. 0.. 0
Swearingen, Van	Account	6.. 7.. 0	6.. 7.. 0
Taylor, Samuel	Account	3..16..11	
Teagarden, Abraham	Promissory note	4.. 1.. 6	4.. 1.. 6 and interest
Thacker, Amos	Promissory note	2.. 5..10	2.. 5..10
Tomlinson, Nathaniel	Bill obligation	7..11.. 2	15.. 2.. 4
Tostee, Peter	Account	6.. 9.. 9	6.. 9.. 9
Trent, William	Ohio Company Supplies	669.. 0.. 0	669.. 0.. 0
Trent and Croghan	No data		
Tucker, John	Promissory note	5..13.. 5	4.. 5.. 0¾
Volgamore, Joseph	Account embedded Merchandise	3..11.. 6	3..11.. 6
Wafer, Francis		111..10.. 0	111..10.. 0
Waltaker, Conrad		33..11.. 9	22.. 0.. 0
Williams, John, Sr.	No data		
Williams, Remembrance	Account	2.. 1..10	2.. 1..10
Wolf, Jacob	Promissory note	2.. 8.. 6	3..12.. 9
Wood, Thomas	Account	3..11.. 6¾	2..13.. 8
	Total	£3,588.. 0.. 2¾	£4,316.. 7.. 1¾

Appendix C

TABLE OF LAND TRANSACTIONS

Lands of the Ohio Company

	Name	*Location*	*Date*
1.	*Ohio Company Grant*	Pennsylvania	July 12, 1749
2.	*Walnut Bottom*	Maryland	September 11, 1753
3.	*New Store Tract*	Virginia	October 25, 1754
4.	*Walnut Bottom Resurvey*	Maryland	June 30, 1762
5.	*Pleasant Valley*	Maryland	June 14, 1763
6.	*The Cove*	Maryland	June 24, 1763
7.	*Welshman's Conquest*	Maryland	June 25, 1763
8.	*Hunt the Hare*	Maryland	June 25, 1763
9.	*New Store Tract Resurvey*	Virginia	May 5, 1768
10.	*Survey*	Kentucky	May-September, 1775
11.	*Limestone Rock*	Maryland	May 2, 1783

Size Acres	*Price*	*Sale Date Figure*
200,000	Grant	Unpatented, Lost
500	£ 20....0..0	May, 1783
		£ 1407..10..0
869	———	£ 2160.. 0..0
1,250	Grant	Unpatented, Lost
300 }	———	$951 = £ 200
510 }	———	£ 471..5..11
260 }	£ 460..10..0	£ 520..0..0
240 }	———	£ 480..0..0
214	Grant	Sold with New Store Tract
200,000	Grant	Unpatented, Lost
63	£ 50..0..0	Sold with Walnut Bottom
Totals	£ 530	£ 5038..15..1

TABLE OF ABBREVIATIONS IN APPENDIX D

Am. Hist. Rec.	*American Historical Record and Repertory of Notes and Queries. . .*, Benson J. Lossing, ed.
APC	*Acts of Privy Council*
APS	American Philosophical Society
Bailey	*The Ohio Company of Virginia*
Bd. of Tr.	Board of Trade and Plantations
BM Add. MSS	British Museum, Additional Manuscripts
Byars	*B. & M. Gratz. . . Papers*
CDP	Court Docket Papers
CHS	Chicago Historical Society
Conway	*Barons of the Potomac and Rappahannock*, by Moncure D. Conway
Darlington	*Journals of Christopher Gist*, William M. Darlington, ed.
DML	Darlington Memorial Library
Douglass	*A Summary, Historical and Political, of the First Planting, Progressive Improvements and Present State of the British Settlements in North America*, by William Douglass
D.R.	David Ross
DUL	Duke University Library
FCM	Frederick County, Maryland
FCV	Frederick County, Virginia
Fernow	*The Ohio Valley in Colonial Days*, by Berthold Fernow
Fitzpatrick	*The Writings of George Washington*, John C. Fitzpatrick, ed.
Force	*American Archives. . .*, Peter Force, ed.
FPLPR	Free Public Library of Philadelphia, Ridgway Branch
Gipson	*The British Empire Before the Am. Rev.*
G.M.	George Mason
GMM	George Mason Manuscripts
GMP	*George Mercer Papers*, Lois Mulkearn, ed.
Hamilton	*Letters to Washington and Accompanying Papers*, S. M. Hamilton, ed.
HCL	Harvard College Library
Hening	*The Statutes at Large Being a Collection of All the Laws of Virginia. . .*, W. W. Hening, ed.
HHL	Henry L. Huntington Library
HSP	Historical Society of Pennsylvania
HSV	Historical Society of Virginia
JBT	*Journal of the Board of Trade and Plantations*
JCB	*Travels in North America by J. C. B.*
J.P.	Jacob Perkey, Tenant in Ejectment Suit

LC	Library of Congress
Md. HR	Maryland Hall of Records
Md. HS	Maryland Historical Society
Md. LO	Maryland Land Office
NCSA	North Carolina State Archives
NYCD	*Documents Relative to the Colonial History of New York*
N.F.	Not Found
NYHS	New York Historical Society
NYPL	New York Public Library
OB	Order Book
O.C.	Ohio Company
PA	*Pennsylvania Archives*
PALO	Pennsylvania Land Office
PCR	*Pennsylvania Colonial Records*
PPP	Pennsylvania Provincial Papers, Harrisburg
PROCO	Public Record Office (London), Colonial Office Papers
PROPCR	Public Record Office (London), Privy Council Register
Rowland	*Life of George Mason,* by Kate Mason Rowland
Sparks	*The Writings of George Washington,* Jared Sparks, ed.
Summers	*History of Southwest Virginia, 1746–1786. . . ,* by Lewis Preston Summers
Thwaites and Kellogg	*Documentary History of Dunmore's War. . . ,* R. G. Thwaites and Louise P. Kellogg, eds.
Toner	*Journal of Colonel George Washington*
TQ	*Tyler's Quarterly*
VHSC	Virginia Historical Society *Collections*
VJCC	*Journal (Executive) Council of Colonial Virginia*
VJHB	*Journal of the Virginia House of Burgesses*
VJHD	*Journal of the Virginia House of Delegates*
VMHB	*Virginia Magazine of History and Biography*
VSL	Virginia State Library
Wallace	*Conrad Weiser, 1696–1760, Friend of Colonist and Mohawk,* by Paul A. W. Wallace
WHS	Wisconsin Historical Society
Wilson	*The Ohio Company of Virginia, 1748–1798,* by Samuel Wilson
W.L.	William Lamar
WLCL	William L. Clements Library
W.M.	William Mason
WMQ	*William and Mary Quarterly*
W.S.	William Stewart
WSGC	Western Shore General Court of Maryland

The standard abbreviations are used in the matter of autographs and signatures.

Appendix D

CALENDAR OF OHIO COMPANY DOCUMENTS

Asterisk identifies documents printed in Appendix A.

October 21, 1743	Warrant to Thomas Bladen for 2,000 Acres.	Md. HR, Ct. of Appeals, Judgments, Liber T. H. No. 16 (1815), f. 138. Copy.
	Warrant to Thomas Bladen for 2,000 Acres.	
	Record of Warrant to Thomas Bladen for 2,000 Acres.	Md. LO, Liber L.G. No. D, f. 182.
October 25, 1743	Petition of James Patton and Others.	*VJCC*, V, 134.
	Release of Land in Virginia from the Indians of the Six Nations of the King.	July 2, 1744. PROCO 5: 1330/197.
February 20, 1745	Record of Warrant to Thomas Bladen for 1,900 Acres.	Md. LO, Warrants, Liber L.G. No. D, f. 358.
April 15, 1745	Record of Warrant to Thomas Bladen for 2,000 Acres.	*Ibid.*, f. 396.
April 16, 1745	*Warrant to Thomas Bladen for 3,000 Acres.	*Ibid.*, f. 397.
	Maryland Land Office Entry.	*Ibid.*
April 26, 1745	Land Grant to James Patton and Others.	*VJCC*, V, 173.
	Grants of Land to John Robinson and Others; John Smith and Others; James Patton and Others; and Henry Downes and Others.	*Ibid.*
June 1, 1745	*Survey Calendar, *Walnut Bottom.*	Attached to Survey. Md. LO, Warrants, Liber L.G. No. D, f. 433.
	*Original Survey of *Walnut Bottom* Tract.	Md. LO, Original Surveys, Prince Georges Co. No. 2241.
	*Certificate and Survey of *Pleasant Valley.*	*Ibid.*, Allegany Co. No. 2087.

June 28, 1745	Warrant of Resurvey to Thomas Cresap.	Md. LO, Liber L.G. No. D, f. 433.
	Warrant to Thomas Bladen for 1,329 Acres.	*Ibid.*, f. 434.
November 4, 1745	Grant of Land to John Blair and Others.	*VJCC*, V.
December 27, 1745	Renewal of Warrant to Thomas Cresap.	Md. LO, Liber L.G. No. D, f. 500.
	Entry of Warrant to Thomas Bladen.	*Ibid.*
February 3, 1746	Petition of and Warrant to George Stewart for 4,010 Acres.	Md. LO, Liber P.T. No. 2, ff. 163-64.
March 11, 1746	Survey of *Welshman's Conquest.*	Md. LO, Original Surveys, Prince Georges Co. No. 2289.
June 13, 1746	Certificate of Thomas Bladen for the *Cove.*	*Ibid.*, No. 572.
August 2, 1746	Gov. Thomas Bladen to Gov. George Thomas.	*PA*, I, 692-93.
February 23, 1747	Minute, Privy Council.	*APC*, IV, 55.
April 22, 1747	Grant of Land to William McMachen and Others.	*VJCC*, V.
June 13, 1747	Title Page of Survey of *Hunt the Hare.*	Md. LO, Liber B.C. and G.S. No. 19, f. 406.
	Copy of Survey of *Hunt the Hare.*	
October 20, 1747	Notation of the O.C. Petition of October 20, 1747.	PROCO 5: 1333/155.
October 24, 1747	The O.C. to Thomas Lee.	*GMP*, p. 2.
November 6, 1747	William Gooch to the Bd. of Tr.	PROCO 5: 1326/547-54. Fernow and Bailey.
January 14, 1748	Minute, Bd. of Tr.	*JBT*, 1741–49, p. 368.
January 19, 1748	Minute, Bd. of Tr.	*Ibid.*
	Bd. of Tr. to William Gooch.	PROCO 5: 1366/408-9.
	Bd. of Tr. to the Duke of Newcastle.	*Ibid.*, f. 410
February 10, 1748	Order of King in Council.	PROPCR 2: 100/540.
	Minute, Privy Council.	*APC*, IV, 55.
February 13, 1748	* Thomas Lee to Conrad Weiser.	HSP Peters Papers, II, 89, a.l.s.
February 23, 1748	Orders, Privy Council.	PROCO 5:1327/1-2.

April 6, 1748	Minute, Bd. of Tr.	*JBT*, 1741–49, p. 278.
May 14, 1748	Thomas Lee to Conrad Weiser.	HSP Peters Papers, 102, l.s.
June 16, 1748	William Gooch to the Bd. of Tr.	PROCO 5:1327/7-8, l.s. Fernow.
July 28, 1748	Extract of Letter from Richard Peters to Thomas Penn.	HSP Penn Papers, Off. Corr. IV, 145. Copy.
August 16, 1748	Minute, Bd. of Tr.	*JBT*, 1741–49, p. 336.
August 30, 1748	Minute, Bd. of Tr.	*Ibid.*, p. 341.
September 1, 1748	Minute, Bd. of Tr.	*Ibid.*, p. 342.
September 2, 1748	Minute, Bd. of Tr.	*Ibid.*
	Report to the Lords of the Committee of Council, upon a Letter from S.r W.m Gooch Relating to Applications that Had Been Made to Him for Grants of Land on the Western Side of the Great Mountains.	PROCO 5:1366/411-17. Excerpt in Fernow.
October 20, 1748	Minute, Committee of the O.C.	*GMP*, p. 167.
	William Trent to Richard Peters.	PPP, X, 46. *PA*, XI, 16-17.
November 24, 1748	Order, Privy Council to the Bd. of Tr.	PROCO 5:1327/21-22.
December 8, 1748	Minute, Bd. of Tr.	*JBT*, 1741–49, p. 356.
December 11, 1748	Thomas Lee to Conrad Weiser.	HSP Peters Papers II, 115, a.l.s. Fernow.
December 13, 1748	Minute, Bd. of Tr.	*JBT*, 1741–49, p. 357.
	Report to the Lords of the Comm.ee of Council, with the Dr.t of an Add.l Instruct.n to S.r W.m Gooch Bar.t Lieu.t Gov.r of Virginia.	PROCO 5:1366/421-26. Fernow.
December 14, 1748	Minute, Bd. of Tr.	*JBT*, 1741–49, p. 358.
December 16, 1748	Minute, Bd. of Tr.	*Ibid.*, p. 361.
December 17, 1748	Minute, Bd. of Tr.	*Ibid.*, p. 265.
January 11, 1749	The Petition of John Hanbury and Others.	PROCO 5:1327/53-57. Bailey, pp. 298-305.
	Minute, Privy Council.	PROPCR 2:101/145.

February 7, 1749	William Gooch to the Bd. of Tr.	PROCO 5:1327/167-68.
February 9, 1749	Minute, Privy Council.	PROPCR 2:101/184-86.
February 14, 1749	Minute, Bd. of Tr.	*JBT*, 1741–49, p. 380.
February 16, 1749	Minute, Bd. of Tr.	*Ibid.*, p. 384.
February 20, 1749	Thomas Penn to Richard Peters.	HSP Penn Papers, Saunders Coates, pp. 29-31, a.l.s.
February 22, 1749	Minute, Bd. of Tr.	*JBT*, 1741–49, p. 386.
February 23, 1749	Report to the Lords of the Committee of Council upon the Petition of John Hanbury Merch.[t] and Several Others for a Grant of 500,000 Acres of Land in Virginia.	PROPCR 2:101/189-92.
	Additional Instructions to William Gooch.	PROCO 5:1366/434-39.
	Minute, Privy Council.	PROPCR 2:101/189-92.
	* The Committee of the O.C. to Thomas Lee and Other Members of the Company.	NYPL Emmet MSS, 14853, d.s. *GMP*, pp. 167-68.
	Minute, Committee of the O.C.	*GMP*, p. 3.
March 4, 1749	Minute, Bd. of Tr.	*JBT*, 1741–49, p. 389.
	Bd. of Tr. to William Gooch.	PROCO 5:1366/439-44.
March 16, 1749	Minute, Privy Council.	PROPCR 2:101/215-16.
May 5, 1749	Prohibition of Surveys Beyond the Great Mountains.	*VJCC*, V, 288.
June 1, 1749	* Thomas Lee to Members of the O.C.	NYPL Emmet MSS, 3772, a.l.s.
June 6, 1749	Thomas Penn to James Hamilton.	HSP Penn-Hamilton Corr., p. 3, a.l.s.
June 20, 1749	The O.C. to John Hanbury.	*GMP*, pp. 140-41, 168-69.
June 21, 1749	Minutes and Orders, O.C.	*Ibid.*, pp. 141-42, 168-70.
	Minute, Bd. of Tr.	*JBT*, 1741–49, p. 426
	Minute, Bd. of Tr.	*Ibid.*, p. 428
June 24, 1749	Samuel Smith to John Hanbury.	NCSA Dobbs MSS, a.l.s.

Summer, 1749	Extract from Letter of George Washington to Mrs. Lawrence Washington.	Toner, p. 66.
July 3, 1749	George Croghan to [Richard Peters].	PPP, X, 62-63, a.l.s.
July 5, 1749	Richard Peters to Thomas Penn.	HSP Penn MSS, Off. Corr. IV, 219-27, a.l.s.
July 7, 1749	Instructions of Conrad Weiser.	HSP Peters MSS, II, 121.
July 12, 1749	Five Grants of Land, to Bernard Moore and Others; John Lewis and Others; Peyton Randolph and Others; and William Winston and Others.	*VJCC*. *GMP*, pp. 250-51, and elsewhere.
	List of Early Land Patents and Grants Petitioned for in Virginia up to 1769, Preserved among the Washington Papers.	*VJCC*, V, 295-98. Many copies.
	The Ohio Company Grant.	PROCO 5:1328/333. In print elsewhere.
July 31, 1749	Thomas Penn to James Hamilton.	HSP Penn Letter Book, II, 270-74.
August 2, 1749	Thomas Penn to Richard Peters.	HSP Penn Off. Corr. IV, 219.
September 25, 1749	Minutes, O.C.	*GMP*, pp. 170-71.
October 18, 1749	Thomas Lee to the Bd. of Tr.	PROCO 5:1327/195-200. Fernow.
October 27, 1749	Minute, Virginia Executive Council	*VJCC*, V, 302-3.
November 6, 1749	Order, Virginia Executive Council.	*Ibid.*, p. 306.
	Directions for Surveyors of Land.	PROCO 5:1327/137-66.
November 7, 1749	Lawrence Washington to John Hanbury.	Conway, pp. 272-77.
November 22, 1749	Thomas Lee to James Hamilton.	HSP Gratz Coll. Case 2: Box 32, a.l.s.
November 25, 1749	George Croghan to Richard Peters.	*Indian Treaties Printed by B. Franklin*, p. lvi, footnote 122. Copy of original.
December 1, 1749	Hugh Parker to Robert Smith.	*Ibid.* A commentary.
December 20, 1749	Thomas Lee to James Hamilton.	NYPL MS, a.l.s. *PCR*, V, 423-24.

Late, 1749	George Washington Memorandum.	Fitzpatrick, I, 18.
January 2, 1750	James Hamilton to Thomas Lee.	HSP Penn Off. Corr. IV, 177. *PA*, 4th ser., II, 123-24. Copy.
January 29, 1750	Memorandum of a Meeting of the Committee of the O.C.	*GMP*, p. 171.
February 3, 1750	Samuel Ogle to James Hamilton.	HSP Penn Off. Corr. IV, 179. Copy. *PA*, II, 40-41.
February 22, 1750	* Disposal of Two Shares in the O.C.	Westmoreland Co., Va. Will Book, II, 311-15.
February 27, 1750	Thomas Lee to Conrad Weiser.	HSP Peters Papers, III, 5, a.l.s. Wallace, pp. 298-99.
March 27, 1750	Meeting, O.C.	*GMP*, p. 5.
March 29, 1750	Orders, Committee of the O.C.	*Ibid.*, p. 142.
May 1, 1750	Extract from Letter of Thomas Penn to James Hamilton.	HSP Penn-Hamilton Corr., p. 7, a.l.s. Gipson, *Lewis Evans*, pp. 34-35.
May 24, 1750-March 23, 1750	* Account of James Ross with G.M. and the O.C.	DML, GMM.
May 24, 1750-May 22, 1752	Account of Zacheus Ruth with G.M. and the O.C.	*Ibid.*
May 27, 1750	G.M. to Lawrence Washington.	Conway, pp. 280-81.
June 7, 1750	Conference Held with the Indians at George Croghan's.	*PCR*, V, 440.
June 21, 1750	Thomas Lee to Conrad Weiser.	HSP Peters Letter Books, III, 9, a.l.s.
June 26, 1750	James Hamilton to Lewis Evans.	*PA*, II, 47-49. PPP, XI, 25. Copy.
June 29-August 10, 1750	Account of Jeremiah Jack with the O.C.	DML, GMM.
July, 1750	* Account of John Hammer vs. the O.C.	*Ibid.*
July 10, 1750	Richard Peters to the Proprietors.	HSP Penn Off. Corr. V, 29-35, a.l.s.
July 24, 1750	* Promissory Note of William Richey to the O.C.	DML, GMM.
July 25, 1750	Account of James Findley with G.M. and the O.C.	*Ibid.*

July 28, 1750-March 17, 1751	Account of Thomas Caton with G.M. and the O.C.	*Ibid.*
July 28-September 10, 1750	Account of Remembrance Williams with G.M. and the O.C.	*Ibid.*
August 3-November 8, 1750	Account of Peter Tostee with G.M. and the O.C.	*Ibid.*
August 3, 1750	Account of Thomas Wood with G.M. and the O.C.	*Ibid.*
August 4-24, 1750	Account of Samuel Taylor with the O.C.	*Ibid.*
August 10, 1750-March 14, 1751	Account of Enoch Enochs with G.M. and the O.C.	*Ibid.*
August 27, 1750	Thomas Penn to Richard Peters, Extract from Letter.	HSP Peters Corr. III, 50-54, l.s.
September 11, 1750	Minutes, Committee of the O.C.	*GMP*, pp. 171-73.
	Instructions to Christopher Gist.	*Ibid.*
	Agreement with Christopher Gist about Settlers.	*Ibid.*
	Promissory Note of Thomas Swearingen.	FCV, CDP.
September 14, 1750	* Bond of Aaron Price and Barney Curran.	FCM, Judgment Record H, ff. 575-76.
September 29, 1750	Thomas Lee to the Bd. of Tr.	PROCO 5:1327/231-46.
October 4, 1750	Conrad Weiser to Thomas Lee.	HSP Weiser Corr. I, 28. Copy.
October 5-November 27, 1750	* Account of Abraham Johnson with the O.C.	Photostat, Abraham Johnson Scrapbook, West Virginia University Coll. Original in the possession of Mrs. J. H. A. Brown, Keyser, West Va.
October 11, 1750	Minute, Bd. of Tr.	*JBT*, 1750–53, p.97.
October 12, 1750	Minute, Bd. of Tr.	*Ibid.*, p. 98
October 15, 1750	Minute, Bd. of Tr.	*Ibid.*, p. 99.
	Bd. of Tr. to Thomas Lee.	PROCO 5:1366/463-65. Copy.

October 21, 1750-March 29, 1751	Journal of Christopher Gist.	Many imprints.
Autumn, 1750	Lawrence Washington to Robert Dinwiddie.	Sparks, II, 481.
October 28, 1750	Account of Thomas Rutherford with the O.C.	DML, GMM.
November 26-December 26, 1750	* Excerpts from Gist's Journal.	*GMP*, pp. 10, 13, 100, 103.
November 6, 1750	Thomas Lee to the Bd. of Tr.	PROCO 5:1327/137.
December 3, 1750	Minutes, Committee of the O.C.	*GMP*, p. 173.
January 9, 1751	Minute, Bd. of Tr.	*JBT*, 1750–53, p. 147.
1751	Contemporary Notice of the O.C.	Douglass, p. 228.
January 15, 1751	Account of David Cragge with G.M. and the O.C.	DML, GMM.
	Account of Mark McDonough with G.M. and the O.C.	*Ibid.*
February 9, 1751	* Bill of Sale to Hugh Parker for the O.C.	FCM, Deeds, B, ff. 347-48.
February 11, 1751	Lewis Burwell to Conrad Weiser.	HSP Peters MSS, III, 27.
March 1, 1751	* Bill of Sale to Hugh Parker for the O.C.	FCM, Deeds, B, ff. 343-44.
March 8, 1751	Peter Collinson to Arthur Dobbs.	NCSA Dobbs MSS, a.l.s.
March 20, 1751	Robert Dinwiddie to Lawrence Washington	Conway, pp. 278-79.
April 3, 1751	Last Will and Testament of Hugh Parker.	Md. HR, Wills, Liber 28, f. 129.
May 21-24, 1751	Minutes, O.C.	*GMP*, pp. 142-43, 173-75.
May 23, 1751	* Articles of Agreement and Co-partnership for the O.C.	HSV photostat. Original in the possession of Alvin F. Embrey, Fredericksburg, Va.
May 27, 1751	Frederick Ice to G.M. and Co.	DML, GMM.
May 30, 1751	Warrant to Thomas Cresap for 1,000 Acres.	Md. LO, Warrants, Liber T.I., IV, No. 5, f. 26.
June 8, 1751-February 11, 1752	Account of Providence Mounts with G.M. and the O.C.	DML, GMM.

1751	Virginia Survey Laws of 1751.	Hening, VI, 33-38.
July 9, 1751	Promissory Note of Jacob Wolf to G.M. for the O.C.	DML, GMM.
July 15, 1751	Notation of a Meeting of the Committee of the O.C.	*GMP*, p. 175.
July 16, 1751	Instructions to Christopher Gist.	*Ibid.*, pp. 31-32, 175, 252.
July 17, 1751	Promissory Note of Abraham Teagarden to G.M. for the O.C.	DML, GMM.
	Promissory Note of John Tucker to G.M. for the O.C.	*Ibid.*
July 26, 1751	Bond of John Adam Long to G.M. for the O.C.	*Ibid.*
July 27, 1751	Promissory Note of Jasper Sutton to G.M. for the O.C.	*Ibid.*
July 31, 1751	Order to Pay Christopher Gist.	*VJCC*, V, 349.
August, 1751	* G.M. and Co. vs. Daniel Ashcraft.	Md. HR, FCM, Docket, f. 154.
August 10, 1751	Robert Dinwiddie to the Bd. of Tr.	PROCO 5:1327/417-18.
August 21, 1751	Lewis Burwell to the Bd. of Tr.	*Ibid.*, ff. 355-58.
August 24, 1751	Promissory Note of William Patterson to G.M. for the O.C.	DML, GMM.
September 19, 1751	[Matthew Rowan] to S.S. [Samuel Smith].	NCSA Dobbs Papers.
October 4, 1751	Bond of John and Isaac Pearis to G.M. for the O.C.	DML, GMM.
October 8, 1751	Promissory Note of Jacob Hood to G.M. for the O.C.	*Ibid.*
October 25, 1751	Promissory Note, with Penal Bond, of Jonathan Coburn to G.M. for the O.C.	*Ibid.*
October 26, 1751	Renewal of Grants of Land to John Blair and Others and to William McMacken and Others.	*GMP*, pp. 51, 251. Printed also elsewhere.
October 28, 1751	Promissory Note of William Castleman to G.M.	DML, GMM.
November 21, 1751	Notice of the Arrival of Dinwiddie and a Cargo of O.C. Goods for the O.C.	*Va. Gazette.*
November 26, 1751	Renewment of Warrant to Thomas Cresap for 1,000 Acres.	Md. LO, Warrants, Liber T.I., No. 5, f. 182.

January 20, 1752	Robert Dinwiddie to the Bd. of Tr.	PROCO 5:1327/453-54.
January 23, 1752	Dinwiddie to Cresap.	*VHSC*, III, 17-18.
February 20, 1752	Thomas Cresap to Conrad Weiser.	HSP Peters MSS, III, 54. Copy.
February 23, 1752	* Warrant of G.M. vs. John Tucker.	FCV, CDP.
February 24, 1752	* Petition of G.M. vs. William Castleman.	*Ibid.*
	Warrant of G.M. vs. William Castleman.	*Ibid.*
	Warrant of G.M. vs. Abraham Teagarden.	*Ibid.*
	Petition of G.M. vs. Jacob Wolf.	*Ibid.*
	Warrant of G.M. vs. Jacob Wolf.	*Ibid.*
March 3, 1752	Instructions to the Commissioners by the Virginia Council.	*VJCC*, V, 376.
March 11, 1752	Minute, Bd. of Tr.	*JBT*, 1750–53, p. 290.
March 12, 1752	Minute, Bd. of Tr.	*Ibid.*
March 17, 1752	G.M. and Co. vs. Van Swearingen.	Md. HR, FCM, Docket, Original Writs, f. 36.
	G.M. and Co. vs. John Johnson.	*Ibid.*, f. 40.
	G.M. and Co. vs. John Williams, Sr.	*Ibid.*
	G.M. and Co. vs. Joseph Volgemore.	*Ibid.*, f. 41.
	G.M. and Co. vs. John Williams.	FCM, Judgment Record G, 1752–53, f. 65.
March 28, 1752	Promissory Note of John Cunningham to G.M. and the O.C.	DML, GMM.
March 31, 1752	* Bond of James Martin to G.M. for the O.C.	*Ibid.*
April 10, 1752	Advertisement of a Meeting of the O.C.	*Va. Gazette.*
April 14, 1752	Additions to the Accounts Sent from Virginia, Concerning the Limits of that Colony.	PROCO 5:1327/429-40.
April 25, 1752	Instructions to Joshua Fry, Lunsford Lomax, and James Patton.	*VMHB*, XIII, 143-50.
April 28, 1752	Instructions of the O.C. to Christopher Gist about the Logstown Indian Conference.	*GMP*, pp. 52-54, 176, 269-71.

May 3, 1752	Petition of G.M. vs. Jacob Hood.	FCV, CDP.
May 4, 1752	Petition of G.M. and the O.C. vs. Remembrance Williams.	*Ibid.*
	Warrant of G.M. and the O.C. vs. Remembrance Williams.	*Ibid.*
May 5, 1752	Petition of G.M. and the O.C. vs. John Cunningham.	*Ibid.*
	Petition of G.M. and the O.C. vs. John Cunningham.	*Ibid.*, Duplicate.
	Warrant of G.M. and the O.C. vs. John Cunningham.	*Ibid.*
	Petition of G.M. and the O.C. vs. William Richey.	*Ibid.*
	Warrant of G.M. and the O.C. vs. John Richey.	*Ibid.*
	Petition of G.M. and Co. vs. Jasper Sutton.	*Ibid.*
	Warrant of G.M. and Co. vs. Jasper Sutton.	*Ibid.*
May 7, 1752	Advertisement of a Meeting of the O.C.	*Va. Gazette.*
May 18, 1752	Petition of G.M. and the O.C. vs. Samuel Taylor.	FCV, CDP.
	Warrant of G.M. and the O.C. vs. Samuel Taylor.	*Ibid.*
June 1-13, 1752	Minutes, Logstown Treaty.	PROCO 5:1327/575-614. In print.
June 1, 1752	* Declaration of G.M. vs. Abraham Teagarden.	FCV, CDP.
	Declaration of G.M. vs. John Tucker.	*Ibid.*
June 5, 1752	G.M. and O.C. vs. William Castleman.	FCV, OB, No. 4, 1751–53, f. 181.
	G.M. and Co. vs. Jacob Wolf.	*Ibid.*
	G.M. and Co. vs. James Findley.	*Ibid.*, f. 182.
	G.M. and Co. vs. Jacob Hood.	*Ibid.*
	G.M. and Co. vs. Thomas Swearingen.	*Ibid.*
	G.M. and Co. vs. Peter Tostee.	*Ibid.*
	G.M. and Co. vs. Thomas Wood.	*Ibid.*
	G.M. and Co. vs. Abraham Teagarden.	*Ibid.*, f. 197.
	G.M. and Co. vs. John Tucker.	*Ibid.*
	G.M. and Co. vs. John Tucker.	Copy on reverse of Warrant of June 16, 1752.

	Dinwiddie to the Lords of Trade.	PROCO 5:1327/461-66, a.l.s.
June 8, 1752	Petition of G.M. and Co. vs. James Findley.	FCV, CDP.
	Warrant of G.M. and the O.C. vs. James Findley.	*Ibid.*
	Petition of G.M. and Co. vs. Thomas Swearingen.	*Ibid.*
	Warrant of G.M. and Co. vs. Thomas Swearingen.	*Ibid.*
	Petition of G.M. and Co. vs. Peter Tostee.	*Ibid.*
	Warrant of G.M. and Co. vs. Peter Tostee.	*Ibid.*
	Petition of G.M. and Co. vs. Thomas Wood.	*Ibid.*
	Warrant of G.M. and Co. vs. Thomas Wood.	*Ibid.*
June 13, 1752	Confirmation of the Deed of 1744.	PROCO 5:1330/201-4.
	Warrant of Land Granted to Thomas Cresap by Renewment.	Md. LO, Liber T.I. No. 5, f. 375.
June 15, 1752	Petition of G.M. and the O.C. vs. David Cragge (Craig).	FCV, CDP.
	Petition of G.M. and the O.C. vs. David Craig.	*Ibid.*
	Warrant of G.M. and the O.C. vs. David Cragge (Craig).	*Ibid.*
	Warrant of G.M. and the O.C. vs. Zacheus Ruth.	*Ibid.*
	Warrant of G.M. and the O.C. vs. Thomas Rutherford.	DML, GMM.
June 16, 1752	* Warrant for the Attachment of the Goods, etc. of John Tucker.	FCV, CDP.
	G.M. and Co. vs. Van Swearingen.	Md. HR, FCM, Docket, f. 76.
	G.M. and Co. vs. Conrad Waltaker.	*Ibid.*, Judgment Writs, June, 1754, f. 85.
	G.M. and Co. vs. Conrad Waltaker.	*Ibid.*, Judgment Record G, 1752–53, ff. 212-15.
	G.M. and Co. vs. Richard Chapman.	*Ibid.*, Original Writs, June 1752, f. 86.

	G.M. and Co. vs. John Macfaddin.	*Ibid.*
	G.M. and Co. vs. William Erwin.	*Ibid.*
	G.M. and Co. vs. James Fowler.	*Ibid.*
	G.M. and Co. vs. Jacobus Houghland.	*Ibid.*, f. 94.
	G.M. and Co. vs. John Nicholas.	*Ibid.*
	G.M. and Co. vs. Philip McGuire.	*Ibid.*
	G.M. and Co. vs. Robert Erwin.	*Ibid.*, f. 98.
July 6, 1752	Bond of Robert Lemen to G.M. for the O.C.	DML, GMM.
July 12, 1752	Dinwiddie to the Bd. of Tr.	PROCO 5:1327/469-70.
July 13, 1752	Warrant of G.M. and the O.C. vs. Zacheus Ruth.	FCV, CDP.
August 6, 1752	G.M. and Co. vs. Thomas Swearingen.	FCV, OB, No. 4, 1751-53, f. 249.
	G.M. and Co. vs. Peter Tostee.	*Ibid.*
	G.M. and Co. vs. James Findley.	*Ibid.*
	G.M. and Co. vs. Thomas Wood.	*Ibid.*, f. 250.
	G.M. and Co. vs. Jacob Hood.	*Ibid.*
	G.M. and Co. vs. Enoch Enochs.	*Ibid.*
	G.M. and Co. vs. David Craig.	*Ibid.*
August 8, 1752	Petition of G.M. vs. Jacob Hood.	FCV, CDP.
	Warrant of G.M. vs. Jacob Hood.	*Ibid.*
August 11, 1752	Declaration of G.M. and the O.C. vs. Thomas Caton.	DML, GMM.
	Warrant of G.M. and the O.C. vs. Thomas Caton.	*Ibid.*
	Declaration of G.M. vs. John Adam Long.	FCV, CDP.
	Warrant of G.M. vs. John Adam Long.	*Ibid.*
	Warrant of G.M. and the O.C. vs. Providence Mounts.	*Ibid.*
August 14, 1752	Petition of G.M. and the O.C. vs. Enoch Enochs.	*Ibid.*
	Warrant of G.M. and the O.C. vs. Enoch Enochs.	*Ibid.*
August 18, 1752	* Debt of Frederick Ice to G.M. and the O.C.	DML, GMM.
	G.M. and Co. vs. Joseph Volgemore.	Md. HR, FCM, Docket, f. 119.

	G.M. and Co. vs. Van Swearingen.	*Ibid.*, f. 120.
	G.M. and Co. vs. John Johnson.	FCV, CDP, f. 120.
	G.M. and Co. vs. Richard Chapman.	Md. HR, FCM, Docket, f. 123.
	G.M. and Co. vs. William Erwin.	*Ibid.*
August, 1752	G.M. vs. John Macfaddin.	*Ibid.*, f. 124.
	G.M. vs. James Fowler.	*Ibid.*
August 18, 1752	G.M. vs. Jacobus Houghland.	*Ibid.*, Original Writs, f. 137.
	G.M. and Co. vs. John Nicholas.	*Ibid.*
August, 1752	G.M. and Co. vs. Philip McGuire.	*Ibid.*
	G.M. and Co. vs. Robert Erwin.	*Ibid.*, f. 138.
	G.M. and Co. vs. Joseph Mounts, Sr.	*Ibid.*, f. 143.
	G.M. and Co. vs. John Nicholas.	*Ibid.*
August 18, 1752	G.M. vs. Robert Erwin.	Md. HR, FCM, Judgement Record G, 1752–53, ff. 442-43.
September 1, 1752	Declaration of G.M. for the O.C. vs. Jonathan Coburn.	FCV, CDP.
	Declaration of G.M. and the O.C. vs. Zacheus Ruth.	*Ibid.*
	Declaration of G.M. and Co. vs. Thomas Rutherford.	DML, GMM.
	Warrant of G.M. and the O.C. vs. Providence Mounts.	FCV, CDP.
	Petition of G.M. and Co. vs. Frederick Ice.	*Ibid.*
	Petition of G.M. and Co. vs. Frederick Ice.	*Ibid.*
	Warrant of G.M. vs. Frederick Ice.	*Ibid.*
	G.M. vs. Jonathan Coburn.	FCV, OB, No. 4, 1751–53, f. 270.
	G.M. and Co. vs. Zacheus Ruth.	*Ibid.*
September 2, 1752	G.M. and the O.C. vs. Thomas Caton.	*Ibid.*, f. 283.
	G.M. and the O.C. vs. Providence Mounts.	*Ibid.*
	G.M. and the O.C. vs. John Adam Long.	*Ibid.*, f. 284.

September 14, 1752	G.M. and Co. vs. Enoch Enochs.	*Ibid.*, f. 302.
	G.M. and Co. vs. Jacob Hood.	*Ibid.*
	G.M. and Co. vs. Frederick Ice.	*Ibid.*
September 15-17, 17-19, 1752	Minutes, O.C.	*GMP*, pp. 175-76.
September 19, 1752	Warrant of G.M. and the O.C. vs. Thomas Caton.	FCV, CDP.
October 5, 1752	G.M. and Co. vs. Thomas Caton.	FCV, OB, No. 4, 1751–53, f. 332.
	G.M. and Co. vs. Providence Mounts.	*Ibid.*, f. 333.
October 6, 1752	Item in the *Virginia Gazette.*	
	Advertisement of a Meeting of the O.C.	*Va. Gazette.*
November 4, 1752	Order of Payment for Services at the Logstown Indian Conference.	*VJCC*, V, 410-11.
	Land Grant Petition of John Mercer and Thirteen Partners.	*GMP*, p. 240.
November 6, 1752	Petition of the O.C. to the Governor and Council of Virginia.	*Ibid.*
November 9, 1752	G.M. and the O.C. vs. Enoch Enochs.	FCV, OB, No. 4, 1751–53, f. 350.
	G.M. and the O.C. vs. Frederick Ice.	*Ibid.*, f. 352.
November, 1752	G.M. and Co. vs. Van Swearingen.	Md. HR, FCM, Docket Trials, f. 162.
November 21, 1752	G.M. and Co. vs. John Johnson.	*Ibid.*
	G.M. and Co. vs. Joseph Volgemore.	*Ibid.*
	G.M. and Co. vs. Richard Chapman.	*Ibid.*, f. 166.
	G.M. and Co. vs. William Erwin.	*Ibid.*
	G.M. vs. John Macfaddin.	*Ibid.*
	G.M. vs. James Fowler.	*Ibid.*
	G.M. vs. Robert Erwin.	*Ibid.*, f. 180
	G.M. vs. Nathaniel Tomlinson.	*Ibid.*, f. 190.
	G.M. vs. John Jones.	*Ibid.*
	G.M. and Co. vs. Evan Shelby.	*Ibid.*
	G.M. and Co. vs. Amos Thacker and James Mayors.	*Ibid.*
	G.M. and Co. vs. Catherine and Evan Shelby.	*Ibid.*

	G.M. and Co. vs. John Nicholas.	*Ibid.*, f. 195.
	G.M. and Co. vs. John Nicholas.	*Ibid.*, f. 196.
	G.M. and Co. vs. Joseph Mounts.	*Ibid.*, f. 196.
	G.M. and Co. vs. Jacobus Houghland.	*Ibid.*, f. 201.
	* G.M. vs. Evan Shelby.	FCM, Judgment Record G, 1752–53, ff. 713-15.
	G.M. vs. Amos Thacker and James Mayors.	*Ibid.*, ff. 715-17.
	G.M. and Co. vs. John Nicholls.	*Ibid.*, ff. 726-28.
	G.M. vs. Jacobus Houghland.	*Ibid.*, ff. 737-39.
November 22-23, 1752	Minutes, O.C.	*GMP*, pp. 143-44, 176.
November 29, 1752	Bd. of Tr. to Robert Dinwiddie.	PROCO 5:1366/516-33.
December 5, 1752	* Gawin Corbin's Statement Assigning his Shares of the O.C. to Robert Carter.	CHS Gunther MSS.
December 11, 1752	Warrant of G.M. and the O.C. vs. Jeremiah Jack.	FCV, CDP.
	Warrant of G.M. and the O.C. vs. Richard Leans.	*Ibid.*
	Warrant of G.M. vs. Robert Lemen.	*Ibid.*
	Warrant of G.M. and the O.C. vs. William Patterson.	*Ibid.*
December 13, 1752	Order for Payment to Christopher Gist.	*VJCC*, V, 44.
December 29, 1752	Land Warrant Granted to Thomas Cresap.	Md. LO, Liber T.I. No. 6, f. 23.
January, 1753	James Patton to John Blair.	WHS Draper MSS, 1QQ, 75-77.
January 11, 1753	Warrant of G.M. vs. James Martin.	FCV, CDP.
February, 1753	William Russell or Andrew Lewis Survey in Western Pennsylvania.	*GMP*, opp. 226.
February-April, 1753	Survey for John Blair and Company.	*GMP*, opp. 226.
February 6, 1753	Minutes, Committee of the O.C.	*GMP*, pp. 144-47, 176.
	Richard Peters to Conrad Weiser.	HSP Peters MSS, I, 38.
February 8, 1753	G.M. and Co. vs. Thomas Caton.	FCV, OB, No. 4, 1751–53, f. 392.

	G.M. and Co. vs. James Martin.	*Ibid.*
	G.M. and Co. vs. Richard Lane (Leans).	*Ibid.*
	G.M. and Co. vs. Robert Lemen.	*Ibid.*
	G.M. and Co. vs. William Patterson.	*Ibid.*
February 9, 1753	Declaration of G.M. vs. Jeremiah Jack.	FCV, CDP.
	Warrant of G.M. and the O.C. vs. Jeremiah Jack.	*Ibid.*
	Declaration of G.M. and the O.C. vs. Richard Leans.	*Ibid.*
	Warrant of G.M. and the O.C. vs. Richard Leans.	*Ibid.*
	Declaration of G.M. vs. Robert Lemen.	*Ibid.*
	Warrant of G.M. vs. Robert Lemen.	*Ibid.*
	Declaration of G.M. vs. James Martin.	*Ibid.*
	Warrant of G.M. vs. James Martin.	*Ibid.*
	Declaration of G.M. and the O.C. vs. Thomas Caton.	*Ibid.*
	Declaration of G.M. and the O.C. vs. William Patterson.	*Ibid.*
	Warrant of G.M. and the O.C. vs. William Patterson.	*Ibid.*
February 15, 1753	Robert Dinwiddie to the Committee of the O.C.	N.F.
February 17, 1753	Conrad Weiser to Richard Peters.	HSP Peters Papers, I, 17.
March 9, 1753	G.M. and Co. vs. John Cunningham.	FCV, OB, No. 4, 1751–53, f. 438.
	G.M. and Co. vs. John Hammer.	*Ibid.*
	G.M. and Co. vs. William Richey.	*Ibid.*
	G.M. and Co. vs. Samuel Taylor.	*Ibid.*
	G.M. and Co. vs. Remembrance Williams.	*Ibid.*
March 14, 1753	Petition of G.M. and the O.C. vs. Mark McDonough.	FCV, CDP.
	Warrant of G.M. and the O.C. vs. Mark McDonough.	*Ibid.*
	Warrant of G.M. and the O.C. vs. John Trohawk.	*Ibid.*

	Declaration of G.M. vs. John and Isaac Pearis.	*Ibid.*
	Warrant of G.M. vs. John and Isaac Pearis.	*Ibid.*
March 18, 1753	Petition of G.M. and the O.C. vs. John Hammer.	*Ibid.*
	Warrant of G.M. and the O.C. vs. John Hammer.	*Ibid.*
March 20, 1753	G.M. and Co. vs. Van Swearingen.	Md. HR, FCM, Docket Trials, March, 1753, f. 4.
	G.M. and Co. vs. John Johnson.	FCV, CDP, f. 5.
	G.M. and Co. vs. Joseph Volgemore.	*Ibid.*
March, 1753	G.M. and Co. vs. Richard Chapman.	*Ibid.*, f. 7.
	G.M. vs. John Macfaddin.	*Ibid.*
	G.M. vs. William Erwin.	*Ibid.*
March 20, 1753	G.M. vs. Nathaniel Tomlinson.	*Ibid.*, f. 18.
March, 1753	G.M. vs. James Fowler.	*Ibid.*
March 20, 1753	G.M. vs. Catherine and Evan Shelby.	*Ibid.*, f. 19.
March, 1753	G.M. vs. John Nicholas.	*Ibid.*, f. 24.
	G.M. vs. Jacobus Houghland.	*Ibid.*
	G.M. vs. Robert Erwin.	*Ibid.*
	G.M. vs. John Jones.	*Ibid.*
	G.M. vs. John Nicholas.	*Ibid.*, f. 33.
	G.M. and Co. vs. Joseph Mounts, Sr.	*Ibid.*
	G.M. and Co. vs. Isaac Baker.	*Ibid.*, f. 38.
March 20, 1753	G.M. and Co. vs. Van Swearingen.	FCM, Judgment Record G, 1752–53, ff. 760-62.
	G.M. and Co. vs. Richard Chapman.	*Ibid.*, ff. 797-800.
	G.M. and Co. vs. William Erwin.	*Ibid.*, ff. 800-3.
	G.M. vs. Robert Erwin.	*Ibid.*, 842-44.
	G.M. vs. John Jones.	*Ibid.*, f. 869.
	G.M. and Co. vs. John Nicholas.	*Ibid.*
March 31, 1753	Inventory of the Estate of Hugh Parker.	FCM, Inventories, Liber I, f. 180.
April 3, 1753	G.M. and the O.C. vs. John and Isaac Pearis.	FCV, OB, No. 4, 1751–53, f. 454.

April 4, 1753	G.M. and Co. vs. John Cunningham.	*Ibid.*, f. 463.
	G.M. and Co. vs. George Park.	*Ibid.*
	G.M. and Co. vs. William Richey.	*Ibid.*
	G.M. and Co. vs. Samuel Taylor.	*Ibid.*
	G.M. and Co. vs. Remembrance Williams.	*Ibid.*
	G.M. and Co. vs. John Hammer.	*Ibid.*, f. 466.
	G.M. and Co. vs. Mark McDonough.	*Ibid.*
April 5, 1753	Warrant of G.M. vs. John and Isaac Pearis.	FCV, CDP.
April 10, 1753	William Trent to Governor Hamilton.	PROCO 5:1066/59.
April 12, 1753	Warrant of G.M. and the O.C. vs. Thomas Caton.	FCV, CDP.
April 15, 1753	Thomas Cresap to Daniel Cresap. Assignment of Land.	Md. LO, Liber G. S. No. I, f. 287.
April 16, 1753	Original Survey of Limestone Rock.	Md. LO, Original Surveys, Frederick Co., No. 2424.
April 26, 1753	Notation of George Mercer concerning Proposed Town on Chartier's Creek.	Map. See *GMP*, opposite p. 226.
	Comments of George Mercer on the Blair Company Survey of April, 1753.	Map. See *GMP*, opposite p. 226.
May 1, 1753	Minute, Bd. of Tr.	*JBT*, 1750–53, p. 416.
May 2, 1753	G.M. and the O.C. vs. Thomas Caton.	FCV, OB, No. 4, 1751–53, f. 476.
	G.M. and the O.C. vs. Jeremiah Jack.	*Ibid.*, f. 486.
	G.M. and the O.C. vs. Richard Leans.	*Ibid.*
	G.M. and the O.C. vs. Robert Lemen.	*Ibid.*
	G.M. and Co. vs. James Martin.	*Ibid.*
	G.M. and the O.C. vs. William Patterson.	*Ibid.*
	G.M. and the O.C. vs. John and Isaac Pearis.	*Ibid.*, f. 489.
	G.M. and Co. vs. John Cunningham.	*Ibid.*, f. 494.
	G.M. and Co. vs. William Richey.	*Ibid.*

	G.M. and Co. vs. Jasper Sutton.	*Ibid.*
	G.M. and Co. vs. Samuel Taylor.	*Ibid.*
	G.M. and Co. vs. Remembrance Williams.	*Ibid.*
	G.M. and Co. vs. George Park.	*Ibid.*, f. 495.
May 3, 1753	Warrant of G.M. and the O.C. vs. Thomas Caton.	FCV, CDP.
	Warrant of G.M. and the O.C. vs. Richard Leans.	*Ibid.*
May 4, 1753	Warrant of G.M. and the O.C. vs. Jeremiah Jack.	*Ibid.*
	Warrant of G.M. vs. Robert Lemen.	*Ibid.*
	Warrant of G.M. vs. James Martin.	*Ibid.*
May 6, 1753	James Hamilton to Robert Dinwiddie.	PROCO 5:13/625-28. *PCR*, V, 628-30.
May 8, 1753	Warrant of G.M. and the O.C. vs. William Patterson.	FCV, CDP.
	Warrant of G.M. vs. John and Isaac Pearis.	*Ibid.*
May 10, 1753	Minute, Bd. of Tr.	*JBT*, 1750–53, f. 421.
May 15, 1753	Andrew Montour's Declaration.	*VJHB*, 1752–55, pp. 515-16. PROCO 5:1327/637.
May 21, 1753	Robert Dinwiddie to James Hamilton.	NYPL Emmet MSS, 1752. *PCR*, V, 630-32.
May 26, 1753	William Fairfax to William Trent.	*GMP*, pp. 73-74, 284-85.
May 31, 1753	Robert Dinwiddie to William Trent.	*Ibid.*
June 1, 1753	Acceptance of Judgment by James Martin.	DML, GMM.
June 2, 1753	*Augustine Washington to Robert Carter.	CHS Gunther MSS.
June 2, 1753–September 4, 1755	Account of William Trent and George Croghan with the O.C.	HSP MS.
June 6, 1753	G.M. and Co. vs. Jeremiah Jack.	FCV, OB, No. 5, 1753–54, f. 10.
	G.M. and Co. vs. James Martin.	*Ibid.*
	G.M. and Co. vs. Edward Lane.	*Ibid.*, f. 11.
	G.M. and Co. vs. Robert Lemen.	*Ibid.*

	Matthew Rogers and Jasper Sutton vs. Daniel McCrory and John Collins.	*Ibid.*
	G.M. and Co. vs. William Patterson.	*Ibid.*
	G.M. and the O.C. vs. John and Isaac Pearis.	*Ibid.*, f. 13.
June 7, 1753	G.M. and the O.C. vs. Enoch Enochs.	*Ibid.*, f. 41.
June 8, 1753	G.M. and Co. vs. John Cunningham.	*Ibid.*, f. 58.
	G.M. and Co. vs. Jasper Sutton.	*Ibid.*
	G.M. and Co. vs. Samuel Taylor.	*Ibid.*
	G.M. and Co. vs. Remembrance Williams.	*Ibid.*
	G.M. and Co. vs. George Park.	*Ibid.*, f. 59.
	G.M. and Co. vs. William Richey.	*Ibid.*
June 9-10, 1753	William Fairfax to William Trent.	*GMP*, pp. 79-80.
June 11, 1753	Warrant of G.M. and the O.C. vs. William Patterson.	FCV, CDP.
	Warrant of G.M. vs. John and Isaac Pearis.	*Ibid.*
June 15, 1753	Land Grants to Richard Corbin and Company.	*VJCC*, V, 436-37.
June 16, 1753	Robert Dinwiddie to the Bd. of Tr.	PROCO 5:1327/637-42, a. l. s.
	Method of Taking up Lands in Virginia.	*Ibid.*, 657-72.
June 18, 1753	G.M. vs. John Macfaddin.	FCM, Judgment Record, Liber G, 1752–53, f. 930.
	G.M. vs. James Fowler.	*Ibid.*
	G.M. vs. Evan Shelby.	*Ibid.*, f. 1007.
	G.M. and Co. vs. Joseph Mounts, Sr.	*Ibid.*, f. 1027.
June 19, 1753	G.M. vs. Joseph Volgemore.	Md. HR, FCM, Docket, June, 1753, Trials, f. 53.
	G.M. and Co. vs. John Johnson.	*Ibid.*
	G.M. vs. John Macfaddin.	*Ibid.*, f. 54.
	G.M. vs. James Fowler.	*Ibid.*
	G.M. vs. Nathaniel Tomlinson.	*Ibid.*, f. 63.
	G.M. vs. Evan Shelby's Administrators.	*Ibid.*

	G.M. and Co. vs. Isaac Baker.	*Ibid.*, f. 70.
	G.M. vs. Evan Shelby.	*Ibid.*, f. 74.
	G.M. and Co. vs. Joseph Mounts, Sr.	*Ibid.*, f. 80.
July 10, 1753	Instructions of Robert Dinwiddie to Christopher Gist.	N.F.
	Message of Governor Dinwiddie to the Half King, etc.	*GMP*, p. 286.
July 11-September 14, 1753	Proceedings with Indians at Logstown Conference.	PROCO 5:1328/15-40.
July 25-27, 1753	Minutes, O.C.	*GMP*, pp. 147-49.
	Resolutions, Committee of the O.C.	*Ibid.*, pp. 147-49, 178-79.
July 27, 1753	Committee Instructions to Christopher Gist.	*Ibid.*, pp. 149-50, 179.
	Case of the Ohio Company.	*Ibid.*, pp. 233-87.
August 8, 1753	G.M. and the O.C. vs. William Patterson.	FCV, OB, No. 5, 1753–54, f. 91.
	G.M. and the O.C. vs. Jeremiah Jack.	*Ibid.*, f. 98.
	G.M. and the O.C. vs. Richard Leans.	*Ibid.*
	G.M. and the O.C. vs. John and Isaac Pearis.	*Ibid.*, f. 99.
August 10, 1753	G.M. and Co. vs. Enoch Enochs.	*Ibid.*, f. 115.
	Daniel Cresap's Patent for Limestone Rock.	Md. LO, Book G, No. 2, ff. 106-7.
August 14, 1753	Warrant of G.M. and the O.C. vs. Daniel McCrory and John Collins.	FCV, CDP.
	Warrant of G.M. and the O.C. vs. Richard Leans.	*Ibid.*
August 16, 1753	Minute, Bd. of Tr.	*JBT*, 1750–53, p. 451.
	Minute, Bd. of Tr.	*Ibid.*, p. 452.
	Thomas Penn to Richard Peters.	HSP Peters MSS, III, 75, l.s.
August 21, 1753	G.M. vs. Joseph Volgemore.	Md. HR, FCM, Docket, Trials, August, 1753, f. 96.
	G.M. and Co. vs. John Johnson.	*Ibid.*
	G.M. vs. Nathaniel Tomlinson.	*Ibid.*, f. 101.
	G.M. vs. Evan Shelby's Administrators.	*Ibid.*
August, 1753	G.M. and Co. vs. Isaac Baker.	*Ibid.*, f. 107.

	G.M. and Co. vs. Joseph Mounts, Sr.	*Ibid.*, f. 122. Original Writs.
August 21, 1753	G.M. and Co. vs. John Johnson.	FCM, Judgment Record H, 1754–59, ff. 30-32.
	G.M. and Co. vs. Joseph Volgemore.	*Ibid.*, ff. 32-35.
	G.M. vs. Nathaniel Tomlinson.	*Ibid.*, ff. 87-88.
August, 1753	G.M. and Co. vs. Joseph Mounts, Sr.	*Ibid.*, f. 117.
August 27, 1753	John Fraser to Mr. Young.	*PCR*, V, 659-60.
September 1, 1753	William Fairfax to William Trent.	*GMP*, p. 80.
September 5, 1753	G.M. and the O.C. vs. Jeremiah Jack.	FCV, OB, No. 5, 1753–54, f. 138.
	G.M. and Others vs. Richard Leans.	*Ibid.*
	G.M. and the O.C. vs. William Patterson.	*Ibid.*, f. 139.
	G.M. and the O.C. vs. John and Isaac Pearis.	*Ibid.*, f. 140.
	G.M. and the O.C. vs. Jeremiah Jack.	*Ibid.*, f. 143.
	G.M. and the O.C. vs. Richard Leans.	*Ibid.*
	G.M. and the O.C. vs. William Patterson.	*Ibid.*
	G.M. and the O.C. vs. Abraham Teagarden.	*Ibid.*, f. 156.
	G.M. and the O.C. vs. John Tucker.	*Ibid.*
	G.M. vs. Jonathan Coburn.	*Ibid.*, f. 164.
	G.M. and the O.C. vs. John Adam Long.	*Ibid.*, f. 168.
	G.M. and the O.C. vs. Thomas Caton.	*Ibid.*, f. 177.
September 7, 1753	Warrant of G.M. and the O.C. vs. Jeremiah Jack.	FCV, CDP.
September 11, 1753	Minutes of the Winchester, Virginia Indian Conference.	PROCO 5:1328/48-86.
September 17, 1753	William Fairfax to Dinwiddie.	*Ibid.*, f. 72.

September 21, 1753	Bond of Jeremiah Jack and Jeremiah Jack, Jr. to G.M. and the O.C.	FCV, CDP.
September 26, 1753	N. Walthoe, Clerk of the Virginia Council, to William Trent.	*GMP*, p. 81.
October 2, 1753	G.M. and the O.C. vs. John Adam Long.	FCV, OB, No. 5, 1753–54, f. 190.
	G.M. vs. John Adam Long.	Duplicate on reverse of warrant of October 10, 1753.
	G.M. and the O.C. vs. Thomas Caton.	FCV, OB, No. 5, 1753–54, f. 193.
October 3, 1753	G.M. and the O.C. vs. Jeremiah Jack.	*Ibid.*, f. 204.
October 5, 1753	William Trent to Governor and Council of Virginia.	N.F.
October 6, 1753	Item in the *Virginia Gazette.*	*GMP*, p. 68.
October 10, 1753	Warrant of Attachment vs. John Adam Long.	FCV, CDP.
October 27, 1753	Minutes, Virginia Council.	*VJCC*, V, 443.
October 31, 1753	Robert Dinwiddie to the French Commander.	*GMP*, pp. 74-75.
November 2, 1753	Orders of the Committee of the O.C.	*Ibid.*, pp. 150, 179.
November 6, 1753	Petition of the O.C. to Governor and Council of Virginia.	Commonly dated April 2, 1754, q.v.
November 9, 1753	The Eckerlain Land Grant.	*VJCC*, V, 450.
November 16, 1753	Minute, Bd. of Tr.	*JBT*, 1750–53, p. 456.
November 17, 1753	William Trent to Robert Dinwiddie.	N.F. See PROCO 5:1328/27-44.
November 20, 1753	G.M. vs. Catherine and Evan Shelby.	Md. HR, FCM, Docket, November Term, 1753, f. 135.
November, 1753	G.M. vs. Isaac Baker.	*Ibid.*, f. 140.
November 21, 1753	G.M. and Co. vs. John Johnson.	*Ibid.*, f. 152.
November, 1753	G.M. and Co. vs. Richard Chapman.	*Ibid.*, f. 154.
	G.M. and Co. vs. William Erwin.	*Ibid.*

	G.M. vs. Nathaniel Tomlinson.	*Ibid.*, f. 155.
	G.M. and Co. vs. Joseph Mounts, Sr.	*Ibid.*, f. 159.
November 21, 1753	G.M. and Co. vs. John Johnson.	FCM, Judgment Record H, 1754–59, f. 266.
November, 1753	G.M. and Co. vs. Richard Chapman.	*Ibid.*, f. 268.
	G.M. and Co. vs. William Erwin.	*Ibid.*
	G.M. and Co. vs. Nathaniel Tomlinson.	*Ibid.*, f. 272.
	G.M. and Co. vs. Joseph Mounts, Sr.	*Ibid.*, f. 278.
November 22, 1753	Extract from George Washington's Journal.	Fitzpatrick, I, 23-24.
December 15, 1753	Legardeur De St. Pierre to Dinwiddie.	VSL MS, a.l.s. *GMP*, pp. 175-76.
December 18, 1753	Warrant of G.M. and the O.C. vs. Francis Ross.	FCV, CDP.
December 19, 1753	An Act for Further Encouraging Persons to Settle on the Mississippi.	Hening, VI, 355-56.
January 1, 1754	Extract from George Washington's Journal.	Fitzgerald, I, 30.
January 27, 1754	Robert Dinwiddie to Lord Fairfax.	*VHSC*, III, 48-50.
	Robert Dinwiddie to William Trent.	PROCO 5:14/147-50. *VHSC*, I, 56.
January 29, 1754	Robert Dinwiddie to the Bd. of Tr.	PROCO 5:1328/97-100.
February 3, 1754	George Croghan to James Hamilton.	PPP, II, 119-20, a. l. s.
February 14, 1754	An Act for the Encouragement and Protection of Settlers.	Hening, VI, 417-19.
February 18, 1754	Minutes, Virginia Council.	*VJCC*, V, 461-62.
February 19, 1754	Proclamation of Governor Dinwiddie Concerning Lands in Ohio.	PROCO 5:1333/203-4. *VJCC*, V, 498-510.
	William Trent to George Washington.	See *Va. Gazette*, March 29, 1754.
February 23, 1754	Christopher Gist to George Washington.	*Ibid.*
March 5, 1754	G.M. and Co. vs. Francis Ross.	FCV, OB, No. 6, 1753–54, f. 313.
March 11, 1754	Petition of G.M. and Co. vs. George Parker, Jr.	FCV, CDP.

	Warrant of G.M. and Co. vs. George Parker, Jr.	*Ibid.*
	Declaration of G.M. and the O.C. vs. Francis Ross.	*Ibid.*
	Warrant of G.M. and the O.C. vs. Francis Ross.	*Ibid.*
March 13, 1754	James Hamilton to Robert Dinwiddie.	*PA*, 4th ser., II, 264-66.
March 14, 1754	Notice of Letters of William Trent and Christopher Gist to George Washington.	*Md. Gazette.* Repeated in the *Va. Gazette*, March 29, 1754.
March 19, 1754	G.M. vs. Catherine and Evan Shelby.	Md. HR, FCM, Docket, March Term, 1754, f. 7.
	G.M. vs. Isaac Baker.	*Ibid.*, f. 9.
	G.M. vs. Evan Shelby, Bail of John Johnson.	*Ibid.*, f. 22.
	G.M. and Co. vs. Joseph Volgemore.	*Ibid.*, f. 23.
	G.M. and Co. vs. Joseph Mounts, Sr.	*Ibid.*, f. 27.
	G.M. and Co. vs. Catherine and Evan Shelby.	FCM, Judgment Record H, 1753–59, ff. 324-26.
	Isaac Baker vs. G.M. and Co.	*Ibid.*, ff. 357-59.
	G.M. and Co. vs. Evan Shelby, Jr.	*Ibid.*, ff. 416-17.
	G.M. and Co. vs. Joseph Volgemore.	*Ibid.*, f. 421.
	G.M. and Co. vs. Joseph Mounts, Sr.	*Ibid.*, f. 429.
March 28, 1754	Minute, Privy Council.	*APC*, IV, 244-45.
March 29, 1754	Item, *Va. Gazette.*	*GMP*, p. 84.
April 2, 1754	Petition, O.C.	PROCO 5:1328/155-61. Bailey, pp. 304-9.
	Minute, Privy Council.	PROCO 5:1328/153-54.
	G.M. and the O.C. vs. Francis Ross.	FCV, OB, No. 5, 1753–54, f. 355.
April 3–July 8, 1754	*Expense Account of Thomas and Richard Penn.	HSP Penn MSS, Large Folio, II, 14.
April 4, 1754	G.M. and Co. vs. George Parker.	FCV, OB, No. 5, 1753–54, f. 392.

April 8, 1754	Expense Account of Christopher Gist at Logstown Conference, 1752.	VSL MS.
	Expense Account of William Trent.	HSP MS.
April 16, 1754	Captain Contrecoeur to the Commander of the British Troops at the Monongahela.	*GMP*, pp. 86-87. Printed in many places.
April 17, 1754	A Comment on the Capture of the Fort at the Forks of the Ohio.	*JCB*, p. 56.
April 18, 1754	George Washington to Thomas Cresap.	*GMP*, p. 85.
	Speech from the Half King . . . to the Governors of Virginia and Maryland.	*Ibid.*, pp. 89-90.
April 27, 1754	George Washington to Horatio Sharpe.	Fitzpatrick, I, 43-44.
May 4, 1754	Robert Dinwiddie to Colonel Hunter.	*VHSC*, III, 150-51.
May 7, 1754	Land Grants to Richard Corbin and Others.	*VJCC*, V, 470.
	Deposition of Edward Ward.	PROCO 5:14/193-96. Darlington, pp. 275-78.
May 9, 1754	Item, *Va. Gazette.*	*GMP*, pp. 85-86.
May 16, 1754	Item, *Va. Gazette.*	*Ibid.*, pp. 89-90.
June 5, 1754	G.M. and Co. vs. Francis Ross.	FCV, OB, No. 5, 1753–54, f. 494.
June 14, 1754	Ononraguite to Philip Schuyler.	*Pa. Gazette*, August 15, 1754. *GMP*, pp. 70, 243-44.
June 15, 1754	Warrant of G.M. vs. Jonathan Coburn.	FCV, CDP.
June, 1754	G.M. vs. Joseph Crecraft, Bail of Nathaniel Tomlinson.	Md. HR, FCM, Docket, June, 1754, Judicial Writs, f. 58.
	G.M. and Co. vs. Joseph Mounts, Sr.	*Ibid.*, Original Writs, f. 66.
	G.M. and Co. vs. Joseph Crecraft.	FCM, Judgment Record H, 1753–59, f. 540.
	G.M. and Co. vs. Joseph Mounts, Sr.	*Ibid.*, f. 545.
June 25, 1754	Bd. of Tr. to the Committee of the Privy Council.	PROCO 5:1367/76-87.

1754–1815	Plea of Defendant in a Suit Relating to Old O.C. Lands.	Md. Ct. of Appeals, Judgments, Liber T. H., No. 16 (1815), f. 177.
August, 1754	Robert Dinwiddie to Robert Innes.	*VHSC*, III, 269-70.
August 5, 1754	Governor Dinwiddie to Governor Glen.	*Ibid.*, f. 272.
August 6, 1754	Report of the Bd. of Tr. to the Lords of the Committees of Council.	*JBT*, 1754–58, p. 64.
August 15, 1754	Item from the *Pa. Gazette.*	
August 20, 1754	G.M. vs. Nathaniel Tomlinson.	Md. HR, FCM, Docket, August, 1754, f. 89.
	G.M. vs. John Nicholas.	*Ibid.*
	G.M. and Co. vs. Joseph Mounts, Sr.	*Ibid.*, f. 93.
	G.M. and Co. vs. Nathaniel Tomlinson.	FCM, Judgment Record H, 1753–59, f. 614.
	G.M. vs. John Nicholas.	*Ibid.*
	G.M. and Co. vs. Joseph Mounts, Sr.	*Ibid.*, f. 623.
August 30, 1754	Robert Dinwiddie to Colonel Innes.	*VHSC*, III, 296-98.
September 6, 1754	Robert Dinwiddie to Governor Sharpe.	*Ibid.*, pp. 303-6.
September 10, 1754	Robert Dinwiddie to Lord Fairfax.	*Ibid.*, pp. 312-13.
September 11, 1754	Robert Dinwiddie to Major Carlyle.	*Ibid.*, pp. 318-19.
September 16, 1754	Warrant of G.M. vs. John Adam Long.	FCV, CDP.
September 18, 1754	Robert Dinwiddie to Colonel Innes.	*VHSC*, III, 320-22.
October 25, 1754	G.M. Deed for 220 Acres in Hampshire County.	VSL, N.N. Grants, H, 1751–56, Lot. 14.
	G.M. Deed for 334 Acres in Hampshire County.	*Ibid.*, Lot 15.
	G.M. Deed for 315 Acres in Hampshire County.	*Ibid.*, Lot. 16.
October 30, 1754	Petition of Christopher Gist.	*VJHB*, 1752–55, p. 323.
November, 1754	G.M. vs. Nathaniel Tomlinson.	Md. HR, FCM, Docket, November 11, 1754, f. 122.

	G.M. vs. John Nicholas.	*Ibid.*
	G.M. and Co. vs. Joseph Mounts, Sr.	*Ibid.*, f. 127.
	G.M. vs. John Nicholas.	*Ibid.*, Judgment Record H, 1753–59, f. 696, November Court.
	G.M. vs. Nathaniel Tomlinson.	*Ibid.*
November 19, 1754	G.M. and Co. vs. Joseph Mounts.	*Ibid.*, ff. 709-10.
February 12, 1755	Additional Instructions about Western Land Grants.	*Va. Gazette.*
March 20, 1755	G.M. vs. John Nicholas.	Md. HR, FCM, Dockets, Judgment Writs, 1755, f. 20.
	G.M. and Co. vs. Joseph Mounts, Sr.	*Ibid.*, f. 21.
	G.M. vs. Nathaniel Tomlinson.	*Ibid.*
	*G.M. and Co. vs. Christopher Gist.	*Ibid.*, f. 31.
	G.M. vs. John Nicholas.	*Ibid.*, f. 54.
	G.M. and Co. vs. Nathaniel Tomlinson.	*Ibid.*, f. 23.
	G.M. vs. Nathaniel Tomlinson.	FCM, Judgment Record H, 1753–59, f. 792.
	G.M. and Co. vs. Joseph Mounts, Sr.	*Ibid.*, f. 793.
	G.M. and Co. vs. Nathaniel Tomlinson.	*Ibid.*, f. 797.
	G.M. and Co. vs. Christopher Gist.	*Ibid.*, f. 800.
May 7, 1755	Petition of Christopher Gist.	*VJHB*, 1752–55, p. 244.
May 9, 1755	Petition of Christopher Gist. Disallowed.	*Ibid.*, p. 247.
June 5,1755	G.M. vs. Abraham Teagarden.	FCV, OB, No. 6, 1754–55, f. 283.
	Jury List, Mason vs. Teagarden.	FCV, CDP.
	G.M. vs. Jonathan Coburn.	FCV, OB, No. 5, 1754–55, f. 285.
	Jury List, Mason vs. Coburn.	FCV, CDP.
	G.M. and the O.C. vs. William Patterson.	FCV, OB, No. 6, 1754–55, f. 289.
	G.M. vs. John and Isaac Pearis.	*Ibid.*, f. 290.
	Jury List, G.M. vs. John and Isaac Pearis.	FCV, CDP.
	G.M. vs. John Tucker.	FCV, OB, No. 6, 1754–55, f. 292.

Date	Item	Source
	Jury Item, Mason vs. Tucker.	FCV, CDP.
	G.M. vs. John Adam Long.	FCV, OB, No. 6, 1754–55, f. 304.
	Jury Item in Mason vs. Long.	FCV, CDP.
	G.M. and the O.C. vs. Thomas Caton.	FCV, OB, No. 6, 1754–55, f. 305.
June 6, 1755	G.M. and the O.C. vs. Francis Ross.	*Ibid.*, f. 330.
June 17, 1755	G.M. and Co. vs. Joseph Mounts, Sr.	Md. HR, FCM, Docket, June, 1755, f. 58.
	G.M. and Co. vs. Joseph Mounts, Sr.	FCM, Judgment Record H, 1753–59, f. 856.
August, 1755	G.M. vs. John Nicholas.	Md. HR, FCM, Docket, August Court, 1755, f. 98.
November, 1755	G.M. vs. John Nicholas.	*Ibid.*, f. 130. Trials.
1756	A List of Accounts Due Hugh Parker.	FCM, Inventories Books, Liber 61, ff. 441-44.
February 24, 1756	Robert Dinwiddie to Andrew Miller.	*VHSC*, IV, 349-50.
March, 1756	G.M. vs. John Nicholas.	Md. HR, FCM, Docket, March Court, 1756, Trials, No. 22.
March 25, 1756	Patent of G.M. for *Walnut Bottom.*	Md. LO, Liber G.S., No. 2, ff. 400-2.
June 30, 1756	Deposition of Edward Ward in 1756.	HSP Photostat.
August 5, 1756	G.M. vs. Thomas Caton.	FCV, OB, No. 7, 1755–58, f. 116.
August 17, 1756	G.M. vs. John Nicholas.	Md. HR, FCM, Docket, ff. 90-91.
September 7, 1756	* Writ of Attachment in behalf of G.M. and the O.C. vs. Richard Pearis.	DML, GMM.
September, 1756	List of Indian Goods at Rock Creek belonging to the O.C.	LC George Washington MSS. Hamilton, I, 362-64.
1757	Excerpt from the Representation of the Council and Burgesses of Virginia.	PROCO 5:1329/11.
January 10, 1757	George Washington to the Earl of Loudoun.	HHL, Lo. 2569. Printed from variant text, Fitzpatrick, III, 6-19.

January, 1757	George Washington to the Earl of Loudoun (Extract).	Fitzpatrick, III, 6-7.
February 2, 1757	* G.M. vs. Richard Pearis.	FCV, OB, No. 7, 1755–58, f. 181.
March 4, 1757	G.M. and the O.C. vs. Thomas Caton.	*Ibid.*, f. 216.
March 14, 1757	Extracts from George Croghan's Journal Enclosed in a Letter to Sir William Johnson Received June 25, 1757.	*NYCD*, VI, 267-71. A copy of the journal is found, HHL, Lo. 3040.
April 7, 1757	Thomas Caton vs. G.M.	FCV, OB, No. 7, 1755–58, f. 232.
December 21-22, 1757	Meeting, Committee of the O.C.	*GMP*, p. 179.
January 3, 1758	G.M. and Co. vs. Thomas Rutherford.	FCV, OB, No. 7, 1755–58, f. 352.
February 7, 1758	G.M. and the O.C. vs. Jeremiah Jack.	*Ibid.*, f. 354.
April, 1758	Declaration of G.M. and the O.C. vs. Providence Mounts.	FCV, CDP.
July 6, 1758	G.M. and the O.C. vs. Providence Mounts.	FCV, OB, No. 8, 1758–60, f. 72.
	G.M. and the O.C. vs. Thomas Caton.	*Ibid.*, f. 73.
	G.M. and the O.C. vs. Matthew Rogers and Jasper Sutton, Executors of James Ross.	*Ibid.*, f. 80.
	G.M. vs. Robert Lemen.	*Ibid.*, f. 81.
August 2, 1758	George Washington to Henry Bouquet.	BM Add. MSS, 21641, f. 33, a.l.s. Fitzpatrick, II, 252-60.
September 8, 1758	G.M. vs. Robert Lemen.	FCV, OB, No. 8, 1758–60, f. 119.
	Jury List, Mason vs. Lemen.	FCV, CDP.
November 9, 1758	Morson and Ross vs. William Harrell.	FCV, OB, No. 8, 1758–60, f. 158.
January 30, 1759	Governor Fauquier to the Lords of Trade.	PROCO 5:1329/247-50.
February 7, 1759	Mason and Ross vs. William Harrell.	FCV, OB, No. 8, 1758–60, f. 195.
	G.M. and the O.C. vs. Executors of James Ross.	*Ibid.*, f. 198.
	G.M. and the O.C. vs. Peter Mounts.	*Ibid.*, f. 199.

	Jury List, Mason vs. Mounts.	FCV, CDP.
	G.M. and Co. vs. Francis Ross.	FCV, OB, No. 8, f. 199.
April 11, 1759	* List of Papers Sent by William Trent to Mr. Mercer.	HSP.
July 6, 1759	Minutes, Committee of the O.C.	*GMP*, p. 179.
ca. September, 1759	John Mercer to Governor Fauquier of Virginia.	*GMP*, pp. 93-95.
October, 1759	Payment to Richard Pearis.	Hening, VIII, 129.
October 29, 1759	Adam Stephen to Governor Fauquier.	PROCO 5:1330/55-58.
November 25, 1759	Deed of John Mercer's Share in the O.C.	*GMP*, p. 41.
December 1, 1759	Francis Fauquier to the Lords of Trade.	PROCO 5:1330/51-54.
December 10, 1759	Appointment of George Mercer as Surveyor.	*WMQ*, III, 129.
May 12, 1760	Francis Fauquier to the Lords of Trade.	PROCO 5:1330/9-12, a.l.s.
July 24, 1760	Thomas Cresap to Henry Bouquet.	BM Add. MSS, 21645, f. 163, a.l.s.
August 6, 1760	Thomas Caton vs. G.M. and Co.	FCV, OB, No. 9, 1760–62, f. 86.
	G.M. and Co. vs. Thomas Caton.	*Ibid.*, f. 102.
September 4, 1760	G.M. and Co. vs. Thomas Caton.	*Ibid.*, f. 168.
September 12, 1760	Henry Bouquet to Thomas Cresap.	BM Add. MSS, 21653, ff. 24-25.
October 17, 1760	Minutes, Committee of the O.C.	*GMP*, pp. 150-57, 179-80.
	State of the Company's Case.	*GMP*, pp. 150-51, 180, 287.
November 8, 1760	* George Mercer to William Trent.	HSP Etting Coll., Ohio Co. Papers, a.l.s. Bailey, pp. 347-48.
November 19, 1760	Minute, Bd. of Tr.	*JBT*, 1759–63, p. 141.
December 27, 1760	George Mercer to Henry Bouquet.	BM Add. MSS, 21645, ff. 340-51, a.l.s.
January 16, 1761	Petition of David Ross.	Md. HR, Ct. of Appeals, Judgments, Liber T. H., No. 16 (1815), ff. 69-72.
	Warrant to David Ross.	Md. LO, Liber W.S., No. 2, f. 170.

March 1, 1761	Order, House of Burgesses of Virginia.	*VJHB*, 1758–61, p. 236.
April 8, 1761	Minute, Report, and Resolution, House of Burgesses of Virginia.	*Ibid.*, p. 255.
June 13, 1761	Warrant for the Resurvey of *Walnut Bottom.*	Md. LO, Warrants, Liber W.S., No. 3, f. 190.
August 13, 1761	Deposition of Joseph Tomlinson before the Judges of the Land Office.	Allegany Co., Md., Judgment Record F, ff. 326-31. Copy.
	Deposition, Thomas Prather.	Md. HR, Ct. of Appeals, Judgments, Liber T. H., No. 16, ff. 48-54.
September 7-9, 1761	Minutes, Committee of the O.C.	*GMP*, pp. 18, 151-53, 287-88.
September 9, 1761	Petition Prepared by the Committee of the O.C. to be Presented to the Crown.	Printed 1760–61. *GMP*, Part II, the *Case*, . . . pp. 25-26.
	G.M. to Robert Dinwiddie.	*GMP*, pp. 151-52. Rowland, I, 78.
September 10, 1761	Committee of the O.C. to Messrs. Capel and Osgood Hanbury.	*Ibid.*, pp. 81, 152-53.
October 30, 1761	Proclamation of Bouquet against Hunters and Settlers.	BM Add. MSS, 21657, f. 26, d.s. In print.
November 7, 1761	Minute, Virginia Council.	PROCO 5:1425/24.
November 23, 1761	Royal Order Forbidding Further Western Grants.	*NYCD*, VII, 472-78.
November 30, 1761	Francis Fauquier to the Lords of Trade	PROCO 4:1330.
December 10, 1761	Renewal of Warrant to Resurvey *Walnut Bottom.*	Md. LO, Warrants, Liber W.S., No. 4, f. 178.
January 17, 1762	Francis Fauquier to Henry Bouquet.	BM Add. MSS, 21648, f. 35, a.l.s.
January 21, 1762	Minute, Virginia Council.	PROCO 5:1425/26.
February 8, 1762	Henry Bouquet to Francis Fauquier.	BM Add. MSS, 21648, f. 25, a.c.s.
February 12, 1762	Notice to Surveyors.	*Va. Gazette.*
February 14, 1762	Major James Livingston to Colonel Henry Bouquet.	BM Add. MSS, 21648, f. 30, a.l.s.
March 3, 1762	G.M. and Co. vs. Thomas Caton.	FCV, OB, No. 9, f. 373.
March 12, 1762	Francis Fauquier to Henry Bouquet.	BM Add. MSS, 21648, f. 60, a.l.s.

April 1, 1762	Henry Bouquet to Jeffery Amherst.	*Ibid.*, 21634, f. 12. Copy.
April 3, 1762	Certificate of Survey of *White Oak Level.*	Md. LO, Liber T.H. No. 16, f. 170.
June 30, 1762	Renewal of Warrant to Resurvey *Walnut Bottom.*	Md. LO, Warrants, Liber W.S. No. 5, f. 60.
	Resurvey on *Walnut Bottom.*	Md. LO, Unpatented Certificate, No. 744.
July 27, 1762	John Mercer to Charlton Palmer.	*GMP*, pp. 46-48.
	Case of the O.C.	*Ibid.*, pp. 49-139, 295-96.
August 4, 1762	G.M. and Co. vs. Thomas Caton.	FCV, OB, No. 10, 1762–63, f. 84.
September 9, 1762	G.M. and Co. vs. Thomas Caton.	*Ibid.*, f. 181.
November 4, 1762	G.M. and Co. vs. Thomas Caton.	*Ibid.*, f. 332.
November 11, 1762	Land Office Judges to Horatio Sharpe.	Md. LO, Liber B.C. and G.S. No. 15, ff. 814-18. Copy. In Md. *Rep.* of Ct. of Appeals, III.
	Horatio Sharpe to the Land Office Judges.	*Ibid.*, ff. 818-19.
December 9, 1762	Payment to Captain Richard Pearis.	*VJCC. VMHB*, XVI, 146.
December 26, 1762	Patent to Doctor David Ross for *White Oak Level.*	Md. LO, Liber B.C. and G.S. No. 15, ff. 479-81.
February 17, 1763	Advertisement of Sale of O.C. Lots.	*Md. Gazette.*
	Notice of a Meeting of the O.C.	*Md. Gazette.*
March-April, 1763	Advertisement of Sale of O.C. Lots.	*Pa. Gazette.*
March 2, 1763	Minutes, Committee of the O.C.	*GMP*, pp. 181-82.
March-May, 1763	George Mercer Field Notes of the Charlottesburg Survey.	*GMP*, pp. 165-66.
March 3, 1763	G.M. and Co. vs. Thomas Caton.	FCV, OB, No. 10, 1762–63, f. 430.
March 4, 1763	Thomas Caton vs. G.M. and Co.	*Ibid.*, No. 11, 1763–64, f. 2.
March 29, 1763	*Power of Attorney from G.M. to George Mercer.	Md. HR, FCM, Deeds, Liber H. f. 350.
April 2, 1763	Acts of Pennsylvania about the Indian Trade.	*GMP*, pp. 156-65.

May, 1763	Revision of Virginia Survey Law.	Hening, VII, 645.
May 4, 1763	*G.M. and the O.C. vs. Thomas Caton.	FCV, OB, No. 11, 1763–64, f. 92.
	Jury List. Mason vs. Caton.	DML, GMM.
June 16, 1763	Notice of a Meeting of the O.C.	*Md. Gazette, Pa. Gazette.*
	Advertisement of Sale of Lots by the O.C.	*Ibid.*
June 24, 1763	Patent of G.M. for the *Cove.*	Md. LO, Liber B.C. and G.S. No. 17, ff. 599-600.
June 25, 1763	Patent to G.M. for *Hunt the Hare.*	*Ibid.*, No. 15, ff. 699-700.
	Patent of G.M. to *Welshman's Conquest.*	*Ibid.*, f. 701.
July 4, 1763	*Resolution, O.C.	NYPL Emmet MSS, 13417, d.s. *GMP*, Part II, the *Case. . . .*
	Memorial of the O.C.	PROCO 4:1331/421-30. Submitted July 16, 1765.
	Minutes of a Meeting of the O.C.	*GMP*, pp. 182, 296.
	The O.C. Appointment of George Mercer as London Agent.	*Ibid.*, pp. 182-83.
	Minute, O.C.	*Ibid.*, pp. 182, 296.
	Statement of the Account of Arthur Dobbs with the O.C.	*Ibid.*, p. 183.
August 18, 1763	Advertisement of a Meeting of the O.C.	*Md. Gazette.*
August 31, 1763	*Thomas Hodgkin to David Ross, the Elder.	Allegany Co., Md., Judgment Record F, ff. 353-54. Copy.
September 6, 1763	Petition of Doctor David Ross.	Md. LO, Original Surveys, Allegany Co., No. 2087.
November 8, 1763	*Double Indemnity Bond, G.M. to Thomas Bladen.	LC, GMM.
November 11, 1763	Proclamation of Egremont Stopping Grants.	
February 13, 1764	Francis Fauquier to the Lords of Trade.	PROCO 5:1330/589-96.
March 11, 1764	George Mercer to James Mercer.	Ky. Coll. W.S. Col., Bowling Green, Ky.

April 5, 1764	Deposition of Jarvis Hougham about *Pleasant Valley*.	Allegany Co., Md., Judgment Record F, ff. 331-34.
April 17, 1764	John Mercer to Charlton Palmer.	*GMP*, pp. 184-85.
October 2-3, 1764	Deposition of Providence Mounts.	Allegany Co., Md., Judgment Record F, ff. 334-37. Copy.
June 21, 1765	Minute, Privy Council.	*APC*, IV, 727.
	Minute, Privy Council and Memorial of George Mercer.	PROCO 5:1331/411-30.
July 8, 1765	Unpatented Resurvey and Plot for Limestone Rock.	Md. LO, FCM, Original Unpatented Certificates, No. 555.
March 1, 1767	*G.M. to Col. Tilghman. G.M. Statement of William Trent's Account with George Croghan, enclosing Letter of John Mercer.	HSP John Cadwallader Papers.
May 20, 1767	*Thomas Cresap to James Tilghman.	HSP, a.l.s.
June 26, 1767	Bd. of Tr. to Lords of Com. of Privy Council for Plantation.	PROCO 5:1368/324-28.
	Report of the Lords of Trade to the Privy Council.	*Ibid. GMP*, Part II, the *Case. . . .*
September 21, 1767	George Washington to William Crawford.	Fitzpatrick, II, 467-71, a.l.s.
September 25, 1767	*Receipt for Money Received by William Trent.	HSP John Cadwallader Coll. Box 36, d.s.
ca. October, 1767	Minutes, Committee of the Privy Council.	PROPCR 2:112/425.
October 8, 1767	*George Mercer's Report to Lord Shelburne on the State of Company Affairs.	WLCL Shelburne Papers, L, 93-97.
	*Lord Shelburne to Governor Fauquier.	*Ibid.*, LIV, 67-69. PROCO 5:1345/385-90.
October 10, 1767	*George Mercer to the Committee of the O.C.	LC, MS, AC 2200.
November 21, 1767	*George Mercer to the O.C.	*WMQ*, I, 200-3.
November 27, 1767	Memorial of George Mercer.	PROCO 5:1332/301-6. *GMP*, Part II, the *Case. . .*, pp. 34-35.

December 12, 1767	Minute, Privy Council.	*APC*, V, 119.
December 21, 1767	*John Mercer to Robert Carter.	NYPL Emmet MS, 6302, a.l.s.
January 1, 1768	George Croghan to Richard Lea.	HSP John Cadwallader Papers, Box 36.
January 23, 1768	G.M. to Robert Carter.	Rowland, I, 131-32.
January, 1768	John Tayloe to John Mercer.	Embedded. See *GMP*, p. 211.
January 28, 1768	John Mercer to George Mercer.	*Ibid.*, pp. 186-220.
February 4, 1768	Advertisement of a Meeting of the O.C.	*Va. Gazette.*
February 10, 1768	*Robert Carter to G.M.	HSP Dreer Coll., French Refugees, Colonial Affairs, f. 44.
February 11, 1768	Advertisement of a Meeting of the O.C.	*Md. Gazette.*
February 23, 1768	*John Mercer to Robert Carter.	HSP Dreer Coll., French Refugees, Colonial Affairs, f. 45.
February 25, 1768	Proposed Boundaries for Grants to the O.C.	*GMP*, pp. 229-31.
February 26, 1768	Revision of Boundary Proposals.	*Ibid.*, pp. 231-32.
March 1, 1768	Warrant to Resurvey the New Store Tract.	VSL. Land Office Papers.
March 3, 1768	John Mercer to George Mercer.	*GMP*, pp. 221-29.
March 9, 1768	John Mercer to George Mercer.	*Ibid.*, pp. 297-310.
March 10, 1768	Minute, Virginia Council.	PROCO 5:1435.
March 21, 1768	John Blair to Lord Shelburne.	*Ibid.*, 1346/13-15.
May 5, 1768	Resurvey of the New Store Tract.	VSL.
May 19, 1768	Minute, Bd. of Tr.	*JBT*, 1768–75, pp. 28-29.
May 31, 1768	Minute, Bd. of Tr.	*Ibid.*, pp. 29-30.
June 3, 1768	Minute, Bd. of Tr.	*Ibid.*, p. 30.
June 7, 1768	Minute, Bd. of Tr.	*Ibid.*, p. 31.
June 10, 1768	Minute, Bd. of Tr.	*Ibid.*, pp. 31-32.
November 20, 1769	The Lords of the Committee to the Bd. of Tr. Referral of George Mercer's Memorial.	PROCO 5:1332/299-306.

December 6, 1769	Attestation of Earlier Documents.	*Ibid.*, 1333/144-59. Walthoe List.
December 18, 1769	Memorial, George Mercer on the O.C.	*Ibid.*, 1332/307-10. In *Case* of 1770, *GMP*.
December 27, 1769	Charlton Palmer to George Mercer.	*GMP*, p. 310.
January, 1770	*Memorandum of George Croghan for Mr. Gratz.	HSP Etting Coll., Ohio Company Papers, I, 83, a.d.
January 3, 1770	Minute, Bd. of Tr.	*JBT*, 1768–75, p. 159.
January 31, 1770	Edward Montagu to the Lords of Trade.	PROCO 5:1334/323. *VMHB*, XII, 162-63.
January 24, 1770	Minute, Bd. of Tr.	*JBT*, 1768–75, p. 163.
February 7, 1770	Thomas Walpole to Osgood Hanbury.	*GMP*, p. 311.
March 26, 1770	Conway Richard Dobbs to George Mercer.	*Ibid.*, pp. 311-12.
April 27, 1770	John Stuart to Lord Botetourt.	DML, GMP.
May, 1770	The Case of the Ohio Company.	NYHS imprint. Reproduced in facsimile in *GMP*.
May 7, 1770	The Admission of the O.C. into the Vandalia Co.	PROCO 5:1332/365-66. *Am. Hist. Rec.*, III (1874), 205, and elsewhere.
May 8, 1770	Memorial of George Mercer.	PROCO 5:1333/383. Bailey, p. 319.
June 26, 1770	Minutes, Board of Property.	*PA*, 3rd ser. I, 310.
June 27, 1770	*Indenture between William Cromwell and Samuel Lyon.	Fayette Co., Pa. Deed Book, A, f. 85.
October 18, 1770	List of Virginia Land Grants.	PROCO 5:1348/335-53.
December 6, 1770	G.M. to [Brother of Robert Brent].	LC, GMM, a.l.s.
October 10, 1770	Statement by John Blair about Land Grants.	PROCO 5:1349/22.
January 2, 1771	Lord Hillsborough to William Nelson.	*Ibid.*, f. 63.
April 12, 1771	Minute, Virginia Council.	*Ibid.*, ff. 12-13.
April 17, 1771	William Nelson to Lord Shelburne.	*Ibid.*, ff. 173-76.
May 28, 1771	George Mercer to Conway Richard Dobbs.	NCSA Dobbs MSS, a.l.s.

August 8, 1771	*George Mercer to G.M.	VSL MS, 20624.
October 24, 1771	Robert Carter to George Mercer.	Embedded in letter of December 9, 1771.
December 5, 1771	Advertisement of James Mercer.	*Va. Gazette.*
December 9, 1771	*Robert Carter to James Mercer.	VSL MS.
December 31, 1771	*James Mercer to Robert Carter.	Once in possession of W. G. Chisolm, Leesburg, Va., a.l.s. Now in HSV.
January 9, 1772	General Letter of James Mercer to Members of the O.C. and Additional Special Letter to Philip Ludwell Lee.	*GMP*, pp. 312-15.
January 11, 1772	James Scott to James Mercer.	*Ibid.*, pp. 321-22.
January 13, 1772	Reply Letter to James Mercer from G.M.	*Ibid.*, pp. 315-18, a.l.s.
	Reply Letter to James Mercer from Pearson Chapman.	*Ibid.*, p. 318, a.l.s.
	Reply Letter to James Mercer from Thomas Ludwell Lee.	*Ibid.*, a.l.s.
January 19, 1772	Thomas Ludwell Lee to James Mercer.	*Ibid.*, p. 320, a.l.s.
January 21, 1772	*Richard Lee to James Mercer.	NYPL MS, a.l.s.
February 29, 1772	*Thomas and Rowland Hunt to Robert Carter.	Md. HS, Tench Tightman Papers, 1770–72.
March 5, 1772	Advertisement of a Meeting of the O.C.	*Va. Gazette.*
April 23, 1772	Advertisement of a Meeting of the O.C.	*Md. Gazette.* Also May 14, 1772. *Va. Gazette.* Repeated May 21, 1772.
July 22, 1772	Notice of a Meeting of the O.C.	*Va. Gazette.*
July 27, 1772	*Minutes, Virginia Council.	PROCO 5:1440/43-46.
August 5, 1772	Draft of George Mercer and Samuel Wharton.	*GMP*, p. 324.
August 19, 1772	*Advertisement of Sale of George Croghan's Philadelphia Estate.	*Pa. Gazette.*
August 20, 1772	Samuel Wharton to George Mercer.	*GMP*, pp. 324-25.

October 26, 1772	* Notes on Financial and Legal Transactions of George Croghan.	FPLPR McAllister Coll. MS.
November 21, 1772	William Franklin to George Croghan.	HSP Society Coll.
December 26, 1772	Account of William Trent with George Croghan.	FPLPR MS.
	George Croghan to William Franklin.	HSP MS, Miscellaneous Coll. Copy.
February 13, 1773	Thomas Fairfax to G.M., Deed.	VSL LO, Archives, N.N. Grants, P, 1771–75.
April 5, 1773	Minute, Bd. of Tr.	*JBT*, 1768–75, p. 352.
April 22, 1773	Minute, Bd. of Tr.	*Ibid.*, pp. 352-53.
April 26, 1773	William Franklin to George Croghan.	HSP MS, Miscellaneous Coll., a.l.s.
June 12, 1773	George Croghan to William Franklin.	*Ibid.*
June 16, 1773	Proclamation Warrant to Thomas French for Part of Unpatented *Walnut Bottom* Resurvey.	Md. HR, Warrants, Liber W.S. No. 16, ff. 231-32.
July 22, 1773	Advertisement of a Meeting of the O.C.	*Va. Gazette.*
July 24, 1773	* Robert Carter to John Taswell at Williamsburg.	DUL Carter Papers.
July 29, 1773	Advertisement of a Meeting of the O.C.	*Va. Gazette.*
August 22, 1773	Thomas Glasscock to George Washington.	Hamilton, IV, 251-52, a.l.s.
December 16, 1773	Renewal of Proclamation Warrant.	Md. HR, Warrants, Liber W.S. No. 16, f. 421.
January 3, 1774	Entry of Andrew Lewis, 3,000 Acres.	Fincastle Co. Entry Book A (Montgomery Co., Va., Courthouse).
January 28, 1774	Endorsement of Hancock Taylor.	*Ibid.*, f. 5.
March 2, 1774	John Floyd Appointed Deputy Surveyor of Fincastle County, Virginia.	VSL, Minutes of Fincastle Co., 1773–77. Typescript.
March 6, 1774	Entry of John Lewis.	Fincastle Co., Entry Book A, f. 8.
March 31, 1774	Entry of Samuel Overton.	*Ibid.*, f. 10.
	Entry of Patrick Henry.	*Ibid.*

May 11, 1774	Certificate of Survey of *The Brothers* for Thomas French.	Md. HR, Frederick Co., Original Certificate, No. 653.
July 7-21, 1774	Extracts from the Journal of Thomas Hanson.	Thwaites and Kellogg, pp. 110-33.
July 22, 1774	Sale of Lands of George Croghan.	Byars.
August 2, 1774	William Russell Appointed Deputy Surveyor of Fincastle County, Virginia.	VSL, Minutes of Fincastle Co., 1773–77. See Summers, p. 630.
August 6, 1774	George Mercer to Robert Carter.	NYPL Emmet MS, No. 49, ff. 118-22, a.l.s.
August 13, 1774	William Preston to ———.	Force, 4th ser. I, 707.
November 29, 1774	Patent to Thomas French for *The Brothers*.	Md. LO, Patents B.C. and G.G.
December 4, 1774	Robert Preston Appointed Assistant Surveyor of Fincastle County, Virginia.	VSL, Minutes of Fincastle Co., 1773–77. Summers, p. 633.
January 28, 1775	* John Tayloe to William Preston.	WHS Draper MSS, 4QQ5, a.l.s.
April 1, 1775	George Rogers Clark to Jonathan Clark.	*Ibid.*, 1L 16, a.l.s. In print.
May-June, 1775	Deposition of Hancock Lee in Lexington.	Fayette Co., Ky., Circuit Court Clerks Office, Land Trials Book, ff. 121-22. Wilson, p. 32.
July, 1775	Deposition of Benjamin Ashby.	*Ibid.* Complete Records B, 1805–10, f. 279.
July 17, 1775	John Floyd to Hancock Lee.	*Ibid.*, f. 270.
December 23, 1782	Survey for John Strode.	Fayette Co., Ky., Fayette Surveys D, f. 9 (related to O.C. Survey of 1775).
Early 1783	* Deposition of Robert Johnson.	An 1806 reference to old lines in O.C. Survey as observed in 1783. Fayette Co., Ky., Circuit Court Clerks Office, Complete Records B, 1805–10, f. 280.
January 4, 1783	* Survey for Francis Ash.	Fayette Co., Ky., Fayette Surveys D, f. 385 (related to O.C. Survey of 1775).

January 31, 1783	Survey for John Marshall, Jr.	*Ibid.*, f. 386 (related to O.C. Survey of 1775).
	Survey for Benjamin Ashby.	*Ibid.*, f. 387 (related to O.C. Survey of 1775).
Summer, 1775	Survey for Daniel Morgan.	*Ibid.*, A, f. 20.
	Survey for Daniel Morgan.	*Ibid.*, D, f. 384.
	Survey for John Ashby, Jr.	*Ibid.*, f. 385.
October 2, 1775	Letter from G.M. to William Aylett.	*TQ*, I, 87-88.
December 4, 1775	Kentucky Land Entry of Joseph Blackwell.	Fincastle Co. Entry Book A, f. 28.
	Kentucky Land Entry of Benjamin Ashby.	*Ibid.*, f. 28.
December 7, 1775	Kentucky Land Entry of Richard Lee.	*Ibid.*, f. 30.
	Kentucky Land Entry of Henry Lee.	*Ibid.*, f. 31.
	Kentucky Land Entry of John Morgan.	*Ibid.*, f. 32.
	Kentucky Land Entry of Charles Morgan.	*Ibid.*, f. 33.
	* Kentucky Land Entry of Daniel Leet.	*Ibid.*
	* Marker on the West Side of Russell Cave Pike, Six Miles South of Centerville, Kentucky. Marker No. 20.	
February 26, 1776	Account Rendered to George Mercer by Thomas Walpole.	*GMP*, p. 325.
March 12, 1776	G.M. to Robert Carter.	Rowland, I, 214-15.
March 14, 1776	William Franklin to William Trent.	APS MS.
June 24, 1776	Resolution, Virginia Convention of 1776.	Force, 4th ser., VI, 1044.
July 17, 1777	Account Rendered, Samuel Wharton against George Mercer.	*GMP*, p. 326.
November 6, 1777	Petition Relating to Grants to O.C.	VSL Miscellaneous Petitions, 1777–81, Folder 140/541.
January 8, 1778	Land Office Legislation.	*VJHD*, 1778, p. 106.
January 14, 1778	Land Title Legislation.	*Ibid.*, p. 115.

January 28, 1778	Land Claims Resolution.	*Ibid.*, p. 136.
February 6, 1778	G.M. to James Mercer.	Rowland, II, 291-93.
April 24, 1778	Advertisement of a Meeting of the O.C.	*Va. Gazette.*
October 2, 1778	G.M. to George Mercer.	HCL MS. Fragment.
October 14, 1778	Bill to Establish Land Office.	*VJHD*, p. 11. Bill postponed, *ibid.*, December 5, 1778.
November 4, 1778	Resolution, Virginia House of Burgesses.	*Ibid.*, p. 42.
November 11, 1778	Memorial of Thomas Walker.	*Ibid.*, p. 53.
November 20, 1778	Memorial of the O.C.	VSL MS. Bailey, pp. 320-27.
	Minute, Virginia House of Delegates on Memorial.	*VJHD*, p. 74.
December 12, 1778, probated	Last Will and Testament of Doctor David Ross.	Md. HR, Prince Georges Co., Original Wills, Box 13, p. 10.
May 17-June 4, 1778	Bills for Land Office and Adjusting and Claims.	*VJHD*, pp. 6-37.
June 19, 1779	G.M. to Richard Henry Lee.	LC, GMM, a.l.s.
June 25, 1779	Virginia Land Law.	Hening, X, 35-65.
August 14, 1779	Indenture of William Ross, Jr. to William Stewart.	Prince Georges Co. Land Record, J.R.M. No. 7, ff. 260-64.
November 10, 1779	Advertisement of a Meeting of the O.C.	N.F.
February 4, 1780	* Land Claims of Thomas Gist.	PALO.
	Certification of Title to Thomas Gist.	*Ibid.*, Original Survey.
March 8, 1780	Warrant and Certificate for Lands of Thomas Gist.	*Ibid.*
July 25, 1780	Writ of Ejectment of Ross's Lessees vs. James Guest, Tenant.	Md. HR, WSGC, Original Papers, Box R, 1793.
October, 1780	*David Ross and Others vs. James Guest, Tenant of G.M. and the O.C.	*Ibid.*, Docket, 1780, May Term, f. 45.
April 14, 1781	Robert Carter to John Sutton.	DUL Robert Carter Let-

Date	Document	Source
		ter Books, IV, 55-61. No. 82.
May 11, 1781	* Robert Carter to G.M.	*Ibid.*, f. 75.
May, 1781	David Ross and Others vs. G.M.	Md. HR, WSGC, Docket Book, 1781, May Term, f. 18.
October, 1781	D.R. and Others vs. G.M.	*Ibid.*, October Term, f. 21.
	D.R. and Others vs. G.M.	*Ibid.*, October Term, f. 85.
August 2, 1782	* Last Will and Codicil of James Scott.	Prince William Co., Virginia Will Book G, ff. 180-83.
October 8, 1782	D.R. and Others vs. G.M.	Md. HR, WSGC, Docket Book, 1782, October Term, f. 21.
October 19, 1782	G.M. to Edmund Randolph.	Rowland, II, 23-32, a.l.s.
November 21, 1782	George Mason's Lessee vs. Thomas Troublesome and Charles Clinton.	Washington Co., Md., Judgment Records, No. 1, ff. 34-41. Ejectment Writ.
April 19, 1783	* Deed of Share of the O.C. by Thomas Cresap.	Washington Co., Md., LO, Liber C, ff. 5-6.
April 28, 1783	Resurvey of *White Oak Level*.	Md. HR, WSGC, Original Papers, Box R, 1793.
	Deposition of Thomas Cresap.	*Ibid.*
	Deposition of Jarvis Haugham.	*Ibid.*
	Deposition of Daniel Cresap.	*Ibid.*
	Deposition of James Prather.	*Ibid.*
April 29, 1783	Deposition of Elizabeth Guest.	*Ibid.*
	Deposition of James Gist.	*Ibid.*
May 2, 1783	Validation of Early Surveys of the Loyal Land Co. and the Greenbrier Company.	LC, Campbell-Preston Papers, II. Printed 4 Coll., 32.
	Indenture of Daniel Cresap and Wife to G.M.	Md. HR, Washington Co., Deeds, Book C, ff. 480-82.
May 13, 1783	D.R. and Others vs. G.M.	Md. HR, WSGC, Docket, May Term, 1783, f. 23.
May, 1783	* George Mason's Lessee vs. Charles Clinton.	*Ibid.*, f. 69.

October 21, 1783	D.R. and Others Lessee vs. G.M.	*Ibid.*, October Term, f. 27.
October 24, 1783	Indenture between G.M. and Thomas Beall.	Md. HR, Washington Co., Deeds Book C, ff. 513-16.
October 25, 1783	Indenture between G.M. and Thomas Beall.	*Ibid.*, ff. 516-21.
October 27, 1783	* Bonds of Thomas Beall and Co-Signers to G.M.	Embedded.
May, 1784	D.R. and Others vs. G.M.	Md. HR, WSGC, Docket, 1784, May Term, f. 25.
October, 1784	D.R. and Others vs. G.M.	*Ibid.*, f. 35.
May, 1785	D.R. and Others vs. G.M.	*Ibid.*
July 13, 1785	Indenture of G.M. to James Maccubbin Lingan.	DML, GMM.
	Indenture of G.M. to James Maccubbin Lingan.	Washington Co., Md., Deeds Book D, ff. 353-56.
July 14, 1785	Deed of New Store Tract by G.M. to James M. Lingan.	DML, GMM.
	Indenture of G.M. to James M. Lingan.	Washington Co., Md., Deeds Book D, ff. 356-58.
October, 1785	D.R. and Others vs. G.M.	Md. HR, WSGC, Docket, 1785, October Term, f. 39.
February 28, 1786	* Depositions of Daniel Cresap, John Nicholls, Elizabeth Gist, and James Gist.	*Ibid.*, Original Papers, Box R, 1793.
May, 1786	D.R. and Others vs. G.M.	*Ibid.*, Docket, 1786, May Term, f. 39.
October, 1786	D.R. and Others vs. G.M.	*Ibid.*, f. 56.
May, 1787	D.R. and Others vs. G.M.	*Ibid.*, 1787, May Term, f. 55.
October, 1787	D.R. and Others vs. G.M.	*Ibid.*, f. 65.
May 1, 1788	G.M. to John Francis Mercer.	Rowland, II, 212-14.
May, 1788	D.R. and Others vs. G.M.	Md. HR, WSGC, Docket, 1788, May Term, f. 25.
October, 1788	D.R. and Others vs. G.M.	*Ibid.*, October Term, f. 1.
May, 1789	D.R. and Others vs. G.M.	*Ibid.*, May Term, f. 9.

October, 1789	D.R. and Others vs. G.M.	*Ibid.*, October Term, f. 9.
May, 1790	D.R. and Others vs. G.M.	*Ibid.*, May Term, f. 8.
October 14, 1790	D.R. and Others vs. G.M.	*Ibid.*, October Term, f. 8.
November 22, 1790	Warrant for the Resurvey of *White Oak Level.*	*Ibid.*, Original Papers, Box R, 1793.
March 14, 1791	* Depositions of Daniel Cresap, Sr., James Prather, Christian Burkett, and James Gist.	*Ibid.*
	Resurvey of *White Oak Level* and *Pleasant Valley.*	Md. HR, Resurvey Plot, No. 2.
May 25, 1791	Case Stated in Ejectment Suit, Ross vs. Mason.	Md. HR, WSGC, Original Papers, Box R, 1793.
May, 1791	D.R. and Others vs. G.M.	*Ibid.*, Docket, May Term, 1791, f. 8.
October, 1791	* D.R. and Others vs. G.M.	*Ibid.*, October Term, f. 22, No. 1.
June 4, 1791	Warrant of G.M. vs. Brooke Beall.	*Ibid.*, Original Papers, 1791, Box R, No. 10.
	Warrant of G.M. vs. William Deakins, Jr.	*Ibid.*, No. 11
	Warrant of G.M. vs. James M. Lingan.	*Ibid.*, No. 12.
	Warrant of G.M. vs. Thomas Beall.	*Ibid.*, No. 16.
	Warrant of G.M. vs. William Deakins, Jr.	*Ibid.*, No. 14.
	Warrant of G.M. vs. James M. Lingan.	*Ibid.*, No. 15.
	* Warrant of G.M. vs. Thomas Beall.	*Ibid.*, No. 13.
	Warrant of G.M. vs. Brooke Beall.	*Ibid.*, No. 17.
June 15, 1791	* G.M. vs. Thomas Beall.	*Ibid.*, Original Judgments, 1792, No. 74.
	G.M. vs. Brooke Beall.	*Ibid.*, No. 75.
	G.M. vs. William Deakins, Jr.	*Ibid.*, No. 76.
	G.M. vs. James M. Lingan.	*Ibid.*, No. 77.
	G.M. vs. Thomas Beall.	*Ibid.*, No. 78.
	G.M. vs. William Deakins, Jr.	*Ibid.*, No. 79.
	G.M. vs. Brooke Beall.	*Ibid.*, No. 80.
	G.M. vs. James M. Lingan.	*Ibid.*, No. 81.
September 9, 1791	Minutes, Board of Property of Pennsylvania.	*PA*, 3rd ser. I, 157-59.

October, 1791	* G.M. vs. Signers of Bonds in Land Transactions:	
	vs. Brooke Beall.	Md. HR, WSGC, Docket, 1791, October Term, ff. 212-13.
	vs. William Deakins, Jr.	*Ibid.*
	vs. James M. Lingan.	*Ibid.*
	* vs. Thomas Beall.	*Ibid.*
	vs. William Deakins, Jr.	*Ibid.*
	vs. James M. Lingan.	*Ibid.*
	* vs. Thomas Beall.	*Ibid.*
	vs. Brooke Beall.	*Ibid.*
May, 1792	D.R. and Others vs. G.M.	*Ibid.*, May Term, f. 46.
May 12, 1792	G.M. to John Francis Mercer.	HSP Dreer Coll., Annapolis Convention, a.l.s. Rowland, II, 354-56.
May 18, 1792	G.M. vs. Signers of Bonds:	
	vs. Brooke Beall.	Md. HR, WSGC, Docket, 1792, May Term, ff. 179-80.
	vs. William Deakins, Jr.	*Ibid.*
	vs. James M. Lingan.	*Ibid.*
	vs. Thomas Beall.	*Ibid.*
	vs. William Deakins, Jr.	*Ibid.*
	vs. James M. Lingan.	*Ibid.*
	vs. Thomas Beall.	*Ibid.*
	vs. Brooke Beall.	*Ibid.*
October 16, 1792	Last Will and Testament of G.M.	Fairfax Co., Va., Will Book F, No. 1, f. 95. Rowland, 57-72.
October, 1792	D.R. and Others vs. G.M.	Md. HR, WSGC, Docket, 1792, October Term, f. 55, No. 2.
November 5, 1792	Minutes, Board of Property of Pennsylvania.	*PA*, 3rd ser. II, 51.
January 7, 1793	* Scifa Writ of Martin Cockburn and G.M., Executors of G.M., vs. Thomas Beall.	Md. HR, WSGC, Original Papers, 1793, Box C, No. 74.
	vs. Brooke Beall.	*Ibid.*, No. 75.
	vs. William Deakins, Jr.	*Ibid.*, No. 76.
	vs. James M. Lingan.	*Ibid.*, No. 77.
	vs. Thomas Beall.	*Ibid.*, No. 78.
	vs. William Deakins, Jr.	*Ibid.*, No. 79.

	vs. Brooke Beall.	*Ibid.*, No. 80.
	vs. James M. Lingan.	*Ibid.*, No. 81.
May, 1793	D.R. and Others vs. G.M.	*Ibid.*, Docket, 1790, May Term, f. 59, No. 1.
	D.R. and Others vs. G.M.	*Ibid.*, Judgments J.G., No. 21, f. 217.
	Martin Cockburn and G.M., Executors of G.M., vs. Signers of Bonds:	
	vs. Thomas Beall.	*Ibid.*, Docket, 1793, May Term, ff. 267-68.
	vs. Brooke Beall.	*Ibid.*
	vs. William Deakins, Jr.	*Ibid.*
	vs. James M. Lingan.	*Ibid.*
	vs. Thomas Beall.	*Ibid.*
	vs. William Deakins, Jr.	*Ibid.*
	vs. Brooke Beall.	*Ibid.*
	vs. James M. Lingan.	*Ibid.*
May, 1794	Martin Cockburn and G.M., Executors of G.M., vs. Signers of Bonds:	
	vs. Thomas Beall.	*Ibid.*, 1794, May Term, ff. 286-87.
	vs. Thomas Beall.	*Ibid.*
	vs. Brooke Beall.	*Ibid.*
	vs. Brooke Beall.	*Ibid.*
	vs. William Deakins, Jr.	*Ibid.*
	vs. William Deakins, Jr.	*Ibid.*
	vs. James M. Lingan.	*Ibid.*
	vs. James M. Lingan.	*Ibid.*
October, 1794	Martin Cockburn and G.M. vs. Signers of Bonds:	
	vs. Thomas Beall.	*Ibid.*, October Term, ff 290-91.
	vs. Brooke Beall.	*Ibid.*
	vs. William Deakins, Jr.	*Ibid.*
	vs. James M. Lingan.	*Ibid.*
	vs. Thomas Beall.	*Ibid.*
	vs. Brooke Beall.	*Ibid.*
	vs. William Deakins, Jr.	*Ibid.*
	vs. James M. Lingan.	*Ibid.*
March 10, 1795	Narrative in Ejectment in Suit of Ross vs. Mason.	*Ibid.*, Original Papers, 1797, Box R.

May, 1795	Martin Cockburn and G.M., Executors of G.M., vs. Signers of Bonds:	
	vs. Thomas Beall.	*Ibid.*, Docket, 1795, May Court, ff. 304-5.
	vs. Brooke Beall.	*Ibid.*
	vs. William Deakins, Jr.	*Ibid.*
	vs. James M. Lingan.	*Ibid.*
	vs. Thomas Beall.	*Ibid.*
	vs. Brooke Beall.	*Ibid.*
	vs. William Deakins, Jr.	*Ibid.*
	vs. James M. Lingan.	*Ibid.*
May, 1795	D.R. and Others vs. Christian Perkey.	*Ibid.*, 1795, May Term, f. 276.
October, 1795	D.R. and Others vs. G.M.	*Ibid.*, October Term, 1795, f. 53.
	Martin Cockburn and G.M. vs. Signers of Bonds:	
	vs. Thomas Beall.	*Ibid.*, ff. 288-89.
	vs. Brooke Beall.	*Ibid.*
	vs. William Deakins, Jr.	*Ibid.*
	vs. James M. Lingan.	*Ibid.*
	vs. Thomas Beall.	*Ibid.*
	vs. Brooke Beall.	*Ibid.*
	vs. William Deakins, Jr.	*Ibid.*
	vs. James M. Lingan.	*Ibid.*
1796, probated	Last Will and Testament of G.M., of Lexington.	Fairfax Co., Va.
May, 1796	D.R. and Others vs. G.M.	Md. HR, WSGC, Docket, 1796, May Term, f. 49.
October, 1796	D.R. and Others vs. G.M.	*Ibid.*, October Term, f. 37. Allegany Imparlances.
November 3, 1796	Warrant to Resurvey *White Oak Level*.	*Ibid.*, Original Papers, Box R, 1797.
April, 1797	Resurvey of *White Oak Level* and *Pleasant Valley*.	*Ibid.*
	Account of George Dent with D.R. for Surveying *White Oak Level* and *Pleasant Valley*.	*Ibid.*
May, 1797	D.R. and Others vs. G.M.	*Ibid.*, Docket, 1797, May Term.

September 7, 1797	Writ of Scifa by Martin Cockburn, Surviving Executor of G.M., vs. Thomas Beall.	*Ibid.*, Original Papers, 1797, October Term, No. 140.
	vs. Margaret Beall and Upton Beall, Executors of Brooke Beall.	*Ibid.*, No. 147.
	vs. Francis Deakins, Jr., Executor of William Deakins, Jr.	*Ibid.*, No. 148.
	vs. James M. Lingan.	*Ibid.*, No. 149.
	vs. Thomas Beall.	*Ibid.*, No. 150.
	vs. Margaret and Upton Beall.	*Ibid.*, No. 151.
	vs. Francis Deakins, Jr.	*Ibid.*, No. 152.
	vs. James M. Lingan.	*Ibid.*, No. 153.
October, 1797	Martin Cockburn, Surviving Executor of G.M., vs. Signers of Bonds:	
	vs. Thomas Beall.	*Ibid.*, Docket, 1797, October Term, ff. 445-46.
	vs. Margaret and Upton Beall.	*Ibid.*
	vs. William Deakins, Jr.	*Ibid.*
	vs. James M. Lingan.	*Ibid.*
	vs. Thomas Beall.	*Ibid.*
	vs. Margaret and Upton Beall.	*Ibid.*
	vs. William Deakins, Jr.	*Ibid.*
	vs. James M. Lingan.	*Ibid.*
January 23, 1798	Statement of James Cook, Attorney for William Deakins, Jr.	*Ibid.*, Original Papers, 1798, Box C, May, 1799.
	Statement of James Cook, Attorney for William Deakins, Jr.	*Ibid.*
January 26, 1798	* Statement of John M. Gantt, Attorney for Thomas Beall.	*Ibid.*
	Statement of John M. Gantt, Attorney for Thomas Beall.	*Ibid.*
	Assertion of Payment by James M. Lingan to Martin Cockburn.	*Ibid.*
	Statement of Attorney at Suit for James M. Lingan.	*Ibid.*

May, 1798	Martin Cockburn, Surviving Executor, vs. Executors of Brooke Beall.	*Ibid.*, Docket, f. 405.
October, 1798	Martin Cockburn, Surviving Executor of G.M. vs. Signers of Bonds:	
	vs. William Deakins, Jr.	*Ibid.*, Docket, October Term, 1798, f. 102.
	vs. William Deakins, Jr.	*Ibid.*
	vs. James M. Lingan.	*Ibid.*
	vs. James M. Lingan.	*Ibid.*
May, 1799	Martin Cockburn vs. Signers of Bonds:	
	vs. Thomas Beall.	*Ibid.*, May Term, 1799, f. 616.
	vs. Thomas Beall.	*Ibid.*
	vs. James M. Lingan.	*Ibid.*
	vs. James M. Lingan.	*Ibid.*
August 14, 1799	Indenture of Old D.R. Estate to William Stewart.	Md. LO, Liber J.G. No. 5, ff. 486-88. Also, Prince Georges Co. Deed Book, Liber J.R.M., No. 7, ff. 486-88.
October, 1799	*Martin Cockburn vs. Signers of Bonds:	
	*vs. Thomas Beall.	Md. HR, WSGC, 1799, October Term, f. 475.
	*vs. Thomas Beall.	*Ibid.*
	*vs. James M. Lingan.	*Ibid.*
	*vs. James M. Lingan.	*Ibid.*
April 19, 1800	Writ of Ejectment, William Stewart, Ross Lessee, vs. Jacob Perkey, Tenant.	Md. Ct. of Appeals, Judgment Liber T.H. No. 16, ff. 3-6.
May 13, 1800	William Stewart, D.R. and Others vs. Jacob Perkey.	Md. HR, WSGC, Dockets, f. 25.
October, 1800	W.S., D.R. and Others vs. J.P.	*Ibid.*, f. 30.
May 13, 1801	W.S., D.R. and Others vs. J.P.	*Ibid.*, 1801, f. 28.
October 13, 1801	W.S., D.R. and Others vs. J.P.	*Ibid.*, f. 24.
May 11, 1802	W.S., D.R. and Others vs. J.P.	*Ibid.*, 1802, f. 24.
October 12, 1802	W.S., D.R. and Others vs. J.P.	*Ibid.*, f. 187.
May 10, 1803	W.S., D.R. and Others vs. J.P.	*Ibid.*, 1803, f. 180.

June 28, 1803	*Deed to the Cove from George Mason's Heirs.	Allegany Co., Md. Deed Book C, f. 668.
October 11, 1803	W.S., D.R. and Others vs. J.P.	Md. HR, WSGC, Dockets, October Term, f. 170.
May 8, 1804	W.S., D.R. and Others vs. William Mason.	*Ibid.*, 1804, f. 29.
October, 1804	W.S., D.R. and Others vs. W.M.	*Ibid.*, f. 27.
May 14, 1805	W.S., D.R. and Others vs. W.M.	*Ibid.*, 1805, f. 27.
May, 1805	Memorandum about *Pleasant Valley*.	Allegany Co., Md. October Ct., 1815, Original Papers.
August 9, 1805	Deposition of John Mason about O. C. Land.	Md. LO, Original Surveys, Allegany Co., No. 2087, a.d.s.
September 3, 1805	Petition of the Granddaughters of G.M.	*Ibid.*, a.d.s., J.T. Mason.
September 3, 1805	*Patent of *Pleasant Valley* to the Descendants of G.M.	Md. LO, Patents, J.C. No. 2, ff. 248-49.
October, 1805	William Stewart, David Ross and Others vs. William Mason.	Md. HR, WSGC, Dockets, October Term, 1805, f. 25.
October 8, 1805	W.S., D.R. and Others vs. W.M.	Allegany Co., Md., Docket, October Term, f. 25.
April 21, 1806	W.S., D.R. and Others vs. W.M.	*Ibid.*, April Ct., 1806.
October 13, 1806	W.S., D.R. and Others vs. W.M.	*Ibid.*, October Term, 1806, Trials.
	*Richard Smith, Lessee of W.S. and Others vs. W.M.	Allegany Co., Md., Judgment Record F, ff. 304-57.
	Judgment of the Court.	Allegany Co., Md., Original Files. Copy.
June 15, 1807	William Stewart and Others vs. William Mason.	Md. HR, Ct. of Appeals, Docket, June, Ct., 1807, No. 242.
December 21, 1807	W.S. and Others vs. W.M.	*Ibid.*, December Term, 1807, No. 166.
June 20, 1808	W.S. and Others vs. W.M.	*Ibid.*, June Term, 1808, No. 98.
December, 1808	W.S. and Others vs. W.M.	*Ibid.*, No. 166.
June, 1809	W.S. and Others vs. W.M.	*Ibid.*, No. 55.

December, 1809	W.S. and Others vs. W.M.	*Ibid.*, No. 35.
June, 1810	W.S. and Others vs. W.M.	*Ibid.*, No. 18.
December, 1810	W.S. and Others vs. W.M.	*Ibid.*, No. 6.
June, 1811	W.S. and Others vs. W.M.	*Ibid.*, No. 4.
December, 1811	W.S. and Others vs. W.M.	*Ibid.*, No. 3.
May, 1812	W.S. and Others vs. W.M.	*Ibid.*
December, 1812	W.S. and Others vs. W.M.	*Ibid.*
May, 1813	W.S. and Others vs. W.M.	*Ibid.*
December, 1813	W.S. and Others vs. W.M.	*Ibid.*
May, 1814	W.S. and Others vs. W.M.	*Ibid.*
December, 1814	W.S. and Others vs. W.M.	*Ibid.*
May 29, 1815	*W.S. and Others vs. W.M.	*Ibid.*, May Term, 1815, No. 1.
	W.S. and Others vs. W.M.	*Ibid.*, Judgments, May Ct., 1815, Liber T.H. No. 16, C1815, ff.1-224.
October 9, 1815	*W.S. and Others vs. W.M.	Allegany Co., Md., Docket, Trials to October Ct., 1815.
April 15, 1816	W.S. and Others vs. W.M.	*Ibid.*, Trials to April Ct., 1816.
October 14, 1816	*W.S. and Others vs. W.M.	*Ibid.*, Judgment Record J, October Ct., 1816, ff. 358-402 and K, ff. 1-59.
	W.S. and Others vs. W.M.	*Ibid.*, Docket, October Term, 1816.
	W.S. and Others vs. W.M.	*Ibid.*, Judgment Record K, ff. 58-59.
April, 1817	W.S. and Others vs. W.M.	*Ibid.*, Docket, Judicial, April, 1817.
October, 1817	Richard Smith, Lessee of W.S. and Others, vs. W.M.	*Ibid.*, October Ct., Judicials.
	John Denn, Lessee of W.M. and Others vs. Richard Fenn.	*Ibid.*, "Originals."
October, 1818	Lessee of W.M. and Others vs. William Lamar.	*Ibid.*, October, 1818, Trials.

April, 1819	W.M. and Others vs. W.L.	*Ibid.*, April Ct., 1819.
	W.M. and Others vs. W.L.	*Ibid.*, variant text.
October, 1819	W.M. and Others vs. W.L.	*Ibid.*, October Ct., 1819, Trials.
October 9, 1820	Commission to Take Agreement of Deed of *Pleasant Valley*.	*Ibid.*, Deed Book L, f. 144.
January 27, 1821	Agreement to Acknowledge Deed to *Pleasant Valley*.	*Ibid.*, ff. 144-45.
	*Deed of *Pleasant Valley* to William Lamar.	*Ibid.*
April, 1821	W.M. and Others vs. W.L.	*Ibid.*, Docket, Trials, April Ct., 1821.
October, 1821	*W.M. and Others vs. W.L.	*Ibid.*, October Ct., 1821.

BIBLIOGRAPHY

Abstracts of the Records of Augusta County, Virginia, ed. Lyman Chalkley. 6 vols. Rosslyn, Virginia, 1912.

Acts of the Privy Council of England (Colonial Series), eds. W. L. Grant and James Munro. Hereford, 1920–31.

Alvord, Clarence Walworth, and Lee, Bidgood. *The First Explorations of the Trans-Allegheny Region by Virginians, 1650–1674.* Cleveland: Arthur H. Clark Co., 1912.

Alvord, Clarence Walworth, and Carter, Clarence Edwin. *The New Regime, 1765–1767.* Springfield: Illinois State Historical Library, 1916.

American Archives . . ., ed. Peter Force. 9 vols. Washington, 1837–53.

American Historical Record and Repertory of Notes and Queries . . ., ed. Benson J. Lossing. 3 vols. Philadelphia: Chase & Town [etc.], 1872–[74].

Archives of Maryland . . ., eds. W. A. Browne, *et al.* 65 vols. Baltimore: Maryland Historical Society, 1883–1952.

Bailey, Kenneth P. *The Ohio Company of Virginia and the Westward Movement 1748–1792. A Chapter in the History of the Colonial Frontier.* Glendale, Calif.: Arthur H. Clark Company, 1939.

———. *Thomas Cresap, Maryland Frontiersman.* Boston: Christopher Publishing House, 1944.

Calendar of Virginia State Papers and Other Manuscripts Preserved in the Capitol at Richmond. 11 vols. Richmond, 1875–93.

Calendar of Transcripts of Virginia State Library, ed. John Kennedy. Richmond, 1905.

Cappan, Lester J., and Duff, Stella F. *Virginia Gazette Index*, 1736–1780. 2 vols. Williamsburg, Va.: Institute of Early American History and Culture, 1950.

The Case of the Ohio Company Extracted from Original Papers. London, May, 1770. Only known imprint in the New York Historical Society. Reproduced in reduced facsimile in *George Mercer Papers*, Part II.

Clark, George Rogers. *Papers, 1771–1781*, ed. James Alton James. Springfield: *Collections* of the Illinois State Historical Library, VIII, 1926. Virginia Series, III.

Colonial Records of North Carolina, ed. William L. Saunders. 10 vols. Raleigh, 1886–90.

Colonial Records of Pennsylvania. 16 vols. Philadelphia, 1852–53. Vols. I-X, *Minutes of the Provincial Council.* Vols. XI-XVI, *Minutes of the Supreme Executive Council.* General Index, Philadelphia, 1860.

Conway, Moncure D. *Barons of the Potomac and Rappahannock.* New York: Grolier Club, 1892.

Cresswell, Nicholas. *The Journal of 1774–1777.* New York: Dial Press, 1924.

Decouvertes et Etablissements des Français . . ., ed. Pierre Margry. Paris, 1876–86.

The Diaries of George Washington, 1748–1799, ed. John C. Fitzpatrick. 4 vols. Boston: Houghton, Mifflin Co., 1925.

Dictionary of American Biography, eds. Allen Johnson and Dumas Malone. 22 vols. New York: Charles Scribner's Sons, 1928–44.

Disney, Daniel, Lieutenant of the 4th Regiment. "Orderly Book of 1775." Manuscript in the Library of Congress, Washington, D.C.

Documentary History of Dunmore's War . . ., eds. R. G. Thwaites, and Louise P. Kellogg. Madison: Wisconsin Historical Society, 1905.

Documents Relative to the Colonial History of the State of New York . . ., eds. E. B. O'Callaghan, and J. R. Brodhead. 15 vols. Albany, N.Y., 1856–61.

Douglass, William, M.D. *A Summary, Historical and Political, of the First Planting, Progressive Improvements and Present State of the British Settlements in North America.* Boston, 1751. London reprint, 1755.

Executive Journals of the Council of Colonial Virginia, 1680–1754, eds. H. R. McIlwaine, and W. T. Hall. 5 vols. Richmond, 1925–45.

Fernow, Berthold. *The Ohio Valley in Colonial Days.* Albany, N.Y.: Joel Munsell's Sons, 1890.

Freeman, Douglas Southall. *George Washington, A Biography.* 6 vols. New York: Charles Scribner's Sons, 1948–54.

George Mercer Papers Relating to the Ohio Company of Virginia, comp. and ed. Lois Mulkearn. Pittsburgh: University of Pittsburgh Press, 1954.

Gipson, Lawrence H. *The British Empire Before the American Revolution . . . .* 9 vols. Caldwell, Ida.: Caxton Printers; and New York: Alfred A. Knopf, 1936–49.

———. *Lewis Evans. . . .* Philadelphia: Historical Society of Pennsylvania, 1939.

Gist, Christopher. *Christopher Gist's Journals with Historical, Geographical and Ethnological Notes and Biographies of his Contemporaries, by William M. Darlington.* Pittsburgh: J. R. Weldin & Co., 1893.

Guthrie, Dwight Raymond. *John McMillan, The Apostle of Presbyterianism in the West, 1752–1833.* Pittsburgh: University of Pittsburgh Press, 1952.

Hanna, Charles A. *The Wilderness Trail. . . .* 2 vols. New York: G. P. Putnam's Sons, 1911.

Hendrick, Burton J. *The Lees of Virginia; Biography of a Family.* Boston: Little, Brown & Co., 1935.

Indian Treaties Printed by Benjamin Franklin, 1736–1762, ed. Julian P. Boyd. Philadelphia: Historical Society of Pennsylvania, 1938.

J. C. B. Travels in New France, eds. S. K. Stevens, *et al.* Harrisburg, 1941.

Johnson, Sir William. *The Papers of . . .* , eds. J. Sullivan, A. C. Flick, and M. W. Hamilton. 12 vols. Albany: The University of the State of New York, 1921–53.

Journal of the Commissioners for Trade and Plantations. . . . 15 vols. London, 1920–38.

Journal of the House of Burgesses of Virginia (1619–1776), eds. H. R. McIlwaine and J. P. Kennedy. 13 vols. Richmond: Colonial Press, E. Woddey Co., 1905–15.

Journal of the Senate of the Commonwealth of Virginia. Begun and held in the City of Williamsburg on Monday, the 5th of October in the Year of our Lord, 1778. 2 vols., 1778–79, 1785–90. Richmond, Va.: Thomas White, 1827–28.

Kegley, Frederick Bittle. *Kegley's Virginia Frontier, The Beginnings of the Southwest, The Roanoke of Colonial Days, 1740–1783.* Roanoke: Southwest Virginia Historical Society, 1938.

Kent, Donald H. *The French Invasion of Western Pennsylvania, 1753.* Harrisburg: Pennsylvania Historical and Museum Commission, 1954.

Koontz, Louis F. *Robert Dinwiddie, His Career in American Colonial, Governmental and Westward Expansion.* Glendale, Calif.: Arthur H. Clark Company, 1941.

Letters to Washington and Accompanying Papers, ed. S. M. Hamilton. 5 vols. Society of the Colonial Dames. Boston: Houghton, Mifflin Co., 1898–1902.

Maryland Gazette (Annapolis), issues for the years 1745–77, 1779–1839.

Maryland Historical Magazine. 51 vols. Baltimore: Maryland Historical Society, 1906-date.

Neill, Edward Duffield. *The Fairfaxes of England and America in the Seventeenth and Eighteenth Centuries.* Albany, N.Y., 1868.

Norkus, Nellie. "Francis Fauquier, Lieutenant Governor of Virginia, 1758–1768. A Study in Colonial Problems." Unpublished Ph.D. dissertation, University of Pittsburgh, 1954.

The Ohio Company Papers, Being Primarily Papers of the Suffering Traders of Pennsylvania, ed. Kenneth P. Bailey. Arcata, Calif.: Privately printed, 1947.

Osgood, Herbert L. *The American Colonies in the Eighteenth Century.* 4 vols. New York: Columbia University Press, 1924–25.

Parkman, Francis. *A Half-Century of Conflict. . . .* 2 vols. Boston: Little, Brown & Co., 1892.

Pennsylvania Archives (1664–), eds. Samuel Hazard, *et al.* Nine series, 138 vols. First series, 12 vols. Philadelphia: Joseph Severns & Co., 1852–

56. Third series, 30 vols. Harrisburg: Joseph Severns & Co., 1852–56. Fourth series, 12 vols. Harrisburg, 1900–1902.

Pennsylvania Gazette (Philadelphia), 1728–1815.

Pennsylvania Magazine of History and Biography. 1877-date. 77 vols. *Index* to vols. 1-75. Philadelphia: Historical Society of Pennsylvania, 1954.

Quattrocchi, Anna. "Thomas Hutchins, 1730–1781." Unpublished Ph.D. dissertation, University of Pittsburgh, 1944.

Reports of Cases Argued and Determined in the Court of Appeals of Maryland in 1810, 1811, 1812, 1813, 1814 & 1815, eds. Thomas Harris, Clerk of the Court of Appeals, and Reverdy Johns, Attorney at Law. Annapolis: Jonas Green, 1826.

Reports of the Virginia Commissioners in Kentucky, 1779–1780. Kentucky State Historical Society 1903– . *Register*, XXI. 54 vols.

Rowland, Kate Mason. *Life of George Mason, 1725–1792*. 2 vols. New York: G. P. Putnam's Sons, 1892.

Scharf, John Thomas. *History of Western Maryland, Being a History of Frederick, Montgomery, Carroll, Washington, Allegany, and Garret Counties from the Earliest Period to the Present Day. . . .* 2 vols. Philadelphia: L. H. Everts, 1882.

Slick, Sewell. *William Trent and the West*. Harrisburg, Pa.: Archives Publishing Co., 1947.

The Statutes at Large; Being a Collection of All the Laws of Virginia . . . (1619–1792), ed. W. W. Hening. 13 vols. Richmond, 1809–23.

Summers, Lewis Preston. *History of Southwest Virginia, 1746–1786. . . .* Richmond, Va.: J. T. Hill Printing Company, 1903.

Swem, E. G. *Virginia Historical Index*. 2 vols. Roanoke, Va.: Stone Printing and Manufacturing Company, 1934–36.

Trent, William. *Journal of . . .*, ed. Alfred J. Goodman. Cincinnati: R. Clarke and Co., 1871.

Tyler's Quarterly Historical and Geneological Magazine, 1920–1952. 33 vols. Richmond, Virginia.

Virginia Gazette (Williamsburg), 1736–1780. Twelve various printers.

Virginia Historical Society *Collections*. 11 vols. 1882–92.

Virginia Magazine of History and Biography, 1893-date. 61 vols. Richmond: Historical Society of Virginia, 1893–1957.

Volwiler, Albert J. *George Croghan and the Westward Movement, 1741–1782*. Cleveland: Arthur H. Clark Company, 1926.

Wallace, Paul A. W. *Conrad Weiser, 1696–1760, Friend of Colonist and Mohawk*. Philadelphia: University of Pennsylvania Press, 1945.

The Washington-Crawford Correspondence, Concerning Western Land, ed. C. W. Butterfield.

The Writings of George Washington, ed. Jared Sparks. 12 vols. Boston, 1837.

The Writings of George Washington From the Original Manuscript Sources,

1745–1799, ed. John C. Fitzpatrick. 39 vols. Washington: Government Printing Office, 1931–44.

Western Pennsylvania Historical Magazine, 1918– . 37 vols. Pittsburgh: Historical Society of Western Pennsylvania.

Wharton, Samuel. *Plain Facts; Being an Examination into the Rights of the Indian Nations of America to their respective Countries and a Vindication of the Grant from the Six Nations of Indians to the Proprietors of Indians. . . .* Philadelphia: R. Aitken, 1781.

William and Mary College Quarterly, 1892-date. First series, 1892–1920, 27 vols. Second series, 1921-date, 37 vols. Williamsburg, Virginia.

Wilson, Samuel. *The Ohio Company of Virginia, 1748–1798*. Lexington, Kentucky, 1926.

Wisconsin State Historical Society, *Collections of . . .*, ed. Lyman C. Draper. 20 vols. Madison, Wisconsin, 1855–82.

Index